# Chronicon
# 284-628 AD

John Colet

## ST. PAUL'S SCHOOL
## LIBRARY

# Translated Texts for Historians

This series is designed to meet the needs of students of ancient and medieval history and of others who wish to broaden their study by reading source material but whose knowledge of Latin or Greek is not sufficient to allow them to do so in the original language. Many important Late Imperial and Dark Age texts are currently unavailable in translation, and it is hoped that TTH will help fill this gap and complement the secondary literature in English which already exists. The series relates principally to the period 300-800 AD and will include Late Imperial, Greek, Byzantine and Syriac texts as well as source books illustrating a particular period or theme. Each volume is a self-contained scholarly translation with an introductory essay on the text and its author and notes indicating major problems of interpretation, including textual difficulties.

# Already published

Translated Texts for Historians
Volume 7

# Chronicon Paschale 284-628 AD

Translated with notes and introduction by
MICHAEL WHITBY and MARY WHITBY

Liverpool
University
Press

First published 1989 by
Liverpool University Press
PO Box 147, Liverpool, L69 3BX

Copyright © 1989 Michael Whitby and Mary Whitby

**British Library Cataloguing-in-Publication Data**

Chronicon Paschale 284-628 AD. (Translated texts for historians; v.7).
   1. Roman Empire. Apolitics
   I. Whitby, Michael, *1952*- II. Whitby, Mary, *1951*-
   III. Series
   320.937

   ISBN 0 85323 096 X

Printed in Great Britain at the
University Press, Cambridge

# PREFACE

We have been greatly helped in the production of this book by friends and colleagues: Averil Cameron, Jill Harries, Peter Heather, and James Howard-Johnston have made constructive comments both on points of detail and on general organization; Claudia Rapp has generously examined the Vatican MS in Rome for specific textual problems; Brian Croke has kept us in touch with progress on the Australian Malalas project.

Our knowledge of problems of Constantinopolitan topography is deeply indebted to Cyril Mango's Oxford seminars, and it is to be hoped that the results of these researches will sometime be published in full. (We would not wish to suggest that our topographical discussions represent or anticipate Mango's considered views.)

Margaret Gibson has inspired us with her own enthusiasm and patiently encouraged the work towards completion. Gillian Clark has helped to ensure the smooth running of publishing matters in Liverpool. The maps were kindly drawn for us by Mrs Sandra Mather of Liverpool University.

The volume has been printed from camera-ready copy produced on an Apple Macintosh computer, using the WriteNow programme generously supplied by M.E. Electronics Ltd. of 3 Collins Street, Oxford; we have also been helped with the programme by Dr A. J. M. Wedderburn of the Department of Biblical Criticism, University of St Andrews. This task has been greatly eased by the staff of the St Andrews University computing laboratory, in particular Dr John Ball to whose patience and skill we are much indebted. The cost of laser printing has been met by St Andrews University.

# CONTENTS

# LIST OF ABBREVIATIONS

*Sources*

| | |
|---|---|
| Agath. | Agathias |
| Amm. | Ammianus Marcellinus |
| *Anec. Cramer* | *Anecdota Cramer* |
| *Anth. Graec.* | *Anthologia Graeca* |
| *Anon. Val.* | *Anonymous Valesianus* |
| ASS | *Acta Sanctorum* |
| Cedr. | Cedrenus |
| *Chr. 354* | Chronographer of 354 (*CM* i. 15-148) |
| *Chron. 724* | *Chronicon Miscellaneum ad Annum Domini 724 pertinens* |
| *CP* | *Chronicon Paschale* |
| *CM* | *Chronica Minora* i-iii (*MGH Auct. Ant.* vols. ix, xi, xiii) |
| *Cod. Iust.* | *Codex Iustinianus* (in *CJ*) |
| *CJ* | *Corpus Iuris Civilis* |
| *Cod. Theod.* | *Codex Theodosianus* |
| Const. Porph. | Constantine Porphyrogenitus |
| | *DAI* = *de Administrando Imperio* |
| | *de caer.* = *de Caerimoniis* |
| | *Exc. de insid.* = *Excerpta de Insidiis* |
| | *Exc. de virt.* = *Excerpta de Virtutibus* |
| *CIL* | *Corpus Inscriptionum Latinarum* |
| Euseb. | Eusebius |
| | *HE* = *Ecclesiastical History* |
| | *Triac.* = *Panegyric to Constantine* |
| | *VC* = *Life of Constantine* |
| Evag. | Evagrius |
| *Exc. de insid.* | see Const. Porph. |
| G. Mon. | Georgius Monachus |
| G. Pisid. | George of Pisidia |
| | *BA* = *Bellum Avaricum* |
| | *Exp. Pers.* = *Expeditio Persica* |
| GC | Great Chronographer |

| | |
|---|---|
| *Heracl.* | *Fasti Heracliani* |
| *Hyd.* | *Fasti Hydatiani* |
| *ILS* | *Inscriptiones Latinae Selectae* |
| J. Eph. | John of Ephesus (*HE = Ecclesiastical History*) |
| J. Lyd. | John Lydus (*de mag. = de Magistratibus*) |
| J. Nik. | John of Nikiu |
| Jul. | Julian (*Or. = Orations*) |
| Lact. *DMP* | Lactantius, *de Mortibus Persecutorum* |
| Leo Gramm. | Leo Grammaticus |
| Mal. | Malalas |
| Marc. Com. | Marcellinus Comes |
| Mich. Syr. | Michael the Syrian |
| Nic. | Nicephorus |
| *Notitia* | *Notitia Urbis Constantinopoleos* |
| *Parast.* | *Parastaseis Syntomoi Chronikai* |
| *Patria* | *Patria Constantinopoleos* |
| Philost. | Philostorgius (*HE = Ecclesiastical History*) |
| Proc. | Procopius |
| | *Bld. = Buildings* |
| | *SH = Secret History* |
| *Scal.* | *Barbarus Scaligeri* |
| Soc. | Socrates |
| Soz. | Sozomen |
| Strat. | Antiochus Strategius |
| *Syn. Eccl. Const.* | *Synaxarium Ecclesiae Constantinopolitanae* |
| Theod. | Theodoret |
| | *HE = Ecclesiastical History* |
| | *HR = Historia Religiosa* |
| Theod. Lect. | Theodore Lector |
| Theod. Sync. | Theodore Syncellus |
| Theoph. | Theophanes |
| *Vind. pr. & post.* | *Fasti Vindobonenses priores & posteriores* |
| Zach. | Ps.-Zachariah |
| Zos. | Zosimus |

*Other*

| | |
|---|---|
| AB | *Analecta Bollandiana* |
| AJA | *American Journal of Archaeology* |
| a.m. | *annus mundi* |
| BAR | *British Archaeological Reports* |
| BMGS | *Byzantine and Modern Greek Studies* |
| BNJ | *Byzantinische-neugriechische Jahrbücher* |
| Byz. | *Byzantion* |
| ByzSlav. | *Byzantinoslavica* |
| BZ | *Byzantinische Zeitschrift* |
| Cpl. | Constantinople |
| CQ | *Classical Quarterly* |
| CSCO | *Corpus Scriptorum Christianorum Orientalium* |
| CSHB | *Corpus Scriptorum Historiae Byzantinae* |
| DOP | *Dumbarton Oaks Papers* |
| EHR | *English Historical Review* |
| FHG | *Fragmenta Historicorum Graecorum* |
| GRBS | *Greek, Roman and Byzantine Studies* |
| JHS | *Journal of Hellenic Studies* |
| JÖB(G) | *Jahrbücher der österreichischen Byzantinistik* (*öst. Byz. Gesellschaft*) |
| JRS | *Journal of Roman Studies* |
| JThS | *Journal of Theological Studies* |
| LSJ | Liddell and Scott |
| MGH | *Monumenta Germaniae Historica* Auct. Ant. = *Auctores Antiquissimi* |
| PBSR | *Papers of the British School at Rome* |
| PG | *Patrologia Graeca* |
| PLRE | *Prosopography of the Later Roman Empire* |
| PO | *Patrologia Orientalis* |
| REB | *Revue des études byzantines* |
| REG | *Revue des études grecques* |
| s.a. | *sub anno* |
| TM | *Travaux et Mémoires* |
| YCS | *Yale Classical Studies* |

In the notes, <u>underlining</u> denotes a parallel source which is very close and indicative of a source tradition available to the author of *CP* (cf. p. xxix).

# INTRODUCTION

## (i) *The Chronicle and its context*

The *Chronicon Paschale* or *Easter Chronicle* (hereafter *CP*) is an anonymous chronicle from the early 7th-c., which preserves an account of the salient events of world history from God's creation of the universe down to the time of writing. Thus it fulfills the standard function of a late Roman or Byzantine chronicle, which was to inter-relate Biblical and secular events, to interpret history in specifically Christian terms, and to present the record of true belief from the beginning of the world, through the turning-point of the Crucifixion, down to the present.[1] Like other chronicles, for example the 6th-c. Malalas (the most influential text for later chronographers) or the early 9th-c. George Syncellus and Theophanes, *CP* contains an amalgam of Old and New Testament, Jewish, Christian, and secular material in a mixture that reflects the interests and knowledge of the individual author.[2] Particular attention is paid in *CP* to the dating of major church feasts, especially Easter, and to their connection with the chronology of the Creation,[3] but the text set out to be much more than a treatise on Biblical chronology and computation since the author chose to include a substantial amount of historical information as well. This material is arranged annalistically by individual years,

---

1   For discussion of the historiographical background to the Byzantine chronographic tradition, see Croke, 'Chronicle', and for Malalas, the forthcoming *Studies in the Chronicle of John Malalas* (Byzantina Australiensia); also W. Witakowski, *The Syriac Chronicle of Pseudo-Dionysius of Tel-Mahrē* (Acta Universitatis Upsaliensis, *Studia Semitica Upsaliensia* ix, Uppsala 1987), ch. 2.

2   The method is summarized in the (lacunose) preface to Malalas: 'I thought it right, after abbreviating some material from the Hebrew books written by Moses [...] in the narratives of the chroniclers Africanus, Eusebius of Pamphilia, Pausanias, Didymus, Theophilus, Clement, Diodorus, Domninus, Eustathius and many other industrious chroniclers and poets and learned historians, and to relate as truthfully as possible a brief account of events that occurred in the time of the emperors, up till the events of my own lifetime which came to my hearing, I mean from Adam to the reign of Zeno and those who ruled thereafter.' (after Australian Malalas). For *CP*'s sources, see sec. ii below.

3   For discussion of this aspect of *CP*, see Beaucamp, 'Chronique'.

being dated throughout by consuls, emperors, indictions, and Olympiads, and sometimes by Antiochene or other local Eras, and Ascension dates; a large number of entries also contain specific dates (by Roman and/or Greek, and occasionally Egyptian months), so that all events are located as accurately as possible.[4] Year headings are recorded even when the author had no historical information to insert (as for most of the years between 533 and 601). This general attempt at chronological precision distinguishes *CP* from Malalas, for whom the basic unit of narrative for Roman imperial history was the emperor's reign rather than the individual year.

*CP* provides important evidence for analysing the contents and scope of the urban, specifically Constantinopolitan, chronicle in late antiquity, and hence for understanding one of the main mechanisms for recording historical events in the late Roman world (see further pp. xx-xxii). Much of its information concerns the public life of the city and its emperors: buildings, the affairs of the imperial family, natural disasters, riots, Church matters, the arrival of interesting embassies or of news of major victories. This material consists of notices which vary in length from one line of text to several pages, and in content from a dry factual statement to the more unusual full-length narrative of a story that particularly attracted the author's attention (e.g. the siege of Nisibis in 350, Eudocia and Paulinus, *ss.aa.* 420, 421, 444, or the conversion of Tzath in 522); this information is second-hand (at best), but *CP* usefully preserves material from sources now lost or incomplete, for example a sequence of pro-Arian notices about the emperor Constantius in the 4th c., or the detailed account of the Nika Riot of 532. As the narrative approaches the author's own life, it develops into a major historical source in its own right: it contains a first hand narrative of events in Constantinople in the early 7th-c. – the coup of Heraclius, reactions in the capital to the disasters of the 610s, the crisis of the 626 siege, and the reception of the news of Heraclius' victory in 628. It also quotes official documents verbatim, even when their length might seem disproportionate to the overall economy of the work.[5]

There is no external information about the author, and little direct internal evidence, so that it is only possible to speculate about his personality and status on the basis of interests

---

4    For references, see General Index s.v. Dates.

5    Especially the Three Chapters Edict *s.a.* 552 (48 pages); also the victory dispatch of Heraclius *s.a.* 628; other documents *ss.aa.* 533 (Theopaschite Edict), 615 (letter to Khusro).

observable in the narrative (see further sec. iii). The chronicle gained its accepted title from the long preface, only partly preserved, in which different methods for calculating Easter are reviewed. The connection of this prefatory material with the main text of *CP* was questioned by Mercati,[6] but even if these pages were introduced from elsewhere, there was already enough Easter material in the chronicle to justify the association: occasional calculations in the text (e.g. *s.a.* 344 with nn. 79-80) show the author's concern with the date of Easter, or at least his interest in transcribing calculations found in his sources, while he personally exploited Easter tables (e.g. *s.a.* 609 with n. 414) as an aid to the establishment of exact chronology, which was one of his major interests.

Although the text of *C P* terminates in 628 where one folio (roughly equivalent to 2.5 pages of the standard Bonn text) has been lost from the MS,[7] the scope of the original chronicle and its date of composition can be deduced with reasonable certainty. The main text of the chronicle is preceded by a title, 'Summary of the years from Adam the first-fashioned man, until year 20 of the reign of Heraclius the most pious, and post-consulship year 19, and year 18 of the reign of Heraclius II Constantine his son, indiction 3' (p. 32 Bonn). Unless the author, for an unknown reason, failed to accomplish his objective fully, this title locates the end of the chronicle in 630, after 22 January (the start of Heraclius II's 18th year) but before 1 September (the start of indiction 4);[8] within this period Easter, 8 April 630, perhaps provided an appropriate terminus.

It may be speculated that a fitting climax to this Christian chronological work would have been afforded by an account of the restoration of the Holy Cross to Jerusalem on 21 March 630.[9] The occasion was marked by a grand ceremony in which the emperor Heraclius, the empress Martina, and Patriarch Modestus of Jerusalem participated, and it definitively signalled the end of the years of crusade against the Persians: not only had the 'God-abhorred' Khusro been defeated and overthrown, but also, after much negotiation and searching in Persia, the relic of

---

6    Mercati, 'Study' 412, who even suggests that the title *Chronicon Paschale* is a misnomer. This is not discussed by Beaucamp, 'Chronique', an investigation that ignores the serious MS problems affecting *CP*.

7    Mercati, 'Study' 408-11.

8    See Appendix 1 for discussion of proposed alternative dates for the end of *CP*.

9    For the year, see Mango, 'Deux Études' 112-13.

the True Cross, taken into Babylonian captivity after the fall of Jerusalem in 614, had been recovered.[10] When the news reached Constantinople on 31 March, its proclamation was celebrated in a panegyric by George of Pisidia (*In restitutionem S. Crucis*).[11] This event provided a suitable conclusion for *CP*: the author had marked the loss of the Cross in 614 by a rare attempt at grand writing (pp. 704. 13-705. 2; see n. 437), and had recorded the reception at Constantinople of 'surrogate' relics, the Holy Sponge and Spear (*s.a.* 614); now the recovery of the Cross triumphantly re-established visible proof of the supremacy of Christianity.

There were also ideological reasons for terminating a history now. From the overthrow of Maurice in 602 until the death of Khusro in 628 the Roman and Persian empires had been engaged in a titanic struggle for control of the near east. Throughout the reign of Phocas (602-10) and increasingly in the first half of Heraclius' reign the Romans had been worsted, with the result that all the eastern provinces, including the great cities of Antioch, Alexandria, and Jerusalem, had been lost to the Persians; disasters in the east had been paralleled by reverses in the Balkans, where Avars and Slavs pushed south to reach the Aegean, lay siege to Thessalonica and Constantinople, and penetrate peninsular Greece. In this crisis, Roman campaigns had been vested with a crusading aura in a desperate attempt to rally morale, the fighting had assumed apocalyptic overtones, while a belief had emerged that victory would be followed by a Golden Age of tranquil prosperity in which mankind would be prepared for the Day of Judgement.[12] In 628 Heraclius triumphed over the Persians. Now the Golden Age could begin, in which human chronology and history would have served their function and man would be firmly set in a heavenly time-scale. However, at this moment it was also essential to ensure the accuracy of the human time-scale, from the Creation, through the events of Christ's life, and thence to the present day, by the precise calculation of the Easter festival which confirmed and commemorated the divine salvation of the world. At a more practical level, since moves were being made to achieve a reconciliation with the Monophysites and to establish contacts with Persian Nestorians,[13] the orthodox church had to have up-

---

10  For details of the negotiations, ibid. 109-12.

11  Ed. with Italian trans. Pertusi, *Giorgio* 225-30; for discussion of the date, ibid. 230-7.

12  See Whitby, *Maurice* 240-1, 333.

13  Frend, *Monophysite* 343-7; Mango, 'Deux Études' 114-15.

to-date calculations to ensure that its views would be universally accepted in any argument about the date of Easter.[14]

The chronicle, produced in this time of triumph, was compiled at Constantinople which, with the exception of Thessalonica, was the only major centre to have escaped devastation by Persians or Slavs and Avars.[15] In the capital the 'court poet' George of Pisidia composed panegyrics not only to celebrate Heraclius' wars against the Persians but also to praise the patrician Bonus, who had been left by Heraclius in control of secular administration, and to commemorate great events such as the repulse of the Avar siege in 626 and the recovery of the Cross in 630. Classicizing historiography was being revived by Theophylact Simocatta under the patronage of the Patriarch Sergius;[16] although Theophylact's account terminates in 602 with the death of Maurice and the resumption of war with Persia, his original intention had been to continue his narrative to record at least the reign of Phocas and probably also the Persian war.[17] There seems to have been a revival of, or increase in, literary activity at Constantinople in the 620s, and it is not surprising that attention was also paid to the updating of the chronicle tradition.

The author of CP was not alone among contemporaries in his concern for chronological matters, including the date of Easter. In 618/19 Stephen of Alexandria, the philosopher whom Heraclius had summoned to Constantinople, produced a short chronological treatise for which a concluding chapter on Easter appears to have been composed (or at least revised) in 623 by the

---

14 The timing of the Lenten fast had caused serious trouble in Justinian's reign (probably 546), with the population refusing to eat meat that the emperor had ordered to be put on sale: Mal. 482. 19-483. 2, Michael the Syrian ix. 33. In the 550s Justinian had attempted to bring the celebration of Easter in the Armenian Monophysite church into line with Chalcedonian practice, see Scott, 'Easter' 217-21.

15 CP is sometimes described as 'Chronicon Alexandrinum' (e.g. in Du Cange, Glossarium and MGH), but this merely refers to its evident connections with an Egyptian chronicle (such as survives in the Goleniščev papyrus) for parts of its narrative. Alexandria was in Persian hands from c.616 to 629 (a fact that CP does not record), and so was an unlikely place for the composition of a historical work in the 620s.

16 For Sergius as the patron of Theophylact, see Whitby, Maurice 32-3; J. D. C. Frendo ('History and Panegyric in the Age of Heraclius: the Literary Background to the Composition of the Histories of Theophylact Simocatta', DOP xlii, 1988, 143-56 at 144-5 n. 11) repeats his assertion that Heraclius was Theophylact's patron, but offers no new evidence.

17 Theophylact viii. 12. 14, 14. 10; Whitby, Maurice 46-7.

emperor Heraclius himself.[18] This treatise does not share *CP*'s interest in the theoretical basis for Easter calculations established by the 19-year lunar and 28-year solar cycles, but produces a much more functional connection which linked the dating of Easter to the years of the indiction cycle that had started in the third year of Heraclius' reign.[19] Stephen is also plausibly credited with another chronological work of relevance to *CP*, a consular list (*Fasti Heracliani*) covering the years 226 to 630 that was drawn up on the basis of a list attached to a law code.[20] The list, exactly contemporary with *CP*, indicates a current interest in chronology, although it is evident from several discrepancies between *CP* and *Fasti Heracliani* that there was no interaction between their respective compilers.

*CP* is an interesting and important chronicle, but it seems to have had no influence on the later Byzantine chronographic tradition, either in terms of its historical information or its complex chronological computations: the World Era presented in *CP*, which placed the Creation in 5509 BC (cf. p. xxiii), was not adopted by other writers, and Nicephorus and Theophanes, writing in the late 8th/early 9th cc., did not use *CP* as one of their sources for events of the early 7th c. It is unlikely that many versions of the text were ever produced: perhaps only a single copy survived somewhere in Constantinople (possibly in the Patriarchate), until it was copied in the 10th c. into what is now the oldest surviving exemplar (Cod. Vat. gr. 1941); by this time the archetype had already begun to disintegrate, hence the lacunae in Anastasius' reign and at the start of the Nika Riot (*ss.aa.* 507–17, 531).[21] Much later, in the 16th c., at least three further copies were made from this version, and there are extracts in two MSS of the 15th and 18th cc.,[22] which suggests there was some interest in the contents of *CP*, but this limited rediscovery was too late to influence Byzantine writers.

---

18 Beaucamp, 'Chronique' 460-1; H. Usener, *De Stephano Alexandrino Commentatio* (Bonn 1880), in *Kleine Schriften* iii (Leipzig 1914), 289-317, esp. 289ff, 314ff. For the 7th-c. debate in the West about the date of Easter, see J. Herrin, *The Formation of Christendom* (Oxford 1987), 244, 268-9.

19 Beaucamp, loc. cit.

20 Ed. H. Usener, *CM* iii. 386-410 (the scholium on p. 392 mentions the law); Bagnall, *Consuls* 57.

21 For an important discussion of the Vatican MS and its lacunae, see Mercati, 'Study'.

22 For details, see G. Moravcsik, *Byzantinoturcica* (Berlin 1958) i. 241-2.

(ii) *Sources*

The range of sources used in *CP* is one of the most important, but also most difficult, problems posed by the chronicle. Occasional references to sources, for example Priscus on Attila, Nestorianus on Leo II, or the anonymous 'he says' for Zilgbis (*ss.aa*. 450, 474, 522, with nn. 260, 300, 331) are unhelpful in that they are invariably copied from an intermediate source (probably Malalas) which is not itself named. This topic could only be fully investigated in conjunction with an examination of the source traditions of Malalas and Theophanes, both of which interlock to a certain extent with *CP*; for the present no more than a preliminary outline of the main inter-relationships is possible.[23]

For the 5,800 years, or so, covered by the chronicle before the section here translated, *CP*'s main source for secular historical information was Malalas, but this material is interwoven with Biblical/Christian information to produce a narrative with a much more pronounced religious character than that of Malalas. Thus Malalas was used extensively for the treatment of very early or 'mythological' history down as far as the foundation of Rome, but thereafter there is little secular history in *CP*, and it did not draw on Malalas until the account of Septimius Severus' constructions at Byzantium (Mal. 291. 15-292. 19; *CP* pp. 494. 12-495. 16). For the intervening 900 years, *CP* contains a detailed treatment of Old and New Testament matters, and then of various Christian martyrs. Apart from the Bible, extended passages were derived from the *Ecclesiastical History* of Eusebius of Caesarea, and the *Christian Topography* of the 6th-c. traveller and theologian Cosmas Indicopleustes,[24] with a consular list to provide the basic chronological framework.

For the reign of Diocletian, *CP* still contains only limited secular information: imperial notices in 287 and 293 are loosely paralleled in Theophanes, an imperial victory in 297 in *Fasti Hydatiani* (on which see p. xvii), but the only two long notices are religious, the account of St. Gelasinus (297) being provided by Malalas and that of the Great Persecution (303) by Eusebius.

---

[23] The very complex task of a thorough analysis is too great an undertaking for this volume; the forthcoming publication by the Australian Malalas team of their *Studies in the Chronicle of John Malalas* (Byzantina Australiensia) should make the investigation a more practical proposition.

[24] On the latter, see W. Wolska-Conus, *Cosmas Indicopleustès, Topographie chrétienne* i (Paris 1968) 54-5, 86-93; for other possible sources, see Hunger, *Literatur* 329, with Mercati, 'Study' 404-8.

Whereas Malalas was consulted directly by *CP*, Eusebius may have been used via an intermediary: information in *CP* clearly has affinities with Eusebius *HE*, but there is considerable variation in the closeness of the language (contrast the parallels cited in nn. 13, 15, 24 with those in nn. 16, 37, 40).

From the accession of the Christian emperor Constantine, the source tradition becomes more complex as the author of *CP* started to record more information about the secular history of the Christian Roman Empire. Some material can still be traced to Eusebius (persecution *s.a.* 309, Constantine's victory *s.a.* 312, and probably the inspiration for the chronological computation *s.a.* 325), but parallels in chronicles now become increasingly important. Malalas, intermittently, is the source for some information, in particular for long notices such as the description of the foundation of Constantinople (*ss.aa.* 328, 330) or the material about Julian, Jovian, and Valentinian (*ss.aa.* 363 [St. Domitius onwards], 364, 369). Theophanes presents a number of interesting parallels for imperial information in Constantine's reign (*ss.aa.* 304, 327, 328 [bridge], 337 [death of Constantine, attack on Nisibis]), then for some markedly pro-Arian notices under Constantius (*ss.aa.* 350 [siege of Nisibis], 351), and for Julian's persecution of the Christians (*ss.aa.* 362–3);[25] the Arian material, which has links with the Arian church historian Philostorgius, appears to have been incorporated in a source that was independently available to *CP* and Theophanes.[26] Whereas *CP* was content to record praise of the Arian emperor Constantius, Theophanes was somewhat disconcerted by the heretical implications of the information, and on occasions he attempted to introduce his own corrections (e.g. 33. 19-22; 42. 1-15).

---

[25] The anecdote about the blessed Leontius, who was an Arian (350), and the description of Constantius' benefactions to St. Sophia (360) probably came from the same source. F. C. Conybeare ('Chronicle') suggested that the Arian source terminated in 354 and was compiled by the Andrew who drew up Easter tables for Constantius in that year, but the fact that close parallels with Theophanes continue down to 363 suggests that the 'Arianizing' section of their common source extended that far. Conybeare's discussion was distorted by his desire to demonstrate the existence of a version of *CP* that stopped in 354, a misguided notion that was rightly rejected by Mommsen (*CM* i. 203) and was subsequently repudiated by Conybeare himself ('Codex').

[26] Theophanes is independent since at some points he preserves the Arian material more completely or clearly than *CP*, which cannot therefore have been the intermediary. Like *CP*, Theophanes was influenced by Eusebian material, and it is possible that their common source transmitted both the Eusebian and the Arian information.

The most important, however, of the parallel chronicles for the 4th c. is the *Fasti Hydatiani* (*Hyd.*), a Latin consular list with historical entries that was compiled in Spain in the late 5th c. but which for most of the fourth century (*c.*330–89) reused a historical text composed at Constantinople.[27] Not only are there extensive overlaps of information between the sequences of brief notices in *CP* and *Hyd.* (e.g. 337, death of Constantine; 351, Gallus; 354, 355, 356, 357, 359), but it is also clear that *CP*'s list of consuls was ultimately derived from a Latin list of which the 4th-c. part is preserved in *Hyd.*: certain errors in *CP* can be explained as misunderstandings of Latin terms which survive in *Hyd.* (consuls for 307, 308). *CP* also has links, less precisely definable, with other lists or chronicles, namely '*Barbarus Scaligeri*' which is a Latin translation of a Greek chronicle extending down to 387, and the fragment of an illustrated Alexandrian chronicle of the early 5th c. known as the Goleniščev papyrus.[28] Although only fragments of the latter survive, including parts of the years 385–92, the rich illustrations provide an insight both into the type of lavish production that might be accorded to a chronicle, a genre of literature that is often regarded as rather dry, and into the diffusion around the Mediterranean of a common consular list which was expanded to include annalistic notices.[29] *CP*'s place in this nexus of 4th-c. chronicle material can only be roughly fixed: it appears to be derived ultimately from an expanded Constantinopolitan consular list, written in Latin, which incorporated some 3rd and 4th-c. Alexandrian information characterized by the Egyptian dates still preserved in *CP*; this text provided the framework to which were added isolated long passages from Malalas,[30] some

---

[27]  CM i. 197-247; Bagnall, *Consuls* 54-5.

[28]  Brief discussion of these texts, Bagnall, *Consuls* 52-4.

[29]  Apart from Spain (*Hyd.*), Italy (*Scal.*), Egypt (Goleniščev papyrus), there are also signs that the common text migrated to Armenia, since Conybeare ('Chronicle') produces convincing parallels in Moses of Khoren's history.

[30]  Conybeare ('Codex' 396-7) argued that *CP* did not use Malalas because the Armenian history of Moses of Khoren frequently covered the same ground, sometimes agreeing with Malalas and sometimes with *CP*, so that all three texts might appear to derive independently from a common source. The number of parallel 4th-c. passages in Moses is not great: ii. 83, Constantine as son of the prostitute Helena; ii. 88, general account of foundation of Cpl.; iii. 12, Constantius' death at Mopsuestia, with a mention of Cyril's notice of the apparition of a luminous Cross; iii. 21, Valentinian's punishment of Rhodanus for appropriating the widow's property; iii. 29, Valentinian's death; iii. 33, Theodosius and the temples. Occasionally Moses does include information not in our abbreviated text of Malalas (e.g. on Theodosius), but it is reasonable to

material from Eusebius, and a collection of Arian (and other) notices that appear in Theophanes.

A new section, from the aspect of source affiliations, begins in the 390s when Marcellinus Comes replaces *Hyd.* as the major parallel text both for the list of consuls and for the annual entries down to 468, though in terms of expression Marcellinus is much less close to *CP* than *Hyd.* had been.[31] Marcellinus, writing in Latin at Constantinople under Justinian, used a 5th-c. chronicle which provided detailed information on the house of Theodosius and which was independently available to *CP* (who often has more details than Marc. Com.). This chronicle seems to have directly continued the 4th-c. chronicle shared by *CP* and *Hyd.*, since in *CP* there is no obvious break in information or change in technical factors such as dating formulae.[32] Malalas provided supplementary material, notably long undated stories (e.g. Athenaïs Eudocia, *s.a.* 420; sequence of stories, *s.a.* 450).

From 469 there is another change in source affiliation, since Malalas now takes over as virtually the sole source to be used in *CP*; it seems that the version of the Constantinopolitan chronicle available to the author terminated at roughly this date, since no further notices can be traced to this source.[33] The subsequent reliance on Malalas created dating problems, since the chronology of Malalas, at least until the reign of Justin I (518–27), was not always precise: some notices in *CP* are misplaced simply because Malalas gave no clear indication of dates (e.g. *ss.aa.* 467, Aspar; 469, fire; 484, Armatus). In addition, Malalas did not provide names of consuls, and it is not possible to isolate a list closely parallel to *CP*: in some years, e.g. 483–90, 493–4, *CP*'s consular names have closer affinities with western than with eastern lists, suggesting that the material did not derive directly

infer that this was derived from the original complete version of Malalas.

31 On Marc. Com., see B. Croke, 'The Chronicle of Marcellinus Comes in its Contemporary and Historiographical Context' (unpublished Oxford D.Phil. 1978); also id. 'A.D. 476: the Manufacture of a Turning Point', *Chiron* xiii, 1983, 81-119 at 87-90.

32 Chronicle notices are characterized by Roman dating formulae (Kalends, Nones, Ides), and the frequent use of the expression, 'In the time of these consuls...', for the first notice in a year, and of the title Augustus for emperors (by contrast Malalas tended to use *basileus*, emperor, and rarely referred to consulships other than at the death/accession of an emperor). The distribution of dates, both Greek months (G) and Roman formulae (R), is interesting. AD 284-364: 30R, 11G (excluding the Easter Tables); 364-425: 79R, 69G; 425-57: 4R, 10G; 457-69: 0R, 1G; 470-600: 2R, 15G; 601-28: 0R, 28G.

33 The version available to Marcellinus may have extended slightly further, but from the late 5th c. he could introduce material from his own experience.

from an official version of the *fasti*. However, in 499 *CP* gives the Greek *Kurtos* as the sobriquet of the consul John, who is elsewhere known by the Latin equivalent Gibbus (Hunchback).[34]

This Malalas-based section terminates with the notice of the 533 earthquake after the long account of the Nika Riot in 532 (*s.a.* 531),[35] and it appears that *CP* used a version of Malalas that ended in that year.[36] For the next 50 years there is very little secular information in *CP*: the majority of the years are left blank, as if the author could not find a source that covered the period, and it seems, surprisingly, that he did not know the extended version of Malalas which included much information on Constantinopolitan events down to 565; less unexpectedly, there is no indication of any awareness of the elevated classicizing writings of Procopius or his historical continuators. To compensate for this dearth, the author of *CP* included two long religious edicts issued by Justinian (*ss.aa.* 533, 552: the latter not translated here), and devised a chronological calculation to mark the end of the first great Easter cycle of 532 years (*s.a.* 562): this material reflects personal interests of the author (see further sec. iii).

There are signs of a change with the accession of Maurice in 582: *CP* begins to preserve some precise information about the imperial family (*ss.aa.* 582, 602) and mentions official records in

---

[34] If a western origin is postulated for this section of *CP's fasti*, *Kurtos* would represent the author's translation of this term (cf. *ss.aa.* 307, 308 for comparable, though garbled, translations).

[35] For the dependence of *CP's* account of the riot on Malalas, see Bury, 'Riot' 95-101, 115-16 (though he also identified the *Akta dia Kalopodion* as non-Malalas material, probably unnecessarily; see note B at pp. 112-13 below).

[36] The question of the terminal dates of Malalas is a complex problem, which will be discussed in the forthcoming *Studies in the Chronicle of John Malalas* (Byzantina Australiensia). The first version of Malalas ended at some point in the period 527–32, whereas the continuation of Malalas concluded in 565. Evagrius (*HE* iv. 5) states that he was using a version that finished after the Antioch earthquake in 526, and it is clear from his account of the Nika Riot (iv. 32) that he did not have access to Malalas' version of events: his text of Malalas may have ended with the accession of Justinian in 527. However, it is conceivable that the first version of Malalas treated the years 527–32 as a quasi-appendix, possibly composed after the author had moved from Antioch to Cpl.: at least the coverage of these years continues at the same thorough level as for Justin I's reign, after which there is a marked decline in detail (cf. L. M. Whitby, 'Justinian's Bridge over the Sangarius and the Date of Procopius' *de Aedificiis'*, *JHS* cv, 1985, 129-48 at 138-9); the account of the Nika Riot in particular seems to reflect an extra-palatial tradition (Bury, 'Riot' 94; Scott, 'Malalas' 102), that preserves a narrative of events which is different from the official version, and which Malalas is more likely to have gathered in Cpl. than at Antioch.

connection with the coronation of Maurice's son Theodosius
(590). However, Theophanes had access to a chronicle source for
the period from 565, which preserved much more Constantinopolitan information than is recorded in *CP*. With the accession
of Phocas (602) the change is complete and *CP* re-emerges as a
detailed, and often unparalleled, Constantinopolitan chronicle.
Some information came from official records (Heraclius' non-
consulship, *s.a.* 611; annual formula used after coronation of
Heraclius II, from 613), and the author also included the texts of
two official letters, from the senate to Khusro (615) and from
Heraclius to the people of Constantinople (628),[37] but some
notices are likely to have derived from his personal experience of
events (e.g. Sergius' liturgical innovations, *ss.aa.* 615, 624; parts
of the 626 siege narrative).

At no period, however, can *CP* be treated simply as the
product of a given number of sources whether identifiable or
obscure, in that the author had his own interests which
influenced his selection or presentation of material, and
sometimes he appears to have composed original notices: thus
having copied a long account, from a source shared with
Theophanes, of dynastic changes in the Tetrarchy (*s.a.* 304), he
then introduced a garbled abbreviation of this imperial survey in
the next year; or having incorrectly noted the proclamation of
Constans as Caesar in 317 (contrast *Hyd.* which correctly names
Licinius), he then upgraded Constans to Augustus in 325 (cf. n.
43).   At some points he deliberately divided Malalas-based
information between two separate years (the foundation of
Constantinople, *ss.aa.* 328, 330; Athenaïs-Eudocia, *ss.aa.* 420–1;
Amantius, *ss.aa.* 518–19), in each case probably because it was
clear that the notice covered a substantial period of time, and so
deserved to be spread over more than one year.   He may also
deliberately have changed the day and month of the discovery of
John the Baptist's head in 453 to accord with the date given in an
alternative version of the deposition of the same relic in 391 (cf.
n. 270). Thus, although *CP* is often an accurate transcription of
information from earlier sources, it would be wrong to assume
that an origin can, or should, be found for every word: the
author was prepared on occasions to think about his material
and to adapt it, not necessarily correctly, when he saw fit.

This discussion of sources has touched on the relationship
between *CP* and the urban chronicle tradition at Constantinople
and, since *CP* is our main example in Greek of this tradition, it is

---

[37]  Cf. Scott, 'Justinian' 17-20, and id. 'Malalas' 100, for official origin.

worth attempting to present some tentative conclusions; the following is a simplification of a complex issue, but may nevertheless have some value as a hypothesis. It appears that some form of official record or register did exist at Constantinople, which probably comprised consular *fasti* dating back to the city's foundation and beyond, together with notices of imperial events. This record must have been preserved in some central archive, where it was regularly updated and was available for consultation or copying by interested individuals.

At certain points the record was supplemented by the insertion of extra notices, which transformed the bare *fasti* into a more informative text that can be characterized as an urban chronicle: this comprised more information about the imperial family, important building works, natural disasters and phenomena, riots, some Church affairs, all of which might be accorded a precise date, on the old Roman system of Kalends, Nones, and Ides, and/or by days of the Roman and/or Greek months. This expansion was probably carried out by the individual who added annually the names of the new consuls, and it remained to an extent a personal matter dependent upon the knowledge, interests, or whim of the particular recorder. Throughout the 4th and into the 5th c. this process was carried on, and the continuity of the basic text is reflected in the absence of any noticeable shift in *CP*'s presentation of chronicle information: chronicle terminology (cf. n. 32 above) continues without a break from the late 4th into the 5th c.

However, in the late 5th c. the tradition of adding information seems to have terminated. A factor may have been the major fires that devastated much of the centre of Cpl. in the 460s and 470s. Thereafter the author of *CP* had access to consular *fasti*, although this list had no 'chronicle' information appended to it and did not present the official eastern view of the consular succession (cf. n. 306), as though an individual with a pronounced western connection was now privately continuing the *fasti*-element from the abandoned urban chronicle. The importance of *fasti* diminished after the consulship of Basilius in 541 (the last non-imperial consul). Thereafter individual imperial consulships were noted in official records, since these consulships were used for dating purposes (cf. *CP s.a.* 611), but the lack of a continuous list may account for the errors in *CP* over the consulships of Justin II and Maurice (*ss.aa* 566, 583).

This hypothesis about the termination of the urban chronicle helps to explain *CP*'s dependence on Malalas for events of the late 5th and early 6th cc., and the virtual interruption of its secular record c.532/3: little historical information could be gained from official records. By the 6th c. the urban chronicle tradition had lost its connection with the *fasti*, and instead depended upon individual writers continuing the work of their predecessors: thus the Antioch-centred *Chronicle* of Malalas was extended by the addition of a Constantinople-centred account covering Justinian's reign, and this in turn was extended by the Constantinopolitan accounts of late 6th and early 7th-c. history that were available to Theophanes; the narrative in *CP* of 7th-c. events is a further example of this process. One consequence of the 'privatizing' of historiographical effort was a fragmentation of historical knowledge: in contrast to the extensive overlaps in the 4th–5th cc. between *CP* and *Hydatius* and Marcellinus Comes, which reflect the existence of a form of (semi-)official urban chronicle, by the late 6th c. the absence of parallels between *CP* and John of Antioch, Theophanes, or Nicephorus is striking, an indication of the lack of a comprehensive central record.

(iii) *Interests*

The personal interests of the author of *CP* made a positive contribution to the chronicle. The most obvious of these is chronology, a natural preoccupation for chroniclers who narrated the progress of history from the creation of the world down to the present day,[38] but one which seems to be especially prominent in *CP*:[39] the author marked the start of the reign of each new emperor with a running total of the years since the creation of the world; the cycle of Olympiads is maintained right through to the end of the chronicle, and each year of imperial Roman history is preceded by a note of indiction and regnal years as well as the names of the consuls (or consul); consular references are even included for years when strictly there appeared to be no acceptable designation (e.g. 583);[40] each year

---

[38] Thus Malalas marks the accession of Justinian with a computation (428. 8-429. 9) that includes the observation that the 6,000th year of the world has now passed. Eusebius had prefaced his chronicle with a long essay that explained the systems of dating used by leading nations.

[39] This special interest is stressed in Beaucamp, 'Chronique'. The fullest discussion of *CP*'s complex chronological scheme is Grumel, *Chronologie*, esp. chs. 4-5, which supercedes the investigation of E. Schwartz (Pauly-Wissowa, *Real-Encyclopädie* iii/2, 1899, 246-77).

[40] It should be noted, contrary to the criticism of Bagnall (*Consuls* 56), that *CP* did not misunderstand the use of the post-consular formula; it is often the Bonn

has its heading even when, as is frequent in the 6th c., there were no notices to be inserted. This concern with the precise identification of each year is not present in Malalas, but it is paralleled in the early 9th-c. chroniclers George Syncellus and Theophanes. The desire for precision could give rise to problems: in *CP* Olympiads are not inserted at the correct year (down to Olympiad 273 they are two years early, thereafter only one year); since consular and indiction years began in different months (January, September), it was necessary to choose one to determine the organization of annual entries, and, because the author gave priority to the consular year, indiction-dated entries for the months September to December are placed in years with the preceding indiction year in their heading (e.g. death of Anastasius of Antioch, *s.a.* 610).[41]

The author of *CP* seems to have carried out many of his own chronological calculations, which enabled him to establish the date of the creation of the world as 5509 BC with the Crucifixion in *annus mundi* 5540,[42] and he was concerned to demonstrate the continuing accuracy of this chronology throughout the work. There are major calculations in 325, probably connected with the termination of Eusebius' *History* (cf. n. 48 ad loc.), in 344 when a new Easter table came into operation, replacing that of Anatolius of Laodicea, in 562 at the end of the first great Easter cycle of 532 years from the Crucifixion, in 609 at the start of the narrative of Heraclius' revolt against Phocas, and in 616 for a reason that remains unclear.[43] Most of these key dates are related to events in Christ's life, his birth, baptism, or the Resurrection, and cross-references to the Resurrection or Ascension also date martyrs (Menas, 295; Gelasinus, 297), church councils (Nicaea, 325; Constantinople, 381; Ist Ephesus, 431; Chalcedon, *s.a.* 452),[44]

text which inaccurately reports the formula used (see nn. 302, 378, 388).

[41] Moreover, Olympiads technically began in mid-summer, a complication for the synchronism of different dating methods that is ignored in *CP*, where precise Olympiad dates are rare in notices except for chronological computations.

[42] For discussion of this unique Era, see Grumel, *Chronologie* pt. I, ch. 5, who terms it 'Protobyzantine'; cf. nn. 79-80. It is not known who devised this Era, but it is not impossible that the author of *CP* was responsible.

[43] The 325 calculation shows Eusebian influences (location in text, structure), but the totals of years are different from Eusebius; the 344 calculation and cycle must have originated in a contemporary who was interested in the start of the new Easter table (cf. n. 79 ad loc.). The later computations can be ascribed to the author of *CP* (cf. *s.a.* 609, where he states that he has checked his calculation against the Easter tables and consular lists).

[44] Some Ascension dates were derived from a source, since the dates for the

and the dedication of Constantinople (*s.a.* 330, adding a cross-reference to the foundation of Rome, the city on which it was modelled).[45] *CP* also took over from its sources various secular dating systems, the Antiochene Era from Malalas, and the Era of Diocletian, which was common in Egypt, perhaps from Alexandrian material that had been attached to the 4th-c. urban chronicle.[46] The result is a plethora of dating systems: traditional Roman dates by Kalends, Nones and Ides, and dates by Egyptian, Greek, and Roman months. This mass of dates was presumably intended to convey an impression of accuracy, and is in marked contrast to Malalas: Malalas' main chronological concern was to convince his readers that the world had safely negotiated the great climacteric of the year 6000 and was now launched into the seventh millenium (428. 8-429. 9), but he does not seem to have bothered to give precise dates to many notices before the reign of Justin I. For the author of *CP* every notice had to be placed in a year, and often also be given a more accurate date (sometimes with days of the week, and even hours, e.g. in the account of Heraclius' coup *s.a.* 610, p. 701. 11).

Other interests are analogous to those of other Greek chronicles: *CP* was composed at Constantinople, a city isolated by the military catastrophes of the early 7th c., which may have imposed limitations on the horizons of its author. Furthermore the anticipated readers were fellow inhabitants of the capital, probably officials with, at the least, a modest education: references to churches of St. Thomas and St. Euphemia (*ss.aa.* 454, 464) would scarcely be intelligible to outsiders, who might have been misled by the text into locating both buildings at Rome, and during the 626 siege the author refers to the defenders in the first person plural (e. g. p. 723. 19); in the 7th-c. narrative, precise titles are carefully recorded for the majority of people mentioned.

It is not surprising that imperial and especially urban affairs

martyrs *ss.aa.* 295 and 297, and in the computation *s.a.* 325, place the Crucifixion in the equivalent of AD 29, whereas the dates for the church councils put it in AD 31 (in accordance with *CP*'s own dating for the Crucifixion, and with its computations *ss.aa.* 562, 616).

[45] Malalas, the source for most of the account of Cpl.'s foundation, does not have the complete dating formula preserved in *CP* (cf. *s.a.* 330 with n. 56). For *CP*'s interest in precise dating, compare also the discovery of John the Baptist's head, *s.a.* 453, dated by years from his death as well as by Seleucid and Antiochene Eras. There is also a puzzling reference to the martyrdoms of Peter and Paul, *s.a.* 396.

[46] Cf. also Constantius' death in 361, dated with reference to 'the peace of the churches' as well as the Antiochene Era.

are prominent, for example riots, earthquakes and fires that affected the capital, stories about emperors, their families and associates. On occasion these stories are narrated from a marked Constantinopolitan perspective: for example, the account of Heraclius' revolt in 610 begins with the appearance of his ships off the Hebdomon, and that of Shahin's raid to the Bosporus in 615 with his arrival at Chalcedon. Notices which reflected these interests were copied from the available sources or, in the latter part of the chronicle, composed by the author himself. Thus, an attempt was made to catalogue the very complex changes to the Diocletianic Tetrarchy and the house of Constantine (ss.aa. 304, 305, 335, 337), and very long accounts of the marriage of Athenaïs Eudocia to Theodosius II and of the downfall of Paulinus were taken from Malalas (ss.aa. 420-1, 444). In the light of such notices, there is a significant silence about Heraclius' marriage to Martina: although the births and coronations of Heraclius' children by his first marriage, Epiphania Eudocia and Heraclius II Constantine, and the death of his first wife the Augusta Eudocia are recorded (ss.aa. 611, 612, 613), the marriage to Martina (Heraclius' niece) is ignored and Martina is only mentioned once *en passant*, in connection with the celebration of Easter in 624. The explanation is plain: the marriage had been strongly opposed by the Patriarch Sergius, who had asked the emperor to renounce the incestuous union but been told to mind his own business (Nic. 14. 26-15. 2).

On the other hand warfare did not, it seems, greatly attract the author: he could easily have extracted more information from Malalas about Julian's Persian campaign in 363, and given a much longer account of Justinian's Persian wars of 527-32. Warfare in the Balkans and the western part of the empire is almost completely disregarded: the Balkans had largely slipped beyond imperial control, and links with the west were so tenuous that the remnants of Justinian's reconquests were outside the vision of the average inhabitant of the capital; the author of CP was prepared to accept that the major city of Naissus was in Italy (s.a. 350). Someone with military interests might have said more about the fighting in both the east and the Balkans during Maurice's reign,[47] or in particular about Heraclius' contemporary Persian campaigns. In this respect CP is different from other chronicles, for example Malalas and

---

[47] A narrative was after all being produced by a contemporary, Theophylact Simocatta, and the Cpl. chronicle subsequently used by Theophanes contained some military information.

Theophanes: the latter, writing in the 9th c., preserves more information about military campaigns in the late 6th/early 7th cc. than does the contemporary *CP*. The only warfare which interested *CP* was the direct attack on Constantinople in 626 and the emperor's report, complete with religious overtones, of the triumph over Persia in 628; apart from these narratives, the longest military account is of the Persian siege of Nisibis (*s.a.* 350), where the combination of siege tactics, divinely-assisted defence, and repulse of the Persians would have had strong contemporary resonances. He was also attracted by the story of the senator Arinthaeus making peace with the Persians (*s.a.* 363), a parallel for the senate's attempt to negotiate with Khusro in the 610s.

After chronology the most striking interest of the author is in ecclesiastical affairs (saints, persecutions, martyrdoms), and in particular in the Constantinopolitan Church and the attempts to revise Chalcedonian orthodoxy that were promoted in the 6th c. Thus he notes recent liturgical developments at the capital (*ss.aa.* 615, 624), but also the arrival of relics in the 4th/5th cc., and he lists many of the bishops present at the Constantinopolitan synod in 360, a list that is not preserved in any of the sources parallel to *CP*. The author's lack of enthusiasm for Chalcedonian orthodoxy emerges not only from the brevity of the reference to the Synod of Chalcedon itself (*s.a.* 452) or the omission of Malalas' description of the Chalcedonian Justin I as 'emperor through the will of God' (see n. 327), but more positively in the report of anti-Chalcedonian chanting following the 533 earthquake ('Destroy and burn the document issued by the bishops of the Synod of Chalcedon') or of Justinian's two neo-Chalcedonian ecclesiastical edicts (*ss.aa.* 533, 552). It is tempting to speculate that the end of the chronicle might have mentioned the further 'improvements' to Chalcedonian doctrine advocated by Sergius (the Monothelete/Monergist formulae);[48] these could have been associated with the triumph of the return to Jerusalem of the Holy Cross, with which *CP*'s account probably terminated (cf. pp. xi-xii).

Literary presentation was not a major concern of the author, and his choice of language tends to reflect closely that of his sources. This leads to variations in style depending on the source used, and means that it is difficult to identify personal characteristics: if anywhere these will emerge in the 7th-c. notices, but several of these are transcripts of official material and so do not represent the individual style of the author. His

---

[48] Frend, *Monophysite* 344-6.

language has been described as a version of 'literary Koine',[49] the functional language of administrative and technical texts which was used by the majority of writers who had no desire to impose a classicizing literary veneer on their works. In *CP* elements of spoken Greek are occasionally admitted, perhaps more commonly in reported direct speech (e.g. the Avar Chagan addressing ambassadors, pp. 721. 15-722. 1, where tenses are used loosely) than in the main text. Sentences are sometimes carelessly constructed, being built up with a series of paratactic phrases; subordinate constructions, such as purpose or temporal clauses, are avoided and strings of participles, or article with infinitive constructions, used instead; and the standard connective καί may be alternately omitted or redundant. Very occasionally there are touches of grander writing, for example in the description of the calamitous capture of Jerusalem in 614 and the introduction to the narrative of the 626 siege (see nn. 437, 457).

The author's ecclesiastical interests and Constantinopolitan focus suggest that Gelzer was right to speculate that he belonged to the clergy, perhaps as a member of the staff of St. Sophia under the authority of the Patriarch Sergius (610–37).[50] However, it is unlikely that he was very closely attached to Sergius, since his description of the patriarch's actions in 626 is not as extravagantly panegyrical as that of Theodore Syncellus. He was a person of some education, though with no obvious knowledge of, or interest in, classical literature or ability to compose elegant literary Greek; he was capable of performing complex calculations, was familiar with records and documents, and was interested in precision of time; furthermore it is possible that he had a limited acquaintance with administrative Latin.[51] On the other hand, his abilities as editor seem to have been

---

[49] Browning, 'Language', 110-11.

[50] *Sextus Julius Africanus und die byzantinische Chronographie* (Leipzig 1885), ii. 138. Browning ('Language' 111) describes him as a monk writing for fellow monks: this description may be too narrow.

[51] This suggestion is based on the assumption that the author was responsible for translating the *fasti*/urban chronicle that he used for 4th–5th cc. events; this work had been composed in Latin (as shown by the misunderstandings of the consular entries in *CP ss.aa.* 307, 308), which is not surprising since Latin was the language of imperial administration in the east down to the reign of Justinian. It seems likely that a person who translated the text would then have extended the historical narrative down to his own time, but *CP*'s version of the text terminated in 469, whereafter only Malalas offered historical information. The argument is, of course, highly speculative.

limited: the majority of notices were copied from one source, and the only examples of amalgamation of sources within a notice are the rare insertion of a precise date into material derived from Malalas (e.g. Roman date for the foundation of Constantinople). There are a few instances which suggest that the author was alert to contradictions in his account: thus having antedated the elevation of Constans as Caesar to 317, the author seems to have remembered that Constans' next elevation must be as Augustus, but he can derive little credit from the erroneous adaptation since he proceeded to record the latter elevation under two separate years (325, 335 – both incorrectly; cf. nn. 43, 65 ad locc.). All these factors would be compatible with an administrative appointment in the ecclesiastical bureaucracy.

Examination of source affiliations and the interests of the author does not provide solutions to all puzzling aspects of the text: thus, even granted that the author's copy of Malalas apparently terminated in 532 and that his personal experiences only began towards 600, the dearth of information for the intervening 70 years remains strange. Historians at Constantinople had written about events (e.g. Agathias, Menander) and, if their accounts were too military or too linguistically elevated for a chronicler's tastes, the period was also covered by chronicles, the continuation of Malalas down to 565 and thereafter the lost source that underlies part of Theophanes' account,[52] but the author of *CP* either chose not to use, or did not have access to, such information.

(iv) *Translation*

The text of *CP* is preserved in one damaged 10th-c. manuscript in the Vatican library (Cod. Vat. gr. 1941), and three apographs of no independent value.[53] Our translation is based on the standard edition, that of Dindorf in the Bonn Corpus (1832); this is basically sound, although a new edition is now being prepared by O. Mazal.[54] We have consulted a microfilm of the Vatican manuscript in order to verify points that appeared problematic, and this has resulted in occasional textual correction (noted ad locc.). Our translation begins with the accession of Diocletian in 284, a natural beginning for a work intended for students of late Roman and medieval history; but it is also the point at which

---

52  Whitby, 'Chronicle Source'.

53  Cf. Introduction nn. 21-2 above.

54  See *JÖB* xxxv, 1985, 341.

*CP* begins regularly to contain useful historical information.[55] For reasons of space, we have had to omit from the translation the long doctrinal document which Justinian issued in 551 (*CP s.a.* 552) in connection with the Three Chapters controversy.

We have aimed, like the Australian Malalas team, to keep close to the structure and style of the original, in the belief that this will be most useful to readers unable to consult the original Greek. Before the headings for each year in the text we have inserted (in bold type) an AD date for the consular year beginning on 1 January (since in *CP* the calendar year takes precedence over indiction or regnal years). We have also inserted page numbers of the Bonn text (also in bold type) to facilitate consultation.

In the notes we have attempted to record for each individual notice: (i) parallel texts that may shed light on the source affiliations of *CP*; we have underlined parallels which we considered to be very close and indicative of a source tradition available to the author of *CP*;[56] (ii) to refer to other ancient sources that provide important additional information about events in question; and (iii) to mention useful secondary literature where further discussion and bibliography can be found. We realize that limitations of space, and ignorance, have necessitated selectivity in the second and third categories of citation. We have tried to discuss most fully events and categories of information for which *CP* is an especially important witness: thus the Nika Riot (*s.a.* 531), 7th-c. history, and the topography of Constantinople receive detailed discussion because *CP*'s evidence is of primary importance and is often unparalleled.

Proper names are an inevitable headache: we have Anglicized where this is the familar form and have otherwise tended to Latinize. We have provided cross-references to *PLRE* vols. i & ii where appropriate; unfortunately we have not had access to *PLRE* iii, whose publication is imminent, and this should be consulted for prosopographical information after *c.*528.

---

[55] *CP* does contain interesting items on earlier imperial history, e.g. Hadrian's activities at Gaza (p. 474. 6-9), or the foundation of the *candidati* under Gordian and Philip (pp. 501. 13-17, 502. 14-19), but such notices are isolated; to have chosen an earlier starting-point (e.g. Julius Caesar, the first Roman emperor) would have expanded the volume excessively.

[56] These parallels occur particularly in *Hydatius*, Malalas, and Theophanes, and to a lesser extent in Marcellinus Comes (the parallels between *CP* and Marc. Com. are established more by the number of analogous notices than by close linguistic similarities in particular cases).

**284 [p.510.18]** Diocletian was 33rd Roman emperor for 20 years.                                                                                   In total, 5,814.
Diocletian, after being proclaimed on day 15 before Kalends of October [17 Sept.] in Chalcedon, entered Nicomedia on day 5 before Kalends of October [27 Sept.] **[p.511]** wearing the purple, and on Kalends of January [1 Jan.] he appeared in public as consul.[1]

**285** Indiction 4, year 1, the 2nd consulship of Diocletian Augustus and that of Aristobulus.
The regnal years of Diocletian in the Easter Tables are determined from these consuls.[2]

---

[1]    **284** Introductory heading for new reign: a standard formula, enumerating emperors in sequence from Julius Caesar and adding their regnal length to the cumulative total of years since the Creation.

Diocletian's proclamation as Augustus: the accepted date and place are 20 Nov. at Nicomedia (anniversary distributions on 20 Nov. 299: Chester Beatty Panopolis papyrus, in *Papyri from Panopolis*, ed. T. C. Skeat, Dublin 1964, ii. 162, 170, *al.*; *vicennalia* at Rome on 20 Nov.: Lact. *DMP* 17.1); unless, for reasons unknown, Diocletian established 20 Nov. as the nominal date of his accession, the *CP* date has to be rejected. It is possible that an initial proclamation at Chalcedon was followed by formal accession at Nicomedia (Diocletian's principal residence for most of his reign), but *CP*'s information on the deaths of Diocletian's predecessors Carus, Carinus, and Numerian is very confused and contributes to doubts about *CP*'s reliability at this point.

For the chronology of changes in the imperial college between the accession of Diocletian and the death of Constantine, see Barnes, *NE* 3-8.

[2]    **285** Easter Tables: the calculation of Easter, a movable Feast dependent on the date of the first full moon after the spring equinox, provided considerable scope for disagreement. Various attempts were made to establish a reliable cycle that would fix the date in advance and ensure the simultaneous celebration of this major festival of the Christian year. An important step was taken in the mid-3rd c. by the Egyptian Anatolius, bishop of Laodicea in Syria, who exploited a 19-year lunar cycle for the computation of Easter and probably produced a 95-year table (5 cycles) whose notional beginning was in 258. In order to place the equinox correctly on 21 March, a reform was undertaken at Alexandria in the early 4th c., and the revised cycle was notionally begun either in 303 or one cycle earlier in 284; the latter coincided with the regnal years of Diocletian which were used for dating purposes especially in Egypt, where the new cycle was adopted.

**286** Indiction 5, year 2, consulship of Maximus and Aquilinus.

### Olympiad 267[3]

**287** Indiction 6, year 3, the 3rd consulship of Diocletian Augustus and that of Maximianus Herculius Augustus.

In this year Diocletian declared Maximianus Herculius partner in his reign, at the beginning of the third year of his reign, after he had spent the winter in Nicomedia.[4]

**288** Indiction 7, year 4, the 2nd consulship of Maximianus Herculius and that of Januarius.[5]

**289** Indiction 8, year 5, consulship of Bassus and Quintianus.

**290** Indiction 9, year 6, the 4th consulship of Diocletian Augustus and the 3rd of Maximianus Herculius Augustus.

### Olympiad 268

**291** Indiction 10, year 7, consulship of Tiberianus and Dio.

**292** [p.512] Indiction 11, year 8, consulship of Hannibalianus and Asclepiodotus.

**293** Indiction 12, year 9, the 5th consulship of Diocletian Augustus and the 4th of Maximianus Herculius Augustus.

In this year Maximianus Jovius *nobilissimus* Caesar was adopted into the rule, as well as Constantius, at Nicomedia on day 12 before Kalends of June [21 May].[6]

**294** Indiction 13, year 10, consulship of Constantius Caesar and Maximianus Jovius Caesar.

---

See further Grumel, *Chronologie* pt. I, ch. 3, Richard, 'Comput', and cf. *s.a.* 344 for an Easter computation that includes Diocletian's regnal years.

3    Olympiads: these strictly began in mid-summer and could not correspond exactly to consular-calendar years. Olympiad 267 began in summer 289: down to Olympiad 273 (placed before AD 312) Olympiads are inserted two years early, thereafter one year early. For indictions (which ran from 1 Sept. to 31 Aug.), see n. 30.

4    **287** Maximian: proclaimed Caesar on 21 July 285, he was in fact created Augustus early in 286, probably on 1 April (*Hyd. s.a.* 286); cf. Theoph. 6. 18-19. Maximianus' divine name Herculius reflected his status as the agent of Diocletian Jovius.

5    **288** *cos. post.*: Januarianus.

6    **293** Galerius (Maximianus Jovius) and Constantius: cf. Theoph. 7. 1-2; both were probably created Caesar (in east and west respectively) on 1 March, Galerius at Sirmium and Constantius at Milan (Barnes, *NE* 60-2).

## Olympiad 269

**295** Indiction 14, year 11, consulship of Tuscus and Anullinus.
In year 267 from the Ascension to heaven of the Lord[7] and under the aforementioned consuls, St. Menas was martyred at Cotyaeum in Phrygia Salutaris, on Athyr 15, day 3 before Ides of November [11 Nov.].[8]

**296** Indiction 15, year 12, the 6th consulship of Diocletian Augustus and the 2nd of Constantius Caesar.

**297** Indiction 1, year 13, the 5th consulship of Maximianus Herculius and the 2nd of Maximianus Jovius.

The Persians were soundly defeated by Constantius and Maximianus Jovius.[9]

[p.513] In year 269 from the Ascension to heaven of the Lord and under the aforementioned consuls, St. Gelasinus was martyred at the Heliopolitan city in Libanensis. This man was second mime and, while a public theatrical contest was being held and the populace was watching, the other mimes threw him into a great tub from the bath-house, full of warm water, in mockery of the doctrine of the Christians and the holy baptism. And the same Gelasinus, the second mime, after being baptized and coming up from the tub, clad in white robes, no longer tolerated being on stage, saying, 'I am a Christian; for I saw an awesome glory in the tub, and I will die a Christian.' And when they heard this the people who were watching in the theatre of the Heliopolitan city were exceedingly enraged; and they rushed from the seats onto the stage, forced St. Gelasinus out of the

---

7 **295** Dating from Ascension: used for Christian material, cf. *s.a.* 297. Both these Ascension dates place the Crucifixion in AD 29, at variance with the location of the Crucifixion in *CP* in *a.m.* 5540 (AD 31); this suggests that the dates were derived from a source, probably that responsible for the Egyptian date at the end of the notice.

8 Menas: an Egyptian martyred at Alexandria (hence the Egyptian month Athyr), whose cult only became widespread in the 5th c. His association with Cotyaeum in Phrygia is plausibly connected with the career of the Egyptian Cyrus, native of Panopolis where the cult of Menas was popular; Cyrus, consul, praetorian and urban prefect under Theodosius II, was relegated to Cotyaeum as bishop *c.*441–2. See P. Peeters, *Orient et Byzance: le tréfonds oriental de l'hagiographie byzantine* (Subsidia Hagiographica xxvi, 1950), 32-41; for Cyrus, *CP s.a.* 450 with n. 261.

9 **297** Persian defeat: *CP* has two separate notices (cf. n. 11) which mention different victors; this suggests the use of two sources. Constantius was in Gaul and was not involved. Galerius (Maximianus Jovius) was defeated by the Persians in 297, but conquered them in 298 (Eutropius ix. 24-5; Barnes, *CE* 17-18, *NE* 63).

theatre still wearing his white robes, and stoned and slaughtered him, and so the just man died. And his kinsmen took his corpse and carried it away to the village called Mariamme from which he originated, outside Heliopolis, and there they built a chapel for him.[10]

In the time of the same consuls, the Persians were defeated by Maximianus Herculius Augustus.[11]

**298** [p.514] Indiction 2, year 14, consulship of Anicius Faustus and Severus Gallus.[12]

Olympiad 270

**299** Indiction 3, year 15, the 7th consulship of Diocletian Augustus and the 6th of Maximianus Herculius Augustus.

**300** Indiction 4, year 16, the 3rd consulship of Constantius Caesar and the 3rd of Maximianus Jovius.

Peter was 16th leader of the Alexandrian church for 12 years. Since he conducted himself with considerable rigour in asceticism and openly concerned himself with the community of the churches, in year 9 of the persecution and year 16 of the reign of Diocletian, he was beheaded and adorned with the crown of martyrdom, together with innumerable others as well who were martyred in many cities.[13]

**301** Indiction 5, year 17, consulship of Tatianus and Nepotianus.

**302** Indiction 6, year 18, the 4th consulship of Constantius Caesar and the 4th of Maximianus Jovius Caesar.

In this year the military bread was granted at Alexandria by Diocletian.[14]

---

10 Gelasinus: cf. Mal. 314. 12-315. 11 (undated). According to Malalas, Mariamme was located half a mile outside Damascus. See further W. Weisman, 'Gelasinos von Heliopolis, ein Schauspieler-Märtyrer', AB xciii, 1975, 39-66.

11 Defeat of Persians: cf. Hyd. (without name of victor). Maximianus Augustus was in Africa and was not involved; cf. n. 9.

12 **298** cos. post.: Virius Gallus.

13 **300** Peter of Alexandria: patriarch 300–11; cf. Euseb. HE vii. 32. 31, also ix. 6. 2. Peter was martyred in 311 (the ninth year from the resumption of persecution in 303), but the regnal year of Diocletian relates to Peter's inauguration (not his death).

14 **302** Bread distributions: the expression καστρήσιος ἄρτος is odd (literally 'camp' or 'military bread'; possibly by extension 'imperial' or 'official'), but Scal. 198 (CM i. 290) attests the donation to Alexandria of castrisius (panis is omitted, presumably by mistake). On distributions, see Carrié, 'Distributions' 1078-80. There is one reference to distributions in mid-3rd c. Alexandria (Euseb. HE vii. 21. 9). Action by Diocletian is confirmed by Procopius (SH 26. 41), who states that he decreed that the treasury should give a large amount of grain to the poor

## Olympiad 271

**303** Indiction 7, year 19, the 8th consulship of Diocletian Augustus and the 7th of Maximianus Herculius.

**[p.515]** In year 19 of the reign of Diocletian, on day 25 in the month Dystrus (this would be called March according to the Romans), on the day of the Feast of Easter, imperial edicts were everywhere published, commanding that the churches be razed to the foundations and the divine Scriptures be obliterated by fire, and proclaiming that those in possession of office and dignity should be demoted, while ordinary citizens, if they persisted in the persuasion of Christianity, should be deprived of freedom. Shortly afterwards other edicts were promulgated which commanded that the leaders of the churches, all of them in every place, should first be consigned to chains, then subsequently be compelled by every means to sacrifice; and so as a result of this, many met their end after resolutely contending in diverse ways, but many were weakened and succumbed through cowardice after first making their souls insensible.[15]

In the same year many men everywhere, as we have said, met their end after resolutely contending; and no less too at the Nicomedian city, in which the emperor was residing, Dorotheus and Gorgonius met their end at that time, together with many others from the imperial retinue, and a great choir of martyrs was manifested together. And not long afterwards Anthimus too, bishop of the same Nicomedian church was beheaded and met his end; others perished by fire and more indeed were cast into the sea, **[p.516]** since the executioners were not adequate to suffice for such a very great innumerable throng. Concerning this innumerable throng of martyrs the presbyter Lucian, writing to the Antiochenes, declared, 'The whole choir of martyrs jointly sends you greetings. I bring you good news that Father Anthimus has met his end in the race of martyrdom.' And as regards Nicomedia these things happened, and yet more than these.[16]

---

of Alexandria each year; the grant would have been associated with the visit by Diocletian in winter 301/2.

[15] **303** Edicts of persecution: cf. Theoph. 10. 5-9, Euseb. HE viii. 2. 4-3. 1; also Lact. DMP 12-15. The first edict was published at Nicomedia on 24 Feb., but arrived in Palestine as Easter was approaching (18 April, not 25 March). By directing their attacks against Christian leaders, the authorities hoped to disorganize and undermine the church while avoiding mass persecutions.

[16] Dorotheus, Gorgonius, and Anthimus: cf. Euseb. HE viii. 6. 1, 5-6; CP is the only evidence for Lucian's letter to the Antiochenes, and preserves the sole

**304** Indiction 8, year 20, the 9th consulship of Diocletian Augustus and the 8th of Maximianus Herculius.

Maximianus Herculius was co-emperor with Diocletian, and gave 8 consular donatives. The same Maximianus was emperor for 18 years. And together with Diocletian these two created two Caesars, Diocletian his own son-in-law Galerius Maximianus (for he had Diocletian's daughter Valeria in marriage), while Herculius Maximianus himself too made his own son-in-law Caesar: for Constantius married Theodora the step-daughter of Maximianus Herculius, by whom his children were Delmatius, Constantius, and Hannibalianus. For Constantine, who was emperor after Diocletian and his partners, was son to this Constantius by another union, with Helena.

As has been said then, Diocletian and Herculius Maximianus were emperors together, Diocletian of Rome and Herculius **[p.517]** Maximianus of the Celts. Subsequently Diocletian and Herculius Maximianus, after laying down their sceptres in their lifetime, have given the empire to their individual Caesars, Herculius Maximianus gave the empire to Constantius and Diocletian to Galerius Maximianus. Constantius died after being Celtic emperor for 13 years, and his son Constantine, the bastard whom he had by Helena, succeeded him; for the children borne to him by Theodora were infants. Galerius Maximianus while he was emperor of Rome created two Caesars, Maximinus in the east and in Italy Severus. But the Romans on their own authority set up as emperor Maxentius, the son of Herculius Maximianus. And Galerius Maximianus dispatched Severus the Caesar to kill Maxentius; and Severus was killed in battle. And after being emperor for 16 years Galerius, when he was dying, made Licinius emperor in the east. And so there existed four emperors, Constantine of the Celts, of Rome Maxentius son of Herculius Maximianus, of the east Licinius, and Maximinus who still remained Caesar. But Constantine killed Maxentius in battle, and thus he was sole emperor of the west. And Maximinus, after campaigning against Licinius, made a truce with him so that Licinius retired from the empire. And thus Constantine, on becoming sole emperor, founded Byzantium, after receiving an oracle that the empire of Rome was about to perish, and became a Christian. He was emperor for 31 years, 10

quotation from any of his letters, see G. Bardy, *Recherches sur Saint Lucien d'Antioche et son école* (Paris 1936), 82-5. Other evidence about Lucian (*c.*240–311/12) can plausibly be traced back to Philostorgius (see *HE* pp. 184-201 Winkelmann); he was an important teacher, with Arius and leading exponents of Arian doctrine among those influenced by his works.

months. **[p.518]** And his children were Constantius, Constans, and Constantine. But the troops of Constans killed Constantine, while one Magnentius, a usurper, killed Constans himself. So Constantius was sole emperor, and he made Caesar Gallus, the son of his uncle Constantius, the brother of Delmatius the son of Theodora, making him Caesar in the east.[17]

The most sacred and faithful Constantine the Great, the son of Constantius, was 34th Roman emperor from day 8 before Kalends of August [25 July], for 31 years and 10 months.[18]

In total, 5,846.

**305** Indiction 9, year 1, the 5th consulship of Constantius Caesar and the 5th of Maximianus Jovius.

When Constantine began his reign from the western regions, he had as joint emperors with him the aforenamed, Constantius, Galerius, Maximinus, and Flavius Valerius Severus and Maxentius – Constantius and Severus until the second year of his reign, Maxentius until the seventh year of his reign, and Galerius, Valerius, and Maximinus until the ninth year of his reign.[19]

**306** Indiction 10, year 2, the 6th consulship of Constantius Caesar and the 6th of Maximianus Jovius.

Constantius, father of Constantine the great emperor, **[p.519]** died after being emperor for 13 years, and Maxentius was proclaimed.[20]

---

[17] **304** Survey of imperial succession: cf. Theoph. 10. 18-11. 8, 11. 33-12. 4. Diocletian: Aug. (based in east) 284–305; Maximian: Aug. (based in west) 286–305; Galerius: Caes. 293–305, Aug. 305–11; Constantius: Caes. 293–305, Aug. 305–6; Constantine: Aug. 306–37; Maximinus (Daia): Caes. 305–10, Aug. 310–13; Severus: Caes. 305, Aug. 306–7; Licinius: Aug. 308–24. For clear tables of the various imperial colleges, see Barnes, *NE* 4-8 (plus 12-13 for the usurper Maxentius); other references to Constantine's illegitimacy, ibid. 36.

*CP*'s summary of events following Galerius' death in 311 (after an 18-year reign) is confused: Maximinus (Daia) committed suicide at Tarsus in mid-313 after being defeated by Licinius at Adrianopolis (cf. *CP s.a.* 310/11); in 324 Licinius abdicated in favour of Constantine (who had just won three victories against him).

[18] Proclamation of Constantine: 25 July 306. In *CP* the consular year 310 is omitted, which helps to compensate for the 2-year antedating of Constantine's proclamation. The regnal length is correct.

[19] **305** Imperial college: probably the author's own confused extrapolations from the previous survey (*s.a.* 304); such summaries of imperial colleges are characteristic, cf. *s.a.* 337 with n. 75.

[20] **306** Constantius' death: this was at once followed by the proclamation at York of Constantine (cf. n. 18), and by that of Maxentius at Rome (28 Oct. 306).

Olympiad 272

**307** Indiction 11, year 3, sole consulship of Novius Constantine Augustus.[21]

Maximianus Jovius died after being emperor for 14 years.[22]

Licinius was proclaimed at Carnuntum on day 3 before Ides of November [11 Nov.].[23]

**308** Indiction 12, year 4, consulship again for the tenth time, and the 7th of Maximianus Galerius.

**309** Indiction 13, year 5, the 8th consulship of Maximianus Herculius and that of Galerius Maximus.

The most magnificent martyrs of Christ, shining out over the whole world, naturally astounded those men everywhere who were spectators of their courage, while they made manifest through themselves proofs of the truly ineffable power of our saviour Jesus Christ; it is impossible for a mortal to mention each of them by name. Of the ecclesiastical leaders who were martyred in famous cities, first let there be proclaimed by us on the monuments of pious men as martyr of Christ's kingdom the bishop of the Nicomedian city who was mentioned a little earlier, Anthimus. Of those in Antioch, Lucian, for all his life the excellent presbyter of the diocese there, himself too in Nicomedia **[p.520]** when the emperor was present, after proclaiming the heavenly kingdom of Christ first by word in his defence speech, then also through deeds, died by the furnace. Of those in Phoenicia, Tyrannion bishop of Tyre, Zenobius presbyter of the church in Sidon, Silvanus bishop of Emesa, in extreme old age after being bishop for forty years, became food for beasts with a great choir of martyrs; and of those in Palestine, Silvanus bishop

---

[21]    307–11 Consuls: there are considerable divergences in the records for these years, which reflect the shifting allegiances in the struggle for power in the western part of the empire: see Bagnall, *Consuls* 148-57. But *CP* has added its own errors to this confused picture: Novius Constantine (307) is a garbled version of the Latin record (*Chr. 354; Hyd.*) of a ninth consulship (*novies*) for Maximian, in association with Constantine for the latter part of the year; the phrase 'again for the tenth time' (308) refers to a tenth consulship for Diocletian, which in the Latin texts is recorded simply as X (=10), without Diocletian's name, or *item* X ('similarly 10'); the consuls of 309 (Licinius Aug. & Constantine Caesar) and 311 (8th of Galerius Maximianus Aug. & 2nd of Maximinus Aug.) have been inverted, and those of 310 (Tatius Andronicus & Pompeius Probus were accepted in the east) omitted altogether.

[22]    307 Death of Maximianus Jovius: the author of *CP* is unaware that this was the dynastic name of Galerius, who died in early May 311 (recorded by *CP s.a.* 312). Severus died in 307.

[23]    Licinius' proclamation: 11 Nov. 308 , cf. <u>Hyd.</u>

of Gaza was beheaded along with others, 40 in number, and the Egyptian bishops Peleus and Nilus, with others, died by fire.[24]

**310/11** Indiction 14, year 6, the 2nd consulship of Constantine Augustus and that of Licinius.[25]

Constantine, an emperor pious above emperors and most moderate in all things, son of Constantius, possessing assurance from God the king of all and his only-begotten son our Lord Jesus Christ, when he moved against the most impious usurpers Maximinus Galerius and Maxentius, the sign of the Cross, radiant in the heaven, was seen by him as he set out to do battle against them, with this in radiant Roman letters in its middle and lower part: 'Conquer in this.' And in clear manifestation Maxentius fell at Rome, drowned in the **[p.521]** river Tiber at the Muluvian bridge after being emperor for 6 years,[26] while Galerius Maximinus, when he had been defeated by Licinius, died a fugitive in Cilicia after being emperor for 9 years; he wasted his great army since he was a usurper of low birth.[27]

## Olympiad 273

**312** Indiction 15, year 7, the 3rd consulship of Constantine Augustus and the 2nd of Licinius.

Constantine, victorious, venerable, Augustus, who first cared for the salvation of the Christians oppressed at Rome, taking God as his heavenly ally and invoking Him by prayers, went out with his whole army to court the ancestral freedom of the Romans. With all joy and gladness, together with mere infants and wives of the men of the senate and of the other most distinguished people, along with the whole Roman populace, their eyes and their very souls bright, they welcomed him as redeemer, saviour, and benefactor, with acclamations and utmost joy. But he, possessed of piety towards God as if it were

---

[24] **309** Martyrs: cf. Euseb. *HE* viii. 13. 1-5 and ix. 6. 1, 3. Anthimus was martyred in 303 at the start of Diocletian's persecution (cf. *CP s.a.* 303, p. 515. 19-21), Lucian (cf. n. 16) and the others by Maximinus Daia in 311–12.

[25] **310/11** Consuls: Licinius Augustus and Constantine Caesar were nominated in 309 by Galerius, and this (combined with the inversion of the consuls of 311 and 309, see n. 21) probably lies behind *CP*'s record; after this year *CP* assigns one more consulship to Constantine than other lists, which either ignore the disputed consulship of 307 or discount the Galerian arrangements in 309.

[26] Defeat of Maxentius: for Constantine's vision and campaign in 312, which culminated in the battle of the Milvian bridge, see Barnes, *CE* 42-3.

[27] Maximinus (Daia): defeated by Licinius in Thrace in 313, he then fled east to Tarsus in Cilicia where he committed suicide, see Barnes, *CE* 62-4.

innate, was neither agitated at all by the shouts nor exalted by the praises, since he recognized full well the help from God. He immediately ordered that there be set up in one of the most public places in Rome a trophy of the saving Passion in the hand of his own statue, holding the saving sign in the right hand, **[p.522]** and he commanded that an inscription be inserted on it in these words in the Roman tongue: 'By this saving sign, true proof of courage, I have liberated your city which is saved from the yoke of slavery of the usurper Maxentius. And furthermore, after liberating the senate and Roman people, I restored them to their ancient distinction and splendour.'[28]

Galerius Maximianus, while living in the east, was attacked by a most grievous illness, his body wasting away and sprouting worms; after being treated by innumerable practitioners and receiving no benefit at all, he issued laws not only that Christians be released but also that churches be built.[29]

*From here is the start of Constantinian indictions.*[30]

**313** Indiction 1, year 8, the 4th consulship of Constantine Augustus and the 3rd of Licinius.

Metrophanes was first leader of the church in Byzantium for 10 years.[31]

**314** Indiction 2, year 9, consulship of Volusianus and Anianus.

**315** Indiction 3, year 10, the 5th consulship of Constantine Augustus and the 4th of Licinius.

---

[28]  **312** Constantine's triumph: the same victory as recorded under 310/11 above; cf. Euseb. *HE* ix. 9. 2, 9-11. For his arrival in Rome, and for the statue which was erected in Maxentius' new basilica in the Forum, see Barnes, *CE* 44-7.

[29]  Galerius' illness and edict in favour of Christians: cf. Euseb. *HE* viii. 16. 4-17. 1 (fuller version), and see Barnes, *CE* 39. He died in April/May 311.

[30]  Indictions: the new 15-year cycle, originally devised for tax assessment, began in the eastern provinces on 1 Sept. 312 (for the evidence: Jones, *LRE* 1077 n. 43), and was probably the consequence of the major census exercise initiated by Galerius before his death. All earlier references in *CP* to indiction years are calculated from the spurious association of the start of indictions with the 'first' Roman emperor Julius Caesar (*CP* p. 355. 14-18).

[31]  **313** Metrophanes: bishop 306/7-14. Cedrenus (i. 477. 3-4) describes him as the fourth bishop and dates his inauguration (wrongly) to Constantine's 9th year. Metrophanes is unlikely to have been the first bishop, but from his episcopate there was a continuous succession: see Dvornik, *Apostolicity* 156-8.

**[p.523]** Olympiad 274

**316** Indiction 4, year 11, consulship of Sabinus and Rufinus.
Constantine the Augustus proclaimed his son Constantine as Caesar.[32]
Galerius Maximianus, who was oppressed by terrible dropsy, died at Salona under these consuls.[33]
**317** Indiction 5, year 12, consulship of Gallicanus and Symmachus.[34]
Constantine Augustus proclaimed as Caesars his sons Constans, Constantius, and Crispus on Kalends of March [1 March].[35]
**318** Indiction 6, year 13, the 5th consulship of Licinius and that of Crispus Caesar.
**319** Indiction 7, year 14, the 6th consulship of Constantine Augustus and the 5th of Licinius.[36]
Since heavenly light shone down on the churches of the saviour Christ throughout the entire world, when in every place the buildings which had been torn down by the usurpers were completed from the foundations to immense height, not only were there inauguration ceremonies but also the emperors provided continual legislation on behalf of Christians.[37]

**[p.524]** Olympiad 275

**320** Indiction 8, year 15, the 7th consulship of Constantine Augustus and that of Constantius Caesar.[38]

---

[32] **316** Proclamation of Constantine Caesar: 1 March 317 (*Hyd.*).

[33] Death of Galerius: the fatal illness is recorded *s.a.* 312. Though 'terrible dropsy' fits Galerius' disease, he died in Dardania, not at Salona in Dalmatia. This suggests that there has been some confusion with Diocletian's death at Salona, which the majority of sources date to 316 (though 313 is probably correct: see Lact. *DMP* ed. Moreau vol. ii. 421-3); Barnes, *NE* 31-2, prefers 311/12.

[34] **317** *cos. post.*: Caesonius Bassus; the consuls of 330 were a different Gallicanus and Symmachus.

[35] Caesars: on 1 March 317, Constantine's sons Crispus and Constantine were proclaimed (cf. n. 32), along with Licinius' infant son Licinius (*Hyd.*); Constantius was in fact proclaimed on 8 Nov. 324, Constans on 25 Dec. 333 (*Hyd. ss.aa.*).

[36] **319** *cos. post.*: Licinius Caesar; several consular lists confuse the infant Caesar with his father, see Bagnall, *Consuls* 172-3.

[37] Favours for Christians: cf. Euseb. *HE* x. 2. 1-2.

[38] **320** *cos. post.*: Constantine Caesar (also 321, 324, 329).

**321** Indiction 9, year 16, the 2nd consulship of Crispus and the 2nd of Constantius.

**322** Indiction 10, year 17, consulship of Probianus and Julianus.

**323** Indiction 11, year 18, consulship of Severus and Rufinus.

Alexander was second leader of the church in Byzantium for 7 years.[39]

## Olympiad 276

**324** Indiction 12, year 19, the 3rd consulship of Crispus and the 3rd of Constantius.

The creator of kindred souls and the merciful saviour who shone out over all went before Constantine together with his son Crispus, and prepared the encirclement of the regions which Licinius possessed; and that man was confined on every side, and being slain obtained an end such as he himself saw and heard had befallen those who had briefly been usurpers before him.[40]

**325**[41] Indiction 13, year 20, consulship of Paulinus and Julianus.

In year 295 from the Ascension to heaven of the Lord and year 20 of the reign of Constantine the pious, the same celebrated emperor, supremely entrusted by God with piety, in the **[p.525]** present year 20 of his reign, on day 19 in the month Daisius [June] prepared for a synod of 318 holy fathers to take place in Nicaea and for the symbol of the blameless faith to be defined. Wherefore, God the Lord of the universe also made him victorious over all by the prayers of the holy and blessed fathers who were assembled in the same synod. For Arius with perverted mind did not shudder, the accursed man, to separate and distinguish the ineffable and indivisible unity of the Godhead of the Father and Son.[42]

---

[39]  **323** Alexander: bishop 314–37, probably the 5th (cf. n. 31).

[40]  **324** Campaign against Licinius: cf. Euseb. *HE* x. 9. 4-5.  Constantine attacked and defeated Licinius three times in 324, twice by land and once by sea; Licinius abdicated in return for the sparing of his life, but in spring 325 he was executed for 'plotting', see Barnes, *CE* 76-7, 214.

This is the last notice that can be traced (indirectly) to Euseb. *HE*, which was published in 325/6.

[41]  **325** The information in this year is a mixture of wrongly-dated chronicle material and ecclesiastical information whose precise provenance cannot be identified.

[42]  Synod of Nicaea: the Nicene creed, promulgated on 19 June 325, condemned the Arian doctrine which attempted to deny the full equality of God the Father and God the Son; see Chadwick, *Church* 129-31, and ch. 9 for the subsequent

The most pious Constantine proclaimed as Augustus his son Constans, who was Caesar, on day 6 before Ides of November [8 Nov.],[43] and he celebrated the twentieth anniversary of his reign and held his *vicennalia* in Rome with exceeding brilliance and lavishness, and he cancelled the taxation of craftsmen and tributaries during the year of the same twentieth anniversary, and gave many gifts to the churches everywhere.[44]

Constantine, victorious Augustus, after smashing the battle of Adrianopolis on day 5 before Kalends of July [27 June], and being victorious in the Chalcedonian battle on day 14 before Kalends of October [18 Sept.],[45] killed his son Crispus who was Caesar and had been maligned to him.[46]

In the same year Constantine, sole-ruling emperor of the entire Roman realm, overturned all the idols everywhere and took away all their wealth and possessions, and honoured all the churches of Christ and all the Christians.

[p.526] At this time he campaigned against the enemies of the faith of the Christians and carried off victory by prayer. Wherefore, he has also inaugurated Sunday for the conversion of

---

controversy. The council had probably begun its meetings in early June; Barnes, *CE* ch. 12, esp. 212ff. The precise number of bishops present is unknown, but by the late 4th c. the number 318 (symbolic, as equivalent to the servants of Abraham at Genesis 14. 14) had become accepted: see G. Bardy in Fliche and Martin, *Église* iii. 81-2.

Ascension date: calculated from AD 31; cf. *ss.aa.* 381, 431, 452, for this method of dating church councils.

[43] Constans: Caesar on 25 Dec. 333, Augustus on 9 Sept. 337 (*Hyd. ss.aa.*); Constantius was created Caesar on 8 Nov. 324 (*Hyd.*). *CP* had already antedated the elevation of Constans and Constantius as Caesars to 317, and now seems to have adapted his source material to take account of this earlier error.

[44] *Vicennalia*: celebrations began in Nicomedia in 325 (Jerome, *Chron.*, p. 231. 10-11 Helm), and were continued in Rome in 326 (Jerome, *Hyd.*; in July: Barnes, *CE* 221). Important imperial anniversaries were regularly marked by donatives to officials and soldiers, which were financed in part by the *collatio lustralis*, a tax on artisans and the professions (see Hendy, *Economy* 175-8, also 192-201); Constantine's remission of taxation is an unusual extension of this munificence.

[45] Adrianopolis battle: Constantine defeated Licinius on 3 July 324, i.e. 5 days before Nones (not Kalends) of July: cf. *Hyd.* with correct date; this was followed by a decisive naval engagement in the Bosporus on 18 Sept., cf. *s.a.* 324.

[46] Crispus: accused of sexual misconduct, he was tried by Constantine and executed in summer 326. The precise circumstances are unclear, but the accusation was probably designed to remove the heir apparent and open the succession for the sons of Constantine's current wife Fausta (whose machinations may soon have been revealed, resulting in her suicide); see Barnes, *CE* 220-1.

the pagans throughout the lands in honour of Christ our God, saviour for all men.[47]

*The years from the foundation of the world to the twentieth anniversary of Constantine Augustus are as follows:*

From creation of Adam until the Flood,  2262.

From the Flood to Abraham,  1070.

From birth of Abraham until year 80 of Moses,  505.

From year 81 of Moses, that is from the Exodus of the children of Israel, until year 3 of Labdon, in which Troy was captured, 404.

From year 4 of Labdon to the 2nd year of Solomon, in which began the first construction of the temple,  226.

From year 1 of Solomon until year 50 of Ozios, that is the first Olympiad,  264.

From beginning of the first Olympiad until year 6 of Darius, son of Hystaspes, in which was completed the second building of the temple,  248.

From year 7 inclusive of the said Darius until year 15 of Tiberius, that is of the saving baptism,  557.

[p.527] From year 16 of Tiberius, that is from year 2 inclusive of Olympiad 202, until the twentieth anniversary of Constantine the great emperor and year 2 of Olympiad 276,  297.

In total from creation of the world until the twentieth anniversary of Constantine, 5833 years.[48]

---

[47] Anti-pagan acts: Eusebius (*Triac.* 8, *VC* iii. 54) records confiscations of temple treasures; for this, and pro-Christian measures, see Barnes, *CE* 210-12, 246-9, Jones, *LRE* 89-93.

Sunday observance: for the law of 321, see Barnes, *CE* 51-2, Jones, *LRE* 81.

[48] *Annus mundi*: CP has a similar calculation under year 15 of Tiberius, the year of Christ's baptism (pp. 403. 13-404. 5), although with some differences in the intermediate points of calculation (Adam, Flood, Flight from Egypt, Construction of Temple in year 4 of Solomon, Cyrus king of Persia, Alexander of Macedon), while the total of years from Creation to Christ's baptism is given as 5537, not 5536 as here.

The framework for both calculations can plausibly be traced back to Eusebius, who was concerned to link Hebrew and Graeco-Roman history, and who may (ultimately) be responsible for the location of this survey in *CP*. Eusebius' *HE* and *Chronicle* both terminated in Constantine's 20th year (325/6), and the *Chronicle* probably concluded with a chronological survey, since an earlier version of the work terminated (*c*.311) with a computation which is quoted in Eusebius' *Praeparatio Evangelica* x. 9. 1-11. This is basically similar to *CP*, although there are differences on specific points: thus for Eusebius there were only 408 years between the destruction of Troy in year 3 of Labdon (i.e. Abdon, judge of Israel before Samson) and the first Olympiad in year 50 of Ozios

**326** Indiction 14, year 21, the 9th consulship of Constantine Augustus and the 4th of Constantius Caesar.[49]

**327** Indiction 15, year 22, the 5th consulship of Constantius Caesar and that of Maximus.[50]

The emperor Constantine, after refounding Drepanum in Bithynia in honour of the holy martyr Lucian, named it Helenopolis, with the same name as his mother, and in honour of the holy martyr Lucian he granted it to the present day immunity from taxation to the extent of the environs visible outside the city.[51]

### Olympiad 277

**328** Indiction 1, year 23, consulship of Januarius and Justus.[52]

Constantine the pious crossed the Danube very many times, and made a bridge for it in stone.[53]

In the time of the aforementioned consuls, Constantine the celebrated emperor departed from Rome and, while staying at Nicomedia metropolis of Bithynia, made visitations for a long

(i.e. Uzziah, king of Judah and contemporary of the prophet Isaiah), and only 548 years between year 2 of Darius and year 15 of Tiberius. Eusebius placed the Crucifixion in Tiberius' 18th year (year 3 of Olympiad 202), 1 year earlier than in *CP* (19th year of Tiberius, year 4 of Olympiad 202). (Julius Africanus, the founding father of Christian chronology, had placed the Crucifixion in year 16 of Tiberius, year 2 of Olympiad 202, according Christ a ministry of only one year.) See further, Finegan, *Handbook* pt. I, sec. III, esp. 147-76, and Grumel, *Chronologie* pt. I, ch. 2.

[49] **326** Consuls: 7th of Constantine and 1st of Constantius. *CP* was already crediting Constantine with one more consulship than other lists (cf. n. 25) but now, for no obvious reason, it misses out an eighth consulship (7th of Constantine recorded *s.a.* 320); Constantius had been wrongly credited with Constantine II's consulships in 320, 321, and 324.

[50] **327** *cos. prior*: Flavius Constantius, praetorian prefect 324–7 (*PLRE* i. 225, s.v. Constantius 5).

[51] Drepanum: cf. Theoph. 28. 3-4. Birthplace of Constantine's mother Helena, Drepanum on the south shore of the gulf of Nicomedia was also famous as the site of the tomb of Lucian, the presbyter of Antioch martyred in 312 at Nicomedia (cf. *CP s.a.* 309; Philostorgius ii. 12 records that his remains were transported there by a dolphin). Barnes (*NE* 77) tentatively dated the refoundation to 7 Jan. 328, on the assumptions that it must have followed Helena's death in 327 and probably occurred on the anniversary of Lucian's death: both assumptions are plausible, no more, and *CP*'s date need not be wrong.

[52] **328** *cos. prior*: Januarinus.

[53] Bridge: cf. Theoph. 28. 19-20 (under Constantine's 24th year). The bridge, at Oescus, was used to launch a series of campaigns against the Goths and Sarmatians in the 330s.

time to [p.528] Byzantium. He renewed the first wall of the city of Byzas, and after making considerable extensions also to the same wall he joined them to the ancient wall of the city and named it Constantinople; he also completed the Hippodrome, adorning it with works in bronze and with every excellence, and made in it a box for imperial viewing in likeness of the one which is in Rome. And he made a great Palace near the same Hippodrome, and the ascent from the Palace to the box in the Hippodrome by way of the Kochlias, as it is called. And he also built a Forum which was large and exceedingly fine; and he set in the middle a great porphyry column of Theban stone, worthy of admiration, and he set on top of the same column a great statue of himself with rays of light on his head, a work in bronze which he had brought from Phrygia. The same emperor Constantine secretly took away from Rome the Palladium, as it is called, and placed it in the Forum built by him, beneath the column of his monument, as certain of the Byzantines say who have heard it by tradition. And after making bloodless sacrifice, he named the Tyche of the city renewed by him Anthusa.

The same emperor also built two fine porticoes from the entrance of the Palace as far as the Forum, adorned with statues and marbles, and he named the place of the porticoes Regia. Nearby he also built a basilica with an apse, and set outside great columns [p.529] and statues; this he named the Senate, and he named the place Augustaeum because he had also set up opposite his own a monument of his mother, lady Helena Augusta, on a porphyry column.

Likewise too he completed the bath which is called Zeuxippon, adorning it with columns and varied marbles and works of bronze.[54]

---

[54] Foundation of Cpl.: cf. Mal. 319. 20-321. 15 with only very minor differences (the bronze statue of Constantine came from Ilium and had 7 rays on its head; some Byzantines say that the Palladium is still beneath Constantine's column; extra antiquarian information on the city's Tyche; Septimius Severus' involvement in the Zeuxippon); *CP* has an occasional phrase not contained in the abridged text of Malalas. Hesychius of Miletus (*Patria* 39-41, pp. 16-18 Preger) has another account.

Discussion of Constantine's works: see Dagron, *Naissance* 29-47, and Mango, *Const.* ch. 2.

Hippodrome and imperial box: the box or *kathisma* was located on the east side of the Hippodrome towards the curved end. See further Müller-Wiener, *Bildlexikon* 64-71, R. Guilland, 'Études sur l'Hippodrome de Byzance: le palais du Kathisma', *ByzSlav.* xviii, 1957, 39-76 = *Études* i. 462-98, and Alan Cameron, *Porphyrius the Charioteer* (Oxford 1973), 49-58. F. Millar (*The Emperor in the Roman World*, London 1977, 370 n. 23) states that there is no corroboration for

**329** Indiction 2, year 24, the 10th consulship of Constantine Augustus and the 5th of Constantius Caesar.[55]

**330** Indiction 3, year 25, consulship of Gallicanus and Symmachus.

In year 301 from the Ascension to heaven of the Lord and year 25 of his reign, Constantine the most pious, father of Constantine II Augustus and of Constantius and Constans Caesars, after building a very great, illustrious, and blessed city, and honouring it with a senate, named it Constantinople, on day five before Ides of May [11 May], on the second day of the week, in the third indiction, and he proclaimed that the city, formerly named Byzantium, be called second Rome. He was first to celebrate a chariot-racing contest, wearing for the first time a diadem of pearls and other precious stones. And he made a great festival, and commanded by his sacred decree that the anniversary of his city be celebrated on the same day, and that on the 11th of the same month Artemisius [May] the public bath Zeuxippon be opened, [p.530] which was near the Hippodrome and the Regia of the Palace. He made for himself another gilded monument of wood, bearing in its right hand a Tyche of the same city, itself also gilded, and commanded that on the same day of the anniversary chariot races, the same monument of wood should enter, escorted by the troops in mantles and slippers, all holding white candles; the carriage should proceed around the further turning-post and come to the arena opposite the imperial box; and the emperor of the day should rise and do

---

CP's statement that the Cpl. *kathisma* was modelled on a similar structure in Rome, but the antecedent might be the *pulvinar* from which emperors usually watched races in the Circus Maximus: see J. H. Humphrey, *Roman Circuses* (London 1986), 78-83 with 691 n. 117, and ibid. 595-600 for the box in the Circus of Maxentius outside Rome, which was directly connected by an elevated passage to the nearby imperial palace.

Constantine's column and associated legends: see C. A. Mango, 'Constantinopolitana', *Jahrb. d. deutsch. arch. Inst.* lxxx, 1965, 305-36 at 306-13, and id. 'Constantine's Porphyry Column and the Chapel of St. Constantine', *Deltion tes christianikes archaiologikes etaireias* x, 1980/1, 103-10; also Müller-Wiener, *Bildlexikon* 255-7.

Palace, Augustaeum, adjacent Senate, baths of Zeuxippus: see Mango, *Brazen House* esp. 37-47, 56-60. This Senate-house is also known as Julian's Senate (J. Lyd. *de mag.* iii. 70) which might indicate that Constantine did not construct it; it must be distinguished from the Senate at Constantine's Forum. See also Guilland, 'L'Augoustéon', *Études* ii. 40-54.

Regia: the eastern section of Cpl.'s main street, the Mese; see Guilland, 'La Mésè ou Régia', *Études* ii. 69-79.

55 **329** *cos. post.*: 4th of Constantine Caesar (cf. nn. 38, 49).

obeisance to the monument of the same emperor Constantine and this Tyche of the city.[56]

The same most sacred emperor Constantine continued as emperor in Constantinople; he separated it from the province of Europe, that is from its metropolis Heracleia, and appointed for

[56]   330 Dedication of Cpl. (chariot races and anniversary festival): cf. Mal. 321. 15-322. 15, again with only minor differences.  Malalas contains a Biblical justification for Constantine's elaborate diadem, correctly states that the Zeuxippon was near 'the Regia and the Palace' (the author of CP has presumably miscopied his source), adds the name Anthusa for the city's Tyche, and asserts that the ceremonial act of obeisance in the Hippodrome continued to the present day.  Malalas has a single account covering foundation, buildings and dedication, the last introduced by a second reference to the construction of the Hippodrome (Mal. 321. 15-16).  In CP this Malalas material is divided between the years 328 and 330 and an elaborate date provided for the second notice.  CP's first sentence (with Ascension date) is not in Malalas, and probably originated in a different source (for the Roman date, cf. Hyd.); the Ascension date is calculated from AD 31, 19th year of Tiberius (in accordance with CP's own chronology, cf. n. 48).

Anniversary ceremony: described, or alluded to, in various chapters of Parastaseis (esp. 5, 38 and 56), whose evidence probably originated in a written source connected with the source tradition on which Malalas and CP were based.  Parast. 5 states that the Hippodrome spectacle continued down to the time of Theodosius I, but a version of the ceremony may have been performed under Phocas, cf. n. 427.  The non-Christian connotations of this ceremony involving the Tyche of the new city have aroused suspicions among those who regard Constantine as a complete and orthodox Christian, but it does seem that Cpl. had a Tyche called Anthusa parallel to Flora at Rome: the whole ceremony with its pagan elements should probably be accepted; for discussion, see Dagron, Naissance 37-45.

The Greek term ξόανον, used of Constantine's gilded statue, need not strictly indicate that it was made of wood, but merely of worked material.  The military escort wear a ceremonial dress similar to that of patricians (J. Lyd. de mag. i. 17); the slippers (compagi) are a sandal-like shoe, rather than a military boot, and are worn by Justinian and his escort in the St. Vitale mosaic at Ravenna.

'Arena opposite the imperial box': the noun 'arena' is uncertain.  The MS reading σκάμμα (cf. Mal. 322. 12: σκάμα in MS) signifies a sanded pit (for wrestling, etc.), hence the Hippodrome race track, 'arena'.  However, in accounts of the ceremony in Parastaseis (5, 38) and Patria (ii. 42) the place is called στάμα, 'the stand'; cf. also Const. Porph. de caer. i. 92 (pp. 418. 3, 423. 4-5) for soldiers gathered on the stama at Anastasius' proclamation.  The Australian translators of Malalas (p. 175; a confused note) accept that σκάμα is a textual corruption for στάμα, but still translate σκάμα ('pit').  The problem is also discussed by R. Guilland ('Études sur l'Hippodrome de Constantinople: L'arène', JÖBG vi, 1957, 25-44 at 37-8 = Études i. 451-2).  We have tentatively retained σκάμ(μ)α on the grounds that, whereas the stama was a recognized location within the Hippodrome, σκάμμα ('arena') was a more general term that required the qualifying phrase 'opposite the imperial box'.

the same Constantinople a praetorian prefect and city prefect and the other major officials.[57]

There are from the foundation of Rome until Constantinople was inaugurated 1,080 years.

In this year Alexander bishop of Alexandria died on day 14 before Kalends of May [18 April], on Pharmuthi 22, and Athanasius the great father was elected bishop in his place.[58]

**331 [p.531]** Indiction 4, year 26, consulship of Bassus and Ablabius.

### Olympiad 278

**332** Indiction 5, year 27, consulship of Pacatianus and Hilarianus.

In the time of these consuls bread began to be disbursed to the citizens of Constantinople, from 18th May.[59]

**333** Indiction 6, year 28, consulship of Dalmatus and Zenophilus.

**334** Indiction 7, year 29, consulship of Optatus Patricius and Anicius Paulinus.[60]

Under these consuls took place the inauguration of the church of the Holy Cross, which had been built by Constantine in the

---

[57] Provincial status of Cpl., and its magistrates: cf. Mal. 323. 3-8 who adds that all appointees were Christians and that Cpl. remained in good fortune as an imperial capital. The first city prefect was in fact only appointed in 359: see *CP s.a.*

[58] Alexander of Alexandria: cf. Scal. 228 (CM i. 292) for the Egyptian dating (= 17 April). Athanasius: patriarch 328-73; for his career and involvement in the Arian controversy, see G. Bardy, P. de Labriolle, and J. R. Palanque in Fliche and Martin, *Église* iii. 97-276.

[59] 332 Bread ration: cf. Mal. 322. 17-323. 2 for a more detailed description, undated but placed between his account of Cpl.'s dedication and that of its provincial status; *Parast.* 56 has an allusion in a similar context; also Zos. ii. 32. 1; Philost. ii. 9. Dagron (*Naissance* 530-41) discusses the ration and favours *CP's* date; see also Carrié, 'Distributions' 1071-3. Socrates ii. 13 suggests that there was initially a maximum of 80,000 recipients, assuming a *modius* per person per day.

[60] 334 Optatus: the first known patrician (*PLRE* i. 650, s.v. Optatus 3); in *CP* the title is mistaken for a proper name.

time of the bishop Macarius, on 17th of the month September.[61] Thereafter began the Feast of the Invention of the Cross.[62]

**335** Indiction 8, year 30, the 6th consulship of Constantius Caesar and that of Albinus.[63]

The thirtieth anniversary of Constantine the pious was celebrated in Constantinople-Rome with exceeding lavishness on day 8 before Kalends of August [25 July],[64] and he declared Constans his son Augustus,[65] and he proclaimed as Caesar Dalmatius, the son of his brother Dalmatius the censor, on day 8 before Kalends of October [24 Sept.].[66] Dalmatius was the son of Dalmatius the brother of Constantine the pious; he was a Roman general and consul prior to his [p.532] being proclaimed Caesar.[67] And after appointing Hannibalianus *rex*, he clad him

---

[61]  Holy Cross: the church of the Holy Sepulchre at Jerusalem, whose dedication was celebrated in 335 with a week of festivities (13–20 Sept.). Macarius, bishop of Jerusalem 314–33, received personal instructions from Constantine about the construction of the church (Euseb. *VC* iii. 30-32). On the church, see C. Coüasnon, *The Church of the Holy Sepulchre in Jerusalem* (London 1974), and Rubin, 'Church'.

[62]  Feast of Invention (discovery) of Cross: for the discovery of the relic and the proliferation of stories concerning it, see Hunt, *Pilgrimage* 38-48, and Rubin, 'Church'. The Cross was supposedly discovered during the construction of the church of the Holy Sepulchre, possibly on the same day as the church's dedication, 14 Sept. (not 17 Sept., as in *CP*). There is no contemporary evidence for the discovery of the Cross: Euseb. *VC* iii. 30. 1, the discovery of a proof of the Passion that had been hidden underground, is most naturally interpreted in connection with *VC* iii. 28 as Christ's tomb (Hunt, *Pilgrimage* 8, *contra* Rubin, 'Church' 81-3), since Eusebius nowhere explicitly mentions the discovery of the Cross. Stories concerning the discovery quickly became popular (c.350), towards the end of the 4th c. it was credited to Constantine's mother Helena, and this version is presented in Malalas (319. 14-18). By the 380s the Feast of the Invention was being celebrated. *CP* has none of the elaborate stories, but antedates the start of the Feast. See also n. 438.

[63]  335 *cos. prior*: Julius Constantius, half-brother of Constantine and father of Gallus and Julian (*PLRE* i. 226, s.v. Constantius 7).

[64]  *Tricennalia*: cf. Hyd. The exact anniversary fell on 25 July 336, when Eusebius delivered his panegyric (*Triac.*), but celebration would have been appropriate during the preceding twelve months (Constantine's thirtieth year), as at the *vicennalia*.

[65]  Constans: proclaimed Caesar on 25 Dec. 333 (8 before Kalends of Jan.: *Hyd.*), he was elevated to Augustus on 9 Sept. 337 after Constantine's death, together with his elder brothers Constantine II and Constantius II (*Hyd.*). *CP* has already recorded his elevation to Augustus on 8 Nov. 325.

[66]  Dalmatius: proclaimed Caesar on 18 Sept. 335 (14 before Kalends of Oct.: *Hyd.*).

[67]  Dalmatius the elder: *PLRE* i. 240-1, s.v. Dalmatius 6, half-brother of

in a scarlet mantle and dispatched him to Caesarea in Cappadocia.[68]

Olympiad 279

**336** Indiction 9, year 31, consulship of Nepotianus and Facundus.

**337** Indiction 10, year 32, consulship of Felicianus and Tatianus.

The Persians declared war against the Romans, and Constantine, who had reached year 32 of his rule, set out for the east against the Persians; when he had gone as far as Nicomedia, he gloriously and piously quitted life in a suburb of the same city, on 11th in the month Artemisius [May], having been vouchsafed the saving baptism by Eusebius bishop of Constantinople, after a reign of 31 years and 10 months.[69] And he left behind as Caesars his three sons, Constantine Caesar emperor of the regions of Gaul, being in the twentieth year of rule, Constantius who was Caesar after him in the regions of the east, being in year 11 of rule, and Constans who was Caesar after him and stayed in the regions of Italy, being in the third year of rule, as well as Dalmatius Caesar, son of his brother, in Mesopotamia, himself also being in his third year.[70]

The thrice-blessed Constantine took his rest on 22nd in the month May, [p.533] day 11 before Kalends of June, at the Holy

Constantine, who in addition to holding the title 'censor' had also been consul and a general (his son the Caesar had not been either).

[68] Hannibalianus: see *PLRE* i. 407, s.v. Hannibalianus 2; younger son of Dalmatius the elder, he was declared *rex regum et Ponticarum gentium* (*Anon. Val.* 6. 35) with the intention of appointing him to Armenia and possibly, in due course, to Persia as well.

[69] **337** Persian war, and baptism and death of Constantine: cf. <u>Theoph. 33. 16-20, 23</u> (no date). Theophanes (33. 21-2) asserts that Constantine had earlier been baptized in Rome by Pope Sylvester, and describes as an Arian falsehood the story of his baptism by the Arian Eusebius, but his own version is an anti-Arian fiction: cf. Soc. i. 39 for the baptism at Nicomedia, but omitting Eusebius' name. On the Persian war, see Barnes, *CE* 259. Constantine died on 22 May, 11 before Kalends of June, as recorded below (pp. 532. 22-533. 1); the mistake here may arise from confusion with the dating by the Kalends.

[70] Imperial succession and division: cf. Theoph. 34. 16-18 (inverting the regions assigned to Constantine and Constans). Constantine II had been Caesar for 20 years, Constantius for 12, Constans for 3, and Dalmatius for less than 2. The regnal lengths given here by *CP* contradict the earlier dating to 317 of the elevation of Constantius and Constans, and the (correct) designation of Constans as Caesar is at odds with the two notices of his elevation to Augustus (*ss.aa.* 325, 335).

Pentecost itself;[71] the corpse of Constantine the pious was still lying unburied and guarded in the Palace of Constantinople until his sons knew.

When Constantius in the east in Mesopotamia heard, although the Persian war was still looming, he immediately set out for Constantinople; on arriving there he escorted forth his celebrated father Constantine in such great pomp and glorious imperial procession that it is impossible to speak worthily of it: the army was present under arms as if he were still alive, and the whole city, both because it had been proclaimed by him as Rome and furthermore so many distinctions had come to it, as well as the corn allocations of the annual distributions which had been donated; everyone was in such great grief that it never happened that any emperor before him was so glorified in life and after death.[72] And he was laid to rest in the church of the Holy Apostles in which lie the remains of the holy apostles Andrew, and Luke the evangelist, and Timothy disciple of Paul the apostle.[73]

Sapor the Persian king invaded Mesopotamia to sack Nisibis, and when he had besieged it for 63 days and not overpowered it, he withdrew.[74]

After the death of their father Constantine, Constantine the younger and Constans and Constantius were 35th Roman emperors for 24 years.                                   In total, 5,870.

[p.534] And the younger Constantine was emperor in Constantinople for 1 year, Constans in Rome for 12 years; and after the death of this Constans, Constantius who was their brother was emperor in Rome for the remaining 12 years. Such is the divisional arrangement.[75]

---

71  Death of Constantine with Roman date: cf. Hyd.

72  Funeral of Constantine: see Barnes, CE 261. Eusebius (VC iv. 65-72, a work of which CP shows no knowledge) preserves a rhetorical and emotional account which includes references to the army honouring Constantine as if he were alive. At Cpl. Constantius, together with his brothers, eliminated their father's various step-relatives in a Palace purge (Barnes, CE 261-2). Bread ration: cf. n. 59.

73  Holy Apostles: designed by Constantine as his mausoleum, see Mango, Const. 27, and Grierson, 'Tombs', for later burial arrangements. On the remains of apostles, see nn. 101–2.

74  Shapur's attack on Nisibis: cf. Theoph. 34. 32-35. 1. Shapur seems to have had two objectives in attacking the Romans, to recover Nisibis which Narses had surrendered in 298, and to reassert Persian authority in Armenia which was now a Christian kingdom. Nisibis was attacked in spring 338, and its famous bishop Jacob died at the time of the siege (Chron. 724, CSCO iii/4. 103).

75  Imperial college: Constantine II ruled Britain, Gaul, and Spain until spring

338  Indiction 11, year 1, consulship of Ursus and Polemius.
339  Indiction 12, year 2, the 4th consulship of Constantine II Augustus and the 7th of Constans Augustus.[76]

Olympiad 280

340  Indiction 13, year 3, consulship of Acindynus and Proclus.[77]
341  Indiction 14, year 4, consulship of Marcellinus and Probinus.
342  Indiction 15, year 5, the 5th consulship of Constantius Augustus and the 2nd of Constans Augustus.[78]
343  Indiction 1, year 6, consulship of Placitus and Romulus.

Olympiad 281

344  Indiction 2, year 7, consulship of Leontius and Salustius.
Chronological tables of the nineteen-year cycle for the fourteenth days according to the moon on which Easter is ordered to be celebrated according to the law.[79]  The cycle

340; Constans Africa, Italy, and much of the Balkans (plus Constantine II's provinces after 340) until 350; Constantius Thrace, Asia Minor, the east, and (after 350) the territory of Constans until 361.

[76] 339 Consuls: 2nd of Constantius and 1st of Constans. Other eastern lists do not share this or the following errors in *CP*, which has lapsed into complete confusion over the sons of Constantine. The 'seventh' consulship for Constans (his second is correctly recorded in 342) is probably a continuation of the 'sixth' credited to Constantius in 335, the 'fourth' for Constantine II appears from nowhere, since his four earlier consulships (320, 321, 324, 329) are all credited to Constantius.

[77] 340 *cos. post.*: Proculus. *Scal.* 245 (*CM* i. 293) also has Proclus, but otherwise does not share *CP*'s errors here (though it introduces several of its own).

[78] 342 *cos. prior*: 3rd of Constantius. Through conflation with Constantine II, Constantius had already been credited with a sixth consulship in 335; now, however, the sequence seems to be reckoned from the 'fourth' consulship of Constantine II in 339. From this point Constantius' consulships are overstated by two in *CP*.

[79] 344 Easter tables: for their development in the 3rd–4th c., see Grumel, *Chronologie* pt. I, ch. 3. Grumel argues that this table is an official statement of the reformed computation of 353, dating from that time. In 352 the 95-year table of Anatolius (cf. n. 2) expired and a replacement was necessary. New calculations had to be made, since the date of the spring equinox was now established as 21 March (instead of 22 March), and this change entailed an adjustment to the date of the creation of the world, since it was believed that the sun and moon were created at the equinox and on a Wednesday (4th day of

contains them according to Romans and Syrians, that is Macedonians, and according to Egyptians. The present nineteen-year cycle took its beginning from year 59 of Diocletian, that is from the 21st inclusive of the month March on which the equinox is recognized in the consulship of Leontius and Salustius, under which consuls the year 5,852 from the creation of the world is completed. So the nineteen-year cycle having been completed in the said times and under the said consuls, return again to its first year on the 21st of the month March, indiction 2, accurately recognizing that neither an eight- and fifteen-year cycle, nor a seventeen-year cycle, nor a sixteen-year cycle, can have accuracy, but only a nineteen-year cycle. In the cycle it also has the epacts which it is necessary to place in each year, and the so-called *embolimoi*.[80]

Year 1; epacts 30; Ides of April [13 April]; *embolimos*; 13 Xanthicus; 18 Pharmuthi; year 59.

Year 2; epacts 14; 4 before Nones of April [2 April]; 2 Xanthicus; 7 Pharmuthi; year 60.

Year 3; epacts 22; 11 before Kalends of April [22 March]; 24 Dystrus; 29 Phamenoth; year 61.

Year 4; epacts 3; 4 before Ides of April [10 April]; *embolimos*; 10 Xanthicus; 15 Pharmuthi; year 62.

Year 5; epacts 14; 4 before Ides of April [10 April]; 29 Dystrus; 3 Pharmuthi; year 63.

---

Creation). As a result of calculations at Cpl., the year of Creation was advanced from *a.m.* 5500 to 5509 BC (see Grumel, *Chronologie* pt. I, ch. 5, who calls this the proto-Byzantine era); this required the advance to AD 345 of the start of the new 'natural' lunar cycle (κατὰ φύσιν), the cycle of the sequence of lunar epacts (the age of the moon at the start of the solar year on 1 Jan.) which began in the year after the creation of the world, *a.m.* 2, or to AD 344 of the 'adjusted' cycle (κατὰ θέσιν), the cycle aligned with the year of the world's creation, when there were no epacts. For detailed discussion, see Grumel, *Chronologie* 41-8.

80 Easter calculations: these are presented in the form of a wheel divided into 19 segments, each of which represents one year in the cycle; the introductory preamble is arranged in the centre of the wheel. There is one other comparable table in *CP* (between pp. 372-3), associated with the date of the conception of John the Baptist by his mother Elizabeth (also two tables that respectively explain solar and lunar cycles, between pp. 26-7). The table here is designed to establish the dates of the first full moon (the 14th day of the moon) after the spring equinox, the date of the Jewish Passover as established by (Mosaic) law, and hence the earliest date on which the Christian Easter could fall. The Quartodecimans insisted on celebrating Easter on this day, regardless of the day of the week, but the majority of Christians celebrated it on the first Sunday following the full moon after the equinox. The years in the table refer to the Era of Diocletian, for which cf. n. 2; an *embolimos* is a month intercalated into the lunar year.

Year 6; epacts 25; 14 before Kalends of March [16 Feb.]; *embolimos*; 18 Xanthicus; 23 Pharmuthi; year 64.

Year 7; epacts 6; 7 before Ides of April [7 April]; 7 Xanthicus; 12 Pharmuthi; year 65.

Year 8; epacts 17; 6 before Kalends of April [27 March]; 27 Dystrus; 1 Pharmuthi; year 66.

Year 9; epacts 28; 17 before Kalends of March [14 Feb.]; *embolimos*; 15 Xanthicus; 20 Pharmuthi; year 67.

Year 10; epacts 9; 1 before Nones of April [4 April]; 4 Xanthicus; 9 Pharmuthi; year 68.

Year 11; epacts 20; 9 before Kalends of April [24 March]; 24 Dystrus; 22 Phamenoth; year 69.

Year 12; epact 1; 1 before Ides of April [12 April]; *embolimos*; 12 Xanthicus; 17 Pharmuthi; year 70.

Year 13; epacts 12; Kalends of April [1 April]; 1 Xanthicus; 6 Pharmuthi; year 71.

Year 14; epacts 23; 12 before Kalends of March [18 Feb.]; *embolimos*; 20 Xanthicus; 25 Pharmuthi; year 72.

Year 15; epacts 4; 5 before Ides of April [9 April]; 9 Xanthicus; 14 Pharmuthi; year 73.

Year 16; epacts 15; 4 before Kalends of April [29 March]; 29 Dystrus; 3 Pharmuthi; year 74.

Year 17; epacts 26; 15 before Kalends of March [16 Feb.]; *embolimos*; 17 Xanthicus; 22 Pharmuthi; year 75.

Year 18; epacts 7; 8 before Ides of April [6 April]; 6 Xanthicus; 11 Pharmuthi; year 76.

Year 19; epacts 18; 7 before Kalends of April [26 March]; 26 Dystrus; 30 Phamenoth; year 77.[81]

**345** Indiction 3, year 8, consulship of Amantius and Albinus.

In the time of these consuls the building of the Constantianae

---

81 Text: the MS has several errors, and at three points is inaccurately reported in the Bonn text. Introductory paragraph: ἀνέδραμε (indicative) for MS ἀνάδραμε (imperative, 'return'; noted by Grumel, see below); year 1: year 79 for MS 59; year 5: 13 Pharmuthi for MS 3 Pharmuthi. (We are indebted to Claudia Rapp for examining the Vatican MS, thereby enabling us to reconsider this problematic section.) Most of the MS errors were corrected by Grumel in an important discussion of the tables, *Chronologie* pt. 1, ch. 5, pp. 73-84, esp. 77ff (though there are some discrepancies with his corrected version of the table at p. 232). The following corrections to the MS are necessary. Year 2: epacts 11; year 3: 22 Dystrus, 27 Phamenoth; year 5: 3 before Kalends of April [30 March], 30 Dystrus, 4 Pharmuthi; year 6: 14 before Kalends of May [18 April]; year 9: 17 before Kalends of May [15 April]; year 11: 28 Phamenoth; year 14: 12 before Kalends of April [21 March], 21 Dystrus, 25 Phamenoth; year 17: 15 before Kalends of May [17 April]. All the years of Diocletian are one year out: year 1, AD 344, was the 60th year of the Diocletianic Era.

bath in Constantinople near the Apostles was begun by
Constantius Augustus, from day 17 of the month April.[82]

**346 [p.535]** Indiction 4, year 9, the 6th consulship of
Constantius Augustus and the 3rd of Constans Augustus.[83]

**347** Indiction 5, year 10, consulship of Rufinus and Eusebius.

Olympiad 282

**348** Indiction 6, year 11, consulship of Philippus and Salia.

**349** Indiction 7, year 12, consulship of Limenius and
Catullinus.

In the time of these consuls Constans was killed in Gaul by
Magnentius after ruling for 12 years, and Magnentius was
elevated on day 15 before Kalends of February [18 Jan.],[84] and
Vetranio at Sirmium on Kalends of March [1 March].[85] And
Nepotianus was elevated in the same year at Rome three days
before Nones of June [3 June],[86] and after this a great war came
about between Romans and Magnentians.

**350** Indiction 8, year 13, consulship of Sergius and
Nigrinianus.

The blessed Leontius, the bishop of Antioch in Syria, a man
who was in all respects faithful and devout and zealous for the
true faith, who also had responsibility for hospices for the care of
strangers, appointed men who were devout in their concern for
these, among whom were three men exceedingly zealous in
piety. On account of a certain business matter these men set out
for a place 17 miles distant from Antioch. The name of the place
was a village called Thracon. **[p.536]** A certain Jew encountered
them and travelled with them. The leader of the three brothers

---

[82]  **345** Constantianae baths: sometimes (e.g. *CP* p. 581. 1) called Constantinianae (wrongly suggesting a link with Constantine rather than Constantius), they
were located to the south-east of the Holy Apostles, and only completed in 427
(*CP s.a.*). See Mango, *Const.* 41; Janin, *Const.* 219-20; G. Prinzing and P. Speck,
'Fünf Lokalitäten in Konstantinopel', 179-81, in Beck, *Studien.*

[83]  *cos. prior*: 4th of Constantius, see n. 78.

[84]  **349** Death of Constans, proclamation of the usurper Magnentius: cf. *Hyd.*
for the same material correctly placed in 350. The coup was promoted by
Constans' *comes rei privatae* Marcellinus (*PLRE* i. 546, s.v. Marcellinus 8);
Magnentius was a high-ranking German army officer, see *PLRE* i. 532.

[85]  Vetranio: *magister peditum per Illyricum* (*PLRE* i. 954, s.v. Vetranio 1); cf.
*Hyd. s.a.* 350, and see further *CP* pp. 539-40 (*s.a.* 350) and notes below.

[86]  Nepotianus: cf. *Hyd. s.a.* 350; nephew of Constantine, he was killed by
Magnentius' troops after a reign of 28 days (*PLRE* i. 624, s.v. Nepotianus 5); cf.
Theoph. 44. 5-7 (giving his reign as 3 months).

was a very devout man named Eugenius. While they were travelling together, Eugenius began and initiated a discussion with the Jew concerning the faith of the only-begotten Son of God. The Jew being utterly scornful, they found on the road a serpent lying dead. And immediately the Jew said to them, 'If you eat this dead serpent and do not die, I will become a Christian.' And immediately Eugenius took the serpent and divided it into three parts for himself and the two with him; and they ate it in front of the Jew and lived. In them was fulfilled the saving word of the Gospel which says, 'And in their hands they shall lift up serpents, and if they eat anything deadly, it will not do them harm.' The Jew came with them to the hospice and, remaining there, was highly esteemed, having become a Christian.[87]

Constantius the Augustus, who was residing in the eastern regions because of the Persian war, when he heard about the events regarding Magnentius, set out from Antioch for Italy.[88]

Sapor the Persian king invaded Mesopotamia, and besieged Nisibis for 100 days. He assailed it in various ways and used many stratagems, so that he even [p.537] brought a multitude of elephants trained for military support, and mercenary kings and all kinds of war engines with which, if they should be unwilling to yield the city, they threatened to obliterate it from the foundations. When the Nisibenes held out against surrender, Sapor thereupon decided to inundate it with the nearby river. But the Nisibenes defeated their enemies by prayers, since they had the favour of God. For when the waters were about to level the structure of the walls in a collapse, part of the wall was affected advantageously in accordance with God's will, as will be shown in what follows: for it came about that the city was protected and the enemy withstood by the waters, so that many in fact perished. And they, even after they had suffered this, were threatening to enter through the collapsed part of the wall: they brought up the armed elephants and prevailed upon the horde to apply more vigorously to the battle, devising stratagems with all kinds of war-engines. But the soldiers

---

87 350 Miracle: Leontius, patriarch of Antioch 344–58, 'zealous for the true faith', was an Arian who actively opposed the orthodox party at Antioch (Philost. iii. 18); Gospel quotation: Mark 16. 18. CP's account of the 4th c. shows several signs of favour towards Arians, especially Constantius; this material was probably transmitted to CP by the Arian church historian Philostorgius, or a similar intermediary text.

88 Constantius in East: cf. Theoph. 43. 32-44. 2, 4-5. Philost. iii. 22 (p. 49. 4-6 Winkelmann) puts Constantius at Edessa.

guarding the city gained victory through God's providence. For they filled the whole place with weapons of every kind, and killed the majority of the elephants with their catapults; the remainder fell in the quagmires of the ditches, while others turned away to the rear after being struck; they killed more than ten thousand of the infantry, and a thunderbolt from heaven fell on the rest; there were black clouds and lashing rain and claps of thunder terrified all, so that the majority of them perished from fear.

[p.538] And the new Pharoah, Sapor, was confined on every side and worsted, being dreadfully submerged by the waves of fear. When he was on the point of destroying it, and the wall had sustained a very large cleft, and the city was on the point of surrendering thereafter, a vision was revealed to Sapor by day, at the very hour when he was fighting: it was a man running around on the walls of Nisibis, and the apparition was in the shape of Constantius the Augustus. Hence Sapor was more enraged against the inhabitants of Nisibis, saying: 'Your emperor is of no avail: let him come out and fight, or you hand over the city.' But they said, 'It is not right that we should hand over the city, since our emperor Constantius the Augustus is absent.' Hence, as a result of this, Sapor was more enraged since, according to the apparition which he had, they were lying, and he said, 'For what purpose are you lying? With my own eyes I behold your emperor Constantius running around on the walls of your city.' And Sapor, who had been variously assailed by God in this, withdrew unsuccessful, after threatening his magi with death. And after learning the reason, they recognized the power of the angel which had appeared with Constantius, and they interpreted it to him. And Sapor, when he understood the cause of the danger, was afraid and ordered that the war-engines be burnt and that all that he had prepared in respect of military equipment be destroyed. He himself, together with his own men, [p.539] driven out in flight, gained his homeland, although the majority perished from pestilential disease beforehand. This is reported in a letter of Valageses, bishop of Nisibis, which sets out the details of these things. [89]

---

[89]   Siege of Nisibis: cf. Theoph. 39. 13-40. 13 for essentially the same account, but clarifying some details (his subsequent long accounts of Constantius' actions and Julian's persecutions are also sometimes clearer). Theophanes, however, omits CP's emphasis on the divine favour for the Arian Constantius signified by Shapur's vision; he also omits Shapur's dialogue with the Nisibenes and gives a different version of the vision in which an angel, brilliantly clad, appeared on top of the wall holding Constantius by the hand (this version is reflected in CP's

While Constantius the Augustus was leaving for the war against Magnentius, before he arrived, Constantia the sister of Constantius clad Vetranio in purple as emperor on Kalends of March [1 March] at Naissus in Italy, and raised up the illustrious man for the battle with Magnentius. And after this Constantius, having arrived in the part of Italy where the war was, received Vetranio with great honour.[90] And after this he made a tribunal on a high place in the Campus; in the presence of the army and

reference to 'the angel which had appeared with Constantius'). Theophanes does not mention Vologeses, third bishop of Nisibis (c.350–361/2) and builder of the extant baptistery (see further Fiey, *Nisibe* 29-33).

Persian tactics: the precise details are hazy, since panegyrical or religious matters, including the prominent role of Vologeses, are the focus of the main sources, Jul. *Or.* i. 27-8, ii. 62-6; Ephraem the Syrian, *Nisibene Hymns* i-iii, xi. 14-18, xiii. 14-20 (ed. E. Beck, *CSCO* Scr. Syri 92-3, Louvain 1961), and *Nicomedene Memre* x. 145-56, xv. 53-62, 97-208 (ed. C. Renoux, *P O* xxxvii/2-3, 1975). However, it is clear that key elements were an attempt to undermine the walls by flooding and a subsequent failed assault involving elephants: see further the useful discussion by C. S. Lightfoot, 'The Eastern Frontier of the Roman Empire with Special Reference to the Reign of Constantius II' (unpubl. Oxford D. Phil., 1981), 92-103 (with notes, 118-29), to which this note is greatly indebted; also M. Maróth, 'Le Siège de Nisibe en 350 ap. J.-Ch. d'après des sources syriennes', *Acta Antiqua* xxvii, 1979, 239-43.

Deliverance of Nisibis: elsewhere the unexpected escape is attributed primarily to the prayers of Jacob, first bishop of the city, or more accurately to his posthumous appearance on the walls: for discussion of the various legends, see P. Peeters, 'La Légende de Saint Jacques de Nisibe', *AB* xxxviii, 1920, 285-373. Theodoret (*HR* i. 12) may reflect the process whereby the bishop took over credit from the emperor, in that Shapur is said to mistake Jacob for the emperor because he appeared to be wearing the purple and diadem. (In Theodoret, *HE* ii. 30 the apparition dressed in imperial purple is kept separate from Jacob's ascent to the walls and efficacious prayers.) For a divine defender at Cpl., cf. *s.a.* 626 with n. 476.

[90] Proclamation of Vetranio: cf. Theoph. 44. 7-12 (wrongly placed in Constantius' 21st year); also Philost. iii. 22 (p. 49. 7-12 Winkelmann); an official version is presented in Julian's panegyrics for Constantius, esp. *Orr.* i. 31-3, ii. 76-8. The elderly Vetranio was proclaimed in Illyricum at Sirmium (Soc. ii. 25; Soz. iv. 1; correctly recorded by *CP s.a.* 349), not Naissus; *CP*'s Italy is an error probably caused by the reference to Italy at p. 539. 9. Constantius, who met Vetranio in Illyricum, did not advance into Italy until late 351.

Constantina (not Constantia): her motives are uncertain. The chronicle version suggests that she was attempting to reduce the threat of Magnentius' usurpation by timely action while her brother was involved in the east, but she may well have had her own imperial ambitions – she had been proclaimed Augusta in her own right by her father Constantine (Philost. iii. 22, 28), and in 335-7 had been married to Hannibalianus, Constantine's step-nephew, and his candidate for the throne of Armenia (and probably also Persia, cf. n. 68); in 351 she married Gallus Caesar, brother of Julian, see *PLRE* i. 222, s.v. Constantina 2.

with Vetranio also standing beside him Constantius declared publicly that it was fitting for empire that power belong even to him who inherited this from imperial ancestors; and it was also expedient for the commonwealth that public affairs and whatever was fitting for these be duly administered under a single power.

In all these things God was with Constantius, guiding his empire. For he himself indeed took great care for the churches of Christ. And when Vetranio had been emperor for ten months, in accordance with the aforementioned public declaration Constantius removed the purple, and at the same time granted him fellowship of his table at dinner; [p.540] with all honour and an escort and many favours, he dispatched him to live in the city of Prusa in Bithynia, receiving payments and provisions in abundance. Since Vetranio was a Christian and attended the church for services, he undertook almsgiving to the poor as well as honouring the leaders of the church until his death.[91]

**351** Indiction 9, year 14, post-consulship of Sergius and Nigrinianus.[92]

Constantius Augustus, being sole emperor, proclaimed as Caesar and colleague in his rule his cousin Gallus, renaming him

---

[91] Constantius' speech and deposition of Vetranio: cf. Theoph. 44. 22-45. 5 (under Constantius' 21st year, in association with his two-week visit to Rome for his *vicennalia* in 357), but omitting the sentences on God's favour for Constantius and the emperor's care for the churches. In Constantius' speech, we have translated Theophanes' aorist, 'who inherited', διαδεξαμένῳ, in preference to CP's future, 'who would inherit', διαδεξομένῳ.

Vetranio was forced to abdicate on 25 Dec. 350 in Illyricum (9 months before Mursa) when Constantius, who for some time had been subverting Vetranio's troops, clinched their allegiance with a harangue that apparently became famous (cf. Jul. *Or*. ii. 77; Zos. ii. 44). Socrates ii. 28 stresses the sympathy and generosity of Constantius' treatment of Vetranio.

From Theophanes' narrative it appears that the common source of CP and Theophanes erroneously narrated these events *after* the defeat of Magnentius at Mursa in Pannonia, and placed the speech at Rome in the Campus Martius. It is possible that CP tried to correct his source by narrating Vetranio's deposition before the battle of Mursa, but he did not realize that he should also have removed from the story the references to Italy.

[92] **351** The MS, misreported in the Bonn text, correctly records the post-consulship. Since consuls were an important dating mechanism, it was necessary to create a formula for the occasions, increasingly common from the mid-4th c., when no consul was appointed (or the men appointed by eastern or western emperors were not accepted in parts of the empire). The solution was the post-consular formula, which simply involved counting from the last recognized consulship: thus the consular dates for 542-65 are provided by reckoning from the consulship of Basilius in 541.

Constantius, on Ides of March [15 March]; he dispatched him to Antioch in the east, since the Persians were pressing.[93]

The sign of the Cross of Christ was seen in Jerusalem at this time: it was about the third hour on the day of Pentecost, the Nones of May [7 May], when it extended radiant in the heaven from the Mount of Olives as far as Golgotha, the place where the Lord was crucified facing east, and from where the Lord was taken up; encircling the apparition of the precious Cross was a corona whose shape was like the rainbow. And at the same hour it was seen in Pannonia by Constantius the Augustus and the army which was with him in the war against Magnentius.[94] And when Constantius began to be victorious, Magnentius joined battle with him near the city of Mursa, as it is called; Magnentius was defeated and fled to Gaul with a few men.[95]

[p.541] Constantius, who was also called Gallus, the afore-mentioned Caesar, stayed in the east and in Antioch.[96]

---

[93] Proclamation of Gallus: cf. Hyd., Theoph. 40. 15-18; also Philost. iii. 25. Constantius, accepting that a single ruler could not cope with all military threats, remained in the west to fight Magnentius and then the Alamanni on the Rhine frontier, while Gallus (PLRE i. 224-5, s.v. Constantius 4), now married to the emperor's ambitious sister Constantina, was sent east.

[94] Apparition of Cross in sky: cf. Hyd., Theoph. 41. 33-42. 1 (wrongly dated to Constantius' 19th year and divorced from the campaign against Magnentius, which he also misdates); CP has misplaced the phrase 'from where the Lord was taken up', which should be connected with the Mount of Olives not Golgotha, so that the reference to the Ascension is confused. Philostorgius iii. 26 records the vision at greater length, noting the connection with the civil war. For an Arian writer the apparition was a sign of divine favour for Constantius, as potent as Constantine's vision before the battle of the Milvian bridge.

The apparition was reported to Constantius in a letter from Cyril bishop of Jerusalem, which confirms the precise date and place (PG xxxiii. 1165-76); the Cross was visible for several hours to the whole city, and after the vision the populace rushed to church. Cyril favourably compared this vision in the sky with the discovery under Constantine of the relic of the Cross in the earth. The connection of the Cross with Jerusalem and the city's possession of a relic (cf. n. 62) were probably exploited by Cyril as part of his attempt to elevate the see of Jerusalem above Caesarea, see Rubin, 'Church'. Theophanes (42. 1-2) alludes to Cyril's account, and then digresses to argue that his reference to Constantius as 'most pious' did not signify that Cyril condoned the emperor's Arianism.

[95] Defeat of Magnentius: after an initial success over Constantius near Atrans, Magnentius was bloodily defeated at Mursa in Pannonia on 28 Sept. 351 (Hyd.).

[96] Gallus at Antioch: for his cruel conduct, see Amm. xiv. 1, 7. 1-3.

Olympiad 283

**352** Indiction 10, year 15, the 7th consulship of Constantius Augustus and that of Constans Caesar.[97]

**353** Indiction 11, year 16, the 8th consulship of Constantius Augustus and the 2nd of Constans Caesar.

**354** Indiction 12, year 17, the 9th consulship of Constantius Augustus and the 3rd of Constans Caesar.

In this year Magnentius again joined battle at Montus Seleucus, was defeated, and fled alone to Gaul to the city of Lugdunum; and when he had slain his own brother, then he also killed himself, four days before Ides of August [10 Aug.].[98]

**355** Indiction 13, year 18, consulship of Arbetio and Lullianus.

In this year Gallus, who was also Constantius, was summoned from the city of the Antiochenes by Constantius the Augustus on a charge that he had killed a praetorian prefect and a *quaestor* contrary to the will of Constantius the Augustus, and he was killed on the island of Istrus.[99] And he put the purple on Julian, the brother of the same Gallus who was also Constantius, and appointed him Caesar [p.542] on day 8 before Ides of October [8 Oct.]; Constantius Augustus gave to him in marriage his sister Helena, and dispatched him to Gaul.[100]

---

[97]   **352** *cos. post.*: Constantius Caesar (i.e. Gallus); also 353 and 354, when *Heracl.* (*CM* iii. 399) makes the same error.

[98]   **354** Defeat and death of Magnentius: cf. Theoph. 44. 14-16, without date, but adding that he killed his mother as well as his brother before committing suicide; also Soc. ii. 32. Magnentius, forced to abandon Italy in 352, was defeated in 353 at Mons Seleucus in south-east Gaul (precise location unknown), after which he committed suicide at Lyons (Lugdunum) on 11 Aug. (*Hyd. s.a. 353*: 3 before Ides of Aug.); a second brother, the Caesar Decentius, committed suicide at Sens on 18 Aug. 353 (*Hyd.*; cf. Theoph. 44. 16-17). Constantius then exacted cruel revenge on the usurper's supporters (Amm. xiv. 5).

[99]   **355** Death of Gallus (in 354): the circumstances are recorded at greater length by Philost. iii. 28-iv. 1, Amm. xiv. 7. 9-19, 11. 1-23, and Soc. ii. 34. Constantius, worried by reports of Gallus' behaviour in Antioch (not all of them true, see Amm. xiv. 11. 3-4, 24), sent the praetorian prefect Domitian to recall him to the west; an argument ensued in which Gallus' *quaestor* Montius sided with Domitian, but Gallus had both men killed. Subsequently Gallus obeyed Constantius' summons to report to Milan, but he was tried *in absentia* and executed at Flanona on the east coast of the Istrian peninsula (*Hyd. s.a.* 354).

[100]   Proclamation of Julian (at Milan): cf. Theoph. 45. 5-9 (wrongly located at Cpl., but with additional details); the correct date was day 8 before Ides of Nov., i.e. 6 Nov. 355 (*Hyd. s.a.*; cf. Soc. ii. 34). For the fullest account, see Amm. xv. 8 (proclamation, marriage, and arrival in Gaul), xvi-xviii, xx (Julian's successes in Gaul); Bidez, *Julien* pt. 2, Browning, *Julian* ch. 5.

## Olympiad 284

**356** Indiction 14, year 19, the 10th consulship of Constantius Augustus and that of Julian Caesar.

In the time of these consuls, on day 1 in the month Panemus [July], the remains of Timothy who had been the holy disciple of Paul the apostle and first bishop elected at Ephesus in Asia, were brought to Constantinople with all honour, and laid to rest in the Holy Apostles beneath the holy altar.[101]

**357** Indiction 15, year 20, the 11th consulship of Constantius Augustus and the 2nd of Julian Caesar.

In the time of these consuls, on day 3 in the month Dystrus [March], the remains of the holy apostles Luke and Andrew were brought to Constantinople through the zeal of Constantius the Augustus, with zeal and piety, amidst psalmody and hymnody, and were laid to rest in the Holy Apostles.[102]

Constantius Augustus came to Rome with great display and pomp for his *vicennalia*. **[p.543]** His wife Eusebia the empress also came with him, and they passed 14 days in Rome.[103]

**358** Indiction 1, year 21, consulship of Datianus and Cerealis.

**359** Indiction 2, year 22, consulship of Eusebius and Hypatius.

In the time of these consuls in the month Hyperberetaeus [October] there was a great and violent earthquake in Nicomedia about hour 3 of the night. And the city collapsed and was destroyed, and among others the bishop of the same city, named Cecropius, also perished.[104]

---

[101] **356** Relics of Timothy: cf. *Hyd. s.a.* (with Roman date of 1 June). This notice and that following, which point to the piety of Constantius, probably derive from the postulated Arian history of the 4th c.: Philostorgius iii. 2 records these translations in a general chapter devoted to Constantius' acts of piety. On the relics' significance, see Dvornik, *Apostolicity* ch. 4.

[102] **357** Relics of Luke and Andrew: cf. *Hyd. s.a.* (with Roman date). Three consular lists (*Vind. pr. & post., Scal.: CM* i. 293) wrongly date this translation to 336 (30 Nov. *Vind. post.*; 22 June *Scal.*). Although *CP* has an anticipatory reference in the context of Constantine's burial in the Holy Apostles (*s.a.* 337, p. 533. 15-17; cf. also Philost. loc. cit. in n. 101, which is out of chronological sequence), the later date is supported by the involvement of Artemius (*PLRE* i. 112, s.v Artemius 2), who was 'martyred' under Julian (cf. *s.a.* 363 with n. 124).

[103] *Vicennalia*: cf. Theoph. 44. 19-22 (wrongly associated with the Magnentius campaign). The grand ceremony is described by Ammianus xvi. 10. 1-17; Constantius entered Rome on 28 April (*Hyd.*) and left on 29 May (Amm. xvi. 10. 20).

[104] **359** Nicomedia earthquake: cf. Theoph. 45. 25-7; also Philost. iv. 10. Ammianus (xvii. 7. 1-8) records that the disaster struck at daybreak on 24 Aug. (in 358; so too *Hyd.*), and that fires then burned for 5 days. *CP* here gives a

Gratian son of Valentinian was born on day 10 before Kalends of June [23 May],[105] and in the same year for the first time there appeared publicly in Constantinople a prefect of Rome, Honoratus by name, on day 3 before Ides of September [11 Sept.].[106]

## Olympiad 285

360 Indiction 3, year 23, the 12th consulship of Constantius Augustus and the 3rd of Julian Caesar.

In this year, on day 15 in the month Peritius [February] the Great Church of Constantinople was consecrated.[107]

Macedonius bishop of Constantinople was demoted on the grounds of his many personal faults,[108] and Eudoxius was appointed in his place as bishop of the same church; he was enthroned on day 27 in the month Audynaeus [January], in the presence of 72 bishops, Maris, Acacius, Georgius, [p.544] Serra, Uranius, Theodosius, Eusebius, Leontius, Curio, Arabianus, Asinus, Philotheus, Agerochius, Eugenius, Elpidius, Stephanus, Heliodorus, Demophilus, Timotheus, Exeuresius, Megasius, Meizonius, Paulus, Evagrius, Apollonius, Phoebus, Theophilus, Protasius, Theodorus, Heliodorus, Eumathius, Synesius, Ptolemaeus, Eutyches, Quintus, Alphius, Trophimus, Eutychius,

---

Greek date, in contrast to the Roman date for other events in the year.

105 Birth of Gratian: at Sirmium on 18 April 359 (Jerome, *Chron. s.a.; Hyd.*). Gratian was emperor 367–83, see *PLRE* i. 401, s.v. Gratianus 2.

106 Honoratus: see *PLRE* i. 438-9, s.v. Honoratus 2; he was the first city prefect of Cpl. (the New Rome), cf. *Hyd.* with the preferred date 3 before Ides of Dec. 359 (11 Dec.). For ἐν πρώτοις in this sense, 'for the first time', cf. Mal. 321. 17-18, *CP* p. 529. 19 (πρώτοις); also *primum* in *Hyd*. For the prefecture, see Dagron, *Naissance* 215-17, 241-2, and R. Guilland, 'Études sur l'histoire administrative de l'empire byzantin – L'éparque de la ville', *ByzSlav* xli, 1980, 17-32.

107 360 Consecration of St. Sophia: cf. *Hyd.* with Roman date (15 before Kalends of March, in fact one day out because 360 was a leap year). The completion of the Great Church, together with the appointment of a city prefect in 359, was an indication that the new city of Cpl. had now developed into a major urban centre. See further n. 110.

108 Macedonius: bishop of Cpl. 342-60 (but from 346 to 351 his deposed predecessor Paul was also recognized). Although elected by Arian bishops and known as a persecutor of 'orthodox' Nicenes, Macedonius was deposed at the instigation of Constantius (a more thorough Arian). His offence was partly doctrinal, because Macedonius denied the divinity of the Holy Spirit (see Chadwick, *Church* 146), and partly arose from the disputes caused by his decision to move Constantine's body to St. Acacius during building work at the Holy Apostles (either repairs or its transformation from a mausoleum into a church). See further Dagron, *Naissance* 436-42.

Basiliscus, Theomnestus, Vetranio, Philippus, Anastasius, Maxentius, Polyeuctus, Gratianus, Leontius, Metrodorus, Eustathius, Junianus, Trophimus, Oecumenius, Menophilus, Euethius, and the rest.[109]

At the time of the same synod of bishops, not many days after the enthronement of Eudoxius as bishop of Constantinople, the inauguration of the Great Church of the same city was celebrated after a little more than 34 years since Constantine, victorious and venerable, laid the foundations.[110] Its inauguration took place in the time of the aforementioned consuls, on day 16 before Kalends of March, which is day 14 of the month Peritius [February].[111] At the inauguration the emperor Constantius Augustus presented many dedications, great gold and silver treasures, and many gemmed and gold-threaded cloths for the holy altar; in addition also, for the doors of the church diverse golden curtains, and for the outer entrances [p.545] varied gold-threaded ones; so he lavishly bestowed many gifts at that time on the entire clergy, and on the order of virgins and widows and on the hospices. And for the sustenance of the aforenamed and of the beggars, and orphans, and prisoners, he added a corn allocation of greater size than that which his father Constantine had bestowed.[112]

---

[109] Eudoxius: bishop 360–70, recently deposed after a short period as bishop of Antioch (358–9). The 72 bishops had gathered at Cpl., following the separate western and eastern councils at Rimini and Seleucia (Isauria) in autumn 359, as the culmination of Constantius' attempt to re-establish ecclesiastical unity throughout his empire, but it was also appropriate for them to solemnize the change of bishop in the capital. See Dagron, *Naissance* 216-17, 441-4; Jones, *LRE* 117-18. The careful preservation of the majority of names indicates *CP*'s interest in the affairs of the Cpl. church.

[110] St. Sophia: the foundation is attributed to Constantine by some late sources, e.g. the anonymous *Ekphrasis St. Sophiae* 1 (*Patria* p. 74. 6-8 Preger), G. Mon. ii. 627. 4-5, and Cedr. i. 498. 3 (cf. 517. 9-11); however, Dagron (*Naissance* 397-401) reviews the evidence, and plausibly suggests that the allusion in *CP* to Constantine laying the foundations 34 years previously (i.e. in 326) refers to his foundation of Cpl. (in 328). Eusebius, in his panegyrical *VC*, does not give Constantine credit for the church. Although it is possible that Constantine left instructions which Constantius executed (Cedr. i. 523. 4-7), Constantius was primarily responsible for the building.

[111] Date: day 16 before Kalends of March was in fact 15 Peritius/Feb. in 360 (a leap year), the date correctly but inconsistently recorded in the first entry for the year (from a different source); cf. n. 107.

[112] Constantius' generosity: the favourable attitude of *CP*'s source towards the Arian emperor is again revealed in this catalogue of his benefactions. Constantius had in fact halved his father's provision of food for Cpl. in 342 (not mentioned in *CP*) as punishment for the murder of Hermogenes (Soc. ii. 13); this

**361** Indiction 4, year 24, consulship of Taurus and Florentius.

At the beginning of the fourth indiction, because the rebellion of Julian Caesar had been reported to him, he came to the springs of Mompsus at the first staging-post from Cilician Tarsus; after he had first received the holy baptism from Euzoius bishop of Antioch, who was summoned to the same staging-post by the same Constantius, the same Constantius Augustus quitted life on day 3 in the month Dius [November], year of Antioch 410, indiction 5, when year 50 of the peace of the churches had been reached, under the aforenamed consuls Taurus and Florentius.[113]

Julian the apostate, cousin of Constantius and brother of Gallus who was also Constantius, was 36th Roman emperor for 2 years.

In total, 5,872.

**362** Indiction 5, year 1, consulship of Mamertinus and Nevitta.

After the death of Constantius the Augustus the peace of the churches was severed when Julian entered Constantinople on day 11 in the month Apellaeus [December]. And these are the ensuing events.[114]

**[p.546]** Julian, when he learnt of the death of Constantius the Augustus, made manifest his own apostasy and impiety by sending out edicts against Christianity throughout the whole world, and commanded that all the idols be restored.[115] Elated at

was reinstated after a request by Themistius in 357, but *CP* may refer to an extra grant for charitable purposes: see Dagron, *Naissance* 534-5.

[113]  **361** Death of Constantius: cf. Theoph. 46. 13-14 for place and date; Amm. xxi. 15. 2-3, but with incorrect date of 5 Oct. (3 before Nones Oct., for 3 before Nones Nov.); Moses of Khoren iii. 12 (alluding to Cyril's account of the apparition of the Cross, cf. *s.a.* 351); also Philost. vi. 5 for baptism by Euzoius, Arian bishop of Antioch 360–76. Constantius was fighting the Persians when Julian was proclaimed Augustus by his troops at Paris in Feb. 360; subsequent attempts to reach a compromise failed and the breach became open in spring 361 (Amm. xxi; see also Bidez, *Julien* pt. 2, chs. 11-14; Browning, *Julian* ch. 6).

Synchronism: this contains the correct indiction date, 5 (since the new indiction began in Sept.), as opposed to the opening phrase, 'at the beginning of the fourth indiction', which was presumably *CP*'s own inference from the year-heading. It reflects the importance attached to the Arian Constantius by *CP*'s source: cf. Theoph. 46. 16-17 where an *annus mundi* date is given for Constantius' baptism. Constantine's victory over Maxentius in 312 had established the peace of the churches.

[114]  **362** Julian's entry into Cpl.: cf. Hyd. *s.a.* 361 (correctly; with Roman date). Ammianus xxii. 2 describes the welcome given to him by senate and people.

[115]  Julian's measures: for summary, see Jones, *LRE* 121-2. The consequences of Julian's apostasy are recorded, with different selections, by the 5th-c. ecclesiastical historians (Soc. iii; Soz. v; Theod. iii; Philost. vii). Julian himself preferred persuasion and patronage to persecution (e.g. Jul. *Letter* 37), and did not want to strengthen Christianity by the creation of new martyrs; but his

this, the pagans in the east at once arrested and killed at Alexandria in Egypt George, the bishop of the city, and impiously insulted his body: for they put it on a camel and carried it around through the whole city, and after this they gathered together dead bodies of various beasts as well as bones, mixed them with his body, burnt them, and scattered them around.[116]

And in Palestine they dug up and scattered around the remains of St. John the Baptist which lay in the city of Sebaste.

Furthermore, they also dug up from the grave the remains of St. Patrophilus who had been bishop of the church in Scythopolis, and scattered the majority around, but the skull they insolently hung up and affixed as it were in the form of a lamp.

And in Gaza and Ascalon they killed presbyters and virgins, and after this, having cut open and filled their bodies with barley, they threw them to the pigs.

And in Phoenicia they killed Cyril a deacon of Heliopolis and ate his liver, since he had destroyed their idols in the time of Constantine of blessed memory. But it is worth mentioning how the man who cut open the [p.547] deacon and ate his liver destroyed his own life. He lost his putrefied tongue, cast out his shattered teeth, was debilitated in the eyes after great and increasingly violent pain, and tortured throughout his whole body he died horribly.[117]

At Emesa they invaded the great church and set up the idol of Dionysus.[118]

Similarly too in the city of Epiphania in Syria the pagans

lenient treatment of pagan excesses (especially when compared with punishment of Christian violence at Caesarea and Edessa) will have encouraged extremists to settle scores that built up during fifty years of Christianization. Local responses to Julian's edicts varied: a thoroughly Christian city like Antioch ignored the emperor's wishes even though he was present, whereas Cyzicus or (Syrian) Hierapolis reacted enthusiastically. See further Bidez, *Julien* pt. 3, chs. 5, 9, 13; Browning, *Julian* ch. 9.

116 George: cf. also Soc. iii. 2-3, Soz. v. 7, Philost. vii. 2. Ammianus (xxii. 11) records that he was killed during a riot to celebrate the death of Artemius, *dux* of Egypt (cf. *s.a.* 363 with n. 124), although the Christians could have prevented this if all men had not hated him; Julian upbraided the Alexandrians for their behaviour (*Letter* 21).

117 Pagan outrages: cf. Theoph. 47. 25-48. 3 (omitting Sebaste), Theod. iii. 7. 1-4 (Gaza, Ascalon, Sebaste, Heliopolis); also Philost. vii. 4 (John the Baptist), Soz. v. 9-10. 7.

118 Emesa: cf. Theoph. 48. 12-13 (crediting Julian with the deed and adding that he pulled down the old church); also Theod. iii. 7. 5.

invaded the church and brought in an idol, with flutes and drums. And the blessed Eustathius who happened to be bishop of the same church, a man devout and pious, when he heard the flutes, enquired where they might be; on learning that they were in the church, being zealous in faith and piety, he was laid to rest immediately he heard, since he prayed not to see these things with his eyes.[119]

Furthermore, when Julian came to Constantinople, while Eudoxius was bishop there, in manifold ways he devised plots against the church for its confusion, and brought these things upon it. He wanted to let loose upon the churches all those who had previously been demoted for various foul heresies, contriving pretexts against the churches of God from the disturbances that arose.[120]

So then, Meletius too, who had been demoted for impiety and other evils, [p.548] returned to Antioch and seized the old church, when those of the clergy who had already been legally demoted by the holy synod also ran to join him.[121] Among these were notably Diogenes a former presbyter, who more than the others ran to join him, and Vitalius a layman, who lived constantly in imposture: and indeed he went much further and afterwards, subsequently aggrieved against Meletius, split off from him and established a heresy which was itself also worthy of ridicule; they are called Vitalians after him to the present day. Apollinarius too, the one who was a Laodicean from Syria, son of a schoolmaster, championed this heresy.[122]

---

[119] Eustathius of Epiphania: the only notice of Julian's anti-Christian actions that cannot be paralleled in a church historian and/or Theophanes.

[120] Encouragement for divisions among Christians: cf. Philost. vii. 4 (p. 81. 6-13 Winkelmann); also Soc. iii. 5 (recall of exiled bishops), Soz. v. 5, Amm. xxii. 5. 3-4. Together with the resumption of imperial patronage for pagans and a corresponding discrimination against those who refused to sacrifice (cf. Soc. iii. 13), this was Julian's most effective weapon against the Christians.

[121] Meletius: an upholder of Nicene orthodoxy, he was briefly bishop of Antioch in 359/60, before being ousted on a disciplinary pretext in favour of the more Arian Euzoius (Theod. Lect. ii. 114). This marked the start of a major schism in the Antioch church that was not healed until 393, and for much of this period Antioch had three bishops, the Arian Euzoius (360–76), the orthodox Paulinus (362–88) who was in communion with Athanasius of Alexandria, and Meletius (360–81) also orthodox but not in communion with Athanasius. For Julian's encouragement of this schism, cf. Theod. iii. 4. 5, Soc. iii. 9, Soz. v. 13.

[122] Heretics: Diogenes is unknown. Vitalius, ordained presbyter by Meletius, subsequently split from him in a personal quarrel and became a devotee of Apollinarius, a vehement anti-Arian who, however, propounded the heresy that Christ lacked a perfect human soul or spirit, since this was replaced by the

**363** Indiction 6, year 2, the 4th consulship of Julian Augustus and that of Salustius.

At this time, certain of those too who were being reviewed on military service were deceived into apostasy, some of them being softened by promises of gifts and rank, others too by constraints applied by their own officers. And a certain Theotecnus, a presbyter of the church in Antioch, deceived by a promise turned voluntarily to idolatry; God forthwith took vengeance on him in the following manner: he became consumed by worms, lost his eyes, ate his tongue, and so died.

Then too Heron, such was his name, a certain Theban bishop, **[p.549]** voluntarily apostasized when he happened to be in the Antiochene city; on him the miraculous power of God exacted vengeance as an example and terror for many. For he rendered him devoid of all care, and inflicting a putrefying disease caused him to expire in public before the eyes of all as he roamed about the streets.

Among these Valentinian also, who was at that time a tribune of a brigade in the so-called cohort of the *Cornuti*, distinguished himself in confession of Christ. For not only did he scorn his rank, but even when subjected to exile he endured nobly and eagerly. How he was subsequently honoured by God in becoming Roman emperor will be shown in the following narrative.[123]

And Artemius, who was *dux* of the diocese of Egypt, since in the period of his office under Constantius the Augustus of blessed memory he had displayed great zeal on behalf of the churches, had his property confiscated and his head cut off in the Alexandrian city, since Julian bore a grudge against him.

And in Dorostolon of Thracian Scythia Aemilianus was also martyred, being consigned to fire by soldiers under the *vicarius*

Divine Word (cf. Soz. vi. 25, and see Bury, *HLRE* [2] i. 350). Apollinarius of Laodicea and his schoolmaster father of the same name, attempted to avoid the consequences of Julian's ban on Christians teaching the pagan classics by transposing the Bible into classical literary genres (Soz. v. 18). 'The one who was a Laodicean' is our conjectural interpretation of a garbled reading in the MS.

123   **363** Pressure on soldiers, Theotecnus of Antioch, Heron, Valentinian: cf. Theoph. 50. 34-51. 11 for the same sequence (adding an anecdote about Jovian, 51. 11-14); also Philost. vii. 13 (Heron, Theotecnus); Sozomen v. 17 records that Julian seduced the troops into sacrificing when they received their pay. For the stories about Valentinian's conduct under Julian, see *PLRE* i. 933-4, s.v. Valentinianus 7; the most extreme is that he was exiled to a desert place for striking a pagan priest. In *CP* the periphrastic 'so-called' is inappropriately applied to 'cohort' rather than to *Cornuti* (as Theoph. 51. 9, Philost. vii. 7), a unit of auxiliaries in the praesental field army.

Capitolinus, and many others in various places, cities, and lands distinguished themselves in confession of Christ, whose number and names it is not easy to declare.

[p.550] At this time a certain Thalassius, who was also called Magnus, being outstanding for licentiousness and profligacy, who even acted as pimp for shameful acts for his own daughter, died when his house collapsed on him.[124]

*Concerning the martyrdom of St. Domitius*

In this year St. Domitius was also martyred in the following manner. For Julian, while setting out on campaign and passing through the Cyrrhestike, saw a crowd standing before the cave of St. Domitius and being cured, and he asked, 'Who is it?'. And when he learnt that he was a monk and that the crowd gathered wishing to be cured and blessed by him, the same Julian made this declaration to St. Domitius through a Christian *referendarius*: 'If you entered the cave to please your God, do not wish to please men, but live alone.' St. Domitius declared to him in return, 'After handing my soul and body over to God long ago, I shut myself away in this cave. But I cannot chase away the crowd who come to me in faith.' And the emperor Julian ordered that the cave be barricaded, and the righteous man remained within. And thus the same St. Domitius met his end.[125]

---

[124] Artemius, Aemilianus, Thalassius: cf. Theoph. 51. 14-27 (with extra details on Thalassius). Ammianus (xxii. 11) records that Artemius was executed because of the serious charges brought against him by the Alexandrians (cf. *PLRE* i. 112, s.v. Artemius 2, and n. 102 above). Dorostolon was an army base at modern Silistra on the Danube in Bulgaria.

Thalassius who 'acted as pimp': we have restored the MS προαγωγεύς (nominative) for the Bonn Text's inaccurate προαγωγούς (accusative).

[125] Domitius: cf. Mal. 328. 5-19. At Antioch Julian had been annoyed by the Christian enthusiasm of the majority of the population, and hoped to find greater reverence for pagan deities away from the city; Domitius was perhaps a victim of Julian's vexation (if the chroniclers' story is true). Julian left Antioch to attack the Persians, and his march eastwards would have taken him through the Cyrrhestike, the vicinity of Cyrrhus (for the route, see Amm. xxiii. 2).

*Referendarius*: a judicial clerk or messenger attached to the emperor; possibly an anachronism, since they are first attested in the law codes only in 427 (Jones, *LRE* 575, 1236 n. 24).

This story, which is not in Theophanes, marks the point at which *CP* switches to Malalas (or material in the Malalas tradition), abandoning the pro-Arian source which he had used in common with Theophanes. The heading printed in the Bonn text appears only in the margin of the MS, and is analogous to similar headings for Artemius and Aemilianus which the editor Dindorf did

At the same time Julian saw in a vision a certain full-grown [p.551] man clad in consular dress who came to him in his pavilion which was pitched near the city of Ctesiphon, in a village called Rasia, and struck him with a spear. And he woke from sleep and cried out, and the eunuch *cubicularii* and the *spatharii*, and the troop guarding the pavilion stood up and came to him with imperial lamps. And Julian, after noticing that he had a wound under the armpit, asked those standing beside him, 'How is the village named where my pavilion is pitched?'. And they said to him, 'Rasia.' And straightway Julian cried out, 'O Helios, you have destroyed Julian.' And he surrendered his soul from loss of blood at hour 5 of the night in the month Daisius, on day 6 before Kalends of July [26 June].[126]  And straightway the army, before the Persian enemy knew of it, departed to the pavilion of Jovian, *comes domesticorum* and a *magister militum* in rank. And while he was unaware of the news of the death of Julian, they brought him to the imperial pavilion as though the emperor Julian had asked for him. And when he entered the pavilion they constrained him and proclaimed him emperor in the same month Daisius, on day 6 before Kalends of July [26 June], before dawn. And the mass of the army, which was at Ctesiphon and encamped a good distance away, did not know of the events until sunrise. So the same Julian died, aged 36 years.[127]

---

not include.

[126] Death of Julian: cf. Mal. 332. 18-333. 6, with minor differences (cuirass rather than consular dress; Asia for Rasia). For the Roman date (not in Mal.), cf. Hyd. Malalas preserves considerable information about Julian's campaign against the Persians, and two versions of the fatal wound, a less miraculous account attributed to the historian Magnus of Carrhae (329. 2-3; 332. 8), and the version shared with *CP*, which is attributed to Eutychianus of Cappadocia (332. 9; little is known, see *PLRE* i. 319, s.v. Eutychianus 3). For detailed narrative of the Persian campaign, and of Julian's death from a wound suffered in a skirmish as the Romans retreated north up the Tigris from Ctesiphon, see Amm. xxiii-xxv. 3 (xxv. 3. 9: the place of death is called Phrygia, which accorded with a prophecy); also Bidez, *Julien* pt. 3, ch. 17, Browning, *Julian* ch. 10.

Julian's devotion to Helios: see Jul. *Or.* vii. 229-34, and P. Athanasiadi-Fowden, *Julian and Hellenism* (Oxford 1981), index s.v. Helios.

*Cubicularii* and *spatharii*: *cubicularii* were attendants of the imperial bed-chamber, traditionally eunuchs, among whom the *spatharii* were bodyguards. However, the first known *spatharius* was Chrysaphius under Theodosius II, so the reference here is anachronistic; cf. n. 264, and see Jones, *LRE* 566-70, Guilland, *Recherches* i. 269-85.

[127] Proclamation of Jovian: cf. Mal. 333. 7-17 (Julian aged 33: he was in fact 31), and Hyd. for the Roman date (5 before Kalends of July, i.e. 27 June, as in Mal.). Jovian, *protector domesticus* under Constantius, was promoted by Julian to be

[p.552] On the same night the most saintly Basil bishop of Caesarea saw in a vision the heavens opened and the saviour Christ seated on a throne, crying out and saying, 'Mercurius, go and slaughter Julian the emperor, he who is against the Christians.' And St. Mercurius, standing before the Lord and wearing an iron breastplate, disappeared when he heard the command. And again he was present, standing before the throne of the Lord, and he cried, 'Julian the emperor is slain and dead, as you ordered, Lord.' And the bishop Basil, terrified at the cry, awoke in confusion. The emperor Julian used to honour him as a man of eloquence and his companion, and he wrote to him constantly. And the bishop Basil went down to the church for the morning service, summoned all the clergy, and told them the mystery of the vision, saying, 'Julian the emperor is slain and dead on this night.' And all urged him to be silent and not to say such a thing.[128]

After the reign of Julian, in the month Daisius [June] the same Jovian became emperor for 8 months, after being crowned by the army in the Persian regions. As soon as he became emperor, in his own voice he personally proclaimed to the whole army and to the senators with him, 'If you wish me to be your emperor, see that we are all Christians.' And all the army and the senate and the brigades of the armies acclaimed him. [p.553] And next, after the same Jovian together with his army left the desert land for the fertile Persian land, he was anxious about how he should depart from the remaining regions of Persia.

But the Persian king Labuarsacius, who had not yet learnt of the death of the emperor Julian, was possessed of great fear and dispatched from the country of Persian Armenia one of his grandees, Surenas by name, on an embassy to the Roman emperor seeking and begging for peace. Jovian the emperor received him gladly and consented to receive the peace embassy, saying that he himself too would send an ambassador to the Persian king. When he heard this, the Persian ambassador

---

primicerius domesticorum, an officer in the regiments of imperial household guards and a second-in-command to the comes domesticorum (Jones, LRE 636-40); see further PLRE i. 461, s.v. Iovianus 3. Magister militum: general in the field army, Jones, LRE 97, 124-5.

[128] Basil's vision: cf. Mal. 333. 18-334. 12, noting at the end that the chronographer Eutropius disagreed in some respects. Eutychianus of Cappadocia (cf. n. 126) is a likely origin for this anecdote, with its unexpected references to Basil's continuing friendship with his former student contemporary, and the clergy's lack of enthusiasm for the news.

St. Mercurius: martyred in the early 250s; see H. Delehaye, Les Légendes grecques des saints militaires (Paris 1909), 91-101, esp. 96ff.

Surenas asked the emperor Jovian to draw up peace terms straightway and at once. And the emperor Jovian selected one of his senators, the patrician Arinthaeus, and handed the whole matter to him, agreeing to abide by what was sanctioned by him, or rather drawn up together with the senate and the Persian ambassador, so as to make peace terms, since Jovian himself was occupied. And he granted an intermission in the war for three days during the council for peace. And between the patrician Arinthaeus the Roman and Surenas the Persian senator it was drawn up that the Romans should give the Persians all the province and the city of Nisibis as it is called, empty, with just its walls alone [p.554] and without the men who inhabited it. And when this had been established and the peace put in writing, the emperor Jovian took with him one of the Persian satraps, Junius by name, who was with the ambassador, for the receipt of the province and its metropolis. And the same emperor Jovian, when he reached the Nisibene city, did not enter inside it, but stopped outside the walls. But Junius, the satrap of the Persians, went into the city at the command of the emperor and affixed a Persian standard to one of the towers, the Roman emperor having commanded that all the citizens together with all their property come out to a man immediately. And Silvanus came out to him, a *comes* in rank and a decurion of the same city, and prostrated himself before the emperor, begging him not to hand over the city to the Persians. But when he did not persuade him (for he said that he had sworn, and did not wish to have a reputation for perjury among all men), Jovian fortified a village which was outside the wall of the city of Amida, linked the same wall to the wall of the city of Amida, called it the village of Nisibis, and made all those from the Mygdonian land live there, including Silvanus the decurion. He immediately brought from Mesopotamia every Christian, and entrusted to Christians the offices and prefectures of all the east.

And after the making of peace terms with the Persians, [p.555] the emperor Jovian departing from the east within a short time set out with the army for Constantinople, in haste on account of the winter; for it was harsh.[129]

---

[129] Proclamation of Jovian, negotiations with Persians, surrender of Nisibis, and Jovian's departure from east: cf. Mal. 334. 13-337. 9 for the same sequence of material, with only minor differences (Jovian is an ardent Christian; as emperor he is too proud, not too occupied, to negotiate directly with a Persian noble; Jovian restored Christianity in Mesopotamia, and made peace with the Persians for a short time). We have repunctuated the text after 'Silvanus the decurion' on

## Olympiad 286

Jovian was 37th Roman emperor for 10 months, 15 days.

In total, 5,873.

**364** Indiction 7, year 1, consulship of Jovian Augustus and Varronianus.

In this year Jovian Augustus died at Dadastana, in the month Peritius, day 12 before Kalends of March [19 Feb.].[130]

Valentinian Augustus was 38th Roman emperor, after Salustius the praetorian prefect and aged patrician had selected the same Valentinian. This was the Valentinian whom Julian the apostate sent to Selymbria because he was thoroughly Christian, making him tribune of a unit there. For Julian recognized in a vision that he would be emperor after him. The praetorian prefect Salustius sent and brought him from Selymbria, and said to the army and senate, 'No-one will make an emperor for Roman affairs like him.' And Valentinian was elevated as Augustus at Nicaea in Bithynia, in the month Peritius, day 5 before Kalends of March [26 Feb.].[131]

the basis of a punctuation mark in the MS (overlooked in the Bonn text): this brings *CP* into agreement with Malalas.

This common account is highly favourable to Jovian, since it absolves him from responsibility for the disadvantageous peace terms agreed with the Persian king Shapur (Labuarsacius is an error for Sabuarsacius, cf. Mal. 335. 4), and does not state the full extent of the Roman loss (5 districts to the east of the Tigris and the city of Singara were also surrendered). Ammianus xxv. 5-9, in a more detailed and critical account, emphasizes the plight of the army stranded on the east side of the Tigris and the disgrace of the agreement: he records that Salutius was the first choice to succeed Julian, attributes Jovian's refusal to enter Nisibis to shame at its surrender, and names Bineses as the Persian who took over the city.

Arinthaeus: one of Julian's commanders, and subsequently consul in 372 (*PLRE* i. 102-3). *Comes*: 'companion', an honorific rank created by Constantine (Jones, *LRE* 104-5).

Peace treaty: see R. Turcan, 'L'Abandon de Nisibe et l'opinion publique', *Mélanges A. Piganiol*, ed. R. Chevallier (Paris 1966), ii. 875-90.

Nisibis: see Fiey, *Nisibe* 35-7. Amida: see A. Gabriel, *Voyages archéologiques dans la Turquie orientale* (Paris 1940), pt. 2, esp. chs. 1, 7.

[130] **364** Death of Jovian: cf. Hyd. with the Roman date of 11 before Kalends of March (13 before Kalends in Eutropius x. 18; 17 Feb. in Soc. iii. 26. 5); also Malalas 337. 9-11, who locates Dadastana in Galatia and gives Jovian's age as 60. For the circumstances, see Amm. xxv. 10. 11-13 (the election as consul of Jovian's infant son Varronianus was taken as a bad omen; Jovian was aged 33).

[131] Elevation of Valentinian: cf. Mal. 337. 12-338. 2 (Valentinian the severe, who is crowned by Salustius), and Hyd. for the place and Roman date. For a fuller and more accurate report, see Amm. xxvi. 1-2. Valentinian had already returned from the exile imposed by Julian (cf. *s.a.* 363, with n. 123), and had been sent by

The same most sacred Valentinian was 38th Roman emperor for 14 years.[132]                                         In total, 5,887.

[p.556] This Valentinian, as soon as he became emperor, replaced the praetorian prefect Salustius and, when he had put him under surety, he posted edicts against him to the effect that if anyone was wronged by him he should approach the emperor Valentinian. And no-one made approaches against Salustius, for he was most thoroughly upright.[133]

In this year Valens, the brother of Valentinian, was elevated as Augustus in Constantinople at the Hebdomon by Valentinian Augustus, in the month Dystrus, day 4 before Kalends of April [29 March].[134]

This Valens the brother of Valentinian was Arian, and had as wife Domnica, by whom he had a son, Galates by name, and two daughters, Anastasia and Carosa,[135] and he founded two baths in Constantinople, the Anastasianae and the Carosianae, in accordance with their names.[136]

Jovian to the west (Amm. xxv. 10. 6-7) but had come back to Ankara by the time of his selection as successor (xxv. 10. 9, xxvi. 1. 5).

Salustius: Secundus Salutius, praetorian prefect of the east 361–5 and 365–7 (*PLRE* i. 814-17, s.v. Secundus 3), not Flavius Sallustius, praetorian prefect of Gaul 361–3 and consul in 363 (*PLRE* i. 797-8, s.v. Sallustius 5). Sources often write Salustius instead of Secundus Salutius: e.g. Jul. *Letter to the Athenians* 281D, Zos. ii. 2. 2. Although Salutius was involved (Amm. xxvi. 2. 1), he was not primarily responsible for Valentinian's elevation; he was an old man in 367 (Zos. iv. 10. 4, cf. Amm. xxv. 5. 3); a career inscription datable to 365–7 (*ILS* 1255) does not mention the title of patrician.

132 Length of reign: under 12 years (until 17 Nov. 375), but the figure has been adjusted to fit *CP*'s incorrect date for Valentinian's death in 378; Malalas 337. 13 gives 16 years.

133 Demotion of Secundus Salutius: cf. Mal. 338. 3-6, and *Suda* s.v. προθέματα (Π 2441) and Σαλούστιος (Σ 64). For his career, see *PLRE* (cited in n. 131); he was deposed after 30 July 365, as a result of intrigues by Valens' father-in-law Petronius (Amm. xxvi. 7. 4), but had been reinstated before 2 Nov.; see further *s.a.* 369.

134 Elevation of Valens: cf. Hyd. Ammianus xxvi. 4. 3 gives the date as 28 March.

Hebdomon: located at the seventh milestone from the centre of Cpl., it seems to have originated as a military parade ground, but developed quickly as a suburban imperial residence at the end of the 4th c. For the remains, see R. Demangel, *Contribution à la topographie de l'Hebdomon* (Paris 1945).

135 Valens' Arianism: cf. Soc. iv. 1. 5. His family: *PLRE* i. 1130, stemma 4; see further ibid. 930-1, s.v. Valens 8.

136 Baths at Cpl.: cf. Theoph. 56. 31-57. 3 (adding a reference to the aqueduct of Valens); the *Notitia* locates the Anastasianae in the ninth region, the Carosianae in the seventh, see Janin, *Const.* 216, 219.

365  Indiction 8, year 1, consulship of Valentinian and Valens.

In this year the sea departed from its proper limits in the month Panemus [July], day 12 before Kalends of September [21 Aug.].[137]

366  Indiction 9, year 2, consulship of Gratian *nobilissimus* and Dagalaiphus.

In the time of these consuls was born Valentinian Augustus, in the month Audynaeus, day 15 before Kalends of February [18 Jan.].[138]

And in the same year the rebel Procopius was arrested [p.557] and killed by Valentinian Augustus in Phrygia Salutaris, on the plain of Nacolia, in the month Daisius, day 12 before Kalends of July [20 June].[139]

367  Indiction 10, year 3, consulship of Lupicinus and Jovian.[140]

In the time of these consuls God showered hail like stones on Constantinople, in the month Daisius, day 4 before Nones of June [2 June].[141]

And in the same year Gratian was elevated as Augustus in Gaul by Valentinian Augustus his father in the month Lous, day 9 before Kalends of September [24 Aug.].[142]

Olympiad 287

368  Indiction 11, year 4, the 2nd consulship of Valentinian Augustus and the 2nd of Valens Augustus.

In the time of these consuls an earthquake occurred in the city of Nicaea so that it was razed, in the month Gorpiaeus, day 5 before Ides of October [11 Oct.].[143]

---

[137] 365  Retreat of sea: cf. *Hyd.* with the date 12 before Kalends of Aug. [21 July], confirmed by Amm. xxvi. 10. 15-19 (cf. also Theoph. 56. 10-21).

[138] 366  Birth of Valentinian II: cf. *Hyd.*

[139] Procopius: cf. *Hyd.*, which does not name the rebel but correctly attributes his capture to Valens (Valentinian was now in the west), and gives the date as 6 before Kalends of June [27 May]. For the revolt, see Amm. xxvi. 5-9: Procopius, already suspect as a relative of Julian, was stimulated to revolt by the harsh exactions of Valens and his father-in-law Petronius; he was finally betrayed by his allies and handed over to Valens. Nacolia is located in central Anatolia, due west of Pessinus.

[140] 367  *cos. post.*: Jovinus.

[141] Hail: cf. *Hyd.* with the date 4 before Nones of July [4 July].

[142] Elevation of Gratian: cf. *Hyd.* (at Amiens); see also Amm. xxvii. 6, and further *PLRE* i. 401, s.v. Gratianus 2.

[143] 368  Nicaea earthquake: cf. *Hyd.*; also Mal. 342. 16-343. 1 (out of chronological sequence, dated Sept.).

369 Indiction 12, year 5, the 3rd consulship of Valentinian Augustus and that of Victor.[144]

In the time of these consuls the most sacred emperor Valentinian slaughtered many senators and provincial officials [p.558] for doing wrong, stealing, and perverting justice. And as for the *praepositus* of his Palace, Rhodanus by name, a man of power and substance who controlled the Palace because he was first and chief eunuch and was held in great honour, he burnt him alive on faggots at the curved end of the Hippodrome, while he was watching the chariot racing.

The same *praepositus* Rhodanus seized property from a certain widowed lady called Berenice, after fabricating a charge against her, because he was a man of power; and she approached the emperor Valentinian against this *praepositus*, and he gave them as judge the patrician Salustius, who condemned the same *praepositus* Rhodanus. And when the emperor learnt of the decision from the patrician Salustius, he ordered the same *praepositus* to give to the widow what he had seized from her. But the same Rhodanus was not persuaded to give up to her what he had seized from her, but appealed against the patrician Salustius. And Salustius, in anger, ordered the woman to approach the emperor when he was watching the chariot racing. And the woman approached the emperor Valentinian in the morning at the 4th race, as the *praepositus* stood near him. And the emperor gave an order, and the *praepositus* was led down from the imperial box while all watched, and was led away to the curved end and burnt. And the emperor bestowed on the woman Berenice all the property of the *praepositus* Rhodanus, and the emperor was acclaimed by all the people [p.559] and the senate as just and severe; and there arose great fear among the evil-doers and those who seized others' possessions, and justice prevailed.

Likewise too when the emperor heard that the lady Marina his wife had bought a suburban estate short of its worth according to its revenue, because she was honoured as Augusta, he sent and had the estate valued, after binding the valuers by oath. And when he learnt that it was worth a far greater price than that for which it was bought, he was angry with the empress and

---

144 369 *cos. prior*: Valentinian Galates, son of Valens. Hereafter *CP* overstates the consulships of Valentinian Augustus by one.

banished her from the city, and gave the estate back to the woman who had sold it.[145]

**370** Indiction 13, year 6, the 4th consulship of Valentinian Augustus and the 3rd of Valens Augustus.

In the time of these consuls the church of the Holy Apostles in Constantinople was consecrated in the month Xanthicus, five days before the Ides of April [9 April].[146]

**371** Indiction 14, year 7, the 2nd consulship of Gratian and that of Probus.

### Olympiad 288

**372** Indiction 15, year 8, consulship of Modestus and Arinthaeus.

**373** Indiction 1, year 9, the 5th consulship of Valentinian Augustus and the 4th of Valens Augustus.

**374** [p.560] Indiction 2, year 10, the 3rd consulship of Gratian Augustus and that of Aequitius.

**375** Indiction 3, year 11, the 4th consulship of Gratian Augustus and the 2nd of Aequitius.[147]

In the time of these consuls the Carosianae gymnasium was inaugurated in the presence of the prefect Vindathnius Magnus.[148]

In the time of the same consuls Valentinian II was elevated as

---

[145] Valentinian's justice: cf. Mal. 339. 20-341. 7 for the same sequence with very minor differences (Valentinian himself instructs the woman to approach him during the racing, and she does this in the fifth race). The *Suda* s.v. Σαλούστιος (Σ 64) contains a brief version of the Rhodanus story. On the office of *praepositus*, see Jones, *LRE* 567-70.

Date: Although Malalas gives no date, he notes the appointment of Salutius (cf. n. 131) as judge by Valentinian 'as soon as he became emperor' (340. 7-8). The story involving Valentinian and Salutius should have occurred in 364 before Valentinian left Cpl. for the west. Marina, however, seems still to have been in favour in 367 when she encouraged Valentinian to proclaim their son Gratian as Augustus (Aurelius Victor, *de caes.* 45. 4); see further *PLRE* i. 828, s.v. Marina Severa 2. It is probable that all the stories about Valentinian, Salutius, and justice came from the same source which celebrated the emperor's severity, but did not precisely date the individual incidents.

Suburban estates: cf. nn. 167, 180 for other evidence for the growth of imperial properties in Cpl. in this period.

[146] 370 Holy Apostles: cf. Hyd. Janin (*Églises* 42) suggested that this consecration followed a rebuilding caused by earthquake damage in 358, but cf. n. 108.

[147] 375 Consuls: post-consulship of the 3rd consulship of Gratian Augustus and of Aequitius. Hereafter *CP* overstates Gratian's consulships by one.

[148] Carosianae baths: cf. Hyd., and above *s.a.* 364 with n. 136.

Vindaonius Magnus: city prefect 375-6, see *PLRE* i. 536, s.v. Magnus 12.

Augustus in the month Dius, day 5 before Kalends of December [27 Nov.] in the city of Aquincum.[149]

## Olympiad 289

**376** Indiction 4, year 12, the 5th consulship of Valens Augustus and that of Valentinian Caesar.[150]

**377** Indiction 5, year 13, the 5th consulship of Gratian Augustus and that of Merobaudes.

**378** Indiction 6, year 14, the 7th consulship of Valens Augustus and the 2nd of Valentinian Caesar.[151]

In the time of these consuls the emperor Valentinian was smitten by sickness and died in the fort of Vergitinae, aged 55 years.[152]

In the time of these consuls Gratian Augustus recalled his mother, the lady Marina.[153]

Gratian, together with Valens and Theodosius the Great, was 39th Roman emperor for 16 years.[154]          In total, 5,903.

[p.561] Theodosius was elevated as Augustus in Sirmium by Gratian Augustus, his wife's brother, in the month Audynaeus, day 14 before Kalends of February [19 Jan.],[155] and he entered

---

[149] Proclamation of Valentinian II: cf. _Hyd._, with the correct date of 10 before Kalends of Dec. [22 Nov.]. Valentinian II (_PLRE_ i. 934-5, s.v. Valentinianus 8), aged only 4, was proclaimed on the sixth day after his father Valentinian's death on 17 Nov. (_Hyd._, Soc. iv. 31. 6-7; Amm. xxx. 10); _CP_ has wrongly placed the latter's death in 378, see n. 152.

[150] **376** _cos. post._: Valentinian II Augustus (also described as Caesar in _Chron. 354_, paschal cycle, _CM_ i. 63).

[151] **378** Consuls: 6th of Valens and 2nd of Valentinian II Augustus.

[152] Death of Valentinian: cf. _Hyd._, correctly located on 15 before Kalends of Dec. [17. Nov.] 375; also Mal. 341. 16-17. He died at Bregetio in Pannonia from a fit of apoplexy after listening to an embassy from the Quadi (Amm. xxx. 6). _CP_'s mistake over the date may have been caused by confusion with the death of Valens in battle against the Goths at Adrianopolis in 378 (recorded by _Hyd._, but not _CP_).

[153] Recall of Marina Severa: the date is unknown, but was presumably 375/6, shortly after Valentinian's death. For her exile, cf n. 145. Malalas 341. 10 wrongly states that Marina was recalled by her son Valerian.

[154] Gratian: Augustus (in the west) for 16 years, but from 367 to 383; the subsequent regnal years in _CP_ relate to Theodosius I, who also reigned for 16 years (379–95).

[155] Elevation of Theodosius: cf. _Hyd._, with _Scal._ 316 and _Vind. prior._ 497 (both _CM_ i. 297), with the correct year 379; independently Mal. 343. 13-15, 344. 9-13 (with reference to his Spanish origins and proclamation by the senate). Theodosius had recently defeated the Sarmatians in Pannonia, a victory that

Constantinople in the month Dius, on day 8 before Kalends of December [24 Nov.].[156]

379 Indiction 7, year 1, consulship of Ausonius and Olybrius.

In the time of these consuls Theodosius the emperor gave the churches to the orthodox, after enacting rescripts everywhere, and expelled from them the so-called Arian Exokionites, and he razed the shrines of the Hellenes to the ground.[157]

The celebrated Constantine, while he was emperor, only closed the temples and shrines of the Hellenes; this Theodosius also destroyed them, including the temple of Balanius at Heliopolis, the great and renowned Trilithon, and made it a Christian church.    Likewise too he made the temple at Damascus a Christian church.    And Christian affairs were further exalted in the course of his reign.[158]

---

went a little way towards restoring Roman morale after the disaster at Adrianopolis. It was only after the death of Flaccilla in 386 that he married Gratian's half-sister Galla (see *PLRE* i. 1130-1, stemmata 4 & 5); cf. n. 167.

[156] Entry into Cpl.: 24 Nov. 380 (Soc. v. 6. 6; *Hyd.* with the date 18 before Kalends of Dec., i.e. 14 Nov.), after further campaigns against the Goths in the Balkans; see *PLRE* i. 904-5, s.v. Theodosius 4.

[157] 379 Religious measures: cf. *Mal. 344. 14-16*. After falling seriously ill in winter 379/80 at Thessalonica, Theodosius had received baptism from the Nicene bishop Acholius; he then began to act against heretics (Soc. v. 6-8, Soz. vii. 4-5, Theoph. 68. 4-7). Pro-Nicene edicts were issued on 27 Feb. 380 from Thessalonica (to Cpl.) and on 30 July 381 from Heracleia (to the province of Asia): *Cod. Theod.* xvi. 1. 2-3; cf. also xvi. 5. 6 (10 Jan. 381).

Arians: the name Exokionites derived from the Exokionion at Cpl., a column outside the Constantinian city walls (Mango, *Const.* 47; Janin, *Const.* 351-2), to which the Arian bishop Demophilus withdrew after Theodosius' edict. At this date Arians were the dominant Christian group in the capital, as shown by the problems encountered by the orthodox Gregory Nazianzen during his brief spell as bishop of Cpl. in 379–81.

[158] Pagans: cf. *Mal. 344. 19-345. 2* (the comparison of Constantine and Theodosius is not in our abridged Malalas, but survives in the Armenian history of Moses of Khoren (iii. 33), which contains some material parallel to Malalas (see Introduction n. 30). *CP* exaggerates Theodosius' harshness to pagans: only in 391 were sacrifices banned and temples closed (survey, Jones, *LRE* 165-9).

Temples: the temple of Zeus Heliopolis at Baalbek (Heliopolis), known as the Trilithon because of three especially large stones in an incomplete outer peristyle (each weighed about 720 tons) was converted into a church to St. Barbara, and that of Jupiter Damascenus into a church to John the Baptist (future site of the great mosque). John of Ephesus, however, records that in 555 the great temple at Baalbek was destroyed by lightning: offerings were apparently still being made at the temple and no-one had been able to destroy its credit (F. Nau, 'Analyse de la seconde partie inédite de l'Histoire Écclesiastique de Jean d'Asie', *Revue de l'Orient chrétien* ii, 1897, 455-93 at 490-1).    Pagans could still be

## Olympiad 290

**380** Indiction 8, year 2, the 6th consulship of Gratian Augustus and that of Theodosius Augustus.

[p.562] In the time of these consuls Gratian Augustus, son of Valentinian the Great, was afflicted in the spleen and remained an invalid for a long time; and as he went up by way of the Kochlias to the Hippodrome of Constantinople to watch the games, his step-mother Justina arranged that he should be slain at the door of the Decimum, as it is called, because he was a Christian; for that lady was Arian.[159]

**381** Indiction 9, year 3, consulship of Syagrius and Eucherius.

In the three hundred and fifty-first year from the Ascension to heaven of the Lord, a synod of 150 holy and blessed fathers was convened in Constantinople. And they confirmed the symbol of orthodoxy by renouncing Macedonius, who was himself also similarly infected in his thinking by Arianism, since the impious man was not reluctant to ordain that the incomprehensibility and invisibility of the coeternity of the Holy Spirit with the Father and the Son was created in time.[160]

discovered at Baalbek in 580 (J. Eph. *HE* iii. 27).

[159] **380** Death of Gratian: cf. Mal. 344. 5-8 for the story of his death in the Cpl. Hippodrome, but omitting the involvement and motive of the Arian Justina and incorrectly giving Gratian's age as 28 (in fact 24). This story is an anti-Arian fiction, since Gratian was in fact killed on 25 Aug. 383 at Lyons in Gaul during the revolt of Magnus Maximus, after being captured by Andragath, one of Magnus' officers (Theoph. 67. 30-68. 3; cf. Marc. Com. *s.a.* 383, Soc. v. 11, Zos. iv. 35. 5-6 with Paschoud's detailed discussion in vol. ii. 2 n. 172 at pp. 413-15). At the time of Gratian's murder, Justina (*PLRE* i. 488-9) was at or near Milan, where her Arian sympathies had led to arguments with bishop Ambrose.

Kochlias: a spiral stair connecting the Palace to the imperial box in the Hippodrome (cf. *CP* p. 528. 7-8, and the description of Justinian's moves during the Nika Riot at p. 625. 17-20 with n. 363, Proc. *Wars* i. 24. 43).

Decimum: a door or chamber behind the imperial box, correctly recognized by R. Guilland, *Études* i. 131-2 (preferable to Janin, *Const.* 187, who described it as a door into the Hippodrome rather than the imperial box); Guilland's further identification of the Decimum with the *triclinium* of the Bronze Doors is speculative. The reference to the Decimum as a means of access into the Palace at Const. Porph. *de caer.* ii. 51 (p. 701. 10-12) does not clarify its precise location. The murder of Armatus is located at the same place, see below *s.a.* 484; and cf. Mal. 387. 13-14 for an attempt on Illus' life (probably in 481).

[160] **381** Synod of Cpl.: Theophanes 68. 21-69. 32 has a detailed account, Mal. 346. 3-5 a brief notice; Marc. Com. (whose chronicle begins in 379) notes the synod.

Ascension date: cf. *ss.aa.* 325, 431, 452 for similar dates for other church councils.

This council (in May) confirmed the orthodoxy of Nicene doctrine, which

**382** Indiction 10, year 4, consulship of Antoninus and the 2nd of Syagrius.[161]

**383** Indiction 11, year 5, consulship of Merobaudes and Saturninus.[162]

In the time of these consuls Arcadius was proclaimed Augustus in Constantinople at the tribunal of the Hebdomon by his father [p.563] Theodosius the Augustus, in the month Audynaeus, day 14 before Kalends of February [19 Jan.].[163]

And in the same year the corpse of Constantia, the daughter of Constantine Augustus, arrived in Constantinople in the month Gorpiaeus, one day before Kalends of September [31 Aug.], and was laid to rest in the month Apellaeus, on Kalends of December [1 Dec.].[164]

Olympiad 291

**384** Indiction 12, year 6, consulship of Richomeres and Clearchus.

In the time of these consuls a Persian ambassador arrived.[165] And in the same year was born Honorius, true brother of

---

Theodosius favoured, and condemned the Arianizing views of the followers of Macedonius, former bishop of Cpl., who denied the divinity of the Holy Spirit; 36 of his followers withdrew from the council rather than subscribe to the doctrine upheld by the majority group of about 150. The triumph of Nicene belief was enshrined (and the end of Arianism signalled) when Theodosius arranged the transfer from Ankara of the relics of Paul, the orthodox bishop of Cpl. whom Macedonius had ousted, and their installation in a basilica constructed by Macedonius (for which see Janin, Églises 394-5). The most significant of the council's decisions was the elevation of Cpl. to second place in the ecclesiastical hierarchy, subordinate only to Rome, in recognition of its status as the New Rome; its bishop was now promoted to the rank of patriarch: see Chadwick, Church 150-1.

[161] **382** Consuls: Antonius and Flavius Afranius Syagrius (the latter to be distinguished from the consul of 381).

[162] **383** cos. prior: 2nd of Merobaudes, consul 377.

[163] Proclamation of Arcadius: cf. Hyd., with the date 17 before Kalends of Feb. (16 Jan.; corroborated by Soc. v. 10. 5); Marc. Com. (year only). Theodosius' eldest son was born c.377, see PLRE i. 99, s.v. Arcadius 5.

[164] Burial of Constantia: cf. Hyd. dating the corpse's arrival to 2 before Ides of Sept. (12 Sept.). She was daughter of Constantius II (not Constantine; error also in Hyd.) and wife of Gratian (PLRE i. 221, s.v. Constantia 2).

[165] Persian embassy: cf. Hyd., Marc. Com. The negotiations, conducted with envoys of Shapur III, resulted in the partition of Armenia between the two empires.

Arcadius Augustus, in the month Gorpiaeus, day 5 before Ides of September [9 Sept.].[166]

385 Indiction 13, year 7, consulship of Arcadius Augustus and Bauto.

Theodosius the Augustus had as first wife before his reign Galla, the daughter of Valentinian the Great. By her he had a daughter with the same name as her mother, Galla, whom he also called Placidia. And both the two women were Arians. And Placidia, when she came to Constantinople with her father Theodosius, founded the mansion of Placidia.[167]

As second wife Theodosius had Flaccilla, who was orthodox, [p.564] by whom he had Arcadius and Honorius. And this Flaccilla founded the Flaccillianon palace.[168]

386 Indiction 14, year 8, consulship of Honorius Caesar and Euodius.

387 Indiction 15, year 9, the 4th consulship of Valentinian and that of Eutropius.[169]

---

[166] 384 Honorius: cf. Hyd., Marc. Com., and see PLRE i. 442, s.v. Honorius 3. 'True brother' because both were the sons of Flaccilla, cf. n. 168.

One fragment of the Goleniščev papyrus, a derivative of an Alexandrian chronicle related to Scal. and Hyd. and hence to CP as well, begins at this point (the last entry is the destruction of the Serapaeum in Alexandria in 392); see Bagnall, Consuls 53-4.

[167] 385 Galla: in 387 Theodosius married Galla (PLRE i. 382, s.v. Galla 2), daughter of Valentinian I and the Arian Justina, as part of the agreement whereby Theodosius was to attack Magnus Maximus and restore Valentinian II (Galla's brother) to the western throne; Valentinian II now abjured the Arian heresy (Theod. v. 15. 3), and it is likely that Justina and Galla did too (Paschoud, Zosime ii. 2, n. 188 at pp. 436-8). Galla Placidia was born c.388 (PLRE ii. 888-9, s.v. Placidia 4); the allusion here to her arrival in Cpl. is probably the result of confusion with her mother's arrival as a refugee from the west, recorded by Marc. Com. s.a. 386.

Palace of Placidia: the Notitia records three palaces of Placidia, two in the first region and one in the tenth; see Janin, Const. 135-6, and for an attempt to distribute these palaces between Galla Placidia mother and daughter, P. Speck in Beck, Studien 144-7. Theodosian princesses were great property magnates, cf. nn. 168 and 180.

[168] Flaccilla: in fact Theodosius' first wife, who died in 386 (PLRE i. 341-2). The inversion of the order of Theodosius' marriages may reflect the reluctance of an orthodox writer to record that the Nicene champion Theodosius married an Arian after an orthodox wife.

Flaccillianon: in the eleventh region of Cpl., cf. s.a. 531 at n. 360, and see Janin, Const. 413.

[169] 387 cos. prior: 3rd of Valentinian II (his 4th is recorded again, correctly, in 390); Scal. terminates in this year.

Olympiad 292

388 Indiction 1, year 10, the 2nd consulship of Theodosius Augustus and that of Cynegius.

389 Indiction 2, year 11, consulship of Timasius and Promotus.

In the time of these consuls Theodosius the emperor came to Rome with his son Honorius, and crowned him there as emperor. And Honorius was emperor there for 14 years.[170]

390 Indiction 3, year 12, the 4th consulship of Valentinian and that of Neoterius.

391 Indiction 4, year 13, consulship of Tatianus and Symmachus.

In the time of these consuls Theodosius Augustus found the head of St. John the Baptist at the house of a certain Macedonian woman living in Cyzicus, recovered it, and laid it to rest for a time in Chalcedon. Finally he built from the foundations a church in the name of the saint at the so-called Hebdomon of Constantinople, and in it he laid the precious head of the Baptist, in the month Peritius, day 12 before Kalends of March [18 Feb.].[171]

Olympiad 293

392 Indiction 5, year 14, the 2nd consulship of Arcadius and that of Rufinus.

393 [p.565] Indiction 6, year 15, the 3rd consulship of Theodosius and that of Abundantius.

---

[170] 389 Coronation of Honorius in Rome: cf. Theoph. 70. 31-3, with the date 5 before Ides of June (9 June); Hyd. records the entry of Theodosius and Honorius into Rome on the Ides of June (13 June) and the granting of a donative, but (correctly) no coronation; similarly Marc. Com. records the entry and donative (also the departure on 1 Sept.). There are traces of this account in the Goleniščev papyrus (VI. verso 1-5).

Theodosius was visiting Rome following the defeat of the usurper Magnus Maximus and the restoration of the young Valentinian II as western emperor. Honorius was not proclaimed Augustus until 393, following the death of Valentinian II, cf. Marc. Com. s.a. He in fact reigned for 28 years (395–423), but the joint reign of Honorius and Arcadius lasted 14 years, 393–408 (CP p. 565. 15-17).

[171] 391 Head of John the Baptist: the same story is in Soz. vii. 21 and Theod. Lect. 268, who explain that the relic had been discovered by 'Macedonian' monks (i.e. followers of the deposed bishop of Cpl. Macedonius: cf. n. 108); Valens wanted to transfer the relic to Cpl., but after a miracle it had been entrusted to a 'Macedonian' holy woman in the village of Cosila in the territory of Chalcedon. CP s.a. 453 has an alternative version of its discovery in Emesa. For the church, see Janin, Églises 413-15.

In the time of these consuls Proclus, former prefect, was beheaded in the month Apellaeus on day 8 before Ides of December [6 Dec.] in Sycae.[172]   And in the same year the Theodosian Forum was inaugurated.[173]

394 Indiction 7, year 16, the 3rd consulship of Arcadius and the 2nd of Honorius.

In the time of these consuls was set up a great statue of Theodosius Augustus in the Theodosian Forum, in the month Lous, on Kalends of August [1 Aug.].[174]

And in the same year Diogenes the usurper was beheaded in Italy.[175]

In this year Theodosius Augustus died in Milan in the month Audynaeus, on day 16 before Kalends of February   [17 Jan.], aged 65 years.

Arcadius was 40th Roman emperor. He set out from Rome, having left his brother Honorius in the same Rome.   And Arcadius was emperor in Constantinople and Honorius in Rome for 14 years.[176]                               In total, 5,917.

---

[172] 393 Proculus: city prefect of Cpl. 388–92, see *PLRE* i. 746-7, s.v. Proculus 6; his execution was connected with the fall of his father Tatianus, praetorian prefect of the east.

Sycae: modern Galata; no remains of the late antique settlement have been identified, but for the late Byzantine (primarily Genoese) town, see A. M. Schneider & M. I. Nomidis, *Galata: topographisch-archäologischer Plan* (Istanbul 1944); also Janin, *Const.* 56-7, 466-7. For executions there, see further nn. 368, 403.

[173] Theodosian Forum: see Mango, *Const.* 43-5 and plan II; Janin, *Const.* 64-8; Müller-Wiener, *Bildlexikon* 258-65; also Guilland, *Études* ii. 56-9.

[174] 394 Theodosius' statue: an equestrian statue on a column, see Mango and Janin, locc. citt. in n. 173. It fell in the earthquake of 478 (cf. GC 1 in Appendix 2 below), and in 543/4 it was transported by Justinian to the Augustaeum to serve as his own famous equestrian monument.

[175] Usurper: Flavius Eugenius (not Diogenes), Augustus 392–4 (*PLRE* i. 293, s.v. Eugenius 6); proclaimed emperor by the Frankish general Arbogast, he was executed on 6 Sept. 394 after Theodosius, prompted by his wife Galla (sister of Valentinian II whose death had been organized by Arbogast), had defeated his army at the river Frigidus (Soc. v. 25. 15-16). Theoph. 71. 2-7, 73. 25-7 has some details; brief notices in *Hyd. s.a.* 392, Marc. Com. *ss.aa.* 391, 394.

[176] Death of Theodosius and succession of his sons: Theodosius died on 17 Jan. 395 at Milan, cf. Marc. Com. *s.a.* (year only). The dying emperor summoned his younger son Honorius from Cpl. and appointed him emperor in the west with Stilicho as guardian, see Theoph. 74. 9-19, with Cameron, *Claudian* 37-40. Arcadius seems to have remained in the east, although Malalas 348. 12-15 states that shortly before Theodosius' death he travelled to Rome to visit Honorius, who was sick.

**395** Indiction 8, year 1, consulship of Olybrius and Probinus.

In the time of these consuls Arcadius Augustus celebrated his marriage in the month Xanthicus, on day 5 before Kalends of May [27 April].[177] And in the **[p.566]** same year the corpse of the great Theodosius arrived in Constantinople in the month Dius, on day five before Ides of November [9 Nov.], and was laid to rest on day 5 before Ides of November [9 Nov.].[178]

And Rufinus, praetorian prefect, was killed at the Hebdomon by the army.[179]

Olympiad 294

**396** Indiction 9, year 2, the 4th consulship of Arcadius Augustus and the 3rd of Honorius Augustus.

This Arcadius, son of Theodosius the Great, had as wife Eudoxia, by whom Theodosius the younger was borne. He also had daughters, Pulcheria and Arcadia and Marina. And two of these, namely Arcadia and Marina respectively founded the Arcadianae bath and the mansion of Marina. And Pulcheria finally married Marcian. But Arcadia founded as well the church of St. Andrew called that of Arcadia.[180]

The 'Constantinopolitan' section of *Hyd.* terminates in this year; see Bagnall, *Consuls* 54-5.

[177] **395** Arcadius' marriage: to Aelia Eudoxia (*PLRE* ii. 410, s.v. Eudoxia 2; cf. *s.a.* 396). This marked the first step in the triumph of the eunuch Eutropius, imperial chamberlain, against the praetorian prefect Rufinus who had hoped to wed his own daughter to the emperor, see Bury, *HLRE* [2] i. 108-9.

[178] Theodosius' corpse: cf. Marc. Com. (year only); Soc. vi. 1. 3 (about 8 Nov.). *CP* is probably wrong to date the corpse's arrival and burial to the same day; it was buried in the Holy Apostles (Theoph. 74. 19).

[179] Death of Rufinus: 27 Nov. 395 (Soc. vi. 1. 4-5) at the hands of the Gothic troops led by Gainas (Bury, *HLRE* [2] i. 112-13); cf. Marc. Com. For his career, see *PLRE* i. 778-81, s.v. Rufinus 18. A hostile view is presented in Claudian's two poems against Rufinus, and his death is described at *in Ruf.* ii. 366-439; see further Cameron, *Claudian* ch. 4.

[180] **396** Children of Arcadius and Eudoxia: the eldest, Flaccilla (cf. *s.a.* 397), is omitted, probably because she died before Arcadius (cf. Soz. ix. 1); the individual births are also recorded under the relevant years.

Arcadianae baths: cf. Marc. Com. *s.a.* 394; on the east side of the ancient acropolis, see Janin, *Const.* 217, 311-12. Mansion of Marina: in the 1st region, ibid. 136 for a later reference. Marriage of Pulcheria: cf. *s.a.* 450. Church of St. Andrew: Janin, *Églises* 27.

The family of Theodosius built up substantial holdings of property at Cpl. (cf. *s.a.* 385 with n. 167), both in the centre and in the newly fashionable suburbs outside the Constantinian walls; many of these became imperial possessions, and continued to exist as individual units for administrative purposes. *CP* has detailed information on the house of Theodosius, often with specific dates and

There are from the time when the holy apostles Peter and Paul died until the aforementioned consuls, that is from the 28th inclusive of the month June, 335 complete years.[181]

**397** Indiction 10, year 3, consulship of Caesarius and Atticus.

**[p.567]** In the time of these consuls Flaccilla *nobilissima* the younger was born, in the month Daisius, on day 15 before Kalends of July [17 June].[182]

**398** Indiction 11, year 4, the 4th consulship of Honorius Augustus and that of Eutychianus.

**399** Indiction 12, year 5, sole consulship of Theodorus.[183]

In the time of these consuls Pulcheria *nobilissima* was born in the month Audynaeus, on day 14 before Kalends of February [19 Jan.].[184]

## Olympiad 295

**400** Indiction 13, year 6, consulship of Stilicho and Aurelian.

In the time of these consuls the *nobilissima* Eudoxia was elevated as Augusta in the month Audynaeus, on day 5 before Ides of January [9 Jan.], and Arcadia *nobilissima* was born in the month Xanthicus, on day 3 before Nones of April [3 Apr.].[185]

And in the same year many Goths were slain in the Lemomacellium.[186] And the church of the Goths was burnt with

even days of the week (though these are not always correct); individual items are shared with other sources, especially Marc. Com., but no other source has the full range of information.

[181] Commemoration of Peter and Paul: their joint Feast was in fact on 29 June; the point of this chronological cross-check is unclear.

[182] **397** Birth of Flaccilla: cf. Marc. Com. (no date); called 'the younger' (*PLRE* ii. 472, s.v. Flaccilla 1) to distinguish her from her paternal grandmother, Flaccilla wife of Theodosius I.

[183] **399** *cos. prior*: Eutropius, who fell from favour during the year and had his name struck from the *fasti*. The deletion is indicated by the plural opening formula, 'In the time of these consuls...' For historical narrative, see Bury, *HLRE* [2] i. 126-7.

[184] Birth of Pulcheria: cf. Marc. Com. (no date); *PLRE* ii. 929-30.

[185] **400** Imperial family: no parallels for *CP*'s dates. Arcadia: *PLRE* ii. 129, s.v. Arcadia 1.

[186] Goth revolt: cf. Marc. Com. *ss.aa.* 399, 400; brief account, Theoph. 76. 10-18. For extensive narrative of these events, see Soz. viii. 4, Soc. vi. 6, Zos. v. 18-21 with Paschoud's notes; see further Bury, *HLRE* [2] i. 129-35, also P. J. Heather, 'The Anti-Scythian Tirade of Synesius' *De Regno*', *Phoenix* xlii, 1988, 152-72. The massacre was the result of the attempt by the Goth military leader Gainas (*PLRE* i. 379-80) to take control of Cpl.

Lemomacellium: (MS reading; Laemo- in Bonn text); mentioned only by *CP*, this might be identical with the Leomacellium, a meat market, attested in

a great multitude of Christians, in the month Panemus, on day 4 before Ides of July [12 July].[187] And Goths were engulfed in the sea at the Chersonese straits in the month Apellaeus, on day 10 before Kalends of January [23 Dec.].[188]

**401** Indiction 14, year 7, consulship of Vincentius and Flavitus.[189]

In the time of these consuls the head of Gainas the Goth was paraded, in the month Audynaeus, on day 3 before Nones of January [3 Jan.].[190]

And in the same year Theodosius *nobilissimus* son of Arcadius Augustus was born in the month Xanthicus, on day 4 before Ides of April [10 Apr.].[191]

[p.568] And in the same year the sea was frozen for 20 days like ice.[192]

**402** Indiction 15, year 8, the 5th consulship of Arcadius Augustus and the 5th of Honorius Augustus.

In the time of these consuls Theodosius II was elevated as Augustus in Constantinople on the tribunal at the Hebdomon by

(e.g.) Cedr. ii. 613. 1. The name was perhaps corrupted from Lemo- to Leo- under the influence of the nickname of Leo I, who was known as the Butcher (Macelles/Macellarius) after he had murdered Aspar (Cedr. i. 607. 14-15). On the uncertain location of the Leomacellium, see Janin, *Const.* 379-80, suggesting the area to the east of the harbour of Theodosius, on the basis of late evidence about churches of St. Acacius.

187 Goths' church: during the suppression of Gainas' revolt, more than 7,000 Goths who had sought refuge in a church adjoining the imperial Palace were killed (Zos. v. 19. 4-5); this was known as the church of the Goths (Soz. viii. 4. 17), probably because it was here that John Chrysostom had permitted the celebration in the Gothic language of orthodox worship (Theod. *HE* v. 30). The majority of Goths, converts to Christianity during the 4th c., were still Arian, but Theodosius' ratification of Nicene doctrine had turned them into heretics: as such they were not allowed to have their own church within Cpl. (Soz. viii. 4. 7), and their desire for freedom of worship had contributed to the discontent exploited by Gainas. In the 570s there was an Arian church at Cpl. for German soldiers, J. Eph. *HE* iii. 13, 26.

188 Goth defeat: after the failure of the revolt, Gainas fled the capital but was defeated by the loyal Goth Fravitta at the Hellespont (Chersonese straits) while trying to cross from Europe to Asia.

189 **401** *cos. post.*: Flavius Fravitta (a reward for the victory over Gainas); see *PLRE* i. 372-3.

190 Gainas' head: cf. Marc. Com. (no date). After his defeat, Gainas fled beyond the Danube where he was killed by the Hun king Uldis (Zos. v. 22).

191 Birth of Theodosius II: cf. Marc. Com. (with Roman date); Theoph. 76. 1-7 (two notices).

192 Frozen sea: cf. Marc. Com., who records that for 30 days mountainous icebergs were carried through the Sea of Marmara.

Arcadius his father, in the month Audynaeus, on day 4 before Ides of January [10 Jan.].[193]

**403** Indiction 1, year 9, consulship of Theodosius II Augustus and Rumoridus.

In the time of these consuls Marina *nobilissima* was born, in the month Peritius, on day 4 before Ides of February [10 Feb.].[194]

## Olympiad 296

**404** Indiction 2, year 10, the 6th consulship of Honorius Augustus and that of Aristaenetus.

In the time of these consuls John bishop of Constantinople was expelled,[195] and the Great Church together with the Senate-house was suddenly burnt by those in possession of it, the so-called Xylocircites, on a Monday at the 6th hour.[196] And Arsacius was created bishop at the Apostles in the month Daisius, on day 6 before Kalends of July [26 June], a Monday.[197]

[p.569] In this year God showered hail like stones the size of nuts on Constantinople, in the month Hyperberetaeus [Oct.], on a Friday at the eighth hour.[198] And Eudoxia Augusta died in the

---

[193] **402** Elevation of Theodosius: cf. Marc. Com. (no date).

[194] **403** Birth of Marina: cf. Marc. Com. (day 3 before Ides of Feb., i.e. 11 Feb.); *PLRE* ii. 723, s.v. Marina 1.

[195] **404** Exile of John Chrysostom: cf. Marc. Com. *s.a.* 403 (incorrect). For the dispute, or clash of personalities, between the empress Eudoxia and the austere and tactless John, which led to his exile, see Soc. vi. 18, Soz. viii, esp. 22, Zos. v. 23-4, Theoph. 79. 4-21; Bury, *HLRE* [2] i. 138-59. J. H. W. G. Liebeschuetz ('Friends and Enemies of John Chrysostom', in *Maistor*, ed. A. Moffat, Canberra 1984, 85-111) argues for a more widespread opposition to John among the eastern senatorial aristocracy.

[196] Fire: cf. Marc. Com. (church and adjacent part of city). St. Sophia and nearby buildings were burnt down on 20 June (Soc. vi. 18. 17-18), the day on which John was banished; responsibility for the fire was variously attributed to John's supporters within St. Sophia or to his opponents outside (Soz. viii. 22. 5). Zosimus (v. 24. 5-8), while lamenting the destruction of the Senate-house which contained several pagan statues, celebrates the miraculous preservation of images of Zeus and Athena.

Xylocircites: the name was derived from the meeting-place of John's supporters during his first exile in 403 or house arrest in 404; this was a wooden circus located outside the Constantinian walls, see Janin, *Const.* 440-1 (accepting the identification of the Xylocircus gate in the Theodosian walls with the Belgrade gate).

[197] Arsacius: he was already aged over 80 (Soc. vi. 19. 1), and only survived until Nov. 405; 26 June 404 fell on a Sunday.

[198] Hail: on 30 Sept., a Friday (Soc. vi. 19. 5).

same month Hyperberetaeus, day 1 before Nones of October [6 Oct.], a Thursday, and was laid in the Holy Apostles in the month Hyperberetaeus, on day 4 before Ides of October [12 Oct.], a Wednesday.[199]

**405** Indiction 3, year 11, the 2nd consulship of Stilicho and that of Anthemius.

**406** Indiction 4, year 12, the 6th consulship of Arcadius Augustus and that of Probus.

In the time of these consuls the gates of the Hippodrome were burnt, together with the Prandiara and the adjacent porticoes, in the month Hyperberetaeus, on day 8 before Kalends of November [25 Oct.], at the third hour of the night.[200]

And in the same year the remains of St. Samuel were conveyed to Constantinople by way of the Chalcedonian jetty, in the month Artemisius, on day 14 before Kalends of June [19 May], with Arcadius Augustus leading the way, and Anthemius, praetorian prefect and former consul, Aemilianus, city prefect, and all the senate; these remains were laid to rest for a certain time in the most holy Great Church.[201]

**407** Indiction 5, year 13, the 7th consulship of Honorius Augustus and the 2nd of Theodosius II Augustus.

In the time of these consuls the *quinquennalia* of Theodosius **[p.570]** II Augustus was celebrated in Constantinople in the month Audynaeus, on day 3 before Ides of January [11 Jan.].[202]

And in this year there was great rain with thunder and

---

199  Death of Eudoxia: cf. Marc. Com. (no date), Theoph. 79. 29; Soc. vi. 19. 6, Soz. viii. 27. 1 (both dating to 4th day after hail-storm).

200  **406** Fire at Hippodrome: no parallels. The Hippodrome gates were the *carceres* (starting-gates for the chariots) at the north end near the Mese.

Prandiara: the identity is uncertain (the name was probably connected with the sale of cloth, πράνδιον); R. Guilland's attempt (*REB* xix, 1961, 407-12 = *Études* i. 45-8) to identify it with the Chalce of the Hippodrome (see further n. 316) is without evidence, see Mango, *Brazen House* 28 n. 27. The only other reference is to its use as the place of Pope Martin's imprisonment in 654 (Janin, *Const.* 170).

Porticoes: i.e. those lining the Mese, just north of the Hippodrome gates.

201  Remains of Samuel: Jerome mentions the enthusiastic welcome given to the relics on their journey from Palestine to Chalcedon (*contra Vigilantium* 5, *P L* xxiii, col. 343); cf. also *PG* lxxxvi (1). col. 213B. The ceremonial, and the presence of secular dignitaries (*PLRE* ii. 93-5, s.v. Anthemius 1, and ii. 15, s.v. Aemilianus 1), illustrates the importance of the growing collection of relics at Cpl.: see Dagron, *Naissance* 408-9, and further *s.a.* 411.

Chalcedonian jetty: the landing-stage at Cpl. for traffic from Chalcedon, located by Janin (*Const.* 235) at the Prosphorion harbour.

202  **407** *Quinquennalia*: cf. Marc. Com. *s.a.* 406 (the start of Theodosius' 5th year).

lightning and earthquake in the month Xanthicus, on Kalends of April [1 April] in the first watch of the night; as a result the bronze tiles of the Forum of Theodosius were swept away to Kainoupolis, and Christ's emblem on the Capitol fell down, and many ships foundered and a considerable number of corpses were cast ashore at the Hebdomon.[203]

In the same year were built the Hippodrome steps to the stoa.[204]

## Olympiad 297

**408** Indiction 6, year 14, consulship of Bassus and Philippus.

In the time of these consuls Arcadius Augustus died in the Palace of Constantinople, in the month Artemisius, on Kalends of May [1 May], and he was laid to rest in the Apostles.[205]

And in the same year there was great rain with thunder and lightning and earthquake in the month Panemus, on day 3 before Nones of July [5 July], a Monday, at hour 1.[206]

Theodosius II was 41st Roman emperor for 42 years.

In total, 5,959.

**409** Indiction 7, year 1, the 8th consulship of Honorius Augustus and the 3rd of Theodosius II Augustus.

**410** Indiction 8, year 2, sole consulship of Varanes.

---

[203] Damage: no parallels. On the Theodosian Forum, cf. nn. 173-4. The bronze tiles will have come from a major public building, perhaps the large basilica in the northern part of the Forum (described by Cedr. i. 610. 15-22).

Kainoupolis: the 'New City', the area of land reclaimed from the Sea of Marmara immediately south-west of the Theodosian Forum, east of the Theodosian harbour, see Mango, *Const.* 18, 45.

Capitol: Mango, *Const.* 30; it is uncertain whether the Christian symbol on this originally pagan temple was a Chi-Rho emblem or a Cross.

[204] Hippodrome steps: the precise reference is uncertain. This construction may have been required after the fire of 406, which damaged the north end (the verb could equally mean 'rebuilt'). There were probably colonnades (i.e. stoae) or vaulted passages behind most of the two long sides of the Hippodrome (cf. the Blues' stoa at Proc. *Wars* i. 24. 49), and the steps could have been part of the internal arrangements for access. Alternatively ἀναβάθρα, 'steps', might refer to the tiers of seating (cf. Mal. 474. 22).

[205] **408** Death of Arcadius: cf. Marc. Com. (no date or details), Soc. vii. 1. 1, Soz. ix. 1. 1; Theoph. 80. 7 has an incorrect Roman date (22 Aug.).

[206] Earthquake: no parallels for this notice (which recalls the earthquake recorded *s.a.* 407). 5 July was a Sunday in 408: the date would be correct for 409. Theophanes 80. 5 records an earthquake at Rome immediately before the deaths of Stilicho and Arcadius (both died in 408).

**411** Indiction 9, year 3, the 9th consulship of Honorius Augustus and the 4th of Theodosius II Augustus.[207]

In the time of these consuls Alaric entered and made Attalus the city prefect revolt.[208]

And in the same year the remains of the holy prophet Samuel were laid to rest in his sanctuary **[p.571]** near St. John Jucundianae in the month Hyperberetaeus, on day 3 before Nones of October [5 Oct.].[209]

## Olympiad 298

**412** Indiction 10, year 4, the 5th and sole consulship of Theodosius II Augustus.

In the present consulship the *praetorium* of Monaxius, city prefect, was burnt by the people of Constantinople because of the shortage of bread, and his carriage was dragged from the First Region as far as the porticoes of Domninus; the two *magistri militum* went to meet them, Varanes the consul and Arsacius, and Synesius the *comes largitionum*, and exhorted them saying, 'Turn back and we will ordain what you wish.'[210]

---

[207] **411** Consuls: for the disagreements between eastern and western lists for 411 and 412, see Bagnall, *Consuls* 356-9; *CP* agrees with the eastern record.

[208] Alaric: in 409 the Visigothic leader, in conflict with the emperor Honorius at Ravenna, established Attalus (*PLRE* ii. 180-1, s.v. Attalus 2) as puppet emperor in Rome, but in mid-410 demoted him again after a brief reconciliation with Honorius. Alaric did not 'enter' Rome until 24 Aug. 410, and died before the end of the year: see Bury, *HLRE* [2] i. 174-85, esp. 180ff. *CP*'s entry is vague, and does not specify that these events occurred in Italy.

[209] Church of Samuel: at the Hebdomon, near the church of John the Baptist whose foundation is recorded *s.a.* 391 (Janin, *Églises* 449-50); the Jucundianae was the site of an imperial palace (Proc. *Bld.* i. 11. 16, rebuilt by Justinian). Cf. *s.a.* 406 for the arrival of Samuel's relics.

[210] **412** Bread riot: cf. Marc. Com. *s.a.* 409 (correct date). Between the death of Arcadius (408) and 414, *CP* was short of information (only this entry is shared with Marc. Com.), which may have contributed to the insertion of this notice in 412 rather than 409. This is the first reference in *CP* to rioting in Cpl., a theme which subsequently attracted the author's attention, and is also present in Marc. Com., *CP*'s parallel source from *c.*380.

Monaxius, city prefect in 408–9 (*PLRE* ii. 764-5), was the recipient of *Cod. Theod.* xiv. 16. 1 (26 April 409), which concerns 500 pounds of gold devoted to famine relief. Varanes (consul in 410, as already recorded by *CP*) and Arsacius were probably *magistri militum praesentales* (*PLRE* ii. 1149-50, s.v. Varanes 1; ibid. 152, s.v. Arsacius 3). Synesius: *comes sacrarum largitionum* in 409 (ibid. 1050, s.v. Synesius 2).

*Praetorium* of city prefect: the location is a problem. The evidence is inadequate, but suggests that the city prefect had more than one *praetorium*

**413** Indiction 11, year 5, sole consulship of Lucius.[211]

**414** Indiction 12, year 6, consulship of Constantius and Constans.

In the time of these consuls Pulcheria, sister of Theodosius II Augustus, was proclaimed *nobilissima* in the month Panemus, on day 4 before Nones of July [4 July].[212]

And in the same year 3 portrait busts of Honorius and Theodosius Augusti, and of Pulcheria Augusta were dedicated in the senate by Aurelian, twice prefect of the sacred praetorians and patrician, in the month Apellaeus, on day 3 before Kalends of January [30 Dec.].[213]

**415** [p.572] Indiction 13, year 7, the 10th consulship of Honorius and the 6th of Theodosius II Augustus.

In the time of these consuls Theodosius II Augustus celebrated his *quinquennalia* in Constantinople in the month Audynaeus, on day 3 before Ides of January [11 Jan.],[214] and the death of Thermuntia, wife of the lord Honorius the Augustus was announced in the month Panemus, on the 3rd day before Kalends of August [30 July], a Friday.[215]

---

(quite apart from buildings associated with the praetorian prefect), one located towards the eastern end of the Mese, another somewhere to the north of St. Irene; for detailed discussion, see nn. 353, 407, and Janin, *Const.* 165-6. First Region: see Janin, *Const.* 49; this included the Great Palace, the area east of SS Sophia and Irene, and the south-east slope of the former acropolis. It was on the acropolis that the coach-house of the praetorian prefect had been established in the former temple of Aphrodite by Theodosius I (Mal. 345. 19-20), and it is possible that Monaxius' carriage was kept nearby (*CP* p. 588. 7-9 may imply that the coaches of the two prefects were kept together). The porticoes of Domninus flanked a major north-south road that intersected the Mese between the Fora of Constantine and Theodosius (Mango, *Const.* 31 and Plan II).

[211] **413** Consuls: Heraclianus, the western consul, had his name struck from all records in Aug. 413, following his attempted usurpation, see Bagnall, *Consuls* 360-1.

[212] **414** Elevation of Pulcheria: she was proclaimed Augusta, not *nobilissima*; cf. Marc. Com. (no date); she acted as regent for the young Theodosius II (Soz. ix. 1).

[213] Portrait busts: nothing is known about these, though Aurelian (*PLRE* i. 128-9, s.v. Aurelianus 3) was himself granted a gilded statue by the Cpl. senate in return for his services (*Anth. Graec.* xvi. 73). For the two Senate buildings at Cpl., cf. n. 54: Janin (*Const.* 155) identifies this one with the Senate at the Augustaeum.

[214] **415** *Quinquennalia*: a doublet for the notice *s.a.* 407; a celebration to mark his 15th anniversary was due in 416/7.

[215] Thermantia (not Thermuntia): *PLRE* ii. 1111-12; second wife of Honorius for about 6 months, she had been repudiated by him in 408 at the disgrace and death of her father Stilicho.

And in the same year in the month Gorpiaeus on the 8th day before Kalends of October [24 Sept.], a Friday, it was announced that the barbarian Ataulph had been killed in the northern regions by the lord Honorius. And lamps were lit, and on the following day chariot racing was held, so that a processional entry was also made.[216]

In the same year the inauguration of the Great Church of Constantinople was celebrated in the month Gorpiaeus, on day 6 before Ides of October [10 Oct.], the Lord's Day.[217] And the remains of Joseph the son of Jacob, and of Zacharias, the father of St. John the Baptist, were conveyed to Constantinople by way of the Chalcedonian jetty, in the month Gorpiaeus, on day 6 before Nones of September [31 Aug.], a Saturday; the same remains were borne in two caskets by Atticus, patriarch of Constantinople, and Moses, bishop of Antaradus in Phoenicia, the two men sitting in carriages; these were laid to rest in the Great [p.573] Church, with Ursus, city prefect, in attendance, and all the senate.[218]

And a golden statue of the lord Theodosius II Augustus was dedicated in the senate by Aurelian, twice praetorian prefect and patrician.[219]

---

[216] Death of Ataulph: Visigoth king, 410–15 in succession to Alaric. After being defeated in south Gaul by Boniface, he had withdrawn to Spain where he was murdered by a servant (Olympiodorus 26; see also PLRE ii. 176-8, s.v. Athaulfus; narrative in Bury, HLRE [2] i. 194-200).

This notice, and some nearby (e.g. Thermantia; damage to Constantine's column, and victory over Attalus s.a. 416) have a slightly different dating formula (the definite article is inserted before the Roman date) when compared with adjacent material that has parallels in Marc. Com.; this might indicate a change of source, though the evidence is too tentative to be pressed.

[217] Great Church: cf. Marc. Com. (no date); a rededication after its destruction in the fire of 404 (cf. CP s.a.).

[218] Relics: for similar transfers, cf. ss.aa. 356, 357, 406 (with n. 201 on Chalcedonian jetty). Atticus was patriarch 406–25, Ursus city prefect in 415–16 (PLRE ii. 1192, s.v. Ursus 3). The involvement of Moses suggests that the relics had been discovered at Antaradus (modern Tartus in Syria): although Joseph had died in Egypt, he had ordered that his remains be returned to the promised land (Exodus 13. 19).

CP's Roman date is impossible, since in Sept. there are only 4 days before the Nones. The date would be correct for Oct., i.e. 2 Oct., which fell on a Saturday in 415 (whereas 31 Aug. was a Tuesday).

[219] Statue: a partial doublet for the notice under 414, probably originating in a different source since a different noun is used to describe the monument (ἀνδριάς instead of στηθάριον).

## Olympiad 299

**416** Indiction 14, year 8, the 7th consulship of Theodosius II Augustus and that of Palladius.

In the time of these consuls a great stone tore away during the night from the lower stonework of the porphyry column on which stood Constantine the great emperor, in the month Dystrus, on the 5th day before Kalends of April [28 Mar.], as Tuesday was dawning. And in the same year all the drums of the same column were bound.[220]

And a theatrical spectacle was performed in the presence of Ursus, city prefect, to celebrate the victory against Attalus the usurper, in the month Daisius, on the 4th day before Kalends of July [28 June], a Wednesday. And chariot racing was also held for the same victory in the month Panemus, on Nones of July [7 July].[221]

[p.574] And in the same year the lord Theodosius II entered Constantinople from Heracleia, in the month Gorpiaeus, 1 day before Kalends of October [30 Sept.], a Saturday, after receiving the golden crown in accordance with custom in the Theodosian Forum from Ursus, city prefect, and the senate.[222]

**417** Indiction 15, year 9, the 11th consulship of Honorius and the 2nd of Constantius.

In the time of these consuls there occurred a great earthquake in the evening, on a Friday in the month Xanthicus, on day 12 before Kalends of May [20 April]. It was on the same day as the Passion of our Lord Jesus Christ.[223]

---

[220] **416** Porphyry column: cf. *s.a.* 328 with n. 54 for its erection in Constantine's Forum.

[221] Attalus: proclaimed emperor (again, cf. n. 208) by the Visigoths in 414, he had been abandoned by them in 415 and handed over to Honorius, who had him mutilated and exiled (Olympiodorus fr. 14, Philost. xii. 4-5, Marc. Com. *s.a.* 412); see Bury, *HLRE* [2] i. 198-9.

[222] Theodosius' entry into Cpl.: the reason for his absence in Heracleia is unknown, but his presence there is attested by *Cod. Theod.* xi. 28. 11 (9 Sept.). Bury (*HLRE* [2] i. 220) suggested that Theodosius, now aged 15, took over formal control of affairs from Pulcheria: the ceremonial entry may be associated with this change. Const. Porph. *de caer.* App. (496. 17-497. 3 Reiske) records that this ceremony was performed when the emperor returned to Cpl. by land; he was offered one crown of gold and others of laurel, the emperor repaying the cost of the golden one.

[223] **417** Earthquake: Marc. Com. records destruction at Cibyra. *CP*'s cross-reference to Good Friday is correct.

**418** Indiction 1, year 10, the 12th consulship of Honorius and the 8th of Theodosius II Augustus.

In the time of these consuls there was an eclipse of the sun, in the month Panemus, on day 14 before Kalends of August [19 July], on a Friday, at hour 8.[224]

**419** Indiction 2, year 11, consulship of Monaxius and Plintha.

In the time of these consuls on the Lord's Day, after Aetius, city prefect, had entered the Great Church in his robes in the month Peritius, on day 7 before Kalends of March [23 Feb.], when he had prayed and was departing, since he had been summoned to the Palace, a certain Cyriacus, an old man, who had thrust a great knife inside a papyrus roll, as if he were presenting a petition to him, struck him in the right side of the chest so that his mantle and toga were cut through.[225]

[p.575]                    Olympiad 300

**420** Indiction 3, year 12, the 9th consulship of Theodosius II Augustus and the 3rd of Constantius.

When Theodosius II Augustus had progressed in boyhood, he studied in the Palace in his father's lifetime; and after his father's death there studied with him a certain youth named Paulinus, son of a *comes domesticorum*. And Theodosius was fond of him. And when the same Theodosius II Augustus reached manhood, he sought to take a lady in marriage. And he pestered his sister, the lady Pulcheria, who was a virgin: she too, in turn, because she loved her own brother, chose not to be married to anyone. And she, who wished to live together with her brother in the Palace, investigated many unmarried girls, daughters of patricians and of imperial blood. Theodosius said to her, 'I wish to find a young woman who is exceedingly comely, so that no other woman in Constantinople may have such beauty, even one of imperial blood. But if she is not of outstanding beauty, I have no use either for distinguished or imperial blood or wealth, but whosoever's daughter she is, provided that she is exceedingly lovely, [p.576] I will take her.' And when she heard this, the lady Pulcheria sent everywhere in her investigations. And Paulinus too, Theodosius' companion and friend hurried around, wishing to please him on this issue.

---

[224] **418** Eclipse: cf. Marc. Com. (no date), Philost. xii. 8.

[225] **419** Attack on Aetius: as city prefect Aetius (*PLRE* ii. 19-20, s.v. Aetius 1) had responsibility for administering a law that cut down the numbers of staff at the Great Church (*Cod. Iust.* i. 2. 4), and this may have occasioned the attempted assassination.

In the meantime it happened that there came to Constantinople with her relatives a most lovely and eloquent girl, a Hellene named Athenaïs, who was daughter of Heraclitus the philosopher; this Athenaïs was compelled to come to the blessed city to her own aunt, for the following reason. The philosopher Heraclitus her father also had two sons, and when he was about to die, he made a will and as heirs of all the property left by him he named in his will his two sons Valerian and Gesius; in the same will he said, 'To Athenaïs my most beloved daughter I wish to be given a hundred *nomismata* and no more; for sufficient for her is her destiny which surpasses all womanly destiny.' And her father Heraclitus the wise Athenian died.

After his demise and the revelation of his dispositions, the same Athenaïs entreated her brothers, since they were senior in age, falling down before them and begging them not to abide by the same will, but that she should receive a one-third share of the paternal property, saying that she had committed no sin, but: 'You yourselves know how I was disposed to our mutual **[p.577]** father, and I do not know for what reason he left me impoverished when he was about to die, and bestowed on me a destiny of riches after his decease.' But her brothers remained intransigent and, enraged, even expelled her from their paternal home. And finally the sister of the woman who had been her mother took her in and protected her, not simply because she was an orphan, but also as a virgin and her sister's child. She took the girl with her and brought her to Constantinople to her other aunt, the sister of her father Heraclitus. And they took her and made a petition against her brothers, and they approached the most pious lady Pulcheria, the sister of Theodosius the emperor; speaking eloquently she told how she had been violently treated by her own brothers. And the same lady Pulcheria, seeing that she was lovely and eloquent, asked her aunts whether she was a virgin. She was told that she had been protected as a virgin by her father, and that she had been guided through many philosophical discourses. Pulcheria bid her to wait together with her aunts, protected by *cubicularii*, while she took, she said, the entreaty from the girl and went to her brother Theodosius the emperor; and she said to him, 'I have found a young girl, pure, well-dressed, with fine features, a good nose, most white as snow, large-eyed, attractive, with fair curly hair and stately step, eloquent, a Hellene, **[p.578]** and a virgin.' And when he heard, he was inflamed since he was young; and after sending for his companion and friend Paulinus, he asked his sister to bring the same Athenaïs to her chamber, as if for some other purpose, in order that he might look at her through the curtain with Paulinus. And she was brought in, and when he saw her he fell in love with her, Paulinus having admired her; he took her and made her a Christian (for she was pagan), and renamed her Eudocia.[226]

421 Indiction 4, year 13, consulship of Eustathius and Agricola.

In the time of these consuls water was let into the cistern of the lady Pulcheria Augusta, in the month Peritius, 1 day before Ides of February [12 Feb.], in the presence of lord Theodosius Augustus.[227]

In this year Theodosius Augustus celebrated nuptials, taking as his wife Athenaïs who was also called Eudocia, in the month Daisius, on day 7 before Ides of June [7 June], and chariot racing was performed in celebration of the same nuptials in the same month Daisius, on day 4 before Ides of June [10 June], and likewise also a theatrical spectacle in the same Hippodrome.[228] And he had by this Athenaïs who was also called Eudocia a daughter, named Eudoxia.[229]

The brothers of the Augusta, when they heard that their sister was empress, fled to Greece in terror; and she sent [p.579] and brought them back under guarantee, and made them dignitaries,

---

[226] 420 Theodosius' wife: cf. Mal. 352. 8-355. 8, for the same story with only a few differences, of which the most significant are that Malalas (also Soc. vii. 21. 8) correctly gives the father's name as Leontius (John of Nikiu 84. 29 has Heraclitus); also Theoph. 83. 19-22, very briefly. At p. 577. 12 we have followed Malalas and translated ἐδίδαξεν, 'she told', for ἐδίδαξαν, 'they told'. The string of epithets in Pulcheria's description of Athenaïs' beauty (CP pp. 577. 20-578. 1) is typical of chronicle descriptions of emperors: see C. Head, 'Physical Descriptions of the Emperors in Byzantine Historical Writing', Byz. 1, 1980, 226-40.

Paulinus: PLRE ii. 846-7, s.v. Paulinus 8; nothing more is known about his family background. Comes domesticorum: commander of imperial household guards, cf. n. 127.

Eudocia: on her origins and the career of Leontius as teacher of rhetoric (not a philosopher), see Cameron, 'Empress' 270-9, who plays down her pagan background but also identifies some true elements in this romantic tale (e.g. the existence of a maternal uncle Asclepiodotus, PLRE ii. 160, s.v. Asclepiodotus 1).

Cubicularii: cf. n. 126.

From this point in Theodosius II's reign, Malalas provided CP with a few long stories (Eudocia, Paulinus, Attila, Cyrus), that are integrated with much briefer 'annalistic' notices frequently shared with Marc. Com.

[227] 421 Cistern: Pulcheria's cistern, otherwise unknown, has probably been confused with that of Aetius, which was constructed in this year (Marc. Com.).

[228] Wedding: cf. Marc. Com. (no date); also Mal. 355. 8-9.

[229] Birth of Eudoxia: in 422 (Marc. Com.); cf. Mal. 355. 9-10.

the emperor Theodosius having promoted them. And the one called Gesius he made praetorian prefect of the Illyrian race, while Valerian he made *magister*; their sister Eudocia said to them, 'If you had not misused me, I would not have been compelled to come to Constantinople, and become empress. So you bestowed the realm which was mine from birth. For it was my good destiny which made you intransigent towards me, and not your attitude towards me.'

The emperor Theodosius made Paulinus advance through every dignity, because he was his friend and had been an intermediary in his marriage and ate with them; and after this he promoted him *magister*. And he was exalted because he had free access to the emperor Theodosius and the Augusta, because he had indeed been their bridal attendant.[230]

In this year a statue of Arcadius was dedicated, which stood on top of the Spiral Column in the Forum of Arcadius at the place called Xerolophus, in the month Panemus, on day 6 before Ides of July [10 July], a Saturday.[231]

In the same year a victory over the Persians was announced, in the month Gorpiaeus, on day 8 before Ides of September [6 Sept.], a Tuesday.[232]

**422** Indiction 5, year 14, the 13th consulship of Honorius and the 10th of Theodosius Augustus.

[p.580] In the time of these consuls there appeared in the sky a star which emitted a ray exceedingly long and white, in the month Dystrus [March] for about 10 nights after the cock-crow; and in the same year there was an earthquake.[233]

**423** Indiction 6, year 15, consulship of Asclepiodotus and Marinianus.

---

[230] Continuation of Athenaïs story: cf. Mal. 355. 11-356. 5 for the same account, with minor differences; CP has deliberately divided the story between two years, presumably to indicate an interval of time.

*Magister*: i.e. *magister officiorum*, see Jones, *LRE* 368-9.

[231] Statue of Arcadius: cf. Marc. Com. (no date); the column itself (spiral because of the sequence of bas reliefs with which it was decorated) had been erected in 402/3 (Theoph. 77. 24). For sketches of the reliefs, see E. H. Freshfield, 'Notes on a Vellum Album containing some original sketches of public buildings and monuments, drawn by a German artist who visited Constantinople in 1574', *Archaeologia* lxxii, 1921-2, 87-104; Müller-Wiener, *Bildlexikon* 250-3.

Xerolophus: the seventh hill of Cpl., and the site of the Forum of Arcadius (Mango, *Const.* 28, 43; Janin, *Const.* 71-2; also Guilland, *Études* ii. 59-62).

[232] Victory over Persians: Marc. Com. refers to a battle; Soc. vii. 18 describes Ardabur's success against the Persians in Arzanene; see also Bury, *HLRE* [2] ii. 4.

[233] **422** Comet: no parallels.

In the time of these consuls Eudocia was proclaimed Augusta, in the month Audynaeus, on day 4 before Nones of January [2 Jan.],[234] and there were many earthquakes on Monday during the tenth hour in the month Xanthicus, on day 7 before Ides of April [7 Apr.].[235]

### Olympiad 301

**424** Indiction 7, year 16, consulship of Victor and Castinus.[236]

**425** Indiction 8, year 17, the 11th consulship of Theodosius Augustus and that of Valentinian Caesar.

In the time of these consuls Valentinian the younger was elevated as Augustus by Theodosius II Augustus, in the month Hyperberetaeus, on day 10 before Kalends of November [23 Oct.].[237]

**426** Indiction 9, year 18, the 12th consulship of Theodosius Augustus and the 2nd of the younger Valentinian Augustus.

**427** Indiction 10, year 19, consulship of Hierius and Ardabur.

In the time of these consuls the bath was inaugurated which was formerly **[p.581]** the Constantinianae, but now the Theodosianae, after Hierius, twice prefect and consul, had completed it in the month Hyperberetaeus, on day 5 before Nones of October [3 Oct.].[238]

### Olympiad 302

**428** Indiction 11, year 20, consulship of Felix and Taurus.

In the time of these consuls the Vandals entered Africa.[239]

---

234  423 Eudocia Augusta: she had been described (prematurely) as Augusta in the Athenaïs story, which CP shares with Malalas as opposed to the Marc. Com. tradition with which this notice is probably to be linked.

235  Earthquake: cf. Marc. Com. (no date).

236  424 Castinus: probably the nominee of the western usurper John, who had seized power following Honorius' death in 423, see Bagnall, Consuls 383; it seems that he was never officially accepted in the east.

237  425 Elevation of Valentinian: cf. Marc. Com. (no date, located at Ravenna). Valentinian III (PLRE ii. 1138-9, s.v. Valentinian 4), infant son of Constantius and Galla Placidia, was installed as nominal western emperor when an eastern army under the Alan Aspar had captured and executed the usurper John at Ravenna; see Bury, HLRE [2] i. 222-4.

238  427 Baths: cf. Marc. Com. (no date or details). Work on these baths had begun in 345, CP s.a. with n. 82. Hierius: PLRE ii. 557, s.v. Hierius 2; his second praetorian prefecture was not until 432.

239  428 Vandals in Africa: Geiseric crossed from Spain in 429; see Bury, HLRE [2] i. 244-9.

**429** Indiction 12, year 21, consulship of Florentius and Dionysius.
**430** Indiction 13, year 22, the 13th consulship of Theodosius Augustus and the 3rd of the younger Valentinian Augustus.
**431** Indiction 14, year 23, consulship of Antiochus and Bassus.
In year 401 from the Ascension to heaven of the Lord, and in year 23 of the reign of Theodosius II Augustus, and of the aforementioned consuls, there took place in Ephesus the third Synod of the 200 holy and blessed Fathers against the impious Nestorius; this was the one which, adhering to the symbol of the correct and blameless faith, renounced the same Nestorius in the name of Christ our true God. For this demented man dared to teach that he who is beyond mortal understanding and who transcends all nature, the Lord Jesus Christ, born of the Virgin, is of mortal substance only, and not at the same time also of divine.[240]

**[p.582]**                    Olympiad 303

**432** Indiction 15, year 24, consulship of Valerius and Aetius.
**433** Indiction 1, year 25, the 14th consulship of Theodosius Augustus and that of Maximus.
In the time of these consuls there was a great conflagration from the Neorion; and the granaries and the bath called Achilles burnt, in the month Lous, on day 12 before Kalends of September [21 Aug.].[241]
**434** Indiction 2, year 26, consulship of Areobindus and Aspar.
**435** Indiction 3, year 27, the 15th consulship of Theodosius Augustus and the 4th of the younger Valentinian Augustus.

---

[240] **431** Nestorian controversy and First Synod of Ephesus: see Soc. vii. 29, 31-5, Theoph. 88. 11-92. 2; cf. Marc. Com. *s.a.* 430. Nestorius, patriarch of Cpl., had explained the unity of God and man in Christ with a formula that referred to the existence of two distinct natures (human and divine) and attacked the belief that Mary was Mother of God rather than Mother of Christ. This resulted in conflict with Cyril of Alexandria, who also wished to reassert the superiority of the see of Alexandria over the upstart Cpl. (cf. n. 160). For discussion of the complex Christological issues and ecclesiastical politics which resulted in the Council of Ephesus, see Bury, *HLRE* [2] i. 350-4; Stein, *BE* i. 300-5; Chadwick, *Church* 194-200; Young, *Nicaea* 213-65.
Ascension dating: cf. *ss.aa.* 325, 381, 452, for other church councils.
[241] **433** Fire: cf. Marc. Com. (large area of northern part of city destroyed in a 3-day fire in Aug.). The harbour of Neorion and its associated granaries were located on the Golden Horn, with the ancient baths of Achilles nearby (Janin, *Const.* 235-6, 216; cf. Mango, *Const.* 18 n. 30, 40).

Olympiad 304

**436** Indiction 4, year 28, consulship of Isidore and Senator.

**437** Indiction 5, year 29, the 2nd consulship of Aetius and that of Sigisvuldus.

In the time of these consuls the younger Valentinian Augustus entered Constantinople, in the month Hyperberetaeus, on day 12 before Kalends of November [21 Oct.]. And he celebrated his nuptials, taking Eudoxia, the daughter of Theodosius and Eudocia Augusti, in the month Hyperberetaeus, on day 4 before Kalends of November [29 Oct.], and by her he had two daughters, Eudocia and Placidia.[242]

**438 [p.583]** Indiction 6, year 30, the 16th consulship of Theodosius Augustus and that of Faustus.

**439** Indiction 7, year 31, the 17th consulship of Theodosius Augustus and that of Festus.

In this year Theodosius Augustus ordered that the walls be made in a circuit on the whole seaward side of Constantinople.[243]

And in the same year Zinzirich the king of the Vandals entered Carthage, in the month Hyperberetaeus [Oct.]; and in the same year he attempted to devastate Sicily.[244]

Olympiad 305

**440** Indiction 8, year 32, the 5th consulship of Valentinian Augustus and that of Anatolius.

---

[242] **437** Marriage of Valentinian III: cf. Theoph. 92. 16-19, Soc. vii. 44; Marc. Com. records that the wedding was celebrated in Thessalonica (the original plan, changed when Valentinian agreed to travel to Cpl.: Soc. loc. cit.), and that the two had long been betrothed (since 424, Marc. Com. s.a.).

Daughters: cf. Mal. 356. 14-16.

[243] **439** Sea walls: the intention was perhaps to safeguard against Vandal sea raiding, and the prefect Cyrus (see below, s.a. 450 with n. 261) is often credited with the construction (e.g. Cameron, 'Empress' 240-1: but the poem of John Geometres discussed by Cameron has no reference to the *building* of walls). Mango (*Const.* 25 n. 12) is inclined to doubt that the order was ever executed, since in the 626 siege of Cpl. there do not appear to have been sea walls (at least on the Golden Horn side). Cyrus is wrongly associated with the construction of Cpl.'s land walls (Theoph. 96. 34-97. 1; Cedr. i. 598. 23-599. 1), an error which is more likely to have occurred if Cyrus had built some walls, perhaps those along the Sea of Marmara.

[244] Capture of Carthage: on 19 Oct.; cf. Marc. Com., dating Geiseric's entry to 23 Oct. See further Bury, *HLRE* [2] i. 254-5; Stein, *BE* i. 324-5; *PLRE* ii. 497. The Vandals attacked Sicily in the next year.

**441** Indiction 9, year 33, sole consulship of Cyrus.

In the time of this man John the Vandal was slain in Thrace.[245]

**442** Indiction 10, year 34, consulship of Eudoxius and Dioscorus.

In the time of these consuls the Huns crossed over, and Attila and Bleda devastated Illyricum.[246]

**443** Indiction 11, year 35, the 2nd consulship of Maximus and that of Paternus.[247]

In the time of these consuls the public bath called Achilles was inaugurated, in the month Audynaeus, on day 3 before Ides of January [11 Jan.].[248]

And [p.584] Theodosius the Augustus entered Constantinople from the expedition to Asia, in the month Lous, on day 6 before Kalends of September [27 Aug.].[249]

Olympiad 306

**444** Indiction 12, year 36, the 18th consulship of Theodosius Augustus and that of Albinus.

In this year, when the emperor Theodosius went in procession to church on the Feast of the Holy Epiphany, it happened that the *magister* Paulinus had an affliction of the foot and stayed away from the procession and made his excuses. And a certain poor man presented to the emperor Theodosius a Phrygian apple, quite exceptionally enormous. And the emperor was

[245] **441** Death of John: cf. Marc. Com. John, *magister militum per Thraciam* (*PLRE* ii. 597, s.v. Ioannes 13), was treacherously slain by Arnegisclus, a subordinate Roman officer, perhaps in connection with preparations for a naval expedition to oust the Vandal Geiseric from Carthage.

[246] **442** Huns: they invaded across the Danube from Pannonia; cf. Marc. Com. See further Bury, *HLRE* [2] i. 273-4; Stein, *BE* i. 291-2.

[247] **443** *cos. post.*: Paterius; Marc. Com. records Paterius correctly, but overlooks Maximus' second consulship.

[248] Baths of Achilles: cf. Marc. Com. (no date); now restored after the fire of 433, cf. n. 241.

[249] *Adventus* of Theodosius: cf. Marc. Com. (no date). Theodosius' visit to Asia (probably the diocese of Asiana) is confirmed by Theodosius, *Novel* 23, issued from Aphrodisias on 22 May and concerned with the restoration of the city of Heraclea (C. Roueché, 'Theodosius II, the Cities, and the Date of the "Church History" of Sozomen', *JThS* xxvii, 1986, 130-2). The preface to this *Novel* explains the visit as the fulfilment of a vow, a reason that might conceal other factors: Theodosius may have retreated from Cpl. in fear of Attila's extensive ravages in Thrace, or the journey might have been connected with the rifts in the imperial household associated with the empress Eudocia's withdrawal to Jerusalem (see n. 250).

astounded and all the senate, and immediately the emperor gave the poor man 150 *nomismata* and sent the apple to the Augusta Eudocia, and the Augusta sent it to Paulinus, the *magister* and friend of the emperor. But the same *magister*, not knowing that the emperor sent it to the Augusta, himself again sent it to the emperor Theodosius, as he departed from the church. And the emperor received it in the absence of the Augusta, and he hid it away, summoned the Augusta and asked her, 'Where is the apple which I sent to you?'. And she said, 'I ate it.' And he made her swear by his own salvation whether she had eaten it or sent it to someone. And she swore that she had sent it to no-one, but had eaten it herself. And he gave a command and the apple was brought, and he showed [p.585] her it. And between them there came about a separation and a breach.

And thereafter Theodosius the emperor suspected the same Paulinus and ordered him to be put to death. And the same lady Eudocia was distressed, because she had been insulted (for it was known everywhere that it was on her account that Paulinus was slain, because he was young and handsome); the Augusta Eudocia asked the emperor Theodosius permission to depart to the Holy Places in order to pray, and he granted it to her.[250] And on her journey from Constantinople to Jerusalem to pray, she arrived at Antioch the Great and spoke in the council chamber a speech of encomium for the same Antioch, seated in the imperial throne which was of solid gold set with gems, and the people of the city chanted for her, and a golden effigy of her was raised up

---

250  444 Eudocia and Paulinus: cf. Mal. 356. 17-357. 19 (undated); also Theoph. 99. 18-28 (under 447/8). Suspicions against Eudocia had probably been aroused by the chamberlain Chrysaphius, who was starting to consolidate his influence over Theodosius. The chronicle version of the apple story presents Eudocia's relations with Paulinus in an innocent light, but there was presumably some more compromising evidence that Chrysaphius could exploit: according to *Patria* iii. 146 (pp. 261-3) Eudocia presented the apple as an explicit love token to Paulinus, who then survived an attempt by Theodosius to have him killed, and founded the church of SS Cosmas and Damian in gratitude for the escape. E. L. Bowie has pointed out that the Phrygian apple is a literary allusion to the apple of discord whose award to Aphrodite in the Judgement of Paris brought about the Trojan War (Phrygian was a synonym for Trojan).

Date: Paulinus was exiled to Cappadocia and killed there, probably in 440 (Marc. Com. *s.a.*), and Eudocia is likely to have withdrawn from the court at about the same time for an extended visit to the Holy Land (Cameron, 'Empress' 258-63, with references to alternative views). Marc. Com. does not mention the Eudocia-Paulinus story, but *s.a.* 444 he records a dispute between Eudocia and Saturninus, *comes domesticorum*, who killed two of her attendants at Jerusalem, but was himself then put to death at her command (cf. Priscus fr. 14. 37-8); Cameron ('Empress' 260-1) suggests this may have influenced the dating in *CP*.

inside the council chamber, and at the so-called Museum they set up to her a bronze monument, and these are standing up to the present day. And after lavishing upon the city of the Antiochenes in Syria money for the grain fund,[251] she set out for the Holy Places, and founded many buildings in Jerusalem, and restored the entire wall of Jerusalem, saying, 'It was on my account that David the prophet said, "And at your good favour let the walls of Jerusalem be built."' And she remained in the same Jerusalem, and after building an imperial tomb for herself there she died, and was laid to rest there in Jerusalem. When she was about to die, she swore that she did not admit the accusation which was brought against her because of Paulinus.[252]

**445 [p.586]** Indiction 13, year 37, the 6th consulship of Valentinian Augustus and that of Nomus.

**446** Indiction 14, year 38, the 3rd consulship of Leontius and that of Symmachus.[253]

**447** Indiction 15, year 39, consulship of Ardabur and Alypius.[254]

---

251 Eudocia at Antioch: the extant Malalas does not preserve any mention of this visit, but it is recorded in the Tusculan fragment (II, pp. 14-16), which indicates that the Antiochene author originally described the occasion; Evagrius (who used Malalas as a source) also mentions Eudocia's impressive speech and the bronze monument. The empress made two journeys to the Holy Land (Evag. i. 21), in 438 and then after the Paulinus affair, and on each occasion she probably passed through Antioch (which lay on the route). Eudocia's visit and bene-factions are usually connected with the earlier pilgrimage (e.g. Downey, *Antioch* 450-1) and CP's version dismissed as a conflation of the two visits, but the narrative sequence in the Tusculan fragment (apple story, then Antioch) indicates that the Antiochene Malalas was responsible for the later context in CP. Although the second pilgrimage resulted from a quarrel in the imperial family, Eudocia's rift with Theodosius was not final until the dispute with Saturninus (cf. n. 250, and see Hunt, *Pilgrimage* 237): she might still have welcomed the chance to behave as a patron at Antioch and obtain benefactions from Theodosius (Evag. i. 20: enlargement of circuit of walls and funds for restoring baths of Valens).

Grain fund: Eudocia's donation is not otherwise attested, but many eastern cities had such funds for subsidizing the purchase of grain (cf. Jones, *LRE* 735), and Eudocia might well have offered a contribution, since her arrival with a large retinue would have increased prices locally.

Museum: originally a shrine to the Muses, it had been converted by Constantine into the *praetorium* of the *comes Orientis* (Mal. 318. 23-319. 4).

252 Eudocia in Jerusalem: cf. Mal. 357. 19-358. 4, and see Hunt, *Pilgrimage* ch. 10. The Biblical reference is Psalms 51. 18, 'And at your good favour will our head be raised up', which provides a 'prophecy' for Eudocia's name (εὐδοκία = 'good favour'). Eudocia died on 20 Oct. 460.

253 **446** *cos. prior*: 3rd of Aetius.

254 **447** *cos. post.*: Calepius.

In the time of these consuls Marcianopolis was captured and Anargiscus, *magister militum per Thraciam*, was slain.[255]

And in the same year there occurred great earthquakes, so that the walls collapsed; for they persisted for some time, so that no-one dared to remain at home, but all fled outside the city, chanting litanies day and night; for there was great peril, such as there had not been from the beginning of time. And some said that fire too had been seen in the heaven. Hence also the commemoration of the litany is celebrated annually up to the present day in the Triconch, because of the forbearance of the beneficent God, on day 8 before Ides of November [6 Nov.]. For amidst such great peril he did not kill any.[256]

## Olympiad 307

**448** Indiction 1, year 40, consulship of Zeno and Postumianus.

**449** Indiction 2, year 41, consulship of Protogenes and Asterius.

In the time of these consuls Marina Augusta, wife of Valentinian Augustus, died in the month Lous, on day 3 before Nones of August [3 Aug.].[257]

**450 [p.587]** Indiction 3, year 42, the 7th consulship of Valentinian Augustus and that of Avienus.

Under these consuls the second Synod in Ephesus took place, and Domnus, bishop of Antioch, and Flavian, bishop of

---

[255] Anargiscus: *PLRE* ii. 151, s.v. Arnegisclus. He was killed during an invasion by Attila's Huns, who overran the Balkans as far as Thermopylae: cf. Marc. Com., and see also Bury, *HLRE* [2] i. 275; Stein, *BE* i. 292-3.

[256] Earthquakes: cf. Marc. Com., who notes the collapse of much of the walls along with 57 towers, a monumental stone structure in the Theodosian Forum, numerous statues, and (contrary to *CP*) the death of many from hunger and the noxious stench. Marcellinus does not mention the popular response, but for this, cf. Theoph. 93. 5-20 (flight to the Campus at the Hebdomon after an earthquake in 437/8). Expiatory supplication was required since earthquakes were regarded as manifestations of divine wrath.

The same earthquake is also recorded in greater detail by *CP s.a.* 450, with the correct date, 26 Jan., and liturgical commemoration at the Campus (cf. n. 262). The annual commemoration at the Triconch does not relate to this earthquake, but to the dust-cloud that gathered over Cpl. on 6 Nov. 472 following the eruption of Vesuvius. See Croke, 'Earthquakes', esp. 140-4.

Triconch: Janin (*Const.* 436-7) identified this among the buildings near to the Capitol (cf. Theoph. 159. 9 for a supplication there).

[257] **449** Death of Marina: cf. Marc. Com. (no date), correctly describing her as Theodosius' sister. Marina was unmarried, whereas Valentinian married Theodosius' daughter Eudoxia, *CP s.a.* 437.

Constantinople, Ibas and Theodoret, and many others were demoted by Dioscorus, bishop of Alexandria.[258]

In the reign of Theodosius and Valentinian Augusti, Attila, who was from the race of the Gepid Huns, marched against Rome and Constantinople with a horde of many tens of thousands. And by means of a certain Goth ambassador he declared to Valentinian emperor of Rome, 'My master and your master Attila commands you through me to make ready a palace for him.' And likewise also to Theodosius the emperor he made the same declaration in Constantinople by means of a certain Goth ambassador. And when Aetius, the first senator at Rome, heard of the exceeding audacity of Attila's senseless dispatch, he departed for Gaul to Alaric, who was hostile to Rome on account of Honorius, and persuaded him to go with him against Attila since he had destroyed many of Rome's cities. And they suddenly rushed upon him when he was encamped near the river Danube, and cut down many thousands of his men. In the engagement Alaric received a wound from [p.588] an arrow and died. Similarly Attila too died, carried off by a downrush of blood through the nostrils during the night while he was sleeping with a Hunnish concubine; the girl was indeed suspected of having killed him herself.[259] The most learned

---

[258] 450 Second Synod of Ephesus: cf. Marc. Com. s.a. 449 (correct). The council was dominated by Dioscorus, his supporters among the monks of Syria and Egypt, and the eunuch Chrysaphius; the result was approval for a Monophysite Christological formula that emphasized the one incarnate nature of Christ and rejected the alternative doctrine of Christ as a unity of two hypostatic natures. See Bury, HLRE [2] i. 355-6; Chadwick, Church 200-2.

This council was often known as the Robber Synod (a name applied by Pope Leo), on account of the excess violence that was used to reach decisions which were soon overturned at Chalcedon (451): neither violence nor repudiation is mentioned in CP, which also omits the Ascension date usually given for synods (cf. n. 42). For CP's attitude to Chalcedon, cf. n. 268.

[259] Campaign and death of Attila: cf. Mal. 358. 6-359. 3 for the same account; both wrongly name as the Roman ally Alaric (the Visigothic leader who had sacked Rome in 410 during his dispute with the emperor Honorius, PLRE ii. 43-8, s.v. Alaricus 1), rather than Theodoric (king of the Visigoths, who were now based in Aquitania in south-west France, PLRE ii. 1070-1, s.v. Theodericus 2), and locate the decisive battle near the Danube rather than at the Catalaunian plain near Troyes in eastern France. Malalas adds an alternative version of Attila's death, that he was murdered after Aetius had suborned one of his guards.

The invasion was precipitated by a request in 450 from Honoria, the ambitious sister of Valentinian III, that Attila should come to rescue her from a marriage that Valentinian was arranging for her; Attila interpreted the request as an offer of marriage, and hence demanded a portion of the empire for himself

Priscus the Thracian has written the history of this war.[260]

He says that in Constantinople Cyrus was appointed praetorian prefect and city prefect. And he used to go in procession as praetorian prefect in the carriage of the prefects, but return seated in the carriage of the city prefect. For he held the two offices for four years, because he was perfectly blameless. And he himself had the idea of lighting the evening lamps in the workshops, and likewise also the night-time ones. And for the whole day the factions chanted for him in the Hippodrome, 'Constantine founded, Cyrus restored.' And the emperor was angry with him because they chanted this, and he confiscated his property, replaced him, made him a cleric, and sent him as bishop to Smyrna in Asia: for the people of that city had already murdered four bishops, and the intention was that they should also kill the same Cyrus. After he had arrived at the city, on the Holy Nativity of our Saviour Jesus Christ, the people of the city of Smyrna, since they suspected that the emperor had made him bishop there because he was a Hellene, asked him to address them. As he was compelled by them, he went up to preach, and after granting [p.589] them peace, he began to speak as follows, 'Brothers, let the birth of our God and Saviour Jesus Christ be honoured in silence, because by hearing alone was he conceived in the Holy Virgin; for he was Word. Glory to Him through the ages. Amen.' And after being acclaimed he stepped down, and he remained there until his death.[261]

---

(Priscus fr. 20. 1, 3), a demand which he tried to enforce by invading Gaul in 451; see F. M. Clover, 'Geiseric and Attila', Historia xxii, 1973, 104-17. After his defeat by the patrician Aetius, the leading Roman general in the western empire (for his career, see PLRE ii. 21-9, s.v. Aetius 7), and Theodoric the Visigoth (who was killed), Attila attacked Italy in 452, but was persuaded to withdraw. He died in 453 of a haemorrhage (Jordanes, Getica 254-5; PLRE ii. 182-3; Bury, HLRE [2] i. 288-96).

[260] Priscus: cf. Mal. 359. 3-4: it is unlikely that either Malalas or CP is derived directly from Priscus (on whom, see Blockley, Historians i. 48-70). Nicephorus Callistus (xiv. 57, PG cxlvi. 1270B-1272C) has a similar muddled story (e.g. Alaric for Theodoric), which he attributes to Eustathius of Epiphania, an early 6th-c. historian (on whom, see Allen, 'Eustathius'). Eustathius appears to have read and garbled Priscus, and transmitted this version to Malalas whose account was then used by CP. Blockley prints this passage of CP (not the equivalent text of Malalas) as Priscus fr. 21, but this seems an optimistic assessment of an account probably derived at third hand; cf. Brunt, 'Epitomes', for the general problem of recovering lost texts from later citations.

[261] Cyrus the prefect: cf. Mal. 361. 14-362. 18, Theoph. 96. 33-97. 15, J. Nik. 84. 48-58. Malalas' version is fuller and diverges more from CP than in other shared stories from Theodosius' reign: e.g. Malalas states that Cyrus was stripped of

In this year in the month Audynaeus [Jan.] during the night of the 26th, Constantinople suffered from an earthquake from the so-called Troadesian porticoes to the bronze Tetrapylon for some time, so that no-one dared to remain at home but all fled outside the city, chanting litanies day and night. And the emperor chanted litanies together with the senate and the multitude and the clergy, barefoot for many days. For there was great peril, such as there had not been from the beginning of time, and some said that fire too had been seen in the heaven. Hence also the remembrance of the litany is celebrated annually even to the present day in the Campus, because of the forbearance of the

---

office on a concocted charge of paganism, and correctly adds that he was made bishop of Cotyaeum in Phrygia (cf. *Life* of Daniel the Stylite 31). Cameron ('Empress' 223) blames *CP* for the erroneous reference to Smyrna, but the suggestion is implausible since Theophanes, the Slavonic Malalas, and John of Nikiu, which are not derived from *CP*, share the error. In the Malalas tradition the Cyrus story is undated, but placed after the death of Attila: this arrangement has determined the incorrect placing of the story in *CP*. In *CP* the story opens with 'he says' (not in Mal.): although this appears to refer to Priscus, the account cannot safely be treated as a fragment of Priscus (cf. n. 260).

   Cyrus' career: see *PLRE* ii. 336-9, s.v. Cyrus 7, and Cameron, 'Empress' 221-5, 256-70; also D. J. Constantelos, 'Kyros Panopolites, Rebuilder of Constantinople', *GRBS* xii, 1971, 451-64. His dual prefecture probably only lasted for two years (439-41; though his urban prefecture, in fact his second, may have started before 439), but was still a most unusual conjunction of offices. He fell from favour towards the end of his sole consulship in 441, a victim, like the empress Eudocia, of the eunuch Chrysaphius. After Theodosius' death (perhaps that referred to here at the end of the story), Cyrus resigned his bishopric and returned to Cpl., where he died *c.*470.

   Lighting: not mentioned in other sources. At Antioch street lighting was provided at private expense, shopkeepers being responsible for maintaining lamps outside their premises (Jones, *LRE* 735); Cyrus presumably undertook to subsidize this expense at Cpl. (see B. Baldwin, *Byz.* l, 1980, 45 = *Studies* 282).

   Buildings: perhaps needed after recent fires and earthquakes; the chanting suggests that these were the chief source of Cyrus' popularity. Little evidence remains: a church to the Virgin can be ascribed to him (Theophylact viii. 8. 11; cf. Janin, *Églises* 193-5, Cameron, 'Empress' 240), an area in the west of the city bore his name (Janin, *Const.* 378-9), he was involved in the restoration of the baths of Achilles (cf. *ss.aa.* 433, 443), and may have built the walls along the Sea of Marmara (cf. n. 243).

   Christmas sermon: see Cameron, 'Empress' 243-5; T. E. Gregory, 'The Remarkable Christmas Homily of Kyros Panopolites', *GRBS* xvi, 1975, 317-24; B. Baldwin, 'Cyrus of Panopolis: a Remarkable Sermon and an Unremarkable Poem', *Vigiliae Christianae* xxxvi, 1982, 169-72 = *Studies* 339-42. It alluded to the contemporary theory, expounded by Proclus (patriarch of Cpl. 434-46) that the Virgin Mary conceived Christ through hearing the divine Word at the Annunciation.

beneficent God.    For amidst such great wrath no-one was killed. [262]

In this year Theodosius Augustus went out to ride, and while he was riding he fell from his horse; and having injured his spine, he entered by litter from the river Leucus, and when he had summoned his sister the lady Pulcheria, [p.590] he spoke to her concerning Marcian the former tribune.  And then again the same emperor Theodosius said to Marcian in the presence of Aspar and all the rest of the senators, 'It has been manifest to me that you must become emperor after me.'  And after some days the same Theodosius died, aged 51 years. [263]

And in the same year Chrysaphius the *spatharius* was slain at the gate of Melantias. [264]

---

[262] Earthquake: cf. Mal. 363. 20-364. 2 (giving the date, 26 Jan., but not the year); the *Syn. Eccl. Const.* (p. 425. 6) specifies that it was a Sunday.  CP has repeated the reference to the day and night litany (which is not in Mal.) from the account of the 447 earthquake.  Croke, 'Earthquakes', has shown that there was no earthquake in 450 (when 26 Jan. did not fall on a Sunday), and that the entry is a doublet for the 447 earthquake (when 26 Jan. *was* a Sunday).  This illustrates the author's method: most of the information recorded in *CP s.a.* 450 was derived from the Malalas tradition (Attila, Cyrus, earthquake, death of Theodosius), which preserved these notices (with others interspersed) in the same order but with no indication of year; in *CP* the first notice (Attila) was placed *s.a.* 450, probably because this was the date of Attila's embassy to Theodosius, and then followed by a sequence of Malalas information: Cyrus (correct date *c.*441/2), earthquake (447), and Theodosius' death (450).

Troadesian porticoes: probably so named because their marble came from the Troad, they flanked part of the western extension of the Mese between the Forum of Arcadius on the Xerolophus and the Constantinian walls.  Bronze Tetrapylon: located at an important crossroads on the Mese between the Fora of Constantine and Theodosius (Mango, *Const.* 28, 30-1 with n. 44).  Campus at the Hebdomon: modelled on the Campus Martius at Rome, see Janin, *Const.* 446-9.

[263] Death of Theodosius and succession of Marcian: cf. Mal. 366. 19-367. 5 (without the reference to the river Leucus, i.e. the Lycus which flowed through the western part of Cpl.); also Marc. Com.; Theoph. 103. 7-16 (giving Pulcheria credit for the appointment of Marcian).  Theodosius died on 28 July.

Marcian: *PLRE* ii. 714-15, s.v. Marcianus 8; he had been *domesticus* to Ardabur and his son Aspar the *magister militum* (*PLRE* ii. 164-9), whose increasing influence at court determined the choice of successor, in conjunction with the wishes of Pulcheria who had benefited from the withdrawal of Eudocia (see Cameron, 'Empress' 263-6).

[264] Death of Chrysaphius: cf. Marc. Com. (no reference to place; Pulcheria responsible for the execution), Mal. 368. 5-9 (beheaded by Marcian because of the testimonies of those injured by him, and as protector and patron of the Greens). The eunuch Chrysaphius (*PLRE* ii. 295-7) had dominated the last decade of Theodosius II's reign; as *spatharius* (the first attested holder of the position) he was captain of the bodyguard in the imperial *cubiculum* (Jones, *LRE* 567-8).

And in the same year Marcian was elevated as Augustus by the Circus at the Hebdomon, in the month Lous, on day 8 before Kalends of September [25 Aug.], a Thursday.[265] As soon as he became emperor, he married the sister of Emperor Theodosius the younger, the lady Pulcheria, who was a virgin aged 54 years. Marcian was 42nd Roman emperor for 7 years.[266]

In total, 5,966 years.

**451** Indiction 4, year 1, consulship of Marcian Augustus and Adelphius.

Pulcheria, the wife of Marcian the emperor, in accordance with a vision, found the remains of the Forty Saints martyred at Sebastea, hidden in the church of St. Thyrsus behind the *ambo*. And Caesarius, consul and prefect, built a church for them outside the Troadesian walls.[267]

## Olympiad 308

**452** Indiction 5, year 2, consulship of Sphoracius and Herculanus.

[p.591] In year 422 from the Ascension to heaven of the Lord, there took place in Chalcedon the fourth Synod of the 630 holy

Melantias Gate: location uncertain, see Mango, *Const.* 32; Melantias itself was a village on the Via Egnatia about 18 miles from Cpl. (cf. n. 459).

265 Elevation of Marcian: cf. Marc. Com. (no date or details). Mal. 367. 6-9 states that he was crowned by the senate, and provides a brief physical description. CP's expression 'by the Circus' (ἀπὸ τοῦ Κερκησίου) is obscure, and Dindorf (n. ad loc.) plausibly suggested it was a corruption of ἐξερκέτου, 'army' (cf. Leo's proclamation *s.a.* 457 for elevation by the army, ὑπὸ τοῦ ἐξερκέτου).

266 Marriage to Pulcheria and regnal length: cf. Mal. 367. 9-11 (reign of 6 years and 5 months).

267 **451** Relics of 40 Martyrs: Sozomen (ix. 2) records that during the patriarchate of Proclus (434–46), Caesarius built a church to St. Thyrsus to serve as his wife's burial place; the relics were discovered near the *ambo* after Pulcheria had a vision, and were placed next to the relics of St. Thyrsus in the same church. Sozomen's account is preferable to CP's: (i) Caesarius, consul in 397 (*PLRE* ii. 249, s.v. Caesarius 1 = Caesarius 6, *PLRE* i. 171), is unlikely still to have been alive in 451; (ii) there is no other evidence for this church of the 40 Martyrs, in spite of Janin's attempt to distinguish it from St. Thyrsus (*Églises* 482-3, 247-8). The Troadesian walls (i.e. the Constantinian walls near the Mese, cf. n. 262), were near the Helenianae, the location attested for St. Thyrsus, which supports the identification of the two churches, cf. Tiftixoglu, 'Helenianai' n. 78 at 97-8.

fathers against the abominable Eutyches and Dioscorus, bishop of Alexandria, who were indeed demoted.[268]

**453** Indiction 6, year 3, consulship of Vincomalus and Opilio.

In the time of these consuls the lady Pulcheria died.[269]

In the time of the aforementioned consuls Vincomalus and Opilio, while Valentinian and Marcian Augusti were emperors, in the month Peritius, on day 12 before Kalends of March [18 Feb.], in the middle week of Lent, in Syromacedonian year 763, Antiochene year 501, and year 425 after the holy Precursor, Prophet, and Baptist John was beheaded, his precious head was found in the Emesene city.[270]

**454** Indiction 7, year 4, consulship of Aetius and Studius.

In this year, when Anthemus was emperor in Rome, the

---

[268]   **452** Synod of Chalcedon: cf. Marc. Com. *s.a.* 451 (correct); the council took place in Oct., indiction 5, in the 14th month after the proclamation of Marcian (Theoph. 105. 21-3). In *CP* the indiction and regnal years are correct, the consular year one year late. The author overlooked the fact that Marcian's 2nd regnal year and indiction 5 both began in 451, consulship of Marcian and Adelphius. The Ascension date is calculated from AD 31, the usual date for the Crucifixion in *CP* (cf. *ss.aa.* 325, 381, with nn. 42, 160, for the Synods of Nicaea and Constantinople), but relates to the incorrect consular year, and so is one year out; this suggests that the chronicler himself made this calculation (cf. Introduction n. 44).

The council partially reversed the decisions of Second Ephesus in 449 (cf. *CP s.a.* 450 with n. 258), where Dioscorus and Eutyches had triumphed. Chalcedon condemned both Nestorian and Monophysite doctrine, endorsed a doctrinal document drawn up by Pope Leo, and reasserted the superior position in the east of Cpl., but many eastern Christians saw its decisions as an unfortunate compromise with Nestorian dual Christology.   The result was to increase divisions within the church; see further Bury, *HLRE* [2] i. 356-9; Stein, *BE* i. 312-15; Chadwick, *Church* 203-5; Young, *Nicaea* 229-40.

In view of the contentious nature of the council, the very brief notice in *CP* may reflect a lack of commitment by the author to Chalcedonian doctrine before the revisions of the 6th c.; note also the lack of criticism of the 'Robber Synod', 2nd Ephesus, *s.a.* 450, and see Introduction p. xxvi.

[269]   **453** Death of Pulcheria: cf. Marc. Com., mentioning her foundation of St. Laurence; also Mal. 368. 18-19, Theoph. 106. 25-9.

[270]   Head of John the Baptist: Marcellinus (*s.a.* 453) preserves a long account of the invention of the relic at Emesa, dated to 24 Feb. in the middle week of Lent. However, Easter 453 fell on 12 April, so that the middle week of Lent began on 15 March, whereas in 452, when Easter fell on 23 March, the middle week started on 24 Feb.   The date of 452 is further supported by a discrepancy in the dating formula: Easter 452 fell in the Syromacedonian (i.e. Seleucid) year 763, although Easter 453 fell in year 501 of the Antiochene Era (see Grumel, *Chronologie* 215, 243, 320). *CP s.a.* 391 records an alternative version of the invention, when the head was deposited in the church of the Baptist at the Hebdomon on 18 Feb., which explains *CP's* incorrect date in this passage.

church of St. Thomas, which is named the Apostoleum, was founded by him near the Boraidion.[271]

455 Indiction 8, year 5, the 8th consulship of Valentinian Augustus and that of Anthemus.

In this year Valentinian Augustus was slain in Rome [p.592] between two laurels, and Maximus was elevated as emperor, and was himself also slain in the same year.[272] And Zinzerich king of the Africans entered Rome and captured Eudoxia, the wife of Valentinian, and her two daughters, Placidia and Honoria; after a short time Leo the emperor ransomed them from captivity. But Zinzerich retained Honoria as bride for Honarich his son.[273]

---

[271] 454 Anthemius: Augustus of the west 467–72, PLRE ii. 96-8, s.v. Anthemius 3. In 453/4 Anthemius married Marcian's daughter Euphemia, and this may have occasioned a summary of other events in Anthemius' life (cf. Mal. 368. 9-12); in 455 he was consul. The exact date of the construction of Anthemius' church is unknown, but it was during Marcian's reign (the notice is wrongly repeated s.a. 468, CP p. 598. 1-2, where the church is also described as 'that of Anthemius').

Church of St. Thomas: CP incorrectly implies that this was at Rome, whereas it was at or near Cpl. The church is most naturally identified with the church of St. Thomas 'in the quarter of Anthemius' near the cistern of Mocius (Janin, Églises 251). However, the area of the Boraïdon has been located near the harbour of Julian on the basis of a reference in John of Antioch's account (fr. 218f. 5) of the overthrow of Phocas in 610 (Janin, Const. 325-6); in this vicinity there was a church of St. Thomas 'in the quarter of Amantius' (Janin, Églises 248-50). But the reference in John of Antioch, though indecisive, might indicate that the Boraïdon was further west, perhaps overlooking the harbour of Caesarius/ Theodosius; this would support the natural identification with the church in the quarter of Anthemius (cf. Tiftixoglu, 'Helenianai' 86-7). Janin, however, located the church of St. Thomas recorded by CP at the suburb of Boradion on the eastern shore of the Bosporus near Kanlica (Monastères 17, Const. 484). The name Boraïdon is traditionally connected with Justinian's nephew Boraïdes; if this connection is correct, the reference is anachronistic in this 5th-c. context.

[272] 455 Death of Valentinian: he was killed (on 16 March) in the Campus Martius by Optila and Thraustila, two dependents of Aetius who had been murdered by Valentinian in 454, cf. Marc. Com.; also Mal. 360. 20-3. The 'two laurels' was apparently a landmark in the Campus Martius (mentioned also in this context by one version of Prosper's Chronicle, CM i. 483-4, with app. crit.).

Maximus: PLRE ii. 749-51, s.v. Maximus 22; he had instigated the murder of Valentinian, but was killed on 31 May in his third month of rule (Marc. Com.) during the Vandal attack on Rome. John of Antioch fr. 201 describes these events at length, probably following Priscus; see also Bury, HLRE [2] i. 298-300.

[273] Vandal attack: cf. Marc. Com., alleging that Geiseric (Zinzerich) was invited by Eudoxia herself, who objected to Maximus forcing himself on her as husband; Theophanes (108. 3-109. 9) also preserves a detailed account. See further Bury, HLRE [2] i. 323-6.

Placidia: although Placidia's ransom is also mentioned s.a. 464 (p. 594. 6-7),

Olympiad 309

**456** Indiction 9, year 6, consulship of Varanes and John.

The emperor Marcian favoured the Blue faction, not only in Constantinople, but also everywhere. And when there was a disturbance from the members of the Green faction, he promulgated his sacred constitution that Greens should not hold public or administrative posts for 3 years.[274]

**457** Indiction 10, year 7, consulship of Constantine and Rufus.

In the time of these consuls Marcian Augustus died, aged 65 years.[275] And Leo the Great was elevated as emperor by the army, in the month Peritius, on day 7 before Ides of February [7 Feb.], and he was emperor for 16 years.[276]					In total, 5,982.

Leo was 43rd Roman emperor for 16 years.

In total, 5,982.

**458 [p.593]** Indiction 11, year 1, consulship of Leo Augustus and Majorian.

**459** Indiction 12, year 2, consulship of Ricimer and Patricius.

In the time of these consuls Theodosius was promoted city

---

Geiseric probably handed her back voluntarily in connection with his diplomatic offensive in 461/2. (Theophanes 110. 5-8 dates her return to 456/7, Malalas 368. 1-4 simply to the reign of Marcian.)

Honoria: in fact Eudocia, elder daughter of Valentinian III and Eudoxia (*PLRE* ii. 410-12, s.v. Eudoxia 2; 407-8, s.v. Eudocia 1), who was already betrothed to Geiseric's son Hunneric.

[274] **456** Factions: cf. Mal. 368. 13-16. Circus factions, and factional allegiance, became more important at Cpl. during the reign of Theodosius II, who had lavished favours on the Green faction (Mal. 351. 5-352. 7), which had his favourite the eunuch Chrysaphius as its patron (Mal. 368. 8). For discussion, see Cameron, *Factions* 288-9, who perhaps unduly minimizes the practical consequences of such patronage of a particular faction (which might have included preference for public and administrative office), and hence underestimates the importance of the ban.

[275] **457** Death of Marcian: on 27 Jan.; cf. Mal. 368. 16-18, Marc. Com., Theoph. 109. 23-4 (with incorrect Roman date). According to Malalas his death was caused by gangrene, five months after his feet had become inflamed because of his anger at the Green riot (which is recorded in the same notice as the imperial succession). Theodore Lector 367 states that he died after participating in the procession to the Hebdomon on 26 Jan. (commemorating the 447 earthquake): for discussion, see B. Croke, 'The Date and Circumstances of Marcian's Decease, A.D. 457', *Byz.* xlviii, 1978, 5-9.

[276] Accession of Leo: cf. Mal. 369. 1-2 (no date); as with Marcian's accession in 450, Malalas records that the emperor was crowned by the senate. Const. Porph. *de caer.* i. 91 preserves a detailed account of the sequence of events and ceremonial in which senate, army, and patriarch were involved.

prefect; and he built the Augustaeum at the side of the Great Church.[277]

And in this year Aspar the *magister militum* began to build the very large cistern near the old wall.[278]

## Olympiad 310

**460** Indiction 13, year 3, consulship of Apollonius and Magnus.

**461** Indiction 14, year 4, consulship of Dagalaïphus and Severianus.

**462** Indiction 15, year 5, the 2nd consulship of Leo Augustus and that of Serpentius.[279]

**463** Indiction 1, year 6, consulship of Vivianus and Basilius.[280]

In the time of these consuls there was a shortage of bread, so that one loaf was sold for three *folles*.[281]

## Olympiad 311

**464** Indiction 2, year 7, consulship of Rusticius and Olybrius.

In this year St. Symeon the Stylite died, when Ardabur the patrician, the son of Aspar the *magister militum*, was *comes*

---

[277] **459** Augustaeum: the open space between the imperial Palace and St. Sophia, it had received its name under Constantine (Mal. 321. 10-12; CP p. 529. 1-4); Theodosius (*PLRE* ii. 1101, s.v. Theodosius 12: nothing else is known) probably built or restored the surrounding porticoes (Mango, *Brazen House* 46, Janin, *Const.* 59-62).

[278] Cistern of Aspar: in the north-west of the city on the fifth hill, Janin, *Const.* 204-5, Mango, *Const.* 49; the old wall is that of Constantine. Aspar: cf. n. 263.

[279] **462** Consuls: eastern lists record this as a sole consulship of Leo, western lists as Leo and Libius Severus (a usurper proclaimed in the west by Ricimer), see Bagnall, *Consuls* 458-9.

[280] **463** *cos. post.*: Basilius is not recognized in other eastern lists. Marc. Com. has Felix, his 'one inexplicable error', Bagnall, *Consuls* 461.

[281] Bread shortage: no parallels for this notice.

*Follis*: its early history is disputed, see Hendy, *Economy* 339-41. The *follis* originated in the late 3rd c. as a sealed bag containing a specified quantity of base metal coin, but by the early 5th c. at least, the term was being used for a coin. In 498 Anastasius reformed the base metal currency of the eastern empire, probably on the basis of numismatic developments in Vandal Africa or Ostrogothic Italy (ibid. 476-92), and established the relationship of the *follis* to the gold *solidus*. The value of a *follis* in 463 is unknown and it is not impossible that the term has been introduced here anachronistically. CP *s.a.* 618 mentions the introduction of a charge of '3 coins' to beneficiaries of the state ration, while *s.a.* 626 it records that bread cost 3 *folles* before an attempted price rise: see nn. 449, 456.

*Orientis.* And when the Antiochenes chanted and demanded the body of the righteous man, the same Ardabur sent **[p.594]** a Gothic guard and brought the body of St. Symeon to Antioch the Great, and a great church was founded there as his martyrium.[282]

Olybrius was sent to Rome by the emperor Leo and, under compulsion from the Romans there, he was there elected emperor and had as his wife Placidia, the one who had been ransomed, that is to say rescued, from captivity. They founded St. Euphemia's, in the quarter of Olybrius. And by her Olybrius begat Juliana, who became wife of Areobindus the great who fought in single combat in Persia; from them Olybrius the younger was begotten.[283]

465 Indiction 3, year 8, consulship of Basiliscus and Armenarichus.

---

[282] 464 Symeon Stylites: cf. Mal. 369. 10-16 (undated). Symeon died on his column at Qalat Seman (near modern Aleppo in Syria) in 459 (H. Leitzmann, *Das Leben des Heiligen Symeon Stylites*, Texte und Untersuchungen xxxii/4, 231-3); *CP's* dating error was probably caused by reliance on the undated notice in Malalas. For accounts of Symeon's career, see Leitzmann, op. cit.

Ardabur: *magister militum per Orientem* 453–66, see *PLRE* ii. 135–7, s.v. Ardabur 1; he is alleged to have tried once to shoot Symeon as an imposter. Popular enthusiasm for the saint dictated that special measures be taken to prevent disturbances arising from a scramble for relics. The Antiochenes wanted the body as a protection after an earthquake had damaged their walls (cf. Evag. i. 13, and see further Downey, *Antioch* 480-2).

[283] Olybrius: *PLRE* ii. 796-8, s.v. Olybrius 6. He was dispatched to Rome in 472; shortly afterwards the emperor Anthemius was murdered by Ricimer, the Germanic *magister militum*: Mal. 373. 9-375. 11 has a detailed account; cf. also Theoph. 118. 8-10, and see Bury, *HLRE* [2] i. 339-40. Olybrius had been betrothed, or possibly even married, to Placidia in 454/5, only shortly before Geiseric attacked Rome and captured her, with her sister Eudocia and her mother Eudoxia; the date of her release is unknown, but 461/2 is a plausible guess, cf. n. 273.

Church of St. Euphemia: located in Cpl. (though the context in *CP* might suggest Rome); Janin, *Églises* 124-6. The quarter of Olybrius, situated between the Capitol and the Holy Apostles, was the location of Anicia Juliana's subsequent foundation, St. Polyeuctus: Janin, *Const.* 398-9.

Anicia Juliana: born post 461/2, married to Areobindus in 478/9, see *PLRE* ii. 635-6, s.v. Iuliana 3 (ibid. 1309, stemma 3 for the family tree). This Areobindus (*PLRE* ii. 143-4, s.v. Areobindus 1) was in fact the grandson of the Areobindus who fought in single combat against the Persians in 421 (Mal. 364. 3-21).

Olybrius the younger: *PLRE* ii. 795, s.v. Olybrius 3.

This notice, of which nothing can be proved to relate to this year, may have been inserted simply because Olybrius was currently consul (cf. *CP s.a.* 468 for repetition of the notice about Anthemius in his consular year); alternatively it might have been the date of Anicia Juliana's birth, to which a reference (now lost) could have attracted the other family information.

In the time of these consuls Menas, who was prefect of the Watch, being accused of evil deeds, was questioned in the Hippodrome by the senate, and at the command of the emperor a boy tripped him up and threw him on his face in the deep part at the Hippodrome turning-post, and the people took hold of him and began to drag him. And the officials, when they saw what had happened, withdrew in fear. And they dragged the man as far as the estate of Studius; and a certain Goth took a stone and struck him on the ear and killed him. And his corpse was dragged by the people as far as the sea.[284]

[p.595] After thirty days, 8 regions of the city were burnt as a result of God's wrath in the month Gorpiaeus, on 2nd September, a Wednesday in indiction 3, on the Feast-day of St. Mamas.[285]

**466** Indiction 4, year 9, the 3rd and sole consulship of Leo Augustus.[286]

**467** Indiction 5, year 10, consulship of Pusaeus and John.

In the time of these consuls Isocasius the philosopher and *quaestor* was accused of being a Hellene; he was descended by ancestry from Aegae in Cilicia, but was a landowner and inhabitant of Antioch the Great, who had discharged many offices with glory and was a man of great intellect. And he was arrested at the command of the emperor because of the rioting then current in Constantinople, stripped of his rank and

---

[284]  465 Menas: nothing else is known about this incident which, however, illustrates the importance of the Hippodrome as the setting for political theatre. prefect of the Watch: *praefectus vigilum*, a subordinate of the city prefect and responsible for the maintenance of order; see Jones, *LRE* 691-2.

Estate of Studius: site of the famous church and monastery dedicated to John the Baptist, see Müller-Wiener, *Bildlexikon* 147-52, C. Mango, 'The Date of the Studius Basilica at Istanbul', *BMGS* iv, 1978, 115-22. It was situated at the western end of the city, close to the Golden Gate and the Sea of Marmara (id., *Const.* 47).

[285]  Fire: cf. Marc. Com. The correct date was 464 (Sept. of indiction 3: 2 Sept. fell on a Wednesday in 464). Theophanes 112. 19-24, recording the same fire (wrongly dated to indiction 15, i.e. 461), notes that it extended from the Neorion (dockyard on the Golden Horn) to the church of St. Thomas in the quarter of Amantius, located near the harbour of Julian on the Sea of Marmara (Janin, *Églises* 248-50). Evagrius ii. 13 describes the genesis and extent of this fire, one of the most destructive in the history of Cpl.: it spread westwards as far as the church of Homonoia (located in the ninth region, Janin, *Églises* 382) and the Forum Tauri (i.e. Forum of Theodosius, cf. n. 310), so that the eight eastern regions of the city were affected. See further n. 296.

[286]  Consuls: three western lists name Tatianus as Leo's colleague, see Bagnall, *Consuls* 466-7.

conducted to Chalcedon on the far side from Constantinople, to Theophilus governor of Bithynia, who was the one who took his testimony. But Jacob the Cilician, who was the chief physician in the city and was called 'the Cooler', appealed to the emperor. For this Leo loved the same Cooler, as did all the senate and the city, because he was an excellent doctor and philosopher, for whom the senators had even set up his effigies in the Zeuxippon. This man entreated the emperor, asking him that Isocasius be examined in Constantinople by the senate and the praetorian prefect and not by a provincial governor, since he had held the rank of *quaestor*. And the emperor Leo was persuaded and ordered [p.596] that Isocasius be brought from Chalcedon; he was brought forward in the Zeuxippon and examined by the praetorian prefect and consul Pusaeus. And the same Pusaeus spoke as follows against Isocasius, who came out naked before the curtain, his arms bound behind his back: 'Do you see yourself, Isocasius, in what condition you stand?'. And Isocasius said in reply, 'I see, and I am not dismayed. For being mortal, I have fallen upon mortal misfortunes. But pass judgement upon me with justice, as you used to pass judgement in my company.' And when they heard Isocasius, the people of Byzantium who were standing and watching acclaimed the emperor Leo many times. And they carried off the same Isocasius and brought him from the Zeuxippon to the Great Church, and he was catechized and baptized and sent to his own land.[287]

And the same most sacred emperor ordered that Lord's Days

---

[287]  **467** Isocasius: cf. Mal. 369. 17-371. 4 for the same story with minor differences, omitting the reference to disorder in Cpl.; also Theoph. 115. 9-18 (abbreviated version). For his career, see *PLRE* ii. 633-4. The *quaestor* was the imperial adviser most closely connected with the formulation of imperial law, see Jill Harries, 'The Roman Imperial *Quaestor* from Constantine to Theodosius II', *JRS* lxxviii, 1988, 148-72. In 468 Leo banned pagans from the legal profession (*Cod. Iust.* i. 4. 15): the attack on Isocasius may have been a prelude to this.

Jacob: *PLRE* ii. 582-3, s.v. Iacobus 3. He was not a Cilician: this error is not in Malalas, who instead calls him *comes* at this point; Jacob's mother was Greek, his father Damascene, and he was born in Alexandria. His nickname 'the Cooler' derived from his prescription of cold baths, and his provision of free medical advice to the poor earned him great popularity. Like Isocasius, he was a pagan.

Theophilus: otherwise unknown, *PLRE* ii. 1109, s.v. Theophilus 6.

Pusaeus: (ibid. 930), praetorian prefect in 465 and 467 (perhaps continuously), when he would have presided jointly with the *quaestor* Isocasius over the special court of appeal established by Theodosius in 440 (Jones, *LRE* 505-6).

Zeuxippon: the large bath complex between the Great Palace and St. Sophia may have been chosen as the venue for the trial because other grand public buildings had been damaged in the fire of 464.

should be days of rest, on this matter promulgating his sacred law that neither flute nor lyre nor any other musical instrument should sound on the Lord's Day, but all lie idle. And every man complied.[288]

In this year he murdered inside the Palace Aspar the patrician and leader of the senate, who had plotted usurpation, and in a senatorial session his sons Ardabur and Patricius, who were themselves also senators, and he mutilated their bodies. And there was unrest in Constantinople; for they had a multitude of Goths as well as *comites* and other servants [p.597] loyal to them. And so a certain Goth from Aspar's own retinue, a *comes* named Ostrys, entered the Palace with other Goths firing arrows, and when an engagement ensued between the excubitors and Ostrys the *comes*, many were cut down. And being surrounded, he saw that he was defeated and fled taking Aspar's concubine, who was a very lovely and rich Goth. She left with him for Thrace on horseback, and they ravaged the estates. The Byzantines chanted concerning him, 'A dead man has no friend, save only Ostrys.'[289]

The same emperor Leo carried out a great persecution against the followers of the doctrine of the Arian Exokionites. And he sent edicts everywhere that they should not have churches or meet together at all.[290]

In the same year there appeared in the heaven a very great

---

[288] Observance of Sunday: cf. Mal. 371. 5-8, Theod. Lect. 377; the law is preserved in *Cod. Iust.* iii. 12. 9, dated 9 Dec. 469.

[289] Overthrow of Aspar: cf. Mal. 371. 9-372. 2 (undated); also Theoph. 117. 11-32. The Alan Aspar, a key figure in the choice of Marcian and Leo as emperors, found his dominance under threat in 466, when the Isaurian Zeno had exposed the treachery of his son Ardabur with the Persians and received Leo's daughter Ariadne in marriage. However, he was not overthrown until 471 (Marc. Com. s.a.); see *PLRE* ii. 167-8; Bury, *HLRE* [2] i. 316-20. The incorrect date in *CP* was again caused by its use of an undated sequence of information from Malalas.

Ostrys: *PLRE* ii. 814-15, a commander in Aspar's army in Thrace in 467 (Priscus fr. 49), who should probably be identified with Triarius, father of Theodoric Strabo (we owe this point to Peter Heather).

Excubitors: created by Leo as a small (300 strong) but effective new element in the Palace guard, and probably dominated at this time by Zeno's fellow Isaurians; see Jones, *LRE* 658-9; Haldon, *Praetorians* 136-9; Mary Whitby, 'Ceremony' 483-8.

[290] Persecution of Arians: cf. Mal. 372. 3-5 (occasioned by the Arianism of Aspar and Ardabur). Other anti-heretical legislation of Leo is preserved at *Cod. Iust.* i. 5. 9-11.

Exokionites: see n. 157.

sign, called by some a trumpet, by some a spear, and by some a beam; and it appeared for some days.[291]

In the same year Anthemius became emperor and left for Rome; and his laureate image entered Constantinople under Diapherentius, city prefect.[292]

## Olympiad 312

**468** Indiction 6, year 11, the 2nd and sole consulship of Anthemius Augustus.

[p.598] This Anthemius built the church of St. Thomas the Apostle, called that of Anthemius, near the quarter of Borraidon.[293]

In the time of the aforementioned consul, Dinzerich son of Attila was slain by Anagastes the *magister militum per Thraciam*, and his head entered Constantinople while chariot races were being held; it was paraded along the Mese, and carried away to the Xylocircus and fixed on a pole. And all the city went out to view it for a number of days.[294]

**469** Indiction 7, year 12, consulship of Zeno and Marcian.

In this year it rained ash instead of rain in Constantinople; the ash lay on the tiles to a palm's depth. And all trembled, chanting litanies and saying, 'There was fire and it was quenched, and ash

---

[291] Sign in heaven: cf. Theoph. 115. 1-2 (under Leo's 9th year = 465/6). Presumably a comet.

[292] Appointment of Anthemius: cf. Marc. Com.; also Theoph. 114. 21-4 (Leo's 8th year, 464/5). Anthemius, son-in-law of Marcian, had proved a competent commander in the Balkans, cf. n. 271; at this time Geiseric was urging the appointment of Olybrius (married to Placidia, the sister of Eudocia who was Geiseric's daughter-in-law, cf. nn. 273, 283), and Anthemius was clearly intended to forestall the Vandal king's imperial plans: see Bury, *HLRE* [2] i. 334-5.

Laureate image: this was brought from Rome by Heliocrates, and welcomed at Cpl. by Diapherentius, city prefect, and Dioscorus, an ex-prefect; the ceremony is described in Const. Porph. *de caer*. i. 87 (i. 395. 9-396. 7); cf. S. MacCormack, 'Change and Continuity in Late Antiquity: the Ceremony of *Adventus*', *Historia* xxi, 1972, 721-52, at 746-9, and for the analogous reception in Egypt of an image of Justin II, L. S. B. MacCoull, 'The Panegyric on Justin II by Dioscorus of Aphrodito', *Byz*. liv, 1984, 575-85.

[293] **468** Church of St. Thomas: a doublet for the notice *s.a.* 454, inserted here because of Anthemius' consulship.

[294] Death of Dengizich: leader of the Huns *c.*460-9, *PLRE* ii. 354-5. For his attacks on the empire in 466/7, see Priscus frr. 46, 48. Anagastes: *PLRE* ii. 75-6. Xylocircus: see n. 196.

Marc. Com. *s.a.* 469 records the arrival of Dengizich's head: this marks the end of the section in which parallels can be traced between *CP* and Marc. Com.

was found since God was beneficent', in the month Dius, November 11th.[295]

In this year there was a great conflagration in Constantinople, such as never before; for it was burnt from sea to sea. And Leo the emperor departed in terror to the far side to St. Mamas, and stayed in retirement there for six months, and he built there a little harbour and a portico, and the place is named thus, New Portico.[296]

**470** Indiction 8, year 13, consulship of Gordian and Severus.[297]

**471** [p.599] Indiction 9, year 14, the 4th consulship of Leo and that of Probianus.

Olympiad 313

**472** Indiction 10, year 15, consulship of Marcian and Festus.[298]

**473** Indiction 11, year 16, the 5th and sole consulship of Leo.

After the death of Leo the Great, Leo II Augustus was 43rd Roman emperor for 1 year.[299]                                    In total, 5,983.

**474** Indiction 12, year 1, sole consulship of Leo II.

This Leo was induced by his own mother the *nobilissima* Ariadne so that when Zeno the *magister militum* and patrician, his father, did obeisance to him as emperor, he placed an imperial crown on the head of the same Zeno; and Zeno Codisseus the Isaurian was emperor together with his offspring Leo for a short time. And in the 11th month of his consulship

---

[295] **469** Rain of ash: cf. Mal. 372. 6-10 (undated); Theoph. 119. 29-33 (Leo's 17th year, 473/4). The dust was caused by the eruption of Vesuvius in 472, and the event was commemorated on 6 Nov. (Marc. Com. *s.a.*; cf. also Croke, 'Earthquakes'). The litany alludes to the unquenchable fire of hell (e.g. Isaiah 66. 24, Mark 9. 42-8), which God's mercy has extinguished.

[296] Fire: cf. Mal. 372. 11-16 (undated). This resembles the fire of 2 Sept. 464 (already recorded *s.a.* 465), which burnt from the Golden Horn to the Sea of Marmara (cf. Evag. ii. 13). The identification of the two fires is supported by the report in the *Life* of Daniel the Stylite (45-6) that after a fire (datable to 464) Leo resided for a time at the palace of St. Michael, which can be equated with the palace of St. Mamas at Beşiktaş on the Bosporus (Janin, *Const.* 141, 473-4), not far from the oratory to the Archangel Michael at Anaplus.

For both notices in this year CP has again been chronologically misled by reliance on the undated sequence of notices in Malalas.

[297] **470** *cos. prior*: Iordanes.

[298] **472** *cos. prior*: Bagnall (*Consuls* 479) distinguishes this Marcian from the consul of 469; identified *PLRE* ii. 717-18, s.v. Marcianus 17.

[299] **473** Accession of Leo II: Leo I died on 18 Jan., and was succeeded by his grandson, the son of Zeno, cf. Mal. 375. 19-376. 7 (wrong date for Leo's death), Theoph. 119. 11-13, and see *PLRE* ii. 664-5, s.v. Leo 7.

CP had correctly recorded that Leo I was 43rd Roman emperor (*s.a.* 457).

Leo II fell sick in the month Dius, which is also November, and died aged 17 years, as Nestorianus the most learned chronicler wrote in his history up to Leo II. [300]

Zeno Augustus was 44th Roman emperor for 17 years.

In total, 6,000.

**475** Indiction 13, year 1, the 2nd and sole consulship of Zeno Augustus.

**[p.600]**              Olympiad 314

**476** Indiction 14, year 2, consulship of Basiliscus and Armatus.[301]

**477** Indiction 15, year 3, post-consulship of Basiliscus and Armatus.[302]

Zeno the emperor had some matter requested of him by his mother-in-law Verina, and since he did not grant it was the object of intrigue by her; and fearing lest he be slain by one of those in the Palace (for his mother-in-law Verina also lived with him in the Palace), he stayed in retirement at Chalcedon; from there he fled by post-horse and departed to Isauria, even though he was emperor. The empress Ariadne caught up with him, after secretly fleeing to Isauria from her own mother, and lived there together with her husband. And after the flight of Zeno the emperor and Ariadne the Augusta, the lady Verina immediately appointed an emperor by crowning Basiliscus her own brother. And the same Basiliscus was emperor for two years, which are reckoned together with the first and subsequent years of Zeno.

---

[300] **474** Reign of Leo II: cf. Mal. 376. 8-20, with the addition of 9 Peritius, i.e. Feb., as the date of Zeno's coronation, and Antiochene dates for Leo II's consulship and death, correctly said to be at the age of 7. Theophanes 120. 1-7 adds that Leo, held by Verina and Ariadne, crowned Zeno in the imperial box in the Hippodrome. Zeno's original name had been Tarasicodissa (vel. sim.).

Nestorianus: also mentioned in Malalas, but otherwise unknown, apart from an earlier reference in Malalas (324. 11-13) in the context of the death of Constantine.

[301] **476** cos. prior: eastern lists fail to record that this was Basiliscus' second consulship (first in 465), see Bagnall, Consuls 486-7. The MS reading, which is consistent with CP's usual formula, is incorrectly reported in the Bonn text (cf. n. 302).

[302] **477** Consuls: CP accurately records this as post cons. of Basiliscus and Armatus (the MS reading is misreported in the Bonn text); CP is in general less confused by the post-consular formula than is suggested by Bagnall, Consuls 56.

And Basiliscus, as soon as he became emperor, crowned his son Marcus as emperor, and the two were emperors together.[303]

**478** Indiction 1, year 4, sole consulship of Illus.

In this year Zeno the emperor returned with a great throng from Isauria. And when Basiliscus learnt of the **[p.601]** return of the emperor Zeno, he sent Armatus the *magister militum praesentalis*, together with all the forces of the army which he had in Thrace and in Constantinople and the Palace, after making him swear by the Holy Baptism that he would not turn traitor. And Armatus crossed over, taking the countless multitude of the army. And, learning of this in advance, Zeno the emperor sent to the same Armatus, promising him many things, including the post of *magister militum praesentalis* for his lifetime, and to make his son Caesar. And Armatus was won over by Zeno the emperor, turned traitor, and was discovered to be on the side of Zeno the emperor: he did not go to meet Zeno as he approached, but decided to depart by another road. But the emperor Zeno, together with his forces, after setting out by the road from Isauria, crossed from Pylae as it is called, and came to the Palace in Constantinople together with his own men, and was welcomed by the armies and the senate. Basiliscus the emperor suddenly heard that Zeno the emperor had set out and come to the Palace and that everyone had welcomed him, including the lady Verina, Zeno's mother-in-law; Basiliscus took his wife and children and fled to the Great Church of Constantinople to the great baptistery. But the most sacred Zeno displayed the Hippodrome banner, immediately went up, watched the games and was welcomed by the people of the city. And immediately the **[p.602]** emperor sent to the Great Church and removed from Basiliscus and his wife and their son all the imperial insignia, and expelled him with his children and wife, after they had received a guarantee that they would not be beheaded. And the same emperor Zeno sent him and those with

---

303 Flight of Zeno and usurpation of Basiliscus: cf. <u>Mal. 377. 5-378. 11</u> for the same account, adding that Verina appointed her brother Basiliscus and his nephew Armatus as consuls. Zeno withdrew to Chalcedon and thence to Isauria on 9 Jan. 475 (John of Antioch fr. 210), and returned to Cpl. in Aug. 476. *CP* was perhaps misled by the incorrect date in Malalas, where the notice is prefaced, 'After 2 years and 10 months of his reign...' The revolt was inspired by the ambitions of Leo's widow Verina and by general dislike of Zeno as an Isaurian: see Bury, *HLRE* [2] i. 389-91, Stein, *BE* i. 363-4.

Basiliscus: *PLRE* ii. 212-14, s.v. Basiliscus 2. Theophanes 121. 1-3 records his proclamation (in the Campus) and imperial appointments; his son Marcus was proclaimed Caesar. For the inclusion of Basiliscus' regnal years with Zeno's, cf. Mal. 380. 19-20, Theoph. 120. 8-9.

him to the fort of Limnae in Cappadocia. And they were thrown into one tower of the fort and the door was walled up, and the tower and fort itself were guarded by soldiers and a great multitude of Isaurians. And the same Basiliscus and his wife and their children surrendered their souls by starving, and were entombed there in the same tower of Limnae.[304]

479 Indiction 2, year 5, the 3rd and sole consulship of Zeno Augustus.

Olympiad 315

480 Indiction 3, year 6, sole consulship of Basilius.
481 Indiction 4, year 7, sole consulship of Placita.[305]
482 Indiction 5, year 8, consulship of Trocondes and Severianus.
483 Indiction 6, year 9, sole consulship of Faustus.[306]

Olympiad 316

484 Indiction 7, year 10, consulship of Theodoric and Venantius.

In this year the emperor Zeno made Caesar the son of Armatus the *magister militum praesentalis*, whose name was Basiliscus, and [p.603] sat with him to watch the games; and the emperor

---

[304] 478 Return of Zeno: cf. Mal. 378. 17-380. 17 for the same account, with some minor additions including the correct date (indiction 14: AD 476), and Zeno's reliance on the support of the Green faction. Theophanes (121. 3-122. 30, 124. 10-125. 2) supplies details about the reign and fate of Basiliscus (emperor 475–6): he had made himself unpopular by giving strong support to the Monophysites and downgrading the importance of the patriarch of Cpl. He also antagonized Illus, an Isaurian commander and supporter of his coup who had been sent to oppose Zeno in the east; Verina, who had hoped to place her lover Patricius on the throne, was also disenchanted, while Armatus (*PLRE* ii. 148-9) may have been concerned at the publicity given to his affair with Basiliscus' wife Zenonis. Zeno exploited the Hippodrome (where a flag was used to signify the holding of games) to demonstrate the strength, vocal and numerical, of his support: the popular chanting would easily have been heard by Basiliscus in St. Sophia. See Bury, *HLRE* [2] i. 391-3; also Croke, 'Basiliscus'.

Pylae: on the Gulf of Nicomedia just east of Yalova, it served as the major port linking Cpl. with the main eastern highways. Limnae: situated to the east of Sasina, near modern Gölcük (30 miles south of Nevşehir); Theophanes 124. 32 calls the place Cucusus.

[305] 481 Consul: Placidus.

[306] 483 Faustus: sole consul, proclaimed in the west; no consul was proclaimed in the east (though Marc. Com. also records Faustus). In 483–90 and 493–4 *CP* (often Marc. Com. as well) records western consuls who were not widely recognized in the east: see Bagnall, *Consuls ss.aa.* for details.

and the Caesar saw the charioteers.   But the emperor Zeno
reckoned that Armatus the *magister militum praesentalis*, the
father of the Caesar, had perjured himself since he had sworn to
Basiliscus by the Holy Baptism that he would not betray him:
'He was won over by me and betrayed him, and Basiliscus died.
How will he preserve loyalty to my sovereignty? For shortly, if
his son the Caesar grows to manhood, assuredly he will do me
wrong too. I did not do him wrong, but I at once caused him to
remain as *magister militum* and made his son Caesar.' And the
emperor Zeno ordered that Armatus the former consul and
*magister militum* be slain as a perjurer.   And the same Armatus
was slain on the Kochlias of the Palace, at the Decimum, when he
was going up to the Hippodrome to watch the games.   And after
Armatus had been murdered, he then also appointed his son
Basiliscus the Caesar, who was still a boy, as bishop of Cyzicus,
the metropolis of Hellespont, because he had worn the imperial
purple as Caesar, and he confiscated all the property of the same
Armatus.[307]
In these times the people of the Samaritan race in Palestine
seized a pretext and rebelled, and crowned a Samaritan brigand
chief named Justasas.   And he came to Caesarea and watched
chariot races and murdered many people [p.604] while he was
ruler in Palestine.   And the same Justasas also burnt the church
of St. Probus, in the time of Timothy bishop of Caesarea.   And
immediately Asclepiades, the *dux* of Palestine and dignitary of
Caesarea, came with his forces to hunt the brigand, together with
the *Arcadianae*; and he set out against the same Justasas and
engaged with him, and the same Justasas was beheaded and his
head was sent along with his diadem to the emperor Zeno.   The

---

[307] 484 Death of Armatus: cf. Mal. 381. 14-382. 9 (undated) for the same story;
Malalas says Zeno and Basiliscus '*honoured* the charioteers', but lacks the
references to the Kochlias and the confiscation of Armatus' property. For the
phrase ἐπὶ τόπου, 'at once' (p. 603. 9), cf. ἐπὶ τόπῳ, Mal. 382. 4; an alternative
translation would be 'to remain in his position as...' (cf. CP p. 621.1 for τόπος in
this sense). Theophanes (125. 2-13) in a shorter version records that Basiliscus,
saved by his relative the empress Ariadne, was first appointed a reader
(ἀναγνώστης); cf. Candidus (in Photius, *Bibliotheca* cod. 79, p. 469 Blockley), who
specifies that he was reader at Blachernae.

Date: Armatus was not allowed to survive for long after Zeno's restoration
in 476; CP has again been misled by the undated Malalas notice, whereas
Theophanes plausibly places Armatus' death in the same *annus mundi* as Zeno's
return. The date of Basiliscus' appointment to the see of Cyzicus is unknown. In
general for events and chronology, see Croke, 'Basiliscus'.

Kochlias and Decimum: cf. n. 159. The location is identical with the false
story told of Gratian's death *s.a.* 380, 'at the door of the Decimum'.

emperor Zeno immediately made their synagogue, which was in the place called Gargarides, into a great house of prayer for Our Lady the Mother of God and ever-Virgin Mary, and he also restored the church of St. Procopius; he issued an edict that a Samaritan should not hold an administrative post, and he confiscated the property of their wealthy men. And there was fear and peace.[308]

485 Indiction 8 , year 11, sole consulship of Symmachus.

In this year a certain Roman woman of senatorial rank, Juvenalia by name, came to Theodoric, who had become *rex* at Rome, telling him, 'For three years I have been in litigation with the patrician Formus: discharge me.' And after bringing the advocates of both parties, he said to them, 'Unless you give them a decision in the course of tomorrow and the following day and release them, [p.605] I will behead you.' And after sitting through the two days, they declared their opinion on the law, gave them a decision and released them. And Juvenalia lit candles and came to him giving thanks because their case had been discharged. And the same *rex* was angry with the advocates, and he brought them and said to them, 'Why did you not do in three years what you have done in two days, and released them?'. And he beheaded the two advocates from both the parties, and there was fear. And he issued an edict about every law. And he departed from Rome and lived in Ravenna, a city by the sea, until his death. And after his death Atallarich,

---

[308] Samaritan revolt: cf. Mal. 382. 10-383. 4 (undated), who records more accurately that Justasas murdered Christians in Caesarea while Porphyrius was governor of Palestina Prima, that the Samaritans burnt the church of St. Procopius, and that the *dux* Asclepiades was helped by a dignitary of Caesarea called Reges the brigand-catcher. However, the version in CP clearly derived from Malalas, so that no reliance can be placed on its date of 484; Asclepiades and Timothy cannot be dated independently. For discussion, see Avi-Yonah, *Jews* 241-3; Montgomery, *Samaritans* 109-13; Rabello, *Samaritani* 148-50, 375-9 (accepting CP's date, and unnecessarily suggesting that the chroniclers' account has been contaminated by the events of 529).

*Arcadianae*: a body of troops first recruited under Arcadius, possibly identical with the *Arcadiaci*, a detachment with special garrison duties at Cpl. (Bury, *IA* 61).

Gargarides (Gargazi in Mal.): i. e. Mount Garizim, the Samaritans' holy sanctuary; Justinian surrounded the church with a new outer wall after damage in a further Samaritan uprising (Proc. *Bld*. v. 7. 8-17).

Anti-Samaritan legislation: Samaritans (and Jews) had been debarred from public service by Theodosius II in 438 (Theod. *Novel* iii. 2); Zeno was probably now repeating or extending this law; no Samaritan legislation of Zeno is cited in *Cod. Iust*. i. 5, but Procopius (*Bld*. v. 7. 7) mentions punishment by Zeno; cf. Jones, *LRE* 948 with n. 26.

who was from his family, became *rex* at Rome. He was Arian in creed, that is Exokionite.[309]

**486** Indiction 9, year 12, consulship of Longinus and Decius.

**487** Indiction 10, year 13, sole consulship of Boethius.

In this year from divine wrath, an earthquake, Constantinople suffered its second affliction in the month Gorpiaeus, September 26th, over a short distance as far as the Taurus.[310]

## Olympiad 317

**488** Indiction 11, year 14, consulship of Dynamius and Siphidius.

**489** [p.606] Indiction 12, year 15, consulship of Eusebius and Probinus.

**490** Indiction 13, year 16, the 2nd consulship of Longinus and the 2nd of Faustus.[311]

He says that Zeno the emperor asked Maurianus, the most wise *comes*, who had in fact prophesied many things to him (for the same Maurianus knew certain mysteries), who would be emperor after Zeno himself; and he learnt from him that a certain

---

[309] **485** Theodoric and Juvenalia: cf. Mal. 384. 5-385. 2 for the same account, except that Juvenalia had been litigating for 30 years; John of Nikiu 88. 52-5 has 3 years. Theodoric the Ostrogoth set out for Italy in 488, arriving in August 489, defeated Odoacer in northern Italy in 489 and 490, and then blockaded him in Ravenna until 493, see PLRE ii. 1077-84, s.v. Theodericus 7 (esp. 1081ff); Bury, HLRE [2] i. 422-8. If there is any truth in this story, it should be located at Ravenna, the centre of western imperial and Ostrogothic administration, not at Rome which Theodoric rarely visited. Theodoric reigned at Ravenna until 526, being succeeded by his grandson Athalaric (526–34), PLRE ii. 175-6.

Date: unknown, but hardly earlier than 493; Malalas does not date the incident, but places it after a notice of Theodoric's march to Italy and defeat of Odoacer.

Exokionite: see n. 157.

There are similar stories about the severity of royal justice (Valentinian I) in CP s.a. 369.

[310] **487** Earthquake: cf. Mal. 385. 3-5 (undated), adding (5-8) that Nicomedia and Helenopolis in Bithynia also suffered. The 'first affliction' was probably the earthquake of 447 (CP ss.aa. 447, 450). This notice is likely to be misplaced and should be identified with the earthquake of 478 (Theoph. 125. 29-126. 5; Stein, BE ii. 787 for the date), when there was extensive damage; cf. Marc. Com. s.a. 480, Anec. Cramer 112. 11-18, GC 1 (Appendix 2 below).

The Taurus: i.e. Forum Tauri, a synonym for the Forum of Theodosius, on which see n. 173. The name, current by the mid-5th c., probably refers to a distinguished citizen, rather than a statue of a bull (*taurus*), Janin, Const. 64.

[311] **490** *cos. post.*: Faustus, a western aristocrat (PLRE ii. 454-6, s.v. Faustus 9), confused by CP with the consul of 483 (ibid. 451-2, s.v. Faustus 4).

former silentiary would inherit his rule and his wife. And when he heard this the emperor Zeno detained the patrician Pelagius, the former silentiary who had completed his term and reached the rank of patrician, a wise man. And he confiscated his property and ordered that he be put under guard. The excubitors who were guarding him throttled him with a noose at the command of the emperor Zeno. And when the praetorian prefect Arcadius heard, he castigated the emperor Zeno on account of the patrician Pelagius, because he had been murdered. And it came to the ears of Zeno the emperor, and he ordered that Arcadius himself be slain as he entered the Palace. But the praetorian prefect Arcadius learnt of this, and that he had been summoned by the emperor; when he was passing by the Great Church he made out that he wished to pray; and dismounting from his carriage, he entered the Great Church of Constantinople, remained inside there, and was delivered from a harsh death.[312]

**491** **[p.607]** Indiction 14, year 17, sole consulship of Olybrius.

## Olympiad 318[313]

In this year in the month Xanthicus, which is also April, Zeno was attacked by dysentery and died, aged 65 years and nine days.[314]

Anastasius Dicorus, who was from the province of New Epirus, a former silentiary, became 45th Roman emperor in the consulship of Olybrius, son of Areobindus; he was crowned in the month Xanthicus, which is also April, on the 5th day of Holy Week in indiction 14, in year 537 reckoning in accordance with Antioch the Great. And he married the lady Ariadne who had

---

312 Maurianus: cf. Mal. 390. 4-391. 1 for the same story, adding that Pelagius' body was thrown into the sea, and Arcadius' property was confiscated while he took sanctuary, but lacking the introductory 'he says'; also Theoph. 134. 25-135. 6. Maurianus is otherwise unknown, PLRE ii. 737, s.v. Maurianus 2.

Pelagius: PLRE ii. 857-8, s.v. Pelagius 2; Arcadius: praetorian prefect in 490 (ibid. 131, s.v. Arcadius 5).

Silentiary: senior officials within the Palace with formal duties as ushers, see Jones, LRE 571-2. Excubitors, see n. 289.

313 **491** Olympiad: this normally precedes the year heading, but is misplaced in the Vatican MS.

314 Death of Zeno: cf. Mal. 391. 1-4, giving Zeno's age as 60 years and 9 months, and adding the exact date of 9 Xanthicus (April), and the Antiochene year 539.

been wife of Zeno the previous emperor. The same Anastasius was emperor for 27 years.[315]                                  In total, 6,027.

**492** Indiction 15, year 1, consulship of Anastasius Augustus and Rufus.

**493** Indiction 1, year 2, the 2nd consulship of Eusebius and that of Albinus.

**494** Indiction 2, year 3, consulship of Asterius and Praesidius.

**495** Indiction 3, year 4, sole consulship of Viator.

## Olympiad 319

**496** Indiction 4, year 5, sole consulship of Paul.

**497** Indiction 5, year 6, the 2nd and sole consulship of Anastasius Augustus.

**498** Indiction 6, year 7, consulship of John Scythopolites and Paulinus.

[p.608] In the time of these consuls, while chariot races were being held, those of the faction of the Greens appealed to the emperor Anastasius that certain men be released who had been detained by the city prefect for stone-throwing. And the same Anastasius refused the appeal from the people, but in anger he ordered an armed force to go out against them, and there ensued a great riot, and the people came down against the excubitors. And they came to the imperial box and hurled stones against the emperor Anastasius, and among them a certain Moor hurled one right at the emperor Anastasius. And the emperor avoided the stone, since he would have been murdered. And the excubitors, when they saw the audacity of the same Moor, rushed upon him and cut him limb from limb, and so he surrendered his soul. But the people, being confined, threw fire into the Chalce, as it is called, of the Hippodrome; and the whole enclosure was burnt as far as the imperial box. And the public portico as far as the Hexaippion and as far as the Forum of Constantine was completely burnt and collapsed, and breaches appeared everywhere; and after many people had been detained and

---

[315] Accession of Anastasius: cf. Mal. 392. 1-7, lacking the Antiochene date (in fact 539), but adding (7-10) a physical description; Theoph. 136. 20-2. Anastasius came from Epidamnus (Dyrrachium) in Epirus; for his early career, see *PLRE* ii. 78-9, s.v. Anastasius 4. His nickname Dicorus was derived from the fact that his eyes were two different colours (one blue-grey, the other black). The accession ceremony is described at length by Const. Porph. *de caer.* i. 92. Olybrius (the younger): cf. n. 283.

punished, quiet followed, when Plato was promoted city prefect.[316]

He says that the emperor Anastasius, after his success in the Persian war, fortified Doras, a place **[p.609]** in Mesopotamia which is very large and strong, situated between the Roman and Persian boundaries. And he made in it 2 public baths and churches and porticoes and granaries for storage of grain and cisterns for water. The same place is said to have been called Doras for this reason by Alexander of Macedon, because the

---

[316] **498** Faction riot: cf. <u>Mal. 394. 11-395. 5</u> (undated) for the same story, adding that Plato was patron of the Greens; also Const. Porph. *Exc. de insid*. Mal. fr. 38.

Excubitors: cf. n. 289; their prominent role here reflects their importance within the imperial guard at this time.

Date: a problem, since this, like the following notice on Dara, may have been displaced. The sequence of Malalas fragments in the Constantinian *Excerpta* suggests a date between 497 and 501: fr. 37 deals with the Isaurian war of 492-7, and fr. 39 with the riot at the Brytae festival in 501. Cpl. suffered serious rioting at this time, much of it centred in the theatre, perhaps because the Hippodrome had been seriously damaged (either in this riot or in that of 491 which destroyed much the same area: John of Antioch fr. 214b); see further Cameron, *Factions* 226-7. However, the juxtaposition of this notice with that of Dara, which is misplaced from 507, might indicate that this riot also belongs in 507, when Marc. Com. records a Hippodrome riot quelled by armed force: see *PLRE* ii. 891-2, s.v. Plato 3. Plato was still (or again) city prefect in 512 at the time of religious rioting (cf. *CP s.a.* 517), and Victor Tonnensis (*CM* ii. 195), in a composite notice about Plato, places in 513 the destruction associated with the riot recorded here.

Chalce of the Hippodrome: to be distinguished from the bronze entrance gate (Chalce) to the imperial Palace, it should probably be located at the north end of the Hippodrome. The only other reference (*CP s.a.* 610, p. 701. 3), does not help to identify or locate it precisely. It may have been a bronze gate (see Mango, *Brazen House* 27-9), or possibly (on the analogy of the imperial Chalce) a term applied to a more substantial bronze-roofed structure, perhaps that which housed the *carceres* or entry gates for chariots. From the Chalce the fire spread south along the Hippodrome as far as the imperial box (on the east side, towards the curved end), and north into the public porticoes flanking the Mese, as far west as the Forum of Constantine.

Hexaippion: otherwise unattested. Janin (*Const.* 356) suggested a location near the Constantinian Forum, but the phraseology in *CP* perhaps indicates that it marked the eastern limit of this destruction. Etymology suggests that the Hexaippion was the site of a six-horse monument, which might appropriately be located near the northern end of the Hippodrome. The patriographers record at least one multi-horse statue group in this area: *Parast.* 84, four horses above the Hippodrome, perhaps identical with *Parast.* 38, four-horse chariot at the Milion; *Patr.* ii. 35, two horses at the Diippion (perhaps a false etymology, see Mango, 'Diippion' 153-4).

same Alexander struck Darius the Persian king there with a spear, and hence indeed it keeps the name until now.[317]

**499** Indiction 7, year 8, sole consulship of John Kurtos.[318]

### Olympiad 320

**500** Indiction 8, year 9, consulship of Patricius and Hypatius.

**501** Indiction 9, year 10, consulship of Pompeius and Avienus.

**502** Indiction 10, year 11, consulship of Probus and the 2nd of Avienus.[319]

**503** Indiction 11, year 12, consulship of Dexicrates and Volusianus.

### Olympiad 321

**504** Indiction 12, year 13, sole consulship of Cethegus.

**505** Indiction 13, year 14, consulship of Sabinianus and Theodorus.

**506** Indiction 14, year 15, consulship of Areobindus and Messala.

**507** Indiction 15, year 16, the 3rd consulship of Anastasius Augustus and that of Venantius.

. . . . . . . . . . . .[320]

---

[317] Dara: cf. Mal. 399. 13-20 (undated, and without the introductory 'he says'); Theoph. 150. 24-9. In Malalas the origin of Dara's name is simply explained as the place where Alexander captured an unnamed Persian king; in CP the obvious derivation from the name of the king, Darius, is not made explicit, and an alternative link with the 'spear' (δόρυ) is suggested. Malalas adds that the place is 'now' called Anastasiopolis. On Anastasius' Persian war, see Bury, HLRE [2] ii. 10-15.

For construction (first phase 505-7) and physical remains, see J. Crow, 'Dara, a Late Roman Fortress in Mesopotamia', Yayla iv, 1981, 12-20, L. M. Whitby, 'Procopius' Description of Dara (Buildings II. 1-3)', in P. Freeman and D. Kennedy (edd.), The Defence of the Roman and Byzantine East (BAR Int. Series 297, 1986) 737-83.

[318] Consul: John Gibbus (κύρτος), the Hunchback.

[319] **502** cos. post.: Rufus Avienus (PLRE ii. 192-3, s.v. Avienus 2), confused by CP with the consul of 501, Flavius Avienus (PLRE ii. 193, s.v. Avienus 3).

[320] **507** Lacuna: after 507, 10 consular years have been omitted. Ericsson ('Date' 18) suggested that an orthodox copyist removed this section because Anastasius now revealed his Monophysite sympathies, but this is unlikely: the text restarts *before* the accession of the orthodox Justin I (not *with* the accession, as stated by Ericsson), an orthodox reader might have approved of the popular rioting caused by Anastasius' religious innovations in 512 (most of which is lost in the lacuna), and Anastasius, in spite of his Monophysite leanings, was regarded as a good emperor by an orthodox church historian like Evagrius (e.g. iii. 30). After the

[p.610] [517...After going to the property] of the *nobilissima* patrician Juliana, they chanted concerning her husband, 'Areobindus as emperor for Romania.' And Areobindus fled to the far side. And finally the emperor Anastasius went up to the imperial box in the Hippodrome without a diadem. And when they learnt this the entire people went up to the Hippodrome, and by means of an address he controlled the populace of the city.[321]

In this year was built the Long Wall which is called Anastasian.[322]

518 Indiction 1, year 17, sole consulship of Magnus.[323]

In the time of this consul the emperor Anastasius saw in a vision that there was before him a man, full-grown and of graceful stature, who was carrying an inscribed volume; after turning over five leaves of the volume and reading out the name of the emperor, he said to him, 'Behold, on account of your greed, I erase 14.' And with his finger he erased them. And the same emperor Anastasius awoke in agitation, summoned Amantis the *cubicularius* and *praepositus* and told him the

lacuna the text restarts in mid-sentence, which suggests that, as with the lacuna in AD 530–1, a page (or more) had been damaged in, or lost from, the archetype, although here the scribe of the Vatican MS failed to observe the lacuna (the first word of the Greek, 'Juliana', is written with an elaborate capital, as if for the opening of a new notice).

321 Rioting in Cpl.: the correct date is 512, cf. Marc. Com.; Malalas 406. 22–408. 11 (undated) has the fullest account of this riot, and his placing of this notice immediately before the story of Anastasius' deathbed vision in 518 has determined the incorrect location of the story in CP *s.a.* 517. We have supplemented CP's text, which resumes in mid–sentence, from Malalas. The disturbance was caused by Timothy, the Monophysite patriarch of Cpl., who attempted with support from Anastasius and several secular officials to insert a Monophysite formula, 'who was crucified for us', into the Trisagion chant: Frend, *Monophysite* 220.

Anicia Juliana: daughter of Placidia and Olybrius, grand-daughter of Valentinian III, she was known to be a defender of Chalcedonian doctrine (Theoph. 157. 34-158. 4); her imperial connections and religious stance led to the unsuccessful approach to her husband Areobindus (cf. n. 283).

322 Long Walls: these extended from Selymbria on the Sea of Marmara, 40 miles west of Cpl., to the Black Sea. The verb used by CP for the 'building' of the walls (κτίζω) is applicable both to a new construction and to a restoration: Croke, 'Long Wall', argues for the former, Whitby, 'Long Walls', for the latter.

323 518 Date: Indiction 11, year 27. The change to the incorrect indiction and regnal years must have been made by a medieval scribe *after* the 10-year gap had appeared in the MS tradition. The scribe of the Paris apograph noted the intervening 10 indictions, and a reference to indiction 11 is preserved in the notice of Justin I's accession below.

purport of the vision. This Amantis said to him, 'May you live
for ever, emperor; for I too saw a spectacle **[p.611]** this night: as I
stood before your Might, a great pig came behind me, seized in
its mouth the corner of my cloak, shook it, and brought me down
to the ground, and destroyed me by devouring and trampling
me.' And the emperor summoned Proclus the Asian, the philosopher and interpreter of dreams, and related to him the vision,
and likewise too Amantius. And he made clear to them their
purport, that after a short time they would reach their end. And
after a short time the emperor Anastasius fell sick and lay in bed;
and there was lightning and great thunder, and in great
consternation he gave up the spirit, aged 90 years and five
months.[324]

After the reign of Anastasius Dicorus, the most sacred Justin
the Bendarite and Thracian became emperor in the consulship of
Magnus, in the month Panemus, which is also July, on the 9th,
indiction 11, in year 566 reckoning in accordance with the
Antiochenes of Syria. The army of the excubitors who guard the
Palace, together with the people, crowned him and made him
emperor; for he was *comes excubitorum*. And he was emperor
for 9 years.[325]                                            In total, 6,036.

**519** Indiction 2, year 18, consulship of Justin Augustus and
Euthericus.[326]

This Justin, as soon as he became emperor, put to death
Amantius his *praepositus*, and Andrew the *cubicularius*, the

---

[324] Anastasius' vision: cf. Mal. 408. 12-409. 10, 409. 17-20; also Theoph. 163. 31-
164. 8. The significance of the 5 turned pages and the 14 [years] erased is unclear.
For other imperial visions before death, cf. *CP* pp. 550. 20-551. 3 (Julian),
Theophylact i. 2. 1-2 (Tiberius).

Amantius: *PLRE* ii. 67-8, s.v. Amantius 4, and below *s.a.* 519 for his fate.
*Cubicularius* and *praepositus*: cf. nn. 126, 145.

Proclus 'the Asian philosopher': otherwise unknown, *PLRE* ii. 919, s.v.
Proclus 9; he should perhaps be identified with the Athenian philosopher Proclus
who helped Anastasius defeat Vitalian in 515 (ibid., s.v. Proclus 8), although the
latter is said to have died immediately afterwards (Mal. 406. 4).

[325] Accession of Justin I: cf. Mal. 410. 1-6, adding (6-8) a physical description.
Justin was born in Bederiana in Dacia Mediterranea; for his early career, see
*PLRE* ii. 648-51, s.v. Iustinus 4 (accepting 10 July as his date of accession).

*Comes excubitorum*: commander of the key element of the palace guard (cf.
n. 289); Justin's use of the post to secure for himself the throne demonstrated its
importance, and for the next century the *comes* was one of the most prominent
imperial officers, often a relative of the emperor. See Jones, *LRE* 658; Haldon,
*Praetorians* 136 with n. 226 at 408-9; Mary Whitby, 'Ceremony' 484-5.

[326] **519** Date: indiction 12, year 1 (of Justin I); as in 518 it appears that a scribe
has incorrectly altered indiction and regnal years (both correct from 520).

*Lausiacus*, [p.612] and Theocritus *comes*, the *domesticus* of the said Amantius, whom the same Amantius wished to make emperor: he had given money to the same Justin to distribute so that Theocritus might become emperor, and he distributed it. But the army and people, after taking it, did not choose to make Theocritus emperor, but they made the same Justin emperor. And so after he became emperor, he slaughtered them as usurpers who had wished to plot against his rule. And they were slain inside the Palace. [327]

The same emperor recalled the patrician Apion and Diogenianus, a former *magister militum*, and Philoxenus, himself too a former *magister militum*, who had been sent into exile by the previous emperor. And he made Apion praetorian prefect, and Diogenianus former *magister militum per Orientem*, and after a time he made Philoxenus consul. [328]

In the same year there rose on the far side in the east a fear-

---

[327] Death of Amantius: cf. Mal. 410. 8-411. 5, commenting that Justin was made emperor through the will of God. The Malalas notice continues without intermission from Justin's accession, but CP has deliberately divided it, so as to place the execution of Amantius under Justin's 1st year rather than Anastasius' 27th (in CP's original dating); cf. *CP ss.aa.* 328/30 and 420/1 for analogous division of a Malalas story.

Justin's proclamation was preceded by a competition in the Hippodrome which is described at Const. Porph. *de caer.* i. 93; see also Bury, *HLRE* [2] ii. 16-18. As *comes excubitorum* and an illiterate peasant, Justin was powerful yet apparently incapable of personal advancement, so that the eunuch Amantius decided to use him in an attempt to control the succession struggle at Anastasius' death, and have his own *domesticus* Theocritus proclaimed (*PLRE* ii. 1065). Amantius was alleged to have continued these attempts even after Justin's proclamation, and was executed along with his fellow conspirators within 10 days (Proc. *SH* 6. 26; Zach. viii. 1; Marc. Com. *s.a.* 519; Theoph. 165. 24-166. 2; Evag. iv. 2). Amantius and Andrew (*PLRE* ii. 88, s.v. Andreas 10) were both Monophysites, and their opposition to Justin was partly religious.

*Lausiacus*: the appellation is unexplained, but may indicate that Andrew was involved in the administration of the palace of Lausus (on the south side of the Mese near the Hippodrome) which was an imperial property. A building within the Great Palace known as the Lausiakos is attributed (*Patria* iii. 130, p. 257) to Justinian II (AD 685-95, 705-11).

[328] Recall of exiles: cf. Mal. 411. 6-10; also Theoph. 166. 2-5. CP has probably confused some of the titles: Malalas describes Diogenianus and Philoxenus as senators, not former generals, and says that Justin made Diogenianus *magister militum per Orientem*. Apion had been exiled in 510 and made a priest at Nicaea (*PLRE* ii. 111-12, s.v. Apion 2); the date and occasion of the other exiles are unknown (*PLRE* ii. 362, s.v. Diogenianus 4; 879-80, s.v. Philoxenus 8, in the latter case accepting CP's evidence for a position as *magister militum* before 518). Philoxenus was consul in 525.

some star, called a comet, which had a beam issuing downwards; some called it bearded; and men were afraid.[329]

## Olympiad 325

**520** Indiction 13, year 2, consulship of Vitalianus and Rusticius.
**521 [p.613]** Indiction 14, year 3, consulship of Justinian and Valerius.
**522** Indiction 15, year 4, consulship of Symmachus and Boethius.

At this time Tzath, the son of Zamnaxes the Laz king, as soon as his father Zamnaxes died, immediately came up to Constantinople to the most sacred emperor Justin. And after handing himself over, he entreated that he might be proclaimed Laz king by the Roman emperor and become a Christian, and not be appointed by the Persian king in accordance with custom, and be compelled, because he was his subject and appointed king by him, to perform sacrifices and all the Persian rituals. Koades was at this time Persian king, and it was the rule among the Persians that when a Laz king died, another king who, however, belonged to the race of the Laz, be crowned for them by the Persian king of the time. And Tzath was received by the same emperor Justin and baptized; and he became a Christian and married a Roman wife, Valeriana, grand-daughter of Oninus the patrician and former *curopalatus*. He took her and led her away to his own country, when he had been appointed and crowned Laz king by the same emperor Justin: he wore a Roman crown and a white mantle of pure silk, which had instead of **[p.614]** purple a royal gold stripe, in the centre of which was a small true purple medallion of the imperial image of Justin; he also wore a white tunic with a purple border, itself also having royal golden embroidery and likewise bearing the image of the same emperor Justin. For his boots were those of his country, red with pearls, in the Persian manner; and his belt too was likewise adorned with pearls. And he received from the emperor Justin many gifts both himself and his wife Valeriana, because she had once for all been compelled or rather won over to be his wife in foreign realms.

And when Koades the Persian king learnt this, he declared to

---

[329] Comet: cf. Mal. 411. 11-13; Theoph. 166. 6-8; perhaps identical with the comet seen universally at the start of Justin I's reign, according to Syriac chroniclers (e.g. Michael the Syrian ix. 12, vol. ii. 170).

the emperor Justin by means of an ambassador the following words, 'While friendship and peace between us is being discussed and established, you commit hostile acts. For behold, you yourself have appointed the Laz king who is subject to me and is not under the Roman administration, but is under the disposition of the Persians from eternity.' And to this the same emperor Justin made the following declaration to him in return, 'We neither appointed nor won over any of those subject to your sovereignty, but a certain man named Tzath came to our realms and begged, falling down before us, to be delivered from an abominable pagan doctrine and from unholy sacrifices and from the deceit of unjust spirits, and to become a Christian, being deemed worthy of the power of the eternal and heavenly God and creator of all things; and it was not possible to impede one who wished **[p.615]** to come to the better and recognize a true God. And so when he had become a Christian and been deemed worthy of the heavenly mysteries, we dismissed him to his own country.' And thereafter enmity arose between Romans and Persians.[330]

And at the same time Koades king of the Persians won over a *rex* of the Huns named Zilgbis. When the same emperor Justin heard about this, he was extremely aggrieved, since he had himself recently won him over to aid the Romans and sent him many gifts and received from him a compact on oath. But the same Hun, having been won over by the Persians, went off to Koades the Persian king in opposition to the Romans with 20,000 men, intending to make war on the Romans. And the most sacred Justin declared to Koades the Persian king by means of an

---

[330] **522** Conversion of Laz: cf. Mal. 412. 15-414. 16 for the same account with minor divergences (recording the sequence up to Justin's reception of Tzath in a different order); also Theoph. 168. 14-169. 12. 'With a purple border' is Lampe's suggestion (*Lexicon* s.v.) for an otherwise unknown term (παραγαῦδιν), but it may simply denote a particular type of tunic (Du Cange, *Glossarium* s.v.).

Malalas (415. 22) indirectly synchronizes the conversion of Lazica with the death in 521 of Paul (patriarch of Antioch), which is probably correct. At this time Roman–Persian relations were governed by the 7-year truce agreed in 505 (even though it had not been renewed on its expiry in 512). The story well illustrates the importance of religion and ceremonial in Roman diplomacy. For Roman relations with Lazica and other sub-Caucasian principalities, see Bury, *HLRE* [2] ii. 79-80, Stein, *BE* ii. 267-71, Whitby, *Maurice* 216-18. Cf. Mal. 427. 17-428. 4, 431. 16-21 for similar religious diplomacy early in Justinian's reign.

Tzath: *PLRE* ii. 1207, s.v. Ztathius. Oninus: otherwise unknown; Malalas and Theophanes record his name as Nomus, see *PLRE* ii. 787, s.v. Nomus 3.

*Curopalatus*: a Palace official with ceremonial duties, see Jones, *LRE* 372-3, Mary Whitby, 'Ceremony' 469-76.

ambassador, along with a friendly dispatch as if he had written for some other reason, the treachery and perjury of the same Zilgbis *rex* of the Huns, and that he had obtained money from the Romans against the Persians, intending to betray them and to ally with the Roman side at the time of the engagement; he added, 'As brothers we ought to speak in friendship and not be mocked by these dogs.' And when Koades the Persian king discovered this, he questioned Zilgbis, saying to him, 'Did you take gifts from the Romans, having been won over to oppose the Persians?'. And Zilgbis said, 'Yes.' **[p.616]** And Koades was enraged and slaughtered him. And he killed many of his horde during the night, having sent a great throng against them, the Huns being ignorant that the throng had been sent against them by the king of the Persians, but, he says, it was as though men from another country had attacked the Huns and their *rex*. And the remainder of the Huns who were left fled. And thereafter Koades decided, he says, to speak about terms of peace or rather friendship, declaring it to Justin the Roman emperor by means of an ambassador, Broeus.[331]

**523** Indiction 1, year 5, sole consulship of Maximus.


## Olympiad 326


**524** Indiction 2, year 6, the 2nd consulship of Justinian and that of Opilio.[332]
**525** Indiction 3, year 7, consulship of Philoxenus and Probus.
**526** Indiction 4, year 8, sole consulship of Olybrius.
**527** Indiction 5, year 9, sole consulship of Mavortius Romanus.
After the completion of the eighth year and 9 months and 5 days of the reign of the most sacred Justin, the most pious Justinian his kinsman, a man of exceptional magnanimity,

---

[331] Huns: cf. Mal. 414. 17-415. 21 for the same account, inserting 'he says' at different points (the ultimate source is unknown), and calling the Persian envoy Labroeus; also Theoph. 167. 4-20. Zilgbis: *PLRE* ii. 1203-4, s.v. Zilgibis.

For the tradition of diplomatic co-operation between Romans and Persians, particularly against the threat of northern tribes (though tension had begun to increase from the start of the 6th c.), see Whitby, *Maurice* 204-8; also Z. Rubin, 'The Mediterranean and the Dilemma of the Roman Empire in Late Antiquity', *Mediterranean Historical Review* i, 1986, 13-62 at 32-47. However, at the same time, the Huns north of the Caucasus were natural auxiliaries for both Romans and Persians in their conflicts in Iberia, Lazica, and Armenia: thus in 527 Justin unsuccessfully attempted to recruit Huns living near the Crimea to help the Laz and Iberians against the Persians (Proc. *Wars* i. 12. 8).

[332] **524** *cos. prior*: 2nd of Justin.

became joint emperor with him, and was proclaimed together
with his wife Theodora, and crowned by the most sacred Justin
his uncle, in the month Xanthicus, on first April according to the
Romans, in indiction 5, in year 575 of Antioch in Syria, in the
consulship of the aforementioned [p.617] Mavortius Romanus.
This emperor Justinian created great composure in Constantinople and in every city, sending sacred rescripts that those
causing riots or murders be punished, that no-one should throw
stones or commit murders, but that men should watch the games
in good order; and he produced much fear and peace in all the
provinces.[333]

And in the meantime it happened that the emperor Justin fell
sick from the ulcer which he had on his foot from the time when
he was struck by an arrow in the battle, and he died in the month
Lous, on first August according to the Romans, a Lord's Day, at
the 3rd hour, in the present tax period 5.  He died aged 77
years.[334]

And thereafter Justinian Augustus was sole-ruling Roman
emperor for 38 years, 11 months.                In total, 6,075.

The time of his reign is calculated from when he was
proclaimed emperor, that is from the month Xanthicus, April 1st
according to the Romans, indiction 5.[335]

---

[333] 527 Coronation of Justinian: cf. Mal. 422. 9-19, lacking the precise dating
formula, but recording Justinian's generosity to Antioch, and that trouble-makers
were to be punished regardless of their factional loyalty; also Theoph. 170. 24-8
(garbled, mentioning Justin rather than Justinian), 173. 13-17.

Justin's reign had witnessed extensive factional disturbances in many cities,
some of the responsibility for which rested with Justinian, who seems to have
used the Blue faction as a group of aggressive supporters to consolidate his
position as Justin's heir and undermine potential rivals (e.g. the various nephews
of Anastasius): see Bury, HLRE [2] ii. 21-3. With ambition satisfied, Justinian
now attempted to restore order.

Date: Marc. Com. supports CP's date of 1 April; Const. Porph. de caer. i. 95
in a brief description of the ceremony gives 4 April, as does the Slavonic Malalas.
In CP Justin's coronation is dated to 9 July 518, so that the precise regnal length
is slightly wrong.

[334] Death of Justin: cf. Mal. 424. 14-20; also Theoph. 173. 17-19. For the evidence
on Justin's age (75 in Mal., but 77 in Slavonic Malalas), see A. Vasiliev, Justin the
First (Cambridge, Mass. 1950), 63 n. 43, 414 (without stating a preference). John
of Nikiu 90. 47 refers to an old arrow wound in Justin's head which reopened; the
occasion of the wound is unknown.

[335] Regnal length: Malalas 425. 1-5 gives the correct figure, 38 years, 7 months,
13 days, adding a physical description (5-9).

## Olympiad 327

**528** Indiction 6, year 1, the 3rd and sole consulship of Justinian Augustus. The emperor Justinian in the first year of his reign in the month Audynaeus, on first January according to the Romans, in the sixth tax period, scattered and provided for all such a quantity of money as no other emperor did when consul.[336]

[p.618] In the same year the Persians made war on Tzath the Laz king, because he had united with the Romans. And thereafter the same Tzath sent and begged the emperor Justinian for Roman aid. And the emperor Justinian sent to him a multitude of soldiers and three *magistri militum*, Belisarius and Cerycus and Irenaeus the son of Pentadia. And they joined battle and many of the Roman army fell. And the emperor Justinian was angered against the *magistri militum* because from mutual jealousy they had betrayed each other and informed against each other to the emperor, and he replaced them. When the *magister militum* Peter, the former notary of the emperor, had gone out and removed them and taken the expeditionary force from them, together with the Laz he engaged the Persians and they cut down many Persians.[337]

---

[336] **528** Justinian's consulship: his second, since Justin was consul in 524; cf. Theoph. 174. 16-18, Mal. 426. 21-2. Justinian's first consulship in 521 had also been renowned for its lavish celebrations (Marc. Com. *s.a.*).

[337] Campaign in Lazica: cf. Mal. 427. 1-13, naming Gilderic as the first general, saying that many from both sides fell in the initial battle, and concluding with Peter's withdrawal of the army from Lazica rather than a successful battle; Theoph. 174. 19-26, naming Belisarius and concluding with battle. The Slavonic Malalas also has Belisarius.

According to Procopius, Kavadh had attempted to coerce the Iberian king Gurgenes back to his traditional allegiance to Persia and Zoroastrian customs, and Gurgenes had sought refuge in Lazica, which led to the outbreak of war in 527, shortly before Justin's death; Peter was sent to support the Iberians, but was recalled after failing to keep out the Persians; Belisarius and Sittas then made incursions into Armenia, which ended in defeat (*Wars* i. 12).

Irenaeus: *PLRE* ii. 625-6, s.v. Irenaeus 7. Peter: ibid. 870-1, s.v. Petrus 27; he was originally secretary to Justin (Proc. *Wars* ii. 15. 8), hence the title 'former notary'. For Cerycus and Belisarius, see *PLRE* iii (forthcoming).

For the course of the Persian war of 527-32, see Bury, *HLRE* [2] ii. 80-9, Stein, *BE* ii. 283-96. The two main Greek accounts, which cannot be entirely reconciled, are Procopius, *Wars* i. 12ff, and a series of notices in Malalas between pp. 427 and 478. In spite of the length of Malalas' account, this notice of the war's outbreak is the only information derived from it in *CP*, reflecting the author's lack of interest in details of fighting: he perhaps selected this notice about Tzath because he had already described his marriage (*s.a.* 522).

At this time the emperor Justinian restored the suburb that was formerly called Sycae, which is situated opposite Constantinople, both the theatre of this Sycae and the walls; and after granting it the rights of a city he renamed it Justinianopolis. And he also built the bridge by which people can make the journey from the opposite side to the all-blessed city.[338]

The same emperor also completed the public bath, the one in the quarter of Dagistheus, which Anastasius the emperor had formerly begun to build in Constantinople.[339]

[p.619] And the same emperor also made the central court of the Basilica of Illus a great cistern, wishing to send into it the water from the Hadrianic aqueduct. The same emperor restored this aqueduct, which had formerly been constructed by emperor Hadrian for the Byzantines to supply water before Byzantium had a water supply.[340]

**529** Indiction 7, year 2, sole consulship of Decius.

In this year the Justinianic Codex was completed and it was ordered that it be authoritative from the 16th day before Kalends of April [17 March] of the current tax period 7.[341]

---

[338] Sycae: cf. Mal. 430. 18-19. The troops of Vitalian, in revolt against Anastasius, had occupied Sycae (the modern Galata) in 515, when some destruction might well have occurred. These Justinianic works are not mentioned in Proc. *Bld.*; the theatre, but not the walls, are included in the *Notitia* of *c.*425. In the Great Plague of 542 corpses were dumped in the towers (Proc. *Wars* ii. 23. 9).

Bridge: probably the bridge of St. Callinicus across the Barbysses stream at the head of the Golden Horn (mentioned *s.a.* 626, p. 720. 18): there is no other evidence for a late Roman bridge directly connecting Galata and the main city, while Theophanes Continuatus (p. 340. 14-15 Bonn) mentions Justinian's bridge across the Barbysses; cf. *Syn. Eccl. Const.* pp. 143. 13, 854. 18-19, and see Mango, 'Fourteenth Region' 2-5, Janin, *Const.* 240-3.

[339] Baths: cf. Mal. 435. 18-20, Theoph. 176. 24-6; located near the Tetrapylon, see Mango, *Const.* 52, Janin, *Const.* 331-3. Dagistheus: *PLRE* ii. 341.

[340] Water supply: cf. Mal. 435. 20-436. 2, Theoph. 176. 26-7.

Basilica cistern: the extant Yerebatan Serayı, cf. Proc. *Bld.* i. 11. 12-15, and see Janin, *Const.* 208-9, Mango, *Brazen House* 48-51, and G. Downey, 'The Words *stoa* and *basilike* in Classical Literature', *AJA* xli, 1937, 194-211 at 204-5. The Basilica itself is said to have been rebuilt by Illus in 478 (J. Ant. fr. 211, cf. *PLRE* ii. 586-90, s.v. Illus 1).

Aqueduct of Hadrian: see Mango, *Const.* 20, identifying it with the partially extant 'aqueduct of Valens'; for the recurrent problem of Cpl.'s water supply, ibid. 40-2.

[341] **529** Codex: Mal. 437. 3-9 and Theoph. 177. 17-21 record a renewal of old laws followed by brief details of some of the laws; Mal. 448. 6-10 refers to a recodification of ancient laws in a single volume, but none of these passages is linguistically close to *CP*. Only *CP* gives a date, and this is one month early.

In this year in accordance with God's clemency there occurred the Great Death.[342]

530 Indiction 8, year 3, consulship of Lampadius and Orestes.

In this year, when the Samaritans revolted and created for themselves an emperor and Caesar, Irenaeus the son of Pentadia was sent as *magister militum* and put many to death. And certain of them in fear came to Christianity under compulsion, and were received and baptized, and up till the present day they waver between the two: under stringent officials they deceive by appearance and they falsely and wickedly manifest themselves as Christians, but under lax and greedy officials, they conduct themselves as Samaritans and haters of Christians and [p.620] as if ignorant of Christianity, persuading the officials by means of money to favour Samaritans.[343]

The revision of the codes of Gregorius, Hermogenes, and Theodosius had been ordered on 13 Feb. 528, to be carried through by a commission of officials and lawyers whose driving force was Tribonian; the new code, completed within 14 months, was promulgated on 7 April 529 by the constitution *summa rei publicae*, and came into force on 16 Kalends of May (i.e. 16 April). See further Stein, *BE* ii. 402-4; Jones, *LRE* 278-9; Honoré, *Tribonian* 212.

342 Great Death: the reference is uncertain. One possibility is the Great Plague that reached Cpl. in 542, in which case the notice is seriously displaced. Malalas 482. 11 describes the Great Plague as 'the compassion of God', similar to *CP*'s reference in this context to God's clemency. An alternative suggestion (less plausible) is that it refers to the loss of life in the earthquake that struck Antioch in 528, which is recorded by Malalas between the two notices concerning laws (442. 18-443. 7; cf. Theoph. 177. 22-178. 5, immediately following notice on law).

343 530 Samaritans: the revolt of 529 is described at length by Mal. 445. 19-447. 21; also *Exc. de insid.* Mal. fr. 44; briefly Theoph. 178. 22-7. But *CP*'s account shows little similarity except in the mention of Irenaeus (cf. n. 337) putting many to death; the second sentence, with its reference to 'the present day' in the description of subsequent Samaritan conduct was perhaps composed by the author of *CP*, under the influence of trouble in Palestine in Heraclius' reign.

The Samaritans crowned the bandit chief Julian as their leader, and he put on chariot races in the hippodrome at Neapolis, a sign of imperial status, cf. Justasas *s.a.* 484. For details and analysis, see S. Winkler, 'Die Samariter in den Jahren 529/30', *Klio* xliii-xlv, 1965, 435-57; Montgomery, *Samaritans* 113-24. Rabello (*Samaritani* pt. ii) discusses the sources at length, with special reference to *CP* at pp. 435-7, but there is no evidence to support the suggestion that the second part of the notice in *CP* might have been derived from John of Ephesus.

Anti-Samaritan legislation and attempted conversions: cf. Proc. *Bld.* v. 7. 16 (optimistic view), *SH* 11. 24-30 (pessimistic), and see Jones, *LRE* 948-50; Avi-Yonah, *Jews* 241-3. Restrictions placed on the Samaritans in 527 (*Cod. Iust.* i. 5. 12) were renewed or extended in 529 and 531 (*Cod. Iust.* i. 5. 13, 17, 18, 21), but these were partially lifted in 551 at the request of Bishop Sergius of Caesarea who thought this would encourage better behaviour (*Novel* 129, *CJ* iii. 647-50); Justin II reimposed strict disabilities in 572 (*Novel* 144, *CJ* iii. 709-10).

.    .    .    .    .    .    .    .    .    .    .    .    .

Note A: Lacuna.

Following the Samaritan notice (fol. 241v), the Vatican MS has a lacuna of uncertain length, which is inaccurately described in the Bonn text (app. crit. p. 620. 2). The main text of *CP* restarts at the top of a page (fol. 243r) in mid-sentence with the words 'at random' (ὡς ἔτυχεν, p. 620. 14), and continues with a detailed account of the Nika Riot of Jan. 532. The scribe of the Vatican MS, noticing the deficiency in his exemplar, left blank the bottom of folio 241v and the two following pages (fols. 242r and 242v): presumably he hoped to find a better exemplar of the text or other relevant material to fill the space. However, all that he was able to include was a brief version of the *Akta dia Kalopodion* ('Acclamations concerning Calopodius') which he used to preface the narrative of the Nika Riot, by inserting it at the top of the second complete blank page (fol. 242v), leaving the lower half blank: Maas ('Akklamationen' 46) provides a diagram of the arrangement of fols. 242v–243r. The remaining blank areas in the MS were subsequently filled, perhaps in the 11th c. (a century after the transcription of the main text), with 14 notices of various natural disasters drawn from the Great Chronographer, and a list of the Muses. For annotated translation of the Great Chronographer extracts, see Appendix 2.

Note B: Nika Riot, sources.

In spite of the opening lacuna, the surviving narrative in *CP* is the fullest, and alone preserves details of the events of the middle days, but there are also important accounts in <u>Malalas 473. 5-477. 3</u> (with *Exc. de insid.* Mal. fr. 46) and <u>Theophanes 181. 24-186. 2</u>. An extensive account, with greater emphasis on the imperial perspective, but less precise detail, survives in Procopius, *Wars* i. 24. Apart from topographical questions, the best overall study is still Bury, 'Riot', which analyses and correlates the different source traditions (chronicles, Procopius, and brief reports in other sources); see also Cameron, *Factions* 278-80.

The accounts in Malalas, supplemented by some details in *Exc. de insid.* Mal. fr. 46 (translated in Australian Malalas, pp. 281-2), *CP* and Theophanes reveal very considerable similarities; this indicates that much of the material was based on a common source, most probably the original complete text of Malalas (a contemporary, possibly eye-witness, narrative). However, because Malalas survives only in abbreviated form, doubts have been raised about the source of some material preserved only in *CP* and Theophanes, in particular the *Akta dia Kalopodion* (in both *CP* and Theophanes) and the details in *CP* about the middle days of the riot: Bury apparently attributed both to a different source ('Riot' 95 sec. 7, 98 sec. 8, 100; but at 115-16 he conceded that *CP* derived from Malalas information on events of Jan. 16–17); the Australian Malalas team (pp. 275ff) assign the *Akta* to a different source, the central narrative to Malalas.

The origin of the central narrative depends on how severely Malalas has been abridged in the course of its various redactions, first the 565 extended edition, finally the 11th-c. MS that preserves the abridged chronicle (earlier stages of compression might have occurred). Malalas 475. 10-11, 'The throng was enraged and threw fire in other places and murdered people indiscriminately', looks like a summary by an epitomator of the events of Thursday 15th/Friday 16th to

Saturday 17th, events which could be omitted to allow the shortened text to concentrate on the start and conclusion of the riot. In this case it would be reasonable to regard the additional material preserved in *CP* as representative of the original Malalas. For the *Akta*, see note C.

Note C: *Akta dia Kalopodion*

Sources: the origin of *CP*'s account, inserted in the MS lacuna by the first hand of the Vatican MS (10th c.), cannot be determined. Cameron argued (*Factions* 322-9, following Maas, 'Akklamationen' 29, 47) that *CP*'s account was summarized directly from Theophanes, but this is unlikely. (i) The scribe of the Vatican MS was looking for material to fill more than two pages of MS, and Theophanes could have provided sufficient material about events between the Samaritan revolt and the Nika Riot to fill the whole of the lacuna. (ii) Theophanes' version of the *Akta* uses the first person singular for the Greens' chants, rather than first plural as in *CP*. Maas suggested ('Akklamationen' 29) that Theophanes derived his version from the 7th-c. chronicler John of Antioch: this is unprovable, since John's account is completely lost, and it would not solve the problem of *CP*'s account, since there is no evidence that *CP* used John at any point. An economical hypothesis is that the damaged exemplar did in fact contain the *Akta*, either *CP*'s summary account or a longer version that was only partly legible (and hence had to be summarized); the Vatican scribe decided to include this after he had failed to supplement his damaged text from a better exemplar or to find relevant material in other available sources. In this case, the ultimate source for the *Akta* would most probably have been the original Malalas, which provided the bulk of both *CP*'s and Theophanes' accounts of the Nika Riot.

Context: the relevance of the *Akta* to the Nika Riot has been questioned by some scholars (e.g. Maas, 'Akklamationen' 49-51; B. Baldwin, 'The Date of a Circus Dialogue', *REB* xxxix, 1981, 301-6 = *Studies* 389-94), who have suggested that it is wrongly dated in Theophanes and belongs at the end of Justinian's reign. This is unlikely if our suggestions are correct that the *CP* version is independent of Theophanes and originated in Malalas: since *CP*'s text of Malalas terminated *c*.533 (see Introduction p. xix, and n. 373 below), the *Akta* could only belong in the opening years of Justinian's reign. An early date is rightly accepted by Cameron, *Factions* 327; also Bury, 'Riot' 106, Stein, *BE* ii. 450 n. 1. Cameron (*Factions* 326-8, elaborating a suggestion of Bury, 'Riot' 102) claimed that Theophanes transcribed the *Akta* in the context of the Nika Riot under the impression that this represented the factional chanting of 13 Jan. when the Blues and Greens united against Justinian (Mal. 474. 1-14; cf. n. 347). But Theophanes (184. 3-12) described the affair of the prisoners which inspired this chanting *after* the *Akta*, and the confrontational spirit of the *Akta* is quite contrary to the co-operation between the factions that began on 13 Jan.; Cameron (*Factions* 328), states that Theophanes copied out the *Akta* without reading it, but this seems implausible even for Theophanes.

It is not necessary to separate the *Akta* from the Nika Riot: although the *Akta* reveal that the Blues and Greens were at loggerheads shortly before their anti-Justinianic union in the Nika Riot, this sudden shift of opinion, which helped to make the riot unusual, is plausible (cf. Proc. *Wars* i. 24 1-7 on their customary hostility and unexpected union), and by the last day of the rioting traditional divisions were beginning to re-emerge. The lack of reference to Calopodius (cf. n. 345; a less exalted personage than officials like John the Cappadocian and Tribonian) in chanting during the Nika Riot is not a significant difficulty: the focus of popular attention shifted very rapidly in the course of the riot, as indicated by the sudden emergence of Probus and subsequently Hypatius as candidates for the throne.

An alternative defence of the location of the *Akta* was advanced by P. Karlin-Hayter ('Les ῎Ακτα διὰ Καλαπόδιον, *Byz.* xliii, 1973, 84-107 = *Studies* II), who argued that the religious references in the acclamations relate to Justinian's negotiations with Monophysites in 532 and reflect the Greens' opposition to orthodoxy. This was rejected by Cameron (*Factions* 323), and there is insufficient evidence to prove the argument, in spite of P. Karlin-Hayter, 'Factions, Riots and Acclamations', in ead. *Studies* III. 1-10, esp. 6-10.

.    .    .    .    .    .    .    .    .    .    .    .    .    .    .

In the fifth year of the reign of Justinian, in the month January, there occurred the insurrection of Nika as it is called, in the following manner.[344]   After the factions had gone up into the Hippodrome, the members of the Greens chanted acclamations concerning Calopodius the *cubicularius* and *spatharius*: 'Long life Justinian, may you be victorious; we are wronged, o sole good man, we cannot endure, God knows, we are afraid to give a name, lest he prosper more, and we are on the brink of danger. It is Calopodius the *spatharocubicularius* who wrongs us.'   And many insults ensued between the factions of Blues and Greens, and after many taunts against the emperor, the Greens went down, leaving the emperor and the Blues watching the chariot racing.[345]

---

[344]  Nika Riot: for *CP*'s introductory sentence, cf. Theoph. 181. 24-5 (with *Anec. Cramer* 112. 19-20), Theoph. 181. 32.

[345]  *Akta*: cf. Theoph. 181. 32-184. 2 for a very much longer transcript of the *Akta*, translated by Bury, *HLRE* [2] ii. 71-4; also Cameron, *Factions* Appendix C, pp. 318-33, with detailed discussion (although his analysis at pp. 324-5 of the MS tradition of *CP* is mistaken), and P. Karlin-Hayter, 'La Forme primitive des ῎Ακτα διὰ Καλαπόδιον, in ead. *Studies* I. The *Akta* began as an argument between the Green faction and Justinian's herald about the wrongs inflicted on the Greens by Calopodius, but quickly degenerated into a slanging match in which the Blues also intervened.

Calopodius: otherwise unknown, although other eunuchs with this name are attested (Theoph. 155. 20, 233. 8); Karlin-Hayter's suggestion (*Studies* I. 10) that he should be identified with Narses (on whom see n. 364) is unconvincing. *Cubicularius* and *spatharius*: cf. n. 126; *spatharocubicularius*: at this period no more than a convenient combined form rather than a distinct position, see Guilland, *Recherches* i. 283-5.

And the emperor sent to see what they were chanting...[346]

.   .   .   .   .   .   .   .   .   .   .   [347]

'....at random. But when great duress arises, then you do as you are advised.' And the emperor said to them, 'Go out then, and learn for what reason they are rioting.'[348] And there went

---

[346] The scribe of the Vatican MS may have composed this sentence, which does not suit the context of the *Akta* (where the emperor has witnessed the chanting), but seems intended to replace the opening lines of the main text on the next page (from '...at random' to '...they are rioting'); this is indicated by marginal signs in the MS at the relevant places on fols. 242v and 243r: see Cameron, *Factions* 325, who follows Maas, 'Akklamationen' 47-8.

[347] Start of Nika Riot: details of events lost in *CP*'s lacuna are supplied by Mal. 473. 5-475. 1. The riot began on Tuesday 13 Jan., the Ides, a day which was traditionally marked by chariot racing in Cpl. It is likely that discontent against Justinian and his administration had been building up for some time (see n. 349), but the flashpoint was provided by the city prefect's bungled execution of some Blue and Green criminals. At the race meeting on the 13th the factions chanted for pardon to be granted to two survivors of the executions (by chance, one of each colour); this chanting was maintained until the 22nd race (from the probable total of 24) with no response from Justinian, the factions then suddenly combined under the password 'Nika' ('Conquer'), and the riot began with the firing of the *praetorium* of the city prefect. On the 14th, Justinian unsuccessfully attempted to re-establish calm by offering another series of games, but this only led to the firing of the Hippodrome seating, with the result that part of the public portico as far as the Zeuxippon was burnt. Cf. *s.a.* 498 for similar causation of a riot.

Date: *CP*'s account is inserted *s.a.* 531, one year early; although the consular heading for 531 is lost in the lacuna, the next chronological entry, at p. 629. 8, relates to 532.

[348] The main text of *CP* resumes at this point in mid-sentence with the words 'at random' (ὡς ἔτυχεν). It is now the second or third day of the riot, Wednesday 14th or Thursday 15th: in Malalas these events are placed on the 14th, but his account is severely abridged at this point, and the next reference in *CP* to a day is Friday 16th (p. 622. 6-7).

The emperor and his supporters are closeted in the Great Palace after the offer of games had failed to appease the rioters (Mal. 474. 20-475. 1; cf. Proc. *Wars* i. 24. 10), and an unidentified speaker is criticizing Justinian's failure to listen to advice. A plausible speaker is the empress Theodora for whom Procopius composed a defiant harangue that scorned Justinian for contemplating flight by sea (*Wars* i. 24. 33-7: the language of *Wars* i. 24. 34 recalls *CP* p. 620. 14-15). Procopius artistically inserted this speech to highlight the dramatic climax of his account, namely the proclamation of Hypatius as emperor and his approach to the Hippodrome on the last day of the riot, Sunday 18th, but it is likely that the option of retreat by sea to Heracleia was discussed rather earlier (Theoph. 184. 27-30), some time *before* the loyal troops to whom Justinian had considered fleeing were summoned into the capital (these had arrived on the 17th: *CP* p. 622. 15-18). If this speculation is correct, Theodora had perhaps

out from the Palace the patrician Basilides who was taking the
[p.621] place of the *magister* Hermogenes in Constantinople, and
Constantiolus. And after halting the masses mobbing outside
the Palace, they silenced them and addressed them in these
words, saying, 'What are you seeking to accomplish by your
rioting?'. And they chanted against the praetorian prefect John
the Cappadocian, and Rufinus the *quaestor*, and the city prefect
Eudaemon. And after hearing this they referred it to the
emperor. And immediately he replaced John the praetorian
prefect, and made praetorian prefect instead of him the patrician
Phocas the son of Craterus. He also replaced Rufinus the
*quaestor* and made *quaestor* instead of him the patrician
Basilides who was deputizing for the *magister*, as said above.
And he replaced the city prefect Eudaemon, and made city
prefect instead of him Tryphon, the brother of Theodore former
city prefect.[349]

urged Justinian not to encourage the rioters further by a display of panic, but to
attempt to quell their wrath by limited measures (such as the dismissal of John
the Cappadocian, whom Theodora detested).

[349] Dismissal of officials: cf. Mal. 475. 1-8 (noting that Mundus also
accompanied Basilides and the *magister militum* Constantiolus), Proc. *Wars* i. 24.
11-18.

Basilides: praetorian prefect of the east and subsequently of Illyricum in the
520s, he served as *quaestor* for two years (532–4), and then succeeded
Hermogenes as *magister officiorum* (535–9): see Stein, *BE* ii. 433 (also *PLRE* iii,
forthcoming, which should be consulted hereafter for prosopography), and C.
Mango, 'Anthologia Palatina, 9. 686', *CQ* xxxiv, 1984, 489-91.

Hermogenes: *magister officiorum*; he was currently engaged in the
negotiations which produced the Endless Peace with Persia (Proc. *Wars* i. 22. 16-
17).

Constantiolus: *magister militum per Moesiam* in 528, and sent by Justinian to
investigate the cause of the Roman defeat at Callinicum in 531 (Mal. 437. 23-438.
20, 465. 12-14, 466. 13-18).

John: appointed praetorian prefect in 531, he had shown a talent for
increasing official revenues (Proc. *Wars* i. 24. 13-14). Zachariah of Mitylene (ix.
14; cf. J. Lyd. *de mag*. iii. 70) provides useful supplementary information: John's
administration provoked numerous people to flock to Cpl. to complain; these
complaints favoured and supported one of the factions (probably the Greens
who were known to oppose Justinian); this resulted in numerous protests against
John and the emperor before the two factions merged and the Nika Riot began.
John was reinstated as praetorian prefect by Oct. 532. He was at some time
patron and ardent supporter of the Greens (J. Lyd. *de mag*. iii. 62), a stance he
probably adopted *after* his reinstatement, to avoid a repetition of his downfall.

Rufinus: see *PLRE* ii. 954-7, s.v. Rufinus 13; like Hermogenes, he was
currently engaged in peace negotiations with Persia, and Tribonian, not he, was
*quaestor* (correctly in Mal. 475. 4-5). For Tribonian's avarice, see Proc. *Wars* i. 24.
16, and on the office of *quaestor*, cf. n. 287. Tribonian was reinstated as *quaestor*

But the people remained mobbing outside the Palace. And when this was known, the patrician Belisarius the *magister militum* came out with a multitude of Goths and cut down many until evening.[350] And thereafter they set fire to the bronze-roofed entrance of the Palace, and it was burnt, together with the portico of the *scholarii* and the *protectores* and *candidati*, and there was a breach. And similarly both the Senate-house, by the Augustaeum as it is called, was burnt, and the whole of the Great Church **[p.622]** together with its awesome and marvellous columns was completely demolished on all four sides.[351] And

in 535 (Honoré, *Tribonian* 57).

Eudaemon: as city prefect, he had been responsible for the incident which immediately provoked the riot, the bungled execution of some faction members (Mal. 473. 5-474. 1, Theoph. 184. 4-14; cf. Proc. *Wars* i. 24. 7, and n. 347).

Phocas, son of Craterus: *PLRE* ii. 881-2, s.v. Phocas 5.

Tryphon: *Exc. de insid.* Mal. fr. 46 mentions his appointment only at the end of the Nika Riot. He may be the Tryphon sent to reorganize taxation in Africa in 534 (Proc. *Wars* iv. 8. 25). His brother Theodore had been city prefect four times in the period 500-26 (*PLRE* ii. 1096, s.v. Theodorus 57).

[350] Belisarius: cf. Mal. 475. 8-10. Following his defeat by the Persians at Callinicum in 531, Belisarius had been replaced by Mundus as commander of the eastern armies and recalled to Cpl. (Mal. 466. 13-18; Proc. *Wars* i. 21. 2, with Averil Cameron, *Procopius*, London 1985, 157-8).

Goths: possibly men who had not followed Theodoric from the Balkans to Italy (e.g. *PLRE* ii. 226, s.v. Bessas); alternatively *bucellarii* of Belisarius, personal retainers of their individual paymaster.

[351] Fire: cf. Theoph. 184. 19-21, 25-7; the latter section records the destruction of St. Sophia in similar language to *CP*, but places it after the destruction of the hospice of Samson which *CP* puts on Friday 16th; Theophanes gives no precise dates. Malalas (474. 17-19) records that the Chalce ('the bronze-roofed entrance of the Palace') as far as the *scholae*, the Great Church and the public portico were burnt on 13 Jan. in the fire which destroyed the *praetorium* of the city prefect (cf. n. 347), before Justinian conceded the demands for the dismissal of officials. *CP*, which appears to place the destruction on Thursday 15th, is the most detailed account at this point (Mal. 475. 10-11 is a generalized summary, see note B, pp. 112-13 above), and likely to be the most reliable, but confusion about which buildings were destroyed at each stage of the riot may well have developed very soon after the events: for discussion, see Bury, 'Riot' 102-3. The 'breach' was likely to be a gap between buildings caused by the fire, as at *CP* p. 608. 16.

Chalce and adjacent buildings: see Mango, *Brazen House*, esp. ch. 2, with map at p. 23. The quarters of the guards were near the Chalce, but the precise location is unknown (ibid. 73); see also R. Guilland, 'Autour du Livre des Cérémonies. Le Grand Palais. Les quartiers militaires', *ByzSlav*. xvii, 1956, 58-97 = *Études* i. 3-40.

Scholarii: the largest element in the imperial guard, numbering 5,500 at the start of Justinian's reign and enrolled in eleven regiments or *scholae* (3,500 regulars plus 2,000 supernumeraries), although the majority of regular *scholarii* were based outside Cpl. with perhaps no more than 500 in the Palace itself.

from there the people went down again mobbing towards the
harbour of Julian to the house of Probus; and they sought to take
arms from him and chanted, 'Probus, emperor for Romania.'
And they threw fire into the house of the same patrician Probus;
and after a little had been burnt, the fire failed and was
quenched.[352]

And on the Friday, day 16 of the same month, the people went
to the *praetorium* of the prefects, and threw fire there, and the
roofs of the two imperial houses were burnt and of the same
*praetorium* only where the archives were. For a north wind blew
and drove the fire away from the *praetorium*;[353] and the bath of

Procopius (*SH* 24. 15-23) and Agathias (*Hist.* v. 15. 1-6) comment, in similar
terms, on their degeneration into ceremonial units, but this criticism may be
extreme: in the Nika Riot their support or disloyalty seems to have been a
significant factor (*CP* p. 626. 11-14; cf. n. 363). *Protectores*: a separate element
within the guard, whose military effectiveness also declined by the 6th c.
*Candidati*: a small component of the *scholarii*, but important because the 40
*candidati praesentales* were in constant attendance upon the emperor. See further
Jones, *LRE* 613-14, 657-9, and Frank, *Scholae*; also Haldon, *Praetorians* 119-41,
Mary Whitby, 'Ceremony' 463-8.

352 Probus: cf. Theoph. 184. 21-4 (recording the chant as, 'Another emperor for
the city', and that Probus' house was destroyed). Although Probus, nephew of
the emperor Anastasius (*PLRE* ii. 912-13, s.v. Probus 8), was not present to
respond to the attempted proclamation (cf. the flight of Areobindus in 512: *CP*
*s.a.* 507), he briefly suffered exile and confiscation of property after the
suppression of the riot (cf. n. 369). His house, near the harbour of Julian on the
Sea of Marmara, was located downhill and only a short distance south-west of
the Palace and Hippodrome. Bury observed ('Riot' 119) that it was only at this
point that the overthrow of Justinian became the object of the rioters.

353 Friday 16th, *praetorium*: the *praetorium* of the city prefect had been burnt
on Tuesday 13th (Mal. 474. 14-17, cf. Theoph. 184. 14-15 and see n. 347) when the
rioters were asking the prefect to pardon the convicted faction members who had
escaped execution. This *praetorium* was located towards the eastern end of the
Mese (cf. n. 407). Although enough of the building might have survived to
attract attention again, a north wind could not have blown the fire directly from
it to St. Irene, which was located to the north-east. Furthermore, *CP* states that
the *praetorium* of the prefects was burnt, which may suggest some joint building
used by both city and praetorian prefects, to be distinguished from their
individual *praetoria*. Another *praetorium* (perhaps that of the praetorian
prefect), located much further west on the south side of the Mese between the
Fora of Constantine and Theodosius (Mango, *Const.* 31 n. 52), was too distant to
be relevant to these events. Janin (*Const.* 166-9) failed to distinguish the two
*praetoria* on the Mese; the discussion of Guilland (*Études* ii. 36-9) does not clarify
this complex issue. Bury ('Riot' 116) repunctuated with a full stop after 'away
from the *praetorium*', so as to understand that there were two separate fires, thus
allowing the *praetorium* to be located away from the other buildings, but this is
not the natural interpretation of the text. The alternative is to assume that the

Alexander was burnt and the hospice of Eubulus in part and St. Irene [...] which had been built by Illus the Isaurian, who rebelled against Zeno the emperor. And the great hospice of Samson was burnt, and those who lay sick in it perished.[354]

And on the Saturday, that is the 17th of the same month Audynaeus [Jan.], the soldiers who had come from the Hebdomon and Regium and Athyras and from Calabria joined combat with the people, since the people were murdering men at random, and dragging them away and throwing them into the sea like dung; and similarly too they were murdering women. And many faction members fell.[355] And when the crowds saw

prefects had a joint building to the north of St. Irene somewhere on the old acropolis of Byzantium (cf. Janin, *Const.* 165-6). The coach-house of the praetorian prefect was located in this region (Mal. 345. 19-20; cf. n. 210).

'The two imperial houses': identity uncertain, but they were perhaps separate buildings associated with this joint *praetorium* for the city and praetorian prefects. The text might be rendered, 'only the roofs of the two imperial houses of the *praetorium* were burnt, where the archives were' (see Australian Malalas, p. 277), but we have preferred Bury's interpretation ('Riot' 116).

Archives: the rioters were naturally interested in destroying the prefects' records: the city prefect kept records of disciplinary matters, the praetorian prefect taxation and other financial records, matters which had all contributed to the build-up of tension before the explosion of the riot. Cf. Theoph. 297. 2-3 for the destruction of the city prefect's records in a riot in 608, and J. Lyd. *de mag.* iii. 13 for the location of *scrinia* (archives) in the *praetorium* of the praetorian prefect; also *de mag.* iii. 19 for judicial archives stored under the Hippodrome.

[354] Spread of fire: cf. Theoph. 184. 24-5 (bath of Alexander and hospice of Samson burnt after house of Probus, before St. Sophia).

Bath of Alexander: otherwise unknown (Janin, *Const.* 216). Hospice of Eubulus: attested under Justin I (Mal. 411. 19-20; cf. *Patria* iii. 120, p. 254); see Janin, *Églises* 558. Their location is unknown, but if *CP*'s list preserves the route along which the fire spread, they would have been to the north of St. Irene.

St. Irene: a foundation of Constantine the Great (Janin, *Églises* 103-6; Dagron, *Naissance* 392-3; Müller-Wiener, *Bildlexikon* 112-17); no connection with Illus is attested. There may be a brief lacuna at this point (or perhaps the author of *CP* omitted a few words), so that a reference to the porch of the Basilica has been lost: this was one of the buildings burnt down in the riot (*Anec. Cramer* 112. 24, Great Chronographer 7, Theoph. 181. 29), and Illus is said to have rebuilt the Basilica in 478 (cf. n. 340).

Hospice of Samson: situated north of St. Sophia, between it and St. Irene, cf. Proc. *Bld.* i. 2. 14-15, and see Janin, *Églises* 561-2; Müller-Wiener, *Bildlexikon*, plates 19, 95, 99; F. Halkin, 'Saint Samson le xénodoque de Constantinople', *Riv. di Stud. biz. e neoell.* xiv-xvi, 1977-9, 5-17, for a text about the founder and the hospice with a reference to various destructions by fire during civil disturbances (ch. 10).

[355] Saturday 17th: cf. Theoph. 185. 1-2 (corpses thrown into sea and women murdered). The entry of loyal troops stationed in Thrace marked the turning-

themselves being hit, they went into the Octagon which **[p.623]** is between the Basilica of the Skindressers and the public portico of the Regia. And the soldiers, when they saw that they were unable to enter, threw fire down upon them, and set alight the Octagon, and as a result of this fire the region around St. Theodore in the quarter of Sphoracius was burnt, except for the oven [sacristy] of the holy church. But the entire portico of the silversmiths, and the house of Symmachus, the former consul *ordinarius*, and St. Aquilina, as far as the arch of the other portico of the Forum of Constantine, was burnt.[356] And fleeing from there, the people threw fire at the Liburnon at the Magnaura, but after a mass rush had taken place, it was quenched immediately.[357]

point in the riot: Justinian, having contemplated flight to these troops earlier in the riot (see n. 348) had probably sent messages to summon them to forgather at the Hebdomon just outside the city walls and then enter *en masse*.

Regium was sited on Küçük Çekmece, about 12 miles beyond the Hebdomon, Athyras near Büyük Çekmece, a further 10 miles, and Calabria, perhaps to be identified with the 11th-c. fort of Calobria mentioned by Nicephorus Bryennius (iv. 5-6, ed. A. Meineke, Bonn 1836), further still.

356 Fires: the soldiers had to fight to reach the city centre, and their main confrontation with the rioters occurred on the section of the Mese called the Regia, between the Constantinian Forum and the Palace (cf. *CP* p. 528. 19-21); the soldiers could only dislodge their opponents by setting fire to more of the city. *Exc. de insid. Mal. fr.* 46 records destruction from the Palace as far as the Forum and the *Arca* (Treasury); Theophanes 184. 15-17 (misplaced, see Bury, 'Riot' 116-17) mentions the burning of the arch of the Forum and the silversmiths' shops, together with the palace of Lausus.

Octagon, Basilica of Skindressers, St. Theodore Sphoracius: although precise locations are problematic, these were all situated north of the Mese, near its eastern end, (Janin, *Const.* 160-1, 98, *Églises* 152-3; also Guilland, *Études* ii. 3-13, somewhat confused). From here the fire spread westwards along the Mese towards Constantine's Forum.

Oven of St. Theodore: located in the sacristy (σκευοφυλάκιον), it was probably used to prepare the holy oil and consume Eucharistic bread which had been spoiled (Mathews, *Churches* 161, Taft, *Great Entrance* 191 n. 49). The word σκευοφυλακίον is added in the margin of the Vatican MS, and is probably a gloss.

Portico of the silversmiths: Janin, *Const.* 88-9.

House of Symmachus: location unknown. Several Symmachi were western consuls, most recently (in 522) Symmachus brother of Boethius, who might have had property in Cpl., see S. J. B. Barnish, 'Transformation and Survival in the Western Senatorial Aristocracy, *c.* AD 400–700', *PBSR* lvi, 1988, 120-55 at 140ff.

St. Aquilina: to the south of the Mese (Janin, *Églises* 17).

Arch: the circular Forum of Constantine was surrounded by porticoes with a monumental arch to east and west (probably spanning the Mese and linking the porticoes); see Janin, *Const.* 62-4, Mango, *Const.* 25.

357 Magnaura and Liburnon: problematic. Janin (*Const.* 117-18, 382) identified

On the Lord's Day, that is on the 18th of the same month, early in the morning the emperor went up into the Hippodrome to his own box, carrying the Holy Gospel. And when this was known, all the people went up, and the entire Hippodrome was filled by the crowds. And the emperor swore an oath to them, saying, 'By this Power, I forgive you this error, and I order that none of you be arrested, – but be peaceful; for there is nothing on your head, but rather on mine. For my sins made me deny to you what you asked of me in the Hippodrome.' And many of the people chanted, 'Augustus Justinian, may you be victorious.' But others chanted, [p.624] 'You are forsworn, ass.' And he desisted, and the emperor himself went down from the Hippodrome;[358] and he immediately granted dismissal to those in the Palace and said to the senators, 'Depart, each is to guard his own house.'[359]

And when they had gone out, the people met Hypatius the patrician and Pompeius the patrician; and they chanted,

the Magnaura as a separate building within the Great Palace complex and the Liburnon as a nearby building or monument; see also Guilland, *Études* i. 141-50. Mango (*Brazen House* 57-8) plausibly equated the Magnaura with the Senate at the east end of the Augustaeum (already burnt, *CP* p. 621. 20-1), and associated the Liburnon with the marble statue (mentioned in the *Notitia*) of a *liburnon*, a type of ship, commemorating a naval victory.

[358] Sunday 18th, Justinian in Hippodrome: cf. Mal. 475. 11-16 (saying that some people chanted for Hypatius). Justinian was attempting to repeat the *coup de theatre* effected by Anastasius in 512 (*CP s.a.* 507) when the emperor's bareheaded appearance in the Hippodrome had defused the crisis caused by the rioting over the Trisagion and had allowed the imperial authorities to reimpose order. Justinian was less successful, but his speech attracted some favourable chanting which indicated that the populace's unanimous opposition to him was beginning to falter. The offer of pardon, although made under extreme pressure (and unlikely ever to have been honoured in full), had at least to be plausible, and Justinian's speech illustrates one aspect of the populace's relationship with the emperor in the Hippodrome, namely that their requests had some claim to be met. This passage is not discussed by Cameron in his treatment of the question at *Factions* ch. 10.

[359] Dismissal of senators from Palace: Procopius (*Wars* i. 24. 19-22) places the dismissal of Hypatius and Pompeius on the previous evening (the fifth day of the riot), but notes that the people only discovered this on the following morning, which explains the timing recorded in *CP*. As nephews of Anastasius, Hypatius (*PLRE* ii. 577-81, s.v. Hypatius 6) and Pompeius (ibid. 898-9, s.v. Pompeius 2) might be thought to have ambitions on the throne: Procopius gives Justinian's suspicions as the reason for their dismissal, but this inference was probably based on subsequent events. The assertion in *CP* that the dismissal of senators was more general suggests that Justinian had a positive strategy: now that he had been joined by sufficient troops to quell the riot by force, he wanted individual senators to use their personal retinues to secure their homes and so prevent the rioters from using strongly-fortified senatorial palaces as defensive refuges.

'Hypatius Augustus, may you be victorious.' And the people took the same patrician Hypatius to the Forum of Constantine, wearing a white mantle, and they carried him on high to the steps of the column of the monument of Constantine the emperor, and the people brought from the palace of Placillianae, as it is called, imperial insignia which were stored up there, and they put them on the head of the same Hypatius, and a golden torque upon his neck. And when this was made known to the emperor, the Palace was locked up; and the masses of the people took the same Hypatius and Pompeius the patrician and Julian the former praetorian prefect and led the same Hypatius away to the imperial box, wishing to bring out imperial purple and a diadem from the Palace and crown him as emperor. And all the people who were in the Hippodrome chanted for him, 'Augustus Hypatius, may you be victorious.'[360]

And Hypatius himself, foreseeing that the ways of the people are fickle, and that the emperor would regain control, secretly sent Ephraem the *candidatus*, in whom he had confidence, and declared to the emperor Justinian, 'See, I have assembled together all your enemies in the Hippodrome; do what you command.' [p.625] And the same Ephraem departed to the Palace, and when he wanted to gain entry and speak his message to the emperor, a certain *a secretis* Thomas met him, who was the emperor's doctor and especially loved by him, and he said to the *candidatus*, 'Where are you going to? There is no-one inside; for the emperor has departed from here.' And Ephraem turned back and said to Hypatius, 'Master, God prefers that you be emperor; for Justinian has fled, and there is no-one in the Palace.' And after hearing this, Hypatius seemed to sit more confidently

---

360 Proclamation of Hypatius: cf. Mal. 475. 16-22 (abbreviated), with *Exc. de insid.* Mal. fr. 46. Procopius (*Wars* i. 24. 22-31) emphasizes the involvement of senators and claims that Hypatius was crowned with a gold necklet since imperial regalia were lacking. In fact the torque was a military insignia used at coronations (e.g. Const. Porph. *de caer.* i. 91, p. 411. 6; i. 93, p. 429. 3), and the reference in *Exc. de insid.* Mal. fr. 46 to Hypatius being raised on a shield increases the resemblance to the military aspect of an imperial coronation. The white mantle was traditional for inauguration ceremonies (e.g. *de caer.* i. 86, pp. 391. 14-15, 392. 12, on *candidati*).

Placillianae (= Flaccillianae) palace: cf. nn. 168, 362.

Julian: *CP* is the sole evidence for his involvement. This Julian was probably the author of two epigrams on the cenotaph subsequently erected by Justinian for Hypatius (*Anth. Graec.* vii. 591-2). R. C. McCail (*JHS* lxxxix, 1969, 87-8) regards the poems as bitter and ironic, plausibly in view of Julian's connection with Hypatius, although Alan Cameron (*GRBS* xix, 1978, 264-6) has doubted this interpretation.

in the imperial box of the Hippodrome and to listen to the people's acclamations for him and the insulting utterances which they spoke against the emperor Justinian and against the Augusta Theodora.[361] And there came too from Constantianae 250 young Greens, wearing breastplates. These young men came armed, supposing that they would be able to open up the Palace and lead him into it.[362]

But the most sacred emperor Justinian, after hearing of the audacious actions by the people and Hypatius and Pompeius, immediately went up by the Kochlias, as it is called, to the Pulpita, as they are called, behind the box of the Hippodrome, to the *triclinium* which has the bronze doors, which were locked. With the emperor himself were Mundus [p.626] and Constantiolus and Basilides and Belisarius and certain other senators. And he also had the armed guard of the Palace, together with his own *spatharii* and *cubicularii*.[363]

---

[361] Hypatius in imperial box: cf. Mal. 475. 22-4 (no mention of Ephraem), Theoph. 185. 2-6 (rumour that Justinian and Theodora had fled to Thrace). CP's unique account of Hypatius' attempt to betray his popular supporters corroborates the variant allegation in Procopius ('some say...' Wars i. 24. 31) that Hypatius' entry into the Hippodrome was duplicitous, since he was still favourably disposed towards Justinian; for his reluctance, cf. Wars i. 24. 56, and lemma on *Anth. Graec.* vii. 591.

*a secretis*: secretary to the consistory, see Jones, LRE 574, 605; *candidatus*: cf. n. 351 and see further n. 363.

[362] Greens: the arrival of 250 armed Greens from Constantianae (the vicinity of the Constantianae baths, cf. n. 82) might suggest that the Greens were more enthusiastic than the Blues in their opposition to Justinian, who had normally favoured the Blues. Theophanes (185. 6-8) mentions 200 Greens from Flacianae: since the Flaccillianae palace (in the 11th region, which included the Holy Apostles) was located not far from the Constantianae baths (in the adjacent 10th region), the same general area of the city is designated. The Flaccillianae palace seems to have been under the control of Justinian's opponents: not only were coronation insignia found there (CP p. 624. 10), but its use was suggested as a base for Hypatius instead of the Great Palace (Proc. Wars i. 24. 30).

[363] Justinian approaches the imperial box: cf. Theoph. 185. 8-13, Mal. 476. 1-3 (confused paraphrase, omitting reference to Justinian). Following Theophanes and the Paris apograph of CP, we have translated 'action by the people' (παρά), not 'action concerning' (περί), the reading of the Vatican MS at p. 625. 16. Procopius (Wars i. 24. 43-7) highlights Belisarius' actions, but helps to clarify CP's narrative: Belisarius challenged the guards to open the doors, but they preferred to maintain neutrality until the outcome was clear; Belisarius then reported his failure to Justinian and expressed despair at the guards' disobedience.

'Armed guard': CP p. 626. 12-14 indicates that the defecting guards mentioned by Procopius included excubitors and *scholarii*. The 'armed guard of the Palace' said here to be loyal to Justinian could therefore be identified as

And after this had happened, Narses the *cubicularius* and *spatharius* went out secretly, and through his own efforts and those of his men suborned certain of those of the Blue faction by distributing money. And they broke away and began to chant, 'Augustus Justinian, may you be victorious. Lord, preserve Justinian and Theodora.' And the whole throng in the Hippodrome raised a cry. But some trouble-makers from the Green faction rushed on them and stoned them.[364] And subsequently those who were in the Palace, after deliberation, took the guard present inside, after suborning in addition certain of the excubitors and *scholarii* (for even these had broken away with the people); and they came out with their own men and dashed into the Hippodrome, Narses by way of the gates, the son of Mundus by the curved end, others by the single door of the imperial box into the arena, and others by the palace of Antiochus and the Gate of the Corpse, as it is called. And they began to strike the people at random, so that none of the citizens or visitors who were present in the Hippodrome survived;

*candidati* (cf. p. 627. 9-10, and see Alan Cameron in *CR* xxii, 1972, 137); however, Ephraem the *candidatus* was disloyal, while Zachariah (ix. 14: Mundus accompanied by *scholarii*) suggests that other *scholarii* may also have remained loyal. The insubordination of excubitors, the prime element in the imperial guard at this period (cf. n. 289), reflects the gravity of the situation. For the different units of guards, cf. n. 351; *spatharii* and *cubicularii*: cf. n. 126.

Kochlias and Pulpita: this description of Justinian's moves provides important evidence for the arrangement of the rooms behind the imperial box. The Pulpita are also mentioned at Mal. 387. 13-14 (attempt to murder Illus in *c*.481), and Const. Porph. *de caer*. i. 86 (p. 391. 16-18), describing the election of a *candidatus*: the emperor has gone up to the Hippodrome, while the *candidatus* stands at the door which was after the former site of the Pulpita where there was 'now' a vaulted staircase built by Justinian. The Latin term *pulpitum* denotes a platform, stage or balcony, and the Pulpita linked the top of the Kochlias, the spiral stair leading from the Palace, with the chambers immediately behind the imperial box, where the Decimum was also located, cf. n. 159 and Guilland as cited there.

Bronze doors: these doors, which opened from a reception hall (*triclinium*), separated the imperial box, where the emperor was in public view, from the interior of the Palace.

364 Narses' bribery: cf. Mal. 476. 3-7, Theoph. 185. 13-17. This timely bribery destroyed the rioters' cohesion, although its fragility had already been shown by the divided chanting during Justinian's appearance in the Hippodrome; it seems that the Blues now returned to their traditional loyalty to Justinian, perhaps worried that the alternative candidate Hypatius might favour the Greens who appeared to be his most enthusiastic supporters.

Narses: he subsequently became one of Justinian's most trusted and successful generals, who completed the reconquest of Italy in the 550s (Stein, *BE* 356-8 and index at 885).

among them even Antipater, the tax-collector of Antioch Theopolis, was slain. And immediately the *magister militum* Belisarius and his entourage opened the doors to **[p.627]** the imperial box, dashed in with *spatharii*, arrested Hypatius together with Pompeius the patrician, his first cousin, and led them to the emperor Justinian. When these had been brought in, they fell down before him, saying, 'Master, it was a great labour for us to assemble the enemies of your power in the Hippodrome.' And the emperor said to them, 'You did well; nevertheless, considering that they obeyed you when you commanded them, why did you not do this before the whole city was burnt?'. And he said to his eunuchs and *spatharii*, and to Eulalius the bearded and the *candidati*, 'Take them and shut them away.' And they took them down into the Palace and shut away Hypatius and Pompeius in solitude.[365] And on the same day, according to those who have estimated the number, 35,000 citizens and visitors were slain at the Palace. And no longer did any faction member appear anywhere at all, but there was quiet until evening.[366]

---

[365] Massacre in Hippodrome: cf. Mal. 476. 7-19, Theoph. 185. 17-26. Procopius (*Wars* i. 24. 47-54) concentrates on the actions of his hero Belisarius who, after finding a direct attack on the imperial box to be too dangerous, advanced on the crowd and supposedly provided an example to the hesitant Mundus; Justinian's nephews Boraïdes and Justus are credited with the physical arrest of Hypatius (i. 24. 53). Hypatius and Pompeius were brothers, not cousins.

Hippodrome entrances: the sources diverge about the various points of entry to the Hippodrome, but *CP* is most detailed. Narses seems to have attacked from the north end (the *carceres*), the son of Mundus from the south (the curved end). Procopius (*Wars* i. 24. 52) states that Mundus himself entered through the Gate of the Corpse, which should perhaps be located on the west side of the Hippodrome (*Patria* iii. 201, p. 278, has a false etymology that derives the Gate's name from the Nika massacre); *Exc. de insid.* Mal. fr. 46 (somewhat confused) records that Mundus entered from the imperial box above the doors, and Belisarius from below the box. The palace of Antiochus, in part of which a church of St. Euphemia was subsequently located, was at the north-west end of the Hippodrome (Janin, *Const.* 310, Müller-Wiener, *Bildlexikon* 122-5, cf. Mango, *Const.* 58). For discussion of the Hippodrome entrances, see also Guilland, *Études* i. 509-41.

*Spatharii*: in the mid-6th c. this title began to be applied more generally to guardsmen, not only eunuchs, of any officer (Haldon, *Praetorians* 138-9 with n. 238; also 155-6), but the *spatharii* associated with Belisarius (*CP* p. 627. 1) are not identified as his personal guard; in Justinian's order (*CP* p. 627. 8-9) eunuchs and *spatharii* are linked, in contrast to the *candidati* (on whom, see nn. 351, 363).

[366] Casualties: cf. Mal. 476. 19-20, Theoph. 185. 26-8. Figures vary, from 30,000 (*Exc. de insid.* Mal. fr. 46, cf.*Wars* i. 24. 54) to 50,000 (J. Lyd. *de mag.* iii. 70), or 80,000 (Zach. ix. 14), but indicate a significant loss from a total population of 3/400,000 (Mango, *Const.* 51). The 'visitors' will have included the people who

And on the next day, which was Monday, the 19th of the same month Audynaeus [Jan.], Hypatius and Pompeius the patricians were slain, and their corpses were thrown into the sea.[367] And the corpse of Hypatius appeared by the shore, and the emperor ordered that it be dumped in the midst of the other executed convicts, and that a tablet be placed above his corpse on which was inscribed, 'Here lies the emperor of the Luppa.' [p.628] After some days he ordered the man's kinsmen to take his corpse and bury it. And his kinsmen took it and buried it in the *martyrium* of St. Maura; but Pompeius' body appeared nowhere.[368] All their belongings were confiscated. And the remaining patricians who had been present with them fled, some to monasteries and others to houses of prayer, and their houses were placed under seal. And certain men suffered both confiscation and banishment. And there arose great imperial terror. And the emperor, having subsequently learnt of the message given by Thomas the *a secretis* to Ephraem the *candidatus*, beheaded Thomas and banished Ephraem to Alexandria the Great.[369]

had flocked to the capital to complain against John the Cappadocian (J. Lyd. *de mag.* iii. 70). The special mention of Antipater the Antiochene tax-collector (*vindex*; p. 626. 21) probably reflects the interests of CP's source, the Antiochene Malalas.

367 Monday 19th, deaths of Hypatius and Pompeius: cf. Mal. 476. 21-2, Theoph. 185. 28-30; Proc. *Wars* i. 24. 56-7. Victor Tonnensis (*s.a.* 530) adds that they were slain by night and their corpses thrown into the Rheuma (i.e. the Bosporus); according to the lemma of *Anth. Graec.* vii. 591, Hypatius was slain on the island of Prinkipos, the largest of the Princes' Islands in the Sea of Marmara. Zachariah ix. 14 claims that Justinian wished to spare Hypatius and Pompeius, but was compelled to execute them by an irate Theodora.

368 Burial of Hypatius: CP's reference to the recovery of the corpse is hard to reconcile with the evidence of the funerary epigrams by Julian (*Anth. Graec.* vii. 591-2), which relate to a cenotaph, see Alan Cameron, 'The House of Anastasius', *GRBS* xix, 1978, 259-76 at 266-7.

'Emperor of the Luppa': obscure. An interpretation is suggested by an exchange in the *Martyr Acts of Babyla* 1. 2 (*ASS* January 24, p. 571), '*Lupus tibi visus sum et non rex, biothanate*', 'Did I seem to you to be a wolf, not a king, you convict', where the nouns are common to this passage of CP (king/emperor, convict, and *lupus*/Luppa, literally 'wolf', but with overtones of 'whore', *vel. sim.*). Hypatius was being exposed among the dead criminals as the king of the whores.

St. Maura: an Egyptian martyr; the church (Janin, *Églises* 329-30) was in Sycae (Galata), apparently a regular place for executions, cf. nn. 172, 403. It appears that Hypatius' body was taken to Sycae to be dumped with the bodies of other criminals, and his family then buried him nearby.

369 Other punishments: cf. Theophanes 185. 30-186. 1, who specifies that 18 other patricians, together with *illustres* and consulars were punished (18

And on the 20th of the same month Audynaeus [Jan.], a Tuesday, all of Constantinople was quiet, and no-one dared to go out, but only the shops which provided food and drink for needy people were open. And business remained untransacted and Constantinople was without commerce for a number of days.[370]

The emperor Justinian immediately announced his victory to all the cities under his sovereignty, and the destruction of the usurpers who had risen against him; and he undertook to build the Great Church zealously and better, and the Palace, [p.629] and all the public places of the city which had been burnt. And he built inside the Palace bakeries and granaries for the storage of grain; and likewise too a cistern for water in case of popular crises, after ordering the city prefect to punish those from the Blue faction who had sided with the Greens and the remaining factions against him. [371]

Olympiad 328

**532** Indiction 10, year 5, the 2nd post-consulship of Lampadius and Orestes.

**533** Indiction 11, year 6, the 4th and sole consulship of Justinian Augustus.[372]

In this year in the month Dius, November according to the Romans, in the 12th indiction, there was a great earthquake in

illustres and senators in Exc. de insid. Mal. fr. 46). Procopius (SH 12. 12, 19. 12) alleges that confiscation of senatorial property was Justinian's purpose in 'managing' the Nika Riot, but this is contradicted by his statement (Wars i. 24. 57-8) that everyone received back their confiscated property, including the children of Hypatius and Pompeius (cf. Mal. 478. 18-21 for their brother Probus and cousin Olybrius).

370 Quiet: cf. Theoph. 186. 1-2, also Exc. de insid. Mal. fr. 46 (no Hippodrome games for a considerable time).

371 Justinian's reactions: cf. Mal. 476. 22-477. 3. For the restoration of buildings, see Proc. Bld. i.

Punishment of Blues: the instructions to the city prefect (Tryphon) suggest that many Blues had survived the Hippodrome massacre (they perhaps withdrew after the chanting inspired by Narses' bribery); however, their desertion to the Greens at the start of the riot had been an act of treachery that disrupted one of the emperor's mechanisms for controlling the populace (namely ensuring the vocal support of one significant group), and as such deserved punishment (cf. Mal. 488. 6-13 for another occasion when Blues were punished for embarassing Justinian). CP's allusion to 'the remaining factions', the Reds and Whites, is the only indication that they played a part in the Nika Riot, which is often referred to as the insurrection of the Prasinobenetoi ('Green-Blues').

372 **533** Consul: 3rd of Justinian, cf. n. 336.

Constantinople without damage, late in the evening, so that all the city gathered in the Forum of Constantine, and chanted litanies and said, 'Holy God, holy and mighty, holy and immortal, who was crucified on our account, have mercy on us.' And they remained all night in vigil, praying. But when morning came, the entire people who had been chanting litanies cried out, 'Victorious is the fortune of the Christians. Crucified one, save us and the city; Augustus Justinian, may you be victorious. Destroy, burn the document issued by the bishops of the Synod of Chalcedon.'[373]

[p.630] And on the 20th of the same month Dius [Nov.], in the 12th indiction, the same emperor Justinian published his sacred edict in Constantinople; and to the city of Rome, and to Jerusalem, and to the great Theopolis of the Antiochenes in Syria, and to the great city of the Alexandrians in Egypt, and to Thessalonica the city of the Illyrian race, and to Ephesus city in Asia, he sent his same sacred edict, which ran as follows:[374]

---

[373] Earthquake: cf. Mal. 478. 8-11 (brief allusion to popular litanies).

Chant: the orthodox Trisagion with the addition of the words 'who was crucified on our account'; this encapsulates Monophysite Christology that the God Christ suffered Crucifixion as an undivided entity (Frend, *Monophysite* 167-8, 263). *CP*'s inclusion of the criticism of the Synod of Chalcedon is notable. Justinian, though a supporter of Chalcedon, had since 530/1 been trying to effect a reconciliation with Monophysite opponents of the Synod, and during 532 there were discussions in Cpl. between representatives of the two sides; see Frend, *Monophysite* 261-7; S. P. Brock, 'The Orthodox-Oriental Orthodox Conversations of 532', *Apostolos Barnabas* xli, 1980, 219-28. Although Monophysites were most strongly entrenched in Egypt and the eastern provinces, they also had substantial support in the capital, as a result both of the regular migration of people from provinces to the centre and of the support of the pro-Monophysite Theodora. The author of *CP* was clearly sympathetic to attempts to shift orthodoxy away from rigid adherence to Chalcedon, as confirmed by the inclusion of Justinian's Theopaschite edict of 533 and 'Three Chapters' edict of 551 (*s.a.* 552), whereas *Novel* 42 (AD 536), which confirmed Chalcedonian doctrine after talks had failed to produce a reconciliation, is ignored.

This is the last notice that *CP* shares with Malalas, and it appears that the version of Malalas used by *CP* terminated in this year. Hereafter *CP*'s information on Justinian is very patchy: there are two long doctrinal documents (*ss.aa.* 533, 552), and a chronological computation (562), but otherwise only a mention of the revision of the Codex in 533, and of the rededication of St. Sophia (*s.a.* 563).

[374] Theopaschite edict: Justinian first issued a Theopaschite edict on 15 March 533 (*Cod. Iust.* i. 1. 6), addressed to the people of Cpl., Ephesus, Caesarea, Cyzicus, Amida, Trapezus, Jerusalem, Apamea, Justinianopolis, Theopolis (Antioch), Sebastea, Tarsus, and Ancyra. This was followed by letters to Patriarch Epiphanius in Cpl. (26 March, *Cod. Iust.* i. 1. 7) and to Pope John II (6 June, *Cod. Iust.* i. 1. 8), in both of which the Synod of Chalcedon was specifically

*'Emperor and Caesar Justinian, pious, victorious, triumphant, greatest, ever-venerable, Augustus, to our citizens.*

'In serving the Saviour and Master of all Jesus Christ, our true God, in all things we strive, as far as it is possible for mortal mind to comprehend, to imitate his leniency. And having found some mastered by the disease and madness of Nestorius and Eutyches, the enemies of God and of the most holy catholic and apostolic church, who refuse to name, properly and in accordance with truth, the holy and glorious ever-Virgin Mary as Mother of God, we have striven that these men be taught the correct faith of the Christians. And they, being incurable and concealing [p.631] their error, go about, as we have learnt, confusing the souls of the more simple and tempting them to sin, and speaking against the holy catholic and apostolic church. Therefore we have considered it necessary to dissolve the falsehoods of the heretics, and to make clear to all what are the beliefs of the holy catholic and apostolic church of God. Her most devout priests make proclamation, and we too, following them, make manifest the matters relating to the hope in us, not devising a new faith (may that never be!), but refuting the madness of those who share the opinions of the impious heretics, which indeed we have already done at the outset of our reign and made clear to all.

'For we believe in one God, Father Almighty, and in one Lord Jesus Christ the Son of God, and in the Holy Spirit, worshipping one being in three substances, one Godhead, one Power, a consubstantial Trinity. And at the end of days we acknowledge Jesus Christ the only-begotten Son of God, who is from the true God, who was begotten from the Father before the ages, who is co-eternal with the Father, the one from whom are all things, and through whom are all things, who came down from the heavens, and was made flesh from the Holy Spirit and the holy, glorious ever-Virgin Mother of God Mary, and was made man; he endured a Cross on our behalf under Pontius [p.632] Pilate, and was buried and rose again on the third day, and we recognize as being of one and the same both the miracles and the sufferings which he voluntarily endured in the flesh. For we know that

mentioned as a constituent of orthodox belief. Pope John did not signal his acceptance of the doctrine until 25 March 534, and CP's record indicates that by Nov. 533 Justinian had decided to cut short debate by reissuing his edict to the main metropolitan sees, this time including Rome, Thessalonica (the seat of the papal vicar of Illyricum), and Alexandria (the centre of potential opposition from the Monophysite side).

God the Word and Christ are not different, Christ the one and the same, consubstantial with the Father in divinity, and the same consubstantial with us in humanity, but we accept and acknowledge the unity in substance. For the Trinity remained a trinity even when one of the Trinity, God the Word, was made flesh; for the Holy Trinity does not admit an addition of a fourth personage. Therefore, since these things are so, we anathematize all heresy, and specifically Nestorius who worships a human being, and those who have shared or share his opinions, men who distinguish our one Lord Jesus Christ the Son of God and our God, and do not acknowledge, properly and in accordance with truth, the holy and glorious ever-Virgin Mary as *Theotokos*, that is Mother of God, but say that there are two sons, one God the Word from the Father, and another the son of the holy ever-Virgin Mother of God Mary, denying that he has been made in grace and relationship and kinship to God the Word and God himself, and not acknowledging that our Master Jesus Christ the Son of God and our God, who was made flesh and became man and was crucified, is one of the consubstantial Trinity. For he alone **[p.633]** is worshipped and glorified together with the Father and the Holy Spirit.

'And we anathematize also Eutyches the madman and those who have shared or share his opinions, who introduce illusion and deny the true incarnation of our Lord and Saviour Jesus Christ from the holy ever-Virgin Mother of God Mary, that is to say they deny our salvation and do not acknowledge that he is consubstantial with the Father in Godhead. And in the same way we anathematize also Apollinarius the soul-destroyer and those who have shared or share his opinions, who say that our Lord Jesus Christ the Son of God and our God is only man, and introduce mixture or confusion into the incarnation of the only-begotten Son of God; and all who have shared or share their opinions.'

All the bishops received a copy of this in their own cities, and published it in the churches.[375]

---

375 Doctrine: Justinian had sought reconciliation by focusing on the oneness of Christ, which could be emphasized by stating that the Christ who suffered in the flesh was one of the Trinity (the Theopaschite formula), without precise definition of how the divine–human unity was achieved. Condemnation of acknowledged heretics could support this attempt: Nestorius, the arch-enemy, had elevated the human qualities of Christ the Son by regarding the Virgin Mary as Christotokos rather than Theotokos (cf. n. 240); Eutyches, a radical Monophysite theologian condemned at Chalcedon, had argued that Christ's humanity was different from normal humanity in that his flesh was the incarnate Word; and Apollinarius, had argued that Christ's mind was divine not human

**534** Indiction 12, year 7, the 5th consulship of Justinian Augustus and that of Paulinus.[376]

In the time of these consuls the Justinianic Codex was revised, with the addition to it also of the constitutions subsequent to it. And it was ordered **[p.634]** that, the previous edition being made void, it should be valid from the 4th day before Kalends of January [29 Dec.], in indiction 13.[377]

**535** Indiction 13, year 8, sole consulship of Belisarius.

## Olympiad 329

**536** Indiction 14 , year 9, post sole consulship of Belisarius.

**537** Indiction 15, year 10, the 2nd post sole consulship of Belisarius.[378]

**538** Indiction 1, year 11, sole consulship of John.

---

(cf. n. 122). The doctrines of Eutyches and Apollinarius were being exploited by Julianists, a schismatic Monophysite group that threatened to overtake the main Monophysite group led by Severus of Antioch. Thus anathemas against these people might conciliate mainstream Monophysites, whereas the edict did not mention Dioscorus patriarch of Alexandria, another casualty of Chalcedon, who remained a hero for most Monophysites in spite of his support for Eutyches. This Theopaschite solution, although it accorded with Monophysite views, failed to achieve a reconciliation, since it did not contain a specific condemnation of the Synod of Chalcedon, which had too many overtones of Nestorian doctrine (and hostility to Cyril of Alexandria) to be tolerated. For further discussion, see Frend, *Monophysite* 267-9 (and index on individuals).

CP's version of the edict has some minor divergences from the text in *Cod. Iust.*: the longest is the omission by CP of 'for as he is perfect in divinity, so the same is perfect in his humanity also', which should have followed the statement on consubstantiality (p. 632. 6). Although it is possible that the November edict differed slightly in phraseology, it is more likely that CP accidentally omitted a few phrases in transcription, since there is also one serious error in CP's text: Apollinarius 'the soul-destroyer' in fact claimed that Christ lacked a human mind (ἄνουν) not that he was 'only man' (ἄνθρωπον μόνον, p. 633. 10). The edict is discussed by Scott, 'Justinian' 16-17; there is, however, no justification for Scott's subsequent inference that the copy of the November text used by the author of CP was 'more reliable' than the March version preserved in *Cod. Iust.* ('Malalas' 100 n. 6).

[376] **534** *cos. prior*: 4th of Justinian.

[377] Revision of Justinianic Codex: the first version, produced in 529, had rapidly been rendered out of date by the speed of Justinian's reforming legislation at the start of his reign. The revision, produced by the second law commission under Tribonian, was enacted on 16 Nov. 534 (Honoré, *Tribonian* 56-7 & ch. 7).

[378] **536, 537** First and second post-consulships of Belisarius: the Bonn text misrepresents the correct MS readings.

**539** Indiction 2, year 12, sole consulship of Apion, son of Strategius.

## Olympiad 330

**540** Indiction 3, year 13, sole consulship of Justin II.[379]
**541** Indiction 4, year 14, sole consulship of Basilius.[380]
**542** Indiction 5, year 15, post sole consulship of Basilius.
**543** Indiction 6, year 16, the 2nd post sole consulship of Basilius.

## Olympiad 331

**544** Indiction 7, year 17, the 3rd post sole consulship of Basilius.
**545** Indiction 8, year 18, the 4th post sole consulship of Basilius.
**546** Indiction 9, year 19, the 5th post sole consulship of Basilius.
**547** [p.635] Indiction 10, year 20, the 6th post sole consulship of Basilius.

## Olympiad 332

**548** Indiction 11, year 21, the 7th post sole consulship of Basilius.
**549** Indiction 12, year 22, the 8th post sole consulship of Basilius.
**550** Indiction 13, year 23, the 9th post sole consulship of Basilius.
**551** Indiction 14, year 24, the 10th post sole consulship of Basilius.

## Olympiad 333

**552** Indiction 15, year 25, the 11th post sole consulship of Basilius.

In this year 25 of the reign of Justinian, the 11th after the sole consulship of Flavius Basilius, there took place in Constantinople

---

[379] **540** Consul: Justin son of Germanus, not his cousin Justin son of Vigilantia who was to succeed Justinian in 565 as Justin II.

[380] **541** Basilius: the last non-imperial consul; for discussion see Alan Cameron and D. Schauer, 'The Last Consul: Basilius and his Diptych', *JRS* lxxii, 1982, 126-45, who suggest that Justinian, unable to afford the consulship himself after 534 since wars and building projects were using his resources, was worried that the consulship might provide potential rivals with excessive popular favour, and so declined to appoint any successors to Basilius. In 566 Justin II revived the consulship as an adjunct of the imperial office.

the 5th Synod against the impious and abominable and unclean and pagan doctrines alien from Christianity of Origen and Didymus and Evagrius, the opponents of God, and of Theodore the impious and his Jewish writings, and against the unclean letter to Maris the Persian called that of Ibas, and the foolish writings of Theodoret against the 12 Chapters of Cyril, our most holy father and teacher.[381]

'In the name of God, both Father and his only-begotten Son Jesus Christ our Lord, and the Holy Spirit, [p.636] Emperor and Caesar Flavius Justinian, Alamanicus, Gothicus, Frangicus, Germanicus, Anticus, Alanicus, Vandalicus, Africanus, pious, fortunate, glorious, victorious, triumphant, ever-venerable, Augustus, to the whole company of the catholic and apostolic church.'[382]

---

[381] 552 Fifth Oecumenical Council: held in Cpl. in May 553, Justinian here imposed his doctrinal decisions in the so-called 'Three Chapters' controversy; this was the culmination of his attempts to conciliate Monophysites by denouncing select aspects of Chalcedonian doctrine while maintaining the overall orthodoxy of the Synod of Chalcedon (AD 451). For discussion, see Bury, *HLRE* [2] ii. 383-94, Frend, *Monophysite* 276-82; and for the text of the council's debates, E. Schwartz and J. Straub, *Acta Conciliorum Oecumenicorum* iv. 1 (Leipzig 1971).

Origenists: Origen, the great theological allegorizer of the early 3rd c., had been condemned as a heretic even during his own lifetime (Chadwick, *Church* 100-14), and continued to be condemned even though later Origenists substantially transformed his teaching. Evagrius and Didymus had expounded Origenist doctrines in the late 4th c. In the 530s proponents of Origenist doctrine had become influential in Palestine, spreading pantheistic ideas that rejected the notion of an anthropomorphic deity, and stressed the supremacy of the soul. These had been condemned by Justinian in 543 (Bury, *HLRE* [2] ii. 381-3).

Three Chapters: after the failure of the Theopaschite formula (cf. nn. 374-5), Justinian was persuaded that unity could be achieved by condemnation of certain specific writings by Theodore of Mopsuestia, the intellectual father of Nestorian doctrine, and by Theodoret of Cyrrhus and Ibas of Edessa, two theologians cleared of heresy at Chalcedon but some of whose works revealed Nestorian tendencies and attacked Cyril of Alexandria. To this end, he issued an edict in 544 condemning specific works by these three theologians, and so started the 'Three Chapters' controversy, which the 553 council was intended to resolve. However, opposition in the west and indifference among Monophysites rendered the compromise ineffectual.

[382] Justinian's imperial titles: the list of epithets relating to real or assumed victories is characteristic of the introduction to an imperial edict or official letter; in Justinian's case they reflect victories against the Vandals in Africa, the Goths and Franks in Italy, and Germanic tribes on the Danube, but the omission of Persia, with whom the empire was still at war, is significant.

[**pp.636-84:** Edict of Justinian on Three Chapters controversy][383]


**553 [p.684.16]** Indiction 1, year 26, the 12th post sole consulship of Basilius.

**554** Indiction 2, year 27, the 13th post sole consulship of Basilius.

**555** Indiction 3, year 28, the 14th post sole consulship of Basilius.

Olympiad 334

**556** Indiction 4, year 29, the 15th post sole consulship of Basilius.

**557** Indiction 5, year 30, the 16th post sole consulship of Basilius.

**558 [p.685]** Indiction 6, year 31, the 17th post sole consulship of Basilius.

**559** Indiction 7, year 32, the 18th post sole consulship of Basilius.

Olympiad 335

**560** Indiction 8, year 33, the 19th post sole consulship of Basilius.

**561** Indiction 9, year 34, the 20th post sole consulship of Basilius.

**562** Indiction 10, year 35, the 21st post sole consulship of Basilius.

In this year 35 of the reign of Justinian, and the 21st post-consulship of Basilius, on the 20th of the month March in indiction 10 and the third year of Olympiad 335, there was completed the 532 years of the festal cycle of the holy and life-giving Cross, from when Christ our true God accepted on our behalf voluntary and life-giving death and we Christians began to keep the Feast of his holy Resurrection. And the second

---

383 Three Chapters edict: we have omitted this from the translation on grounds of length (48 pages in the Bonn edition). For the text (Greek and Latin), see also E. Schwartz, 'Drei dogmatische Schriften Iustinians', *Abhandl. d. Bayer. Akad. d. Wiss.* phil.-hist. Abt. xviii, 1939, 73-111. The document in *CP* is not, as might have been expected, a record of the proceedings of the Fifth Council, but rather an edict issued by Justinian in July/Aug. 551 that laid down in advance the decisions which the emperor intended the bishops to endorse. The treatment in *CP* of the Three Chapters controversy (coupled with the lack of reference to the problems and ultimate failure of the initiative) reflects the author's interest in attempts to move away from Chalcedon in the search for a harmonizing formula, cf. nn. 268, 373 and Introduction p. xxvi.

circuit of the festal cycle of 532 years begins from the twenty-first inclusive of the month March of the current tax period, on the day which is recognized as the equinox.[384]

*From St. Gregory's Oration for Easter*

'"I will stand upon my guard," says the admirable Habakkuk, and today with him I too, since authority and insight have been granted me by the [p.686] Spirit, will both watch and learn what is to be seen and what is to be spoken by me. And I stood and I watched. And behold, a man mounted upon the clouds, and he was exceedingly lofty, and his appearance was as an angel's appearance, and his raiment was as the brightness of darting lightning. And he raised up his hand towards the east, and cried in a loud voice; his voice was like a trumpet's voice, and encircling him a multitude as it were of a heavenly host. And he said, "Today there is salvation for the universe, all that is visible and all that is invisible. Christ is risen from the dead; rise up with him! Christ returns to himself; return! Christ is freed from the tomb; be freed from the bonds of sin! The gates of Hades are opened, and death is destroyed, and the old Adam is put aside. And if there is in Christ a new creation, be renewed!". And thus he spake, while they raised the chant which they also raised before, when Christ appeared to us through his birth below, "Glory to God in the highest, and on earth peace, goodwill among men." With them I too say this among you, "Grant that I might also receive a voice worthy of the angel's, reverberating to all the ends of the earth."'[385]

---

[384] **562** Easter cycle: the passage of 532 years from the Crucifixion marked the joint completion of the 19-year lunar and 28-year solar cycles (28 x 19 = 532), which together permitted the accurate calculation of Easter; a new great cycle was due to begin, and so this was an appropriate occasion for a chronological computation.

Date: in *CP* the Crucifixion is placed in *annus mundi* 5540, equivalent to AD 31, so that the 532nd Easter fell in AD 562. The date of Easter was fixed as the first Sunday after the first full moon after the spring equinox (21 March), since this corresponded to the time of the Passion: it is for this reason that the first great cycle is said to end on 20 March and the new cycle begin on the equinox. See further n. 386.

[385] Oration of Gregory: Gregory of Nazianzus xlv. 1 (*PG* xxxvi. 624); the Biblical reference is Habakkuk 2. 1. This passage from Gregory, celebrating both Easter and a new beginning, serves as a rhetorical *auxesis* to enhance the importance of the start of the new Easter cycle. There are a few small changes in *CP*'s version, usually in the form of the addition of redundant terminal nu; one whole clause, 'and the new is accomplished', is omitted after 'old Adam put

Let the beginning of the revolution, that is to say of the circuit of 532 years, be reckoned from year 5 inclusive of Philip the Younger and of Philip his son, the consulship of Decius and Gratian, and year 1 of Olympiad 257: from this point anyone who goes back to the 19th [p.687] year of Tiberius Caesar, that is to say year 4 of Olympiad 202, in which occurred the redeeming Passion of our Lord Jesus Christ, will find a period of 218 years, but going forward to the 8th year of Constantine the greatest emperor, in which the first indiction was established in the consulship of Volusianus and Anianus, he will amass 65 years; from year 9 of Constantine as far as the current indiction 10, year 35 of the reign of Justinian, the 21st year of the sole consulship of Basilius, he will accumulate a period of 249 years, so that in total the years from the redeeming Easter as far as the current year 35 of the reign of Justinian and year 3 of Olympiad 335, are 532.[386]

563 Indiction 11, year 36, the 22nd post sole consulship of Basilius.

In this year 36 of the reign of Justinian, in the month Apellaeus, on December 24th according to the Romans, a Sunday in indiction 12, the festival of inauguration of the holy Great

aside', but this is also missing in some MSS of Gregory's *Orations*.

[386] Computation: the purpose of this chronological verification is to confirm that 532 years have elapsed since the Crucifixion. The basic calculation is straightforward: the Crucifixion occurred in year 4 of Olympiad 202, so that, counting inclusively, the 532-year cycle must terminate in year 3 of Olympiad 335, which is the current year (532 years = 133 Olympiads).

Consulship of Decius and Gratian: the significance of this starting-point is unclear. This consulship in fact occurred in AD 250, after the overthrow of the emperor Philip, but in *CP* it is inserted under year 1 of Olympiad 257, year 4 of Philip (although counting inclusively this could be reckoned as a 5th year), which is equivalent to AD 248. One possibility is that this year was treated as the notional start of the 95-year Easter cycle of Anatolius: the original start of this cycle had probably been in 258 (cf. n. 2), but the reform of 344 had advanced world chronology by nine years (the date of Creation was changed from 5500 to 5509 BC; cf. n. 79); this change could have been applied to the Anatolian cycle, and a further one year's advance caused by the minor difference between Anatolius' 'natural' (κατὰ φύσιν) and *CP*'s 'adjusted' (κατὰ θέσιν) calculations, cf. n. 79.

Year 8 of Constantine: this is used as an intermediate stage because it marked the start of the first indiction cycle (cf. n. 30), and indictions had become a standard dating device; the addition of 65 years to AD 248 gives AD 313. However, the consulship of Volusianus and Anianus is equated with year 9 of Constantine, indiction 2 (AD 314), cf. *CP* p. 522. 19. For further discussion, see Grumel, *Chronologie* 65-8, who suggests that the consulship of Volusianus and Anianus is intended solely to date the creation of the indiction cycle (on the unsupported assumption that indictions were introduced in 314, but antedated to 1 Sept. 312).

Church of God in Constantinople was celebrated for the second time.[387]

### Olympiad 336

**564** Indiction 12, year 37, the 23rd post sole consulship of Basilius.

**565** Indiction 13, year 38, the 24th post sole consulship of Basilius.

**566** Indiction 14, year 39, the 2nd sole consulship of Justin II.[388]

[p.688] In this year on the 14th of the month November in indiction 15, Justinian died, and Justin II Augustus was emperor for 11 years, 8 months.[389]                    In total, 6,087.

The appearance of Justinian the emperor was diminutive, broad-chested, pale, thin-haired, balding at the front, round-faced, handsome, of florid complexion, slightly smiling, with grey-flecked hair, a smooth chin after the Roman fashion, a shapely nose, and palish skin.[390]

**567** Indiction 15, year 1, post 2nd sole consulship of Justin II Augustus.

---

[387] **563** Rededication of St. Sophia: Dec. 562 (indiction 11); cf. _Anec. Cramer_ 114. 26-7 (with dating by Justinian's regnal year), Theoph. 238. 18-19, Mal. 495. 9-10. This followed the reconstruction necessitated by the collapse of much of the dome and east end in May 558 after the earthquake of Dec. 557. The occasion was marked by ceremony and extended celebrations; see further Mary Whitby, 'The Occasion of Paul the Silentiary's _Ekphrasis_ of S. Sophia', CQ xxxv, 1985, 215-28.

[388] **566** Consul: CP's formula is confused. Justin II assumed his first consulship in Jan. 566 (see Corippus, _In laudem Iustini Augusti minoris_ iv, with commentary by Averil Cameron, London 1976). CP had credited the wrong Justin with the consulship of 540, and so, to be consistent, described 566 as 'the 2nd sole consulship of Justin II': the Bonn text incorrectly prints 'the 2nd post sole consulship', and also misprints the MS reading 'Ind. 14, year 39' as 'Ind. 19, year 34'.

[389] Accession of Justin: Justinian died in Nov. 565 (indiction 14; correct in Theoph. 241. 2-3). Justin II ruled for 12 years and 11 months (14 Nov. 565 to 5 Oct. 578). The error in CP's figure for years (but not for months) is accounted for by the post-dating of Justinian's death.

[390] Justinian's appearance: this passage is preserved in the margin of the Vatican MS; cf. _Mal. 425. 5-8_ for much the same description (in a slightly different order and located at the start of Justinian's reign). Malalas calls Justinian 'curly-headed' (οὐλόθριξ) rather than 'balding' (ὀλιγόθριξ), alleges that his beard was greying as well as his hair (CP correctly records that Justinian had no beard), and adds 'magnanimous, Christian'. For another description, see Proc. _SH_ 8. 12-13. There is also a mosaic depiction in St. Vitale at Ravenna, as well as numerous coin images (good reproductions in R. Browning, _Justinian and Theodora_, London 1971).

## Olympiad 337

**568** Indiction 1, year 2, the 2nd post 2nd sole consulship of Justin II Augustus.

**569** Indiction 2, year 3, the 3rd post 2nd sole consulship of Justin II Augustus.

**570** Indiction 3, year 4, the 4th post 2nd sole consulship of Justin II Augustus.

**571** Indiction 4, year 5, the 5th post 2nd sole consulship of Justin II Augustus.

## Olympiad 338

**572** Indiction 5, year 6, the 6th post 2nd sole consulship of Justin II Augustus.

**573** **[p.689]** Indiction 6, year 7, the 7th post 2nd sole consulship of Justin II Augustus.

**574** Indiction 7, year 8, the 8th post 2nd sole consulship of Justin II Augustus.

In this year 8 of his reign, on 7th in the month September in indiction 8, Justin Augustus fell ill and made Tiberius Caesar, renaming him Constantine; he continued as Caesar with him for 4 years.[391]

**575** Indiction 8, year 9, the 9th post 2nd sole consulship of Justin Augustus.

## Olympiad 339

**576** Indiction 9, year 10, the 10th post 2nd sole consulship of Justin Augustus.

**577** Indiction 10, year 11, the 11th post 2nd sole consulship of Justin Augustus.

**578** Indiction 11, year 12, the 12th post 2nd sole consulship of Justin Augustus.

In this year 12 of the reign of Justin, on 26th in the month September in indiction 12, Tiberius II Constantine was crowned by him, and on the 5th of the following month October Justin Augustus died.[392]

---

[391] **574** Justin's illness: Justin suffered a mental derangement in winter 573/4 (the ninth year of his reign), as a result of the disastrous news that the Persians had captured Dara (Theophylact iii. 11. 3; Evag. v. 11). After about a year's illness, the *comes excubitorum* Tiberius was elevated as Caesar to assist in the running of the empire, in a ceremony on Friday 7 Dec. 574 (Theophylact iii. 11. 4-13; J. Eph. iii. 5; Evag. v. 13).

[392] **578** Accession of Tiberius: cf. Theophylact iii. 16. 3-6. Theophanes (249. 22-3) states that Tiberius was crowned by the Patriarch Eutychius.

And Tiberius Constantine was sole ruler for another 4 years.
                                                In total, 6,091.
**579** Indiction 12, year 1, the 1st consulship of Tiberius II
Constantine Augustus.

**[p.690]**                    Olympiad 340

**580** Indiction 13, year 2, post-consulship of Tiberius II
Constantine.
**581** Indiction 14, year 3, the 2nd post sole consulship  of
Tiberius II Constantine.
**582** Indiction 15, year 4, the 3rd post sole consulship of
Tiberius II Constantine.
In this year 4 of his sole rule, Tiberius Caesar fell ill, and on the
fifth of the month August in the present indiction 15 Maurice
Tiberius became Caesar. And on the thirteenth of the month
August he was crowned emperor, after Tiberius II Constantine
had given him as wife his daughter Constantina. And on the
14th of the same month August, Tiberius II Constantine died at
the suburban palace of the Hebdomon; and after his corpse had
been carried by boat to Constantinople, on the following day his
funeral was held and his body laid to rest in the Holy Apostles.[393]
Next Maurice was emperor for 20 years.          In total, 6,111.
**583** Indiction 1, year 1, year without a consul.
And by common consent it was recorded as post-consulship of
Tiberius Constantine of blessed memory year 4.[394]

---

[393] **582** Tiberius' illness: said to have been caused by eating a bowl of
mulberries (Theoph. 252. 5-6). His succession arrangements were rather more
complicated than suggested in *CP*, since Germanus the governor of Africa was
also betrothed to a daughter of Tiberius, Charito, and created Caesar (Theoph.
252. 2-4). The coronation is described at much greater length by Theophylact (i.
1) who, however, wrongly locates the scene in the Great Palace (cf. J. Eph. v. 13
for the Hebdomon). Funeral: Theophylact i. 2. 3-6. See further Whitby, *Maurice*
7-8.

[394] **583** 'Year without a consul': the year could no more have lacked a consul
than any other post-consular year, but the comment reflects the perception of the
consulship at this period as an appendage of the imperial title (cf. the discussion
of Heraclius' 'non-consular' consulship *s.a.* 611, at p. 702. 2-6). In any case
Maurice assumed the consulship on 25 Dec. 583 (Theoph. 253. 24-6, Theophylact
i. 12. 12), a late start which Hendy (*Economy* 193) has attributed to Maurice's
desire to curtail the expenses of the post. In *CP* Maurice's consulship is inserted
*s.a.* 584, so that subsequent post-consulships are one year out.

**[p.691]**                    Olympiad 341

**584** Indiction 2, year 2, the 1st sole consulship of Maurice Augustus.

**585** Indiction 3, year 3, post sole consulship of Maurice Tiberius Augustus.

**586** Indiction 4, year 4, the 2nd post sole consulship of Maurice Tiberius Augustus.

**587** Indiction 5, year 5, the 3rd post sole consulship of Maurice Tiberius Augustus.

Olympiad 342

**588** Indiction 6, year 6, the 4th post sole consulship of Maurice Tiberius Augustus.

**589** Indiction 7, year 7, the 5th post sole consulship of Maurice Tiberius Augustus.

**590** Indiction 8, year 8, the 6th post sole consulship of Maurice Tiberius Augustus.

In this year at the Easter festival, Maurice Tiberius crowned his son Theodosius as emperor. However, it was not posted in the records, and none of the other actions of imperial recognition was performed in his case, except only the coronation.[395]

**591** Indiction 9, year 9, the 7th post-consulship of Maurice Tiberius.

In this year Chosroes the Persian king came to the Romans after suffering an insurrection by his fellow-clansman Baram. And through a Roman alliance he was restored to his own kingdom.[396]

---

[395] **590** Coronation of Theodosius: Maurice's eldest son had been born on 4 Aug. 583 (J. Eph. v. 14; Theoph. 254. 24-5 in the wrong year). The 'other actions' not performed for Theodosius were probably obeisance by the senate and acclamations by the factions (cf. *CP* pp. 703. 20-704. 1).

Records: probably an official list that recorded the precise designation of each year, and of different parts of each year. From the reign of Maurice onwards the author of *CP* displays increasing concern for accuracy in such references to years (cf. pp. 693. 5-9; 694. 13-16; 701. 20-702. 6; 704. 3-9, etc.), and he had probably consulted these records himself.

[396] **591** Khusro II (Chosroes): he had fled to the Roman empire in March 590 in the face of the revolt by the general Vahram Tchobin (who was distantly related to the royal clan: Theophylact iii. 18. 6-10); in the latter part of 590 he agreed terms with Maurice for Roman support, and in summer 591 a grand alliance of Romans, loyal Persians, and Armenians defeated Vahram in Azerbaijan and reinstated Khusro. For discussion, see Whitby, *Maurice* 292-303.

**[p.692]** Olympiad 343

**592** Indiction 10, year 10, the 8th post-consulship of Maurice Tiberius.

In this year Anastasius, patriarch of Antioch, returned to Antioch after the death of Gregory, who had been patriarch and had indeed previously succeeded the same Anastasius.[397]

**593** Indiction 11, year 11, the 9th post-consulship of Maurice Tiberius.

**594** Indiction 12, year 12, the 10th post-consulship of Maurice Tiberius Augustus.

Cyriacus was leader of the most holy church in Constantinople for 12 years; he had been presbyter and *oikonomos* of the same church.[398]

**595** Indiction 13, year 13, the 11th post-consulship of Maurice Tiberius Augustus.

Olympiad 344

**596** Indiction 14, year 14, the 12th post-consulship of Maurice Tiberius.

**597** Indiction 15, year 15, the 13th post-consulship of Maurice Tiberius.

**598** Indiction 1, year 16, the 14th post-consulship of Maurice Tiberius.

**599** Indiction 2, year 17, the 15th post-consulship of Maurice Tiberius.

---

[397] **592** Gregory of Antioch: patron of the historians Evagrius and John of Epiphania and an important official figure in the eastern provinces, he died in summer 592 (Evag. vi. 24; Allen, *Evagrius* 262-3).

Anastasius: a popular and respected patriarch (at least Monophysites appealed to him for arbitration, and Pope Gregory corresponded with him even during his period of demotion), he had been ousted by Justin in 570 for reasons that are obscured by our main source Evagrius (v. 5, with comments by Allen, *Evagrius* 214-17); he was reinstated on 25 March 593.

[398] **594** Cyriacus: the former *oikonomos* (steward) of St. Sophia served as patriarch for 11 years (until Oct. 606) in succession to John Nesteutes who had died on 2 Sept. 595; Cyriacus and his two successors, Thomas (607) and Sergius (610), had all been senior financial administrators in the Constantinopolitan church before being chosen as patriarch: this probably reflects the desire of emperors to have competent controllers of the Church's great wealth, especially after the reign of John Nesteutes, which may have been less prudent (see Theophylact vii. 6. 2-4).

## Olympiad 345

**600** Indiction 3, year 18, the 16th post-consulship of Maurice Tiberius.

**601 [p.693]** Indiction 4, year 19, the 17th post-consulship of Maurice Tiberius.

**602** Indiction 5, year 20, the 18th post-consulship of Maurice Tiberius.

In this year in the month February the marriage of Theodosius the son of Maurice took place over seven days, from day 9 inclusive until day 15 of the same month February.[399]

And on the 6th of the month July in the same indiction 5 an edict was published, and for the remaining part of the year, that is until January of the 6th indiction, it was recorded as follows: 'And in the second consulship of our same most pious lord.'[400]

And in the month November of the same indiction 6 there occurred an uprising against Maurice by Phocas, a soldier, together with the army. And Maurice Tiberius with his wife Constantina and 9 children, namely 6 boys, Theodosius, Tiberius, Peter, Paul, Justin, and Justinian, and three girls, Anastasia, Theoctiste, and Cleopatra, fled on the 22nd of the month Dius, November according to the Romans, by night as Friday 23rd was dawning. On the 23rd of the same month, a Friday, Phocas was crowned by Cyriacus, patriarch of Constantinople, in the venerated church of St. John at the Hebdomon; on the 25th of the said month, a Lord's Day, he entered Constantinople, seated in a chariot; from the Hebdomon he entered by way of the Golden Gate, and the Troadesian porticoes and the whole length of the Mese as far as the Palace, with no-one at all opposing, but everyone acclaiming him.[401]

---

[399] **602** Marriage of Theodosius: cf. Theoph. 283. 35-284. 3; Theophylact viii. 4. 10. The marriage (to a daughter of the patrician Germanus, cf. nn. 406, 411) may actually have been celebrated in Nov. 601 (Theoph.), whereas the week-long festivities were perhaps intended to regain popular goodwill towards the imperial family after the serious rioting on 2 Feb. 602 occasioned by a food shortage; cf. Theophylact viii. 4. 10-11 with notes (Whitby).

[400] Maurice's second consulship: perhaps to be connected with the twentieth anniversary of Maurice's accession, it was probably a further attempt to boost his popularity.

[401] Phocas' coup: cf. Theoph. 286. 14-289. 25, Theophylact viii. 6. 2-10. 10, for more extensive accounts, though only *CP* preserves a sequence of precise dates (cf. Whitby, *Maurice* 24-7). The military revolt had been sparked off when Maurice instructed the Balkan army to winter north of the Danube in order to press home the Roman advantage in their campaigns against the Slavs; after failing to persuade their general Peter to disobey Maurice's order, the army chose

[p.694] Maurice Tiberius, together with his wife and eight of his children, was seized at St. Autonomus, near Praenetus. And on the 27th of the same month, a Tuesday, Maurice himself was slain near Chalcedon, as were Tiberius, Peter, Justin, and Justinian.[402] Peter too, the brother of Maurice, who was *curopalatus*, was also arrested and slain, and other officials were also arrested. Constantine Lardys, the former praetorian prefect, logothete, and curator of the palace of Hormisdas, and Theodosius the son of Maurice were slain at Diadromoi, near Acritas; Comentiolus, the patrician and *magister militum*, was also slain on the far side, near St. Conon by the sea, and his body was eaten by dogs.[403]

the officer Phocas as leader and marched on the capital, apparently with the intention of replacing Maurice by his son or the Caesar Germanus (ibid. 165-9). Maurice was not sufficiently confident to try to defend the capital, and started to flee east.

Phocas' triumphal entry: cf. Theophylact viii. 10. 7-8 (lacking CP's precise route). The church of John the Baptist at the Hebdomon (cf. *s.a.* 391) had been used in proclamation ceremonies of some 5th-c. emperors (e.g. Leo: Const. Porph. *de caer.* i. 91, p. 413. 13), and from there Phocas passed through the Theodosian walls by the ceremonial Golden Gate and then along the entire length of the Mese; for the Troadesian porticoes, cf. n. 262. Phocas' ambitions for the throne were supported by the Green faction (Theoph. 289. 8-10, Theophylact viii. 10. 1), who now probably led the acclamations; there was perhaps also considerable public support for the removal of the parsimonious Maurice.

[402] Death of Maurice's family: Maurice with most of his family had been detained through bad weather and ill health at Praenetus, modern Karamürsel on the south shore of the Gulf of Izmit (Theophylact viii. 9. 9-10); for the church of St. Autonomus, see Janin, *Monastères* 86-7. They were brought back as far as Chalcedon, where the men and boys were slain at the harbour of Eutropius (Janin, *Const.* 238-9), after a factional squabble in Cpl. that Phocas may have misunderstood as support for Maurice (Theophylact viii. 10. 11-11. 6 with notes [Whitby]; Theoph. 289. 25-290. 12).

[403] Maurice's supporters: Theophylact viii. 13. 1-2 records the executions of Peter, Comentiolus, George the second-in-command to Philippicus, and Praesentinus the *domesticus* of Peter. Peter and Comentiolus had both commanded armies in the Balkans in the last years of Maurice's reign, and were disliked by the troops for their attempts to implement Maurice's strategic orders (cf. Whitby, *Maurice* 100-4). *Curopalatus*: from the time of Justin II a post reserved for close relatives of the emperor, see Mary Whitby, 'Ceremony' 476, and cf. n. 330.

Constantine Lardys: cf. Theophylact viii. 9. 11-12, 11. 1-2, 13. 3; he had been deputed to accompany Maurice's son Theodosius in an attempt to obtain support from Khusro II of Persia, but this mission was countermanded. Theophanes (287. 12-16) mentions his unpopularity with the Green faction. Logothete: the first mention of this new senior official, who was probably responsible for a reorganized system of military finances, see Bury, *IA* 86f; Haldon, *Recruitment*

And from the 25th of the same month November for the rest of the year, that is until the month January of the present indiction 6, it was recorded in the records as, 'In year 1 of the reign of Phocas.'[404]
The same Phocas was emperor for 8 years.					In total, 6,119.
**603 [p.695]** Indiction 6, year 1, sole consulship of Phocas Augustus.[405]
In this year Constantina the former queen was put into a monastery. And Philippicus the patrician and *comes excubitorum*, and Germanus, the patrician and father-in-law of Theodosius son of Maurice, were made clerics.[406]

33-4. Palace of Hormisdas: an imperial estate; for *curatores*, see Jones, *LRE* 426.

Diadromoi: near Tuzlaburnu on the north shore of the Gulf of Izmit, see Janin, *Monastères* 53-6.

St. Conon: the monastery was located in Sycae/Galata, on the far side of the Golden Horn (Janin, *Églises* 283-4). It is regularly mentioned in connection with executions or the display of decapitated heads (Mal. 389. 14, 431. 13, 473. 15), which might indicate that the vicinity was a recognized place for capital punishment; cf. also *CP s.a.* 393 for executions at Galata and *s.a.* 531 (p. 628. 2-3 with n. 368) for the burial of Hypatius' executed corpse at St. Maura in Galata.

A further extract from the Great Chronographer, relating to Maurice's overthrow, is inserted in the margin of the Vatican MS beside the notice for 602. See Appendix 2 for translation and notes.

[404]  Records: cf. n. 395.

[405]  603 Phocas' consulship: celebrated at Christmas (Theoph. 292. 5-6); cf. n. 394 for Maurice.

[406]  Constantina: Theophanes 293. 8-23 (*a.m.* 6098 = AD 605/6) provides more details: Germanus was attempting to oust Phocas, and hoped that Constantina would provide a rallying point for those disaffected with the new emperor, but the move was thwarted by opposition from the Greens who were bitterly hostile to Germanus (cf. Theophylact viii. 9. 15). Germanus' attempt may also have been encouraged by rumours that his son-in-law Theodosius had managed to escape to Persia and was now being supported by Khusro II (cf. Sebeos ch. 23, Theophylact viii. 13. 4-5).

Monastery: Theophylact viii. 15. 1 records that Constantina and her three daughters were confined in the house of Leo. According to *Patria* iii. 185 (p. 274) the monastery was known as the Nea Metanoia (Janin, *Églises* 332), which may be identical with the monastery of St. Mamas (mentioned in the same passage) at the Xerocircus/Xylocircus that had been founded by Maurice's sister Gordia, and where the bodies of Maurice and Constantina were buried (Const. Porph. *de caer.* ii. 42, pp. 646. 19-647. 6, Cedr. i. 707. 10-708. 2; Janin, *Églises* 314-19).

Philippicus: husband of Gordia, he had founded a monastery to the Virgin at Chrysopolis to which he now withdrew (Leo Gramm. 138. 12-13, Theoph. 293. 22-3); his involvement in the plot is not specified by the sources.

*Comes excubitorum*: for this officer, cf. n. 325; Tiberius and Maurice had held the post before their elevation to Caesar, and Philippicus was succeeded by Phocas' son-in-law Priscus.

Then, when a faction riot occurred, the Mese was burnt from
the palace of Lausus, and the *praetorium* of the city prefect, as far
as the Treasury opposite the Forum of Constantine of blessed
memory, when Leontius, the former curator of the palace of
Antiochus, was city prefect.[407] John, who was called Crucis, the
controller of the Green faction, was burnt in the Mese between
the *praetorium* of the city prefect and the **[p.696]** Forum.[408]

## Olympiad 346

**604** Indiction 7, year 2, post-consulship of Phocas Augustus.
**605** Indiction 8, year 3, the 1st post-consulship of Phocas
Augustus.[409]
In this year in the month Daisius, June according to the
Romans, on a Saturday, there were beheaded Theodore the
praetorian prefect, John *antigrapheus*, Romanus *scholasticus*,
Theodosius subadjutant of the *magister*, Patricius *illustris*
nephew of Domniziolus who was curator of the palace of
Hormisdas, John and Tzittas, *spatharii* and *candidati*,
Athanasius *comes largitionum*, Andrew *illustris* who was called
Scombrus, and Elpidius *illustris*. Elpidius had his tongue cut
out and his 4 extremities removed; he was paraded on a stretcher

---

407 Riot: the cause is unknown, but Cameron (*Factions* 282) has rightly rejected
theories that it was connected with changes in Phocas' patronage of the factions.

Palace of Lausus: on the south side of the Mese, north-west of the
Hippodrome, see Janin, *Const.* 379, Müller-Wiener, *Bildlexikon* 238-9 and plate
109, Guilland, *Études* ii. 32-5.

*Praetorium* of city prefect: located towards the east end of the Mese (cf. nn.
210, 353). This passage perhaps suggests that the *praetorium* was on the north
side of the street, since it may have been named in conjunction with the palace of
Lausus to signify that both sides of the Mese were burnt from the vicinity of the
Hippodrome as far west as Constantine's Forum. Mango ('Diippion' 156) located
the *praetorium* south of the Mese, citing Const. Porph. *de caer.* i. 79 (pp. 375-6),
but this is not conclusive.

Treasury (*Arca*): cf. *Exc. de insid.* Mal. fr. 46, with n. 356; see also Guilland,
*Études* i. 394.

Leontius: for possible identifications with this man, cf. nn. 425, 443. Palace
of Antiochus: cf. n. 365; an imperial estate like the palace of Hormisdas, cf. n. 403.

408 John Crucis: recently installed as demarch of the Greens (Sergius was
demarch in 602: Theophylact viii. 7. 10), possibly against the wishes of the faction
members (cf. Theoph. 287. 12-15). It is uncertain whether he perished during the
riot or was executed by Phocas as punishment for the destruction. This riot of
'the Greens under Crucis' was sufficiently notorious to be included by Jacob the
Jew in his 'career' of anti-Christian hooliganism (*Doctrina Iacobi* p. 39. 5).

409 **605** Phocas' 2nd post-consulship; all subsequent post-consular headings for
Phocas are one short.

and carried down to the sea; when his eyes had been gouged out, he was thrown into a skiff and burnt. The other people aforementioned were beheaded, on the grounds that they were discovered plotting against the emperor Phocas.[410]

At the same time Constantina the former queen was also beheaded, across the strait at the breakwater of Eutropius near Chalcedon. And the surviving female [p.697] children of her and Maurice, Anastasia, Theoctiste, and Cleopatra, were also killed, together with the daughter of Germanus who had been wife of Theodosius; and Germanus himself was killed with them.[411]

606 Indiction 9, year 4, the 2nd post-consulship of Phocas Augustus.

In this year Cyriacus, patriarch of Constantinople died, in the month Hyperberetaeus, on October 29th according to the Romans, a Saturday. And his funeral was held on the 30th of the

---

[410] Conspiracy: this further plot against Phocas is narrated at greater length by Theophanes (294. 27-295. 13; 297. 12-298. 4), although with some confusion since he records the conspiracy in two versions under the years 607 and 609, with a different person betraying the plot in each year, and makes Theodore and Elpidius, who were executed in 607, reappear in 609. The date of the near-contemporary CP should probably be preferred. Theophanes (297. 16-18) presents Theodore and Elpidius as the prime movers in the plot, states that Theodore was beaten to death (295. 5-6; although at 298. 2-3 he is decapitated), and names Anastasius rather than Athanasius as comes largitionum (297. 20-1).

The plot was apparently triggered by continuing rumours that Maurice's son Theodosius was still alive in the east (Theoph. 294. 30-2), but the involvement of so many senior officials also suggests that the administrative aristocracy of Cpl. was trying to remove Phocas, the choice of the Balkan army and the circus factions, since his defects as a ruler were now being highlighted by Persian successes on the eastern front.

Antigrapheus: head of one of the major bureaux of administration, see Bury, IA 75-6, Jones, LRE 549, 575-6. Scholasticus: a barrister in one of the main lawcourts.

Domniziolus: probably to be distinguished from Phocas' brother Domentziolus (e.g. Theoph. 292. 2); curator of palace of Hormisdas: cf. n. 403.

Spatharii and candidati: formerly separate elements, the spatharii being eunuchs in the cubiculum, while the candidati were part of the scholarii, cf. nn. 126, 351. The conjunction of titles in the case of John and Tzittas reflects an organizational change: see Mary Whitby, 'Ceremony' 467-8; Haldon, Praetorians 155-6.

Comes largitionum: see Bury, IA 86, Jones, LRE 427-8; a late reference to the financial official whose duties were taken over during the 7th c. by the logothete (cf. n. 403).

[411] Execution of Maurice's female relatives and Germanus: they were also implicated in the above plot, cf. Theoph. 295. 7-10. For the harbour of Eutropius at Chalcedon, cf. n. 402.

same month, a Sunday, and his body was laid to rest according to custom in the Holy Apostles.[412]

**607** Indiction 10, year 5, the 3rd post-consulship of Phocas Augustus.

In this year in the month Audynaeus, on January 23rd according to the Romans, Thomas became patriarch in Constantinople; he was a former deacon of the Great Church, *sacellarius* of the patriarch and in charge of appointments.[413]

## Olympiad 347

**608** Indiction 11, year 6, the 4th post-consulship of Phocas Augustus.

**609** Indiction 12, year 7, the 5th post-consulship of Phocas Augustus.

At this point one can prove that from when the thrice-blessed Constantine terminated his life up till the 22nd of the month May in the current tax period 12, the year 7 of the reign of Phocas, 272 years are completed and the 273rd starts from the 22nd of the [p.698] month May in indiction 12. For if in that year Pentecost occurred on the 22nd of the month May, the Resurrection indubitably fell on the third of the month April, so that the first day of that April began on a Friday. Therefore, add a quarter to the 272 years, that is 68, and it becomes 340; divide this by 7, and there is a residue of 4; and so since April began then on a Friday, count Friday, Sabbath, Lord's Day, Monday, and thereafter the 273rd year begins on a Tuesday. It follows then that the April in the current year 12 of the solar cycle, year 19 of the lunar cycle, begins on the third day of the week, which in fact it does. Furthermore I have perused both the Easter tables and the consular lists, and have found that this calculation is concordant. And so from the death of Constantine until now there are 272 years, while from his twentieth anniversary, 284 complete years. Easter indeed fell on third of April 272 years ago in year 13 of the moon's cycle, in the second year of Olympiad 279. There have

---

[412] **606** Death of Cyriacus: cf. Theoph. 293. 26. This notice provides useful confirmation that the 5th-c. practice of burying patriarchs in the Holy Apostles was still maintained, and that the church had not yet become reserved for imperial tombs (earlier evidence cited by Grierson, 'Tombs' 6 n. 26).

[413] **607** Appointment of Thomas: cf. Theoph. 293. 26-8, who dates his election to 11 Oct. (apparently 606, which would precede CP's date for the death of Cyriacus); as *sacellarius* Thomas had been the church's chief treasurer.

been 272 consuls from Felicianus and Tatianus up till the Easter
of year 19 of the solar cycle which is now current.[414]

In this year was completed the composite column which was
built by Phocas the emperor, as well as the cistern, by the [p.699]
eastern part of the church of the 40 Saints near the bronze
Tetrapylon.[415]

---

[414] 609 Chronological computation: this calculation seems to have been
intended as a means of cross-checking the chronological accuracy of the period of
history for which the author of *CP* had himself devised at least part of the
chronological framework; down to Constantine's 20th year, Eusebius provided
the basic framework (see the computation from the creation *s.a.* 325, with n. 48).
This computation enables the revolt against Phocas and the start of Heraclius'
reign to be correctly located in their place in the progress of Christian history.

The author first reckoned the lapse of time from Constantine's death as 272
full years: this could be done by counting Olympiads from year 2 of Olympiad
279 (*CP*'s Olympiad date for Constantine's death) to year 2 of Olympiad 347, a
total of 68 Olympiads. Constantine had died at Pentecost 337, 22 May, which
entailed that Easter in that year fell on 3 April and 1 April fell on Friday. This is
then related to the day for 1 April in the current year: each year the calendar
advances by one day of the week, except in leap years when it advances by two
days, so by taking the time lapse of 272 years, adding an extra day for each leap
year (= 68), and by dividing this figure by seven for the days of the week, the
remainder gives the number of days by which 1 April had advanced from the
base year. The calculation is then cross-checked by reference to Easter Tables and
consular lists (Felicianus and Tatianus were consuls in 337), which involves a
restatement of the conclusions. For lunar and solar cycles, cf. n. 384.

The essentials of the computation are correct (in spite of the occasional
confusions in *CP*'s consular list in the 6th c.). The Bonn text mistakenly records
the years from Constantine's anniversary as 281 (*ΣΠΑ*), misreading the correct
figure in the MS, 284 (*ΣΠΔ*). There is an analogous computation *s.a.* 616.

[415] Column: located to the east of the church of the 40 Martyrs, which had been
built by Tiberius and Maurice on the south side of the Mese between the
Tetrapylon (cf. n. 262) and the Forum of Theodosius; this church had replaced a
*praetorium* (Theoph. 267. 29-31, *Patria* iii. 46, p. 234; Janin, *Églises* 483-6, nos. 3
& 6), probably the *praetorium* of the praetorian prefect, cf. n. 353. Phocas'
column, surmounted by Heraclius' Cross (*CP s.a.* 612), survived into the Middle
Ages, providing useful evidence for topographical reconstruction of Cpl., see
Mango, *Const.* 31 n. 52. *Parast.* 74 records that in the 7th year of his reign
Phocas eagerly organized the erection of a statue of himself behind the Magnaura
(at the east end of the Augustaeum, see n. 357), which was erected only 18 days
before his death; if one can trust that *Parast.* is referring to a different
monument, these constructions suggest that Phocas was trying to stamp his
image on public spaces in the capital, perhaps in an attempt to counter his
growing unpopularity.

Cistern: Mango, *Const.* 51 n. 1; the population of Cpl. was still large enough
to require the maintenance of its extensive water collection and storage
arrangements, and even the thrifty Maurice had contributed to the repair of the
aqueduct system (Theophylact viii. 13. 17).

In this year Africa and Alexandria rebelled; and the Father of Alexandria was slain by opponents.[416] Isacius also was deposed from Jerusalem, and Zacharias, a former presbyter and *skeuophylax* of the church of Constantinople, took his place;[417] and Edessa came under Persian control.[418]

**610** Indiction 13, year 8, the 6th post-consulship of Phocas Augustus.

In this year in the month Dystrus, on March 20th according to the Romans, a Friday, Thomas patriarch of Constantinople died, and his funeral was held on the 22nd of the same month, a Sunday. And on the 18th of the month Artemisius, April according to the Romans, in the same indiction 13, on Easter Eve, Sergius became patriarch of Constantinople; he had been a deacon of the Great Church of Constantinople, responsible for poor relief and guardian of the harbour.[419]

And at the end of the month September in the 14th indiction, it

---

[416] Revolt against Phocas: cf. Theoph. 295. 27-296. 3, 297. 5-10; Nic. 3. 6-4. 1; see A. J. Butler, *The Arab Conquest of Egypt* (2nd ed., Oxford 1978), chs. 1-3; Bury, *HLRE* [1] ii. 203-6. Plotting against Phocas in Africa, which was governed by Maurice's former general Heraclius and his brother Gregory, started in mid-608: the Carthage mint began striking *solidi* for the exarch Heraclius, father of the future emperor, in indiction 11, 607/8, see P. Grierson, 'The Consular Coinage of "Heraclius" and the Revolt against Phocas of 608–10', *Numismatic Chronicle* x, 1950, 71-93. The revolt then received encouragement from enemies of Phocas in the capital, including the emperor's son-in-law Priscus. The first move of the rebels was to stop the grain ships to restrict Cpl.'s food supply, and to this end they also sent Nicetas, son of Gregory, to Egypt to spread the revolt; for events in Egypt, where Phocas' henchman Bonosus arrived to confront the rebels, but was defeated at Alexandria, see J. Nik. 107-9. Theodore, patriarch of Alexandria (608–9), was a supporter of Phocas (J. Nik. 107. 6, 17-18).

[417] Jerusalem: in 609 there was also serious unrest in Antioch and Palestine, which was quelled by Bonosus; he originally planned to kill the patriarch of Jerusalem (Strat. 3. 11-4. 8), and the dispatch of a senior Cpl. priest (*skeuophylax* = sacristan) to replace Isacius was probably part of the reassertion of imperial control.

[418] Persian capture of Edessa: Theoph. 299. 14-15 dates this to May 611 (by implication: indiction 14 at 298. 15); the month may be right, but *CP*'s date of 609 is supported by *Chron. 724* (Seleucid Era 921 = AD 609/10).

[419] **610** Sergius: Theophanes records the change of patriarch in Cpl. only in the tables prefacing the year (p. 296. 12; *a.m.* 6101 = AD 608/9, one year early), but the author of *CP* shows more interest in Sergius (probably his patron) than in the gathering momentum in the provinces of Heraclius' revolt. Easter Day fell on 19 April in 610: the date 18th is correct in the MS, but misreported in the Bonn text, which prints 8th. The description of Sergius as 'guardian of the harbour' is obscure, but suggests the importance of clergy in civic affairs at this time; it may be connected with the reception of grain for poor relief.

was announced that Anastasius, who was patriarch of Antioch, the former *scholasticus*, had been killed by soldiers. [420]

In this year in the month Hyperberetaeus, on October 3rd according to the Romans, indiction 14, a Saturday, a number of ships appeared by the circular fort, and in them indeed was Heraclius the son [p.700] of Heraclius. And then on this day, towards evening, Phocas entered from the suburban palace of the Hebdomon, and came on horseback to the Palace in the city. [421]

And on the following day, that is to say the Lord's Day, when the ships drew near to the city, Bonosus, who had performed the dreadful deeds in Antioch the Great at the injunction of Phocas, and at the instigation of Theophanes of execrated memory, [422] – this Bonosus, who was then in the city, fled after himself setting fire to the vicinity of Caesarius' quarter and being unsuccessful; he went in a skiff to the harbour of Julian to the so-called quarter

---

[420] Anastasius II: patriarch 598/9–609. Theophanes 296. 17-21 records his death under *a.m.* 6101 (AD 608/9), before the dispatch of Bonosus to the east (cf. n. 416), and states that he was mutilated and killed by Jews. Although J. D. Frendo ('Who killed Anastasius II?', *Jewish Quarterly Review* lxxii, 1982, 202-4) raises doubts about the mutilation, Theophanes may still be correct in crediting the murder to the Jews: Jacob the Jew was involved in the disturbances at Antioch in Phocas' reign (*Doctrina Iacobi* p. 39. 7-9), Michael the Syrian (x. 25, p. 379) also blames them for the murder (but at xi. 1, p. 401, the murderers are not identified), and *CP*, though a contemporary witness, only records how the death was reported at Cpl. ('it was announced'). The long interval between Anastasius' death (probably in 609) and the arrival of the news in Cpl. in Sept. 610, was perhaps due to the disorganized state of the empire.

[421] Arrival of Heraclius: there are four other main accounts of Heraclius' coup, John of Antioch fr. 218f, John of Nikiu 109. 25-110. 9, Theoph. 298. 15-299. 8; Nic. 4. 1-5. 7, but *CP* has some unique details and precise dates. It is not always easy to reconcile these accounts, particularly those of *CP* and John of Antioch. *CP* presents the perception of an eye-witness in the capital: Heraclius is not mentioned until his fleet comes into sight. George of Pisidia's *In Heraclium ex Africa redeuntem* celebrates Heraclius' return, but supplies no factual details.

Heraclius, son of Heraclius the governor of Africa, had set out against Phocas with a fleet in mid-summer; after spending some time in the Sea of Marmara while his support increased, he continued his advance on the capital by sea whereas Phocas, expecting him to attack by land, had garrisoned the Long Walls but then had to withdraw.

Circular fort: situated outside the city walls, near the Hebdomon (cf. Proc. *Bld.* iv. 8. 4); Heraclius waited in full view of the city while dissension within the walls undermined Phocas' attempts at opposition.

[422] Bonosus: for his activities in the east, cf n. 416: he had been defeated by Nicetas in Egypt and returned to Cpl. shortly before the appearance of Heraclius. Theophanes 'of execrated memory': otherwise unknown.

of Maurus; being cornered, he threw himself into the sea, and after receiving a sword blow from an excubitor when he was in the sea, he died; when his corpse was cast ashore, he was dragged along, brought to the Ox, and burnt.[423]

And on the 6th of the same month, as Monday was dawning, Photius, the curator of the palace of Placidia, and Probus the patrician seized Phocas stark naked from the Archangel in the Palace, and led him off through the harbour in the direction of the mansion of Sophia; after throwing him into a skiff, they

---

[423] Sunday 4th: CP concentrates on the activities of the villain Bonosus who is presented as a scapegoat, whereas the main alternative account in John of Antioch (fr. 218f. 3-5) emphasizes the role of the circus factions and the equivocal behaviour of Priscus, son-in-law of Phocas and *comes excubitorum* (cf. n. 406). John of Nikiu 109. 25-110. 3 mentions both Bonosus and the significant role of the factions, especially the Greens.

According to John of Antioch, certain Greens liberated Heraclius' mother and fiancée who had been taken hostage; Phocas relied on the circus factions to defend the harbours on the Sea of Marmara at which Heraclius might land, with the Greens taking charge of the harbours of Caesarius and Sophia (i.e. Theodosius and Julian, see Mango, *Const*. 38-40, 55). The Greens set fire to the harbour of Caesarius after being incited by the charioteer Calliopas Trimolaimes who had arrived by boat. (Tiftixoglu, 'Helenianai' 85, plausibly suggests that Calliopas was a disgraced charioteer who had taken refuge with Heraclius and was now being sent back to incite unrest among his former fans.) Bonosus came to the harbour, but was attacked by the Greens and sought refuge in a boat; Priscus throughout had bided his time, first feigning illness, then summoning excubitors and *bucellarii* to the hippodrome of his mansion at the Boraïdon (for which, cf. n. 271), and finally using the charioteer Calliopas to liaise with the excubitors.

Cameron (*Factions* 284-5) used CP's failure to mention the role of the Green faction in the coup as proof that their involvement was unimportant, but CP may be presenting a quasi-official version that was reluctant to give any credit for Heraclius' success to the unruly factions. On the other hand, John of Antioch's presentation of Priscus' actions may reflect the latter's desire to gain maximum credit for his switch of allegiance to the new regime.

Caesarius' quarter: i.e. the vicinity of the harbour of Theodosius. It is impossible to determine who was responsible for the burning of this area: the Greens might have started the fire as an act of rebellion, or Bonosus could have done so in an attempt to curb the Greens' disloyalty (cf. the burning of the Octagon during the Nika Riot, n. 356), but the conflagration marked the end of co-ordinated opposition. The concentration of attention on the harbours might indicate that the rest of this coast was inaccessible, which would support the existence of a sea wall on this side, cf. n. 243.

Quarter of Maurus: near (perhaps to the west of) the harbour of Julian, Janin, *Const*. 387.

The Ox: Forum Bovis, on the Mese between the Forum Amastrianum and that of Arcadius (Mango, *Const*. 28); the site of a furnace (perhaps in the form of an ox's head) used for public burnings, Janin, *Const*. 69-71; cf. *Parast*. 42.

displayed him to the ships; and then they brought him to Heraclius. And his right arm was removed from the shoulder, as well as his head, his hand was impaled on a sword, and thus it was paraded along the Mese, starting from the Forum. His head [p.701] was put on a pole, and thus it too was paraded around. The rest of his body was dragged along on the belly, and was brought in the direction of the Chalce of the Hippodrome.[424] Behind his corpse Leontius the Syrian, the former *sacellarius*, was also dragged: as he was still breathing, someone gave him a blow with a piece of wood by the Chalce of the Hippodrome, and then he died. His head was removed and then his corpse and that of Phocas were borne off to the Ox, where they were burnt. The race-starter and the sergeant of the city prefect, who was nicknamed 'former demoniac', were likewise burnt at the Ox.[425]

And about the ninth hour of the same Monday, Heraclius was crowned emperor in the most holy Great Church by Sergius patriarch of Constantinople.[426] And on the following day,

[424] Death of Phocas: on Monday, which was 5 Oct. Nicephorus 4. 19-25 adds that Phocas was dressed in a black loincloth (the garb of a criminal); John of Antioch fr. 218f. 6 and Nic. 4. 25-7 record an exchange of insults between Heraclius and Phocas before the latter's death. John of Nikiu 110. 5-6 locates Phocas' death in the presence of Heraclius at the church of St. Thomas (near the harbour of Sophia, Janin, *Églises* 248-50), and records the mutilation of his body differently (in retaliation for the rape of Photius' wife).

Palace of Placidia: cf. *CP s.a.* 385 with n. 167; *curatores*: cf. n. 403.

Archangel: there was an oratory dedicated to Michael inside the Palace near the Kochlias, and possibly also a larger chapel (Janin, *Églises* 342, 344 nos. 11, 15: the distinction, solely on grounds of size, is not conclusive).

Mansion of Sophia: located near the harbour of Sophia, where Heraclius was docked (Theoph. 299. 6); see Averil Cameron, 'Sophiae' 13-15.

Forum: that of Constantine; Chalce of the Hippodrome: cf. n. 316.

[425] Phocas' associates: their precise crimes are unknown. Phocas' brother Domentziolus was among the victims burnt at the Ox (Nic. 5. 4-5, J. Ant. fr. 219f. 6). For the Ox, cf. n. 423.

Leontius: as *sacellarius* or treasurer (Bury, *IA* 84-6) he may have been involved in confiscations of property. John of Nikiu (110. 4-5) says that Leontius was killed with Phocas at the church of Thomas after he had co-operated with Phocas in throwing the imperial treasures into the sea. It is uncertain whether this Leontius is to be identified with the city prefect mentioned *s.a.* 603.

Race-starter (μαππάρις): probably a Hippodrome functionary implicated in Phocas' regime through the emperor's exploitation of the Blue faction as vocal and physical supporters. Sergeant (ταξεώτης) of the city prefect: responsible for supervising arrests. Only *CP* mentions these lesser officials.

[426] Coronation of Heraclius: Theophanes 299. 8-14 records that the ceremony was performed in the oratory of Stephen within the Palace (see Janin, *Églises* 473-4), and that immediately afterwards Sergius conducted the marriage of

Tuesday, while a race meeting was being held, the head of Leontius the Syrian was brought in and burnt in the Hippodrome, along with the image of Phocas which, during his lifetime, foolish men wearing white robes had conducted into the Hippodrome with lighted candles. At the same time the Blue flag was also burnt. [427]

**611 Indiction 14, year 1 in the reign of Heraclius Augustus.**

From the 7th inclusive of the month October of the present indiction 14 up till the thirteenth of the month January of the same [p.702] indiction, it was recorded in the records as, 'In the reign of Heraclius'. And from the 14th inclusive of the same month for the ensuing year, namely until the completion of December of year 15 of the tax period, it was recorded as follows, 'And in the consulship of our same most pious lord'. For even though he did not parade in a chariot, still it was decreed that it should be credited to him as a consulship. [428]

In this year in the month Xanthicus, on April 20th according to the Romans, a Tuesday, at the 7th hour, there occurred a great earthquake, with the result that before Pentecost on the 22nd of the same month, a Thursday, it was necessary for a litany to be held in the Campus and the Trisagion to be chanted. [429]

Heraclius and Eudocia. Nicephorus (5. 10-16) mentions that Heraclius initially proposed Priscus as emperor, but was then himself proclaimed by the senate and people. John of Nikiu (110. 9) places the coronation, said to be against the will of Heraclius (cf. CP p. 708. 5-9), in the church of St. Thomas.

[427] Race meeting: the Blues had been closely identified with Phocas in Cpl. and throughout the empire to such an extent that when Heraclius entered the capital they had fled to St. Sophia for asylum (J. Nik. 110. 3). The burning of the Blue flag in the Hippodrome was symbolic punishment and humiliation for these opponents. The ceremony organized by Phocas for the honouring of his image resembles the anniversary celebrations initiated by Constantine (CP p. 530. 2-11); Phocas may have introduced his own image and possibly also revived the ceremony, if it had lapsed, cf. n. 56.

[428] **611** Heraclius' consulship: the Ides (13th) of Jan. were the occasion of the first important race meeting of the new year (at which the Nika Riot broke out in 532), and so provided a suitably festive context to which the fictitious consulship could be attached. Shortage of money is the most likely reason for Heraclius' failure to assume the consulship. From 612 onwards CP's year headings incorporate the fictional consulship. An imperial consulship was now regarded as an essential part of the ruler's title as well as of the dating mechanisms for his reign (cf. n. 394). This notice illustrates the concern of the chronicler, and presumably also of officials in Cpl., with precise chronological definition.

[429] Earthquake: not recorded elsewhere. The Campus Martius at the Hebdomon was an appropriate open space at which to offer prayers to God to avert further manifestations of divine anger, and was used for annual commemorations of the earthquake of 447 (cf. ss.aa. 447, 450 with nn. 256, 262).

And on the 7th of the month July in the same indiction 14, a Wednesday, at hour 8, Epiphania the daughter of Heraclius and Eudocia was born at the suburban palace of Hieria.[430]

## Olympiad 348

**612** Indiction 15, year 2, post-consulship of Heraclius Augustus.

In this year in the month Artemisius, on May 3rd according to the Romans, a Wednesday, Heraclius II Constantine, son of Heraclius and Eudocia, was born in the suburban palace of Sophianae.[431]

And on the 13th of the month August in the same indiction 15, a Sunday, the Augusta Eudocia, who was also called Fabia, died at the suburban palace of Blachernae. And when her body had been conveyed [p.703] by boat to the Palace in the city, on the following day her funeral was held and she was buried at the Apostles.[432]

And on the 4th of Hyperberetaeus, the month October according to the Romans, in indiction 1, a Wednesday, the child Epiphania, who was also called Eudocia, was crowned in St. Stephen in the Palace. Seated in a chariot and escorted by Philaretus the *cubicularius* and *chartularius* and by Synetus the *castrensis*, she departed as is customary to the Great Church.[433]

For the Trisagion chant used at time of earthquake, cf. *s.a.* 533 with n. 373.

430 Birth of Epiphania: cf. Theoph. 299. 18-20 (also recording her baptism at Blachernae on 15 Aug.).

Palace of Hieria: built by Justinian on the Asiatic shore south of Chalcedon (Proc. *Bld.* i. 11. 16-22); a favourite residence for Heraclius (see Janin, *Const.* 148-50).

431 **612** Birth of Heraclius II Constantine: cf. Theoph. 300. 7-9, Nic. 5. 30-1.

Sophianae palace: built by Justin II on the Asiatic shore of the Bosporus, probably at Çengelköy (see Averil Cameron, 'Sophiae' 11-18).

432 Death of Eudocia: cf. Theoph. 300. 9-10, though with the date 14 Aug. (possibly by confusion with the funeral). Nicephorus (7. 12-27) records that Eudocia died of epilepsy, and that her funeral was marred by a strange incident when a foreign maidservant accidentally spat from an upstairs window onto the open coffin and was promptly burnt to death by the outraged crowd of mourners.

Palace of Blachernae: located close to the sanctuary of the Virgin, which was just outside the city walls on the Golden Horn, Janin, *Const.* 123-5; cf. n. 478.

433 Coronation of Epiphania Eudocia: cf. Theoph. 300. 12-14. Oratory of St. Stephen: cf. n. 426. Officials of the imperial bedchamber (*cubiculum*) attended the child: Philaretus was probably *chartularius* (secretary) to the *castrensis* (majordomo), see Jones, *LRE* 567-8.

In the same year in the month Apellaeus, on December 5th according to the Romans, a Tuesday, Priscus the *comes excubitorum* became a cleric, and in his place Nicetas the patrician was made *comes excubitorum*. [434]

In this year the venerable Cross was placed on top of the composite column to the east of the church of the 40 Saints, while Theodore the former notary of the imperial household was city prefect. [435]

**613** Indiction 1, year 3, the 2nd post-consulship of Heraclius Augustus.

In this year in the month Audynaeus, on January 22nd according to the Romans, a Monday, the child Heraclius II Constantine was crowned emperor by his father Heraclius in the Palace; and straightway he ascended into the Hippodrome and there, wearing the crown, he received obeisance from the senators as emperor, and was acclaimed **[p.704]** by the factions; and so, carried by Philaretus, he departed to the Great Church with his father.

And from this 22nd of the month January, it was ordered that

---

[434] Priscus and Nicetas: for details, see Nic. 5. 31-7. 11. Nicetas, the cousin of Heraclius who had been responsible for capturing Egypt from Phocas, had only reached Cpl. in 612, when he was elevated to the rank of patrician. Priscus, son-in-law of Phocas, had been sent by Heraclius to Cappadocia to command operations against the Persians in Caesarea, but he had there fallen out with Heraclius (Nic. 5. 16-29). The baptism of Heraclius II Constantine provided an opportunity to demote Priscus, who was lured to the ceremony by the prospect of being the child's godfather; once inside the Palace away from the protection of his bodyguards, Priscus was forced to become a monk and retired to the monastery of the Chora (the modern Kariye Camii, near the Edirne Gate, Janin, *Églises* 531-8), where he died a year later. At the same time, Heraclius raised his brother Theodore to the post of *curopalatus*, and gave Priscus' command in the east to Philippicus, formerly brother-in-law and general of Maurice, thus establishing the loyalty of a key circle of officials (Bury, *HLRE* [1] ii. 210-11). *Comes excubitorum* : cf. n. 406.

[435] Composite column: the column whose construction by Phocas is recorded *s.a.* 609, cf. n. 415. *Patria* ii. 64 (p. 185) mentions the column with the Cross (wrongly attributing it to Constantine), and Nicephorus Callistus (*PG* cxlvi. col. 121) records a line of the inscription which Heraclius added on this occasion (though Nicephorus claims that the Cross was merely being restored after toppling in an earthquake in Maurice's 18th year; cf. Mango, *Const.* 31). It is not clear how Phocas had intended to decorate the column; Heraclius' choice of a Cross is in accordance with his Christian presentation of his coup, as for example the icons of the Virgin on his boats in 610 (Theoph. 298. 17).

Notary: see Jones, *LRE* 572-5, Guilland, *Recherches* i. 306 (= *REB* xiv, 1956, 133). 'Notary of the imperial household' perhaps distinguishes the post from ecclesiastical notaries; cf. *s.a.* 528 for Peter, former notary of the emperor.

it be recorded, after the introductory 'In the name of...', as 'In the reign of our most sacred lords and greatest benefactors, in year 3 of Flavius Heraclius the most pious, and in year 2 after his consulship, and in year 1 of Flavius Heraclius II Constantine his God-protected son, the eternal Augusti and emperors.'[436]

**614** Indiction 2, year 4, the 3rd post-consulship of Heraclius Augustus.

And from 22nd of the month January, it is recorded as year 2 of the reign of Heraclius II Constantine.

In this year in about the month June, we suffered a calamity which deserves unceasing lamentations. For, together with many cities of the east, Jerusalem too was captured by the Persians, and in it were slain many thousands of clerics, monks, and virgin nuns. The Lord's tomb was burnt and the far-famed temples of God, and, in short, all the precious things were destroyed. The venerated wood of the Cross, together with the holy vessels that were beyond enumeration, was taken by the Persians, and the Patriarch Zacharias also became a prisoner. **[p.705]** And this has not taken a long time to come to pass, not even a whole month, but a few days.[437]

---

[436] **613** Coronation of Heraclius II: Theophanes 300. 14-16 dates this to 25 Dec. 612. Although G. Ostrogorsky (*BNJ* vii, 1930, 29 n. 2; followed by Stein, 'Post-consulat' 891) preferred Theophanes' date because Christmas seemed a suitable occasion for this ceremony, 22 Jan. was regularly taken as the start of Heraclius Constantine's regnal years, and this remains inexplicable unless it was the actual date of his coronation, as recorded by *CP*. Throughout the rest of the chronicle each year is introduced by a sentence recording the change in the regnal year of Heraclius II on 22 Jan.

[437] **614** Capture of Jerusalem: cf. Theoph. 300. 30-301. 5 (*a.m.* 6106, i.e. AD 614/5, one year late); Nic. 15. 5-9. The best account is a sermon by Antiochus Strategius, a monk of the Mar Saba monastery, who witnessed the sack; also Sebeos ch. 24. When the Persian armies approached, the Patriarch Zacharias attempted to negotiate a surrender since there seemed to be no prospect of relief from the emperor, but this was thwarted, apparently by members of the circus factions (Strat. 2. 5).

Date: Strategius (8. 5) records that the attack began on 15 April and that the city was stormed on the 21st day of a siege efficiently prosecuted by the Persian general Shahvaraz; this should be 5 May. Strategius, however, delivered his sermon on 20 May, apparently in commemoration of the day of the sack. Sebeos states that Jerusalem was captured on the 19th day of the siege, 10 days after Easter, the 28th day of the month Margats (equated with 26 May by Macler, ad loc., 19 May by Thomson, *Artsrunik* p. 156 n. 3, who suggests it should be 10 days after Ascension). A date towards the end of May would be consistent with *CP*'s reference to June, if the latter is taken as the date when the disaster was reported at Cpl.

Sebeos records 35,000 captives and 57,000 dead; Strategius numbers the

And on the 14th of Gorpiaeus, the month September according to the Romans, in the third indiction, the precious sponge was fastened onto the life-giving Cross at the third Exaltation and was itself also exalted with it in the most holy Great Church, since it had been dispatched by Nicetas the patrician.

And on the 28th of Hyperberetaeus, the month October according to the Romans, a Saturday, on the eve before the Lord's Day, the precious spear was brought from the Holy Places, since one of those close to the accursed Salvaraz, after it had been captured by them, had given it to the aforementioned Nicetas. And straightway, on the same Lord's Day, it was proclaimed in the most holy Great Church that it had been brought. And on the Tuesday and Wednesday it was venerated by men, and on Thursday and Friday by women.[438]

**615** Indiction 3, year 5, the 4th post-consulship of Heraclius Augustus.

---

dead as 66,509, and records that the local Jewish population contributed to the total by ransoming Christian captives from the Persians and killing them; cf. Theoph. loc. cit. The survivors, led by the Patriarch Zacharias, and the booty including the True Cross were removed to Persia. The fate of the True Cross is uncertain, since Strategius states that the Persians forced the captives to march over it; however, it later became convenient to assert that the relic had survived intact in Persia in the possession of Khusro's Christian wife Shirin, until it was surrendered to Heraclius in 629/30; see further Mango, 'Deux Études' 113-14.

The author of CP seeks to highlight these events, which he clearly regarded as catastrophic, by a brief attempt at an uncharacteristically flowery style, e.g. opening sentence (cf. p. 716. 9-10), tricolon of 'clerics, monks and virgin nuns' (cf. p. 716. 15-16), 'far-famed temples', and the periphrastic last sentence.

[438] Relics: the organization of new religious ceremonies in Cpl. is an aspect of official attempts to restore the morale of the populace after the catastrophe of the capture of Jerusalem, cf. n. 440. The loss of the main relic of the Cross concentrated attention on other physical adjuncts of the Crucifixion. Nicetas, now commander of the Byzantine forces in the east, had so few troops at his disposal that he could do little more than organize support for refugees from Palestine who fled to Egypt; it was presumably during this relief work that he acquired the sacred sponge and spear. At some point Shahvaraz, 'the accursed Salvaraz', became a Christian: for Christianity in his family, see Mango, 'Deux Études' 105-17.

Dates: the Feast of the Invention of the Cross, at which the Cross was exalted, was originally celebrated on 14 Sept. (cf. s.a. 334 with n. 62): this date was subsequently associated with Heraclius' restoration of the Cross to Jerusalem in 630, an event which actually occurred in March. In 614, 28 Oct. fell on a Monday: the date should probably be 26 Oct.

Worship: men and women were segregated in different parts of the church (see Mathews, *Churches* 130-4): the designation of separate days for the sexes would appear to be an extension of this practice to allow both men and women to venerate a centrally-placed relic without coming into contact with each other.

And from 22nd inclusive of the month January it is recorded as year 3 of the reign of Heraclius II Constantine.

In this year, under Sergius patriarch of Constantinople, from the 1st week of Lent, in indiction 4,[439] a chant was introduced after the 'Let it be directed', at the moment when the pre-sanctified gifts are brought to the altar from the sacristy [p.706] after the priest has said, 'In accordance with the gift of your Christ', the congregation at once begins, 'Now the powers of the heavens are invisibly worshipping with us: for behold, the king of glory enters in. Behold, the mystic and perfect sacrifice is being escorted. In faith and fear let us approach, so that we may become partakers in eternal life. Alleluia!'. This is chanted not only during Lent as pre-sanctified offerings are brought in, but also on other days, whenever there are pre-sanctified offerings.[440]

In this year, there was made by law a six-gram silver coin, and imperial payments were made with it, and at half their old rate.[441]

---

[439] 615 Date: the indiction date is one year out – it should either be indiction 3 or the notice belongs in AD 616. See Appendix 3 for discussion of Ericsson's postulated textual transposition.

[440] Liturgical change: the chant was inserted at the Great Entrance, when the consecrated bread and wine were brought into the church; this moment could be treated as symbolic of Christ's entry into Jerusalem, and the new chant may have been meant to focus the congregation's thoughts on the recovery of the Holy City, by increasing their participation in the liturgy at this solemn moment. In the eastern church during Lent, the full mass was only celebrated on Saturdays, Sundays (not counted in the 40 days of fasting), and Holy Thursday (in honour of the Last Supper); on all other occasions pre-sanctified offerings were used, with a special liturgy. On the liturgy, and the sacristy (*skeuophylakion*) of St. Sophia, see further Mathews, *Churches* 155-62, esp. 158; Taft, *Great Entrance* 76, 192-4; Brightman, *Liturgies* i. 345-52. 'Let [our prayer] be directed': Psalm 140 (141). 2.

This information on liturgical changes (cf. *s.a.* 624) reflects the interests of the author of *CP* (probably a member of Sergius' clergy).

[441] Coinage: there appear to have been two elements in the change recorded by *CP*, first the introduction of a new coin, the hexagram (evidence reviewed by Hendy, *Economy* 494-5, and examined in detail by P. Yannopoulos, *L'Hexagramme, un monnayage byzantin en argent du VIIe siècle*, Numismatica Lovaniensia iii, 1978), and second, perhaps more importantly, the tariffing of this new coin at about double its correct value in terms of its precious metal content. Hendy (loc. cit.) states that the bullion and face value of the hexagram were not greatly discrepant, since it turns up in hoards well beyond imperial frontiers, but for export purposes the coin would have been treated as a weight of silver, not as a unit of currency with a specific value. The introduction of this over-valued coin may have been connected with the quinquennial donative that was now due, as well as with the cost of warfare against the Persians and diplomacy in the Balkans.

Law: presumably to enforce the false valuation, since a law was scarcely

And the Persian commander, who was called Saen, came as far as Chalcedon itself and to the regions of Chrysopolis and Ceconium, and he looked across to the opposite side.[442] And after receiving gifts from the emperor Heraclius, who personally approached the harbour of Chalcedon in a fleet, he retired, after proclaiming that if certain of us were dispatched on an embassy to Chosroes, there would be peace. And indeed three ambassadors were dispatched from us, namely Olympius

necessary for the introduction of a new coin, whereas the gold/silver ratio (the point at issue here) was established by law (*Cod. Theod.* viii. 4. 27; *Cod. Iust.* x. 78. 1). Because this new coin was used for imperial payments it effectively halved official expenditure internally; the government must also have stipulated that only gold coin would be accepted for tax payments, as the coins would otherwise quickly have passed full circle.

Financial problems: various stories of lost imperial treasure (Nic. 12. 10-14 for Heraclius; J. Nik. 110. 4 for Phocas) reflect a popular awareness of the difficulties. The report that the bronze ox in the Theodosian Forum was melted down for a military treasury (*Parast.* 42) probably points to a very rare use of bronze for soldiers' pay. Hendy (*Economy* 229 n. 55) assumes that the silver equivalent, 24 pounds, of the melted bronze was sent for the army; however, the concluding sentence of *Parast.* 42 implies that the bronze was struck directly into coins, and Heraclius did mint bronze for some military needs (P. Grierson, *Catalogue of the Byzantine Coins in the Dumbarton Oaks Collection and in the Whittemore Collection* ii, pt. 1, Washington 1968, 220). There were other attempts to reduce expenditure: the bronze *follis* was reduced *c.*616 from approximately 11 to 8 grams, then to 6 grams in the 620s, and 4.5 in the 630s (C. Morrisson, *Catalogue des monnaies byzantines de la Bibliothèque Nationale*, Paris 1970, i. 260). These shortages were not alleviated until Heraclius appropriated the accumulated treasures of the church in 622 (Theoph. 302. 34-303. 3; cf. Nic. 15. 2-4).

[442] Shahin (Saen) at the Bosporus: after capturing Jerusalem in 614, the Persians had advanced across Asia Minor to reach the Aegean at Ephesus and the Bosporus, see C. Foss, 'The Persians in Asia Minor and the End of Antiquity', *EHR* xc, 1975, 721-47. Nicephorus 9. 18-20 notes that Shahin first besieged Chalcedon for a long time. Theophanes records Persian advances to Chalcedon in 607/8 (296. 9-11) and again in 616/7 (301. 15-16, correcting Carthage to Chalcedon), and places embassies from Heraclius to Khusro in 613/4 (300. 21-5) and 617/8 (301. 21-4), but it is likely that there was only one advance to Chalcedon in these years. There is no reason to reject CP's date.

Ericsson's discussion ('Date' 24-7) of the passage is unconvincing: she postulates that this sentence relates to the arrival of Shahvaraz in 626 (the names of the Persian generals being interchanged), and that before the report of Heraclius' diplomacy there must be a lacuna in which Shahin's attack on Chalcedon was recorded, but this entails pressing Nicephorus' brief mention over-precisely; see further Appendix 3.

Chrysopolis: modern Üsküdar, on the Bosporus facing Cpl.; Ceconium was also located on the Bosporus, probably slightly to the north (Janin, *Const.* 494-5, 487).

praetorian prefect, Leontius city prefect, and Anastasius presbyter of the most holy Great Church in Constantinople.[443] They also carried written dispatches from our officials to the apostate Chosroes, whose purport is this:

[p.707] 'God, who fashioned all things and sustains them with his might, bestowed upon the race of men as a gift worthy of his goodness the providence of empire, by means of which we are deemed worthy of an untroubled existence or we discover a remedy if we encounter any adversities. Having regard to this divine thing, by which we mean the imperial providence, and to your superabundant clemency above all else, we beseech that you deem us worthy of pardon for daring to make the present recourse to your might, contrary to the former political institution. For we know that in the preceding period the practice prevailed which, when some dispute sprang up between the two states, encouraged their respective sovereigns to resolve the points of dispute by means of communications to each other. But Phocas who plotted against the Roman state dissolved this arrangement: for after secretly corrupting the Roman army in Thrace, he suddenly attacked our imperial city and killed Maurice who piously ruled over us, and his wife, and in addition his children, relatives, and not a few of the officials. And he was not satisfied with his accomplishment of such great evils, but he did not even render the honour that was appropriate to your superabundant clemency, so that thereafter, incited by our faults,

---

[443] Negotiations: cf. Nic. 9. 20-12. 2, which includes (but only in the Vatican recension) a high-flown speech composed for Shahin, who urged on Heraclius the benefits of peace, promising that he spoke for Khusro and would assist in urging Khusro to agree to terms; he subsequently turned against the ambassadors as soon as he reached Persia; Nicephorus notes that Shahin performed obeisance to Heraclius (9. 23-6) and that Khusro executed him for failing to arrest the 'prisoner' (11. 25-30). In fact Shahin survived to die naturally in 626 (Theoph. 315. 23-4), while *CP*'s emphasis on Heraclius' gifts and personal diplomacy as the important factor in securing Shahin's help seems more plausible. There is no confirmation for Stratos' suggestion (*Byzantium* 116-17) that Shahin was persuaded to negotiate by the surprise approach of an army commanded by Philippicus, an army that subsequently vanishes.

Ambassadors: Nicephorus records the same names, but describes Anastasius as the *oikonomos* of the patriarch; subsequently *CP* also describes Anastasius as *syncellus* (p. 709. 11), the cell-mate of the patriarch: the inclusion on the embassy of a high-ranking ecclesiastic reflects the importance of the church in secular affairs. Leontius: possibly the city prefect mentioned *s.a.* 603 (although he may have been killed in 610: cf. n. 425). In spite of Shahin's assurances, the ambassadors were maltreated in Persia, where they eventually perished (Nic. 20. 16-20).

you brought the affairs of the Roman state to this great diminution.

[p.708] 'When he who is now piously ruling over us, together with his father of eternal memory, discovered what had been done by that corrupter, they planned to liberate the Roman state from the great duress of that man. This they in fact achieved, although they found that state humbled by your might. And after the death of the usurper, our emperor wished to take his relatives and to return to his own father in Africa, after urging us to elect the man we wanted as emperor. With difficulty won over by our entreaties, he accepted the sovereignty; and on account of the disturbance prevailing in the two states, and in addition because of the intestine strife, he did not have an opportunity to do what ought to have been done, to present by means of an embassy the honour that was owed to the superabundant might of your serenity.

'And so we decided to disregard the custom which we mentioned above and, being insignificant men, to employ entreaty to such a supreme king, by sending certain of us indeed who should be deemed worthy of your footsteps. But because of the intervening events, we have not dared to do this until now. However, when Saen the most glorious Babmanzadag, commander of the Persian army, came to the regions of Chalcedon and met our most pious emperor and ourselves, being entreated by all to hold discussions concerning peace, he said that he did not himself have such power, but that concerning this he would make request of [p.709] your beneficence. But now he has also sent us a dispatch by Spadadavar, promising on oath that your superabundant Might would receive in appropriate manner those dispatched by us and send them off unharmed to return to us, and that it was commanded by your beneficence that this be done. We in turn, having confidence in this sequence of events, and above all in God and in your majesty, have sent off your slaves Olympius the most glorious former consul, patrician and praetorian prefect, and Leontius the most glorious former consul, patrician and city prefect, and Anastasius the most God-loved presbyter and *syncellus*; we beseech that they be received in appropriate manner by your superabundant Might, and that they shortly return to us, securing for us the peace which is pleasing to God and appropriate to your peace-loving Might. We beg too of your clemency to consider Heraclius, our most pious emperor, as a true son, one who is eager to perform the service of your serenity in all things. For if you do this, you will procure a two-fold glory for yourselves, both in respect of your valour in war and in respect of your gift of peace. And hereafter we shall be in enjoyment of tranquillity through your gifts, which will be remembered for ever, receiving an opportunity to offer prayers to God for your long-lasting prosperity and keeping your benefaction free from oblivion for the eternal duration of the Roman state.'[444]

[p.710]					Olympiad 349

616 Indiction 4, year 6, the 5th post-consulship of Heraclius Augustus.

And from 22nd inclusive of the month January it is recorded as year 4 of the reign of Heraclius II Constantine.

From the birth of the Lord Christ up till this consulship, 619 years have been completed and 620 have begun. From this total are subtracted the 33 years until his Crucifixion, and there are left 586. Now 586 years ago the month March began on

---

[444] Letter to Khusro: the author of *CP* seems to have had access to an accurate copy of this letter, which displays the periphrastic rhetoric typical of much late Roman diplomacy. The Romans' only resort lay in an appeal to Khusro's better nature, much as Khusro had approached Maurice in 590, but without the supporting argument that legitimate sovereigns should help each other, since Khusro did not accept Heraclius' presentation of himself as the avenger of Maurice. This probably explains why officials, perhaps the senate, rather than the emperor assumed responsibility for the diplomatic initiative (Stratos, *Byzantium* 115-17). Khusro would have rejected overtures from Heraclius as from a usurper, whereas the officials could defend Heraclius' legitimacy as sovereign and offer him to Khusro as a willing adoptive son (*CP* p. 709. 14-17), a similar relationship to that of Khusro to Maurice in 590. Sebeos (ch. 26) preserves a letter that Khusro may have sent in reply to this initiative: Heraclius is presented as a vile slave, a usurper whose God has failed to save him, but is offered pardon, estates, and a pension if he comes to Khusro and asks for forgiveness.

Breakdown in diplomatic relations: Phocas did in fact send the customary embassy at his accession (Theophylact viii. 15. 2-7), whereas Heraclius appears not even to have attempted this courtesy. Khusro had exploited Phocas' tyranny as an excuse for war (Theophylact viii. 15. 7), and Phocas was blamed as far as possible for the manifold humiliations suffered by the Romans in the early 7th c.

Heraclius' reluctance to assume the throne: cf. Nic. 5. 10-16 (he offers the throne to Priscus but is persuaded by senate and people to take it himself); also J. Nik. 110. 9. The elder Heraclius died in Africa after his son's accession (J. Nik. 110. 13).

Babmanzadag: a rendition of the Persian Wohu-manañh, signifying the personification of the Good Spirit (Justi, *IN* 374-5). Spadadavar: more commonly Aspabad in Greek, a military title.

Thursday: for one must add to the 586 the leap years, that is 147, because it is currently a leap year: it comes to 733. Subtract from this 7 times 104, the remainder is 5. Count 5 from the Thursday, and you stop at Monday, which is correct. For the March of the current indiction 4 begins on Monday of the week.[445]

Again if we investigate the periods of the 19-year cycle, we find that 586 years ago, that is to say 30 cycles, it was indiction 11. For 11 up to 11 totals 571; the remainder is 12, 13, 14, 15, 16, 17, 18, 19, 1, 2, 3, 4, 5, 6, 7; for this is the indiction now current.[446] Then if we calculate the moon 586 years ago, we find that on the 23rd of that month March, which was on Friday, it was 14 days old, 5, so that the Passover [p.711] of the Jews when the Lord was crucified began on Friday evening. The Lord rose on the following Sunday, which was the 25th of the same month March. This is consistent with the prior determinations of reputable men in the calculation of the heavenly bodies.[447]

---

[445] **616** Computation: the reason for this further chronological computation is unclear. The calculation in 609 had already served to verify the author's chronology for the start of Heraclius' reign, and this notice merely adds further confirmation that the author had counted the appropriate number of years since the birth of Christ and the Crucifixion. The first part of the calculation is relatively straightforward, and verifies the date by checking the day of the week on 1 March, using the same method as *s.a.* 609 (when 1 April was verifed: cf. n. 414). In AD 31 1 March fell on a Thursday, since the Crucifixion occurred on Friday 23 March in that year (*CP* p. 415. 13). After the passage of 586 years, 1 March would fall 5 days later (counting inclusively), namely on Monday.

[446] 19-year cycle: the second part of the computation provides a further cross-check with reference to the 'indictions' of the 19-year lunar cycle. The Crucifixion had occurred in year 11 of the lunar cycle (*CP* p. 409. 1-2), so that reckoning inclusively from then up to the most recent lunar year 11 gives 571 years (30 cycles of 19, plus one for the inclusive reckoning). Since the Crucifixion occurred 586 years ago, there remained a difference of 15 years between the lunar indiction then and the current one: this difference is then counted through the 19-year cycle, terminating in year 7, the current lunar year.

[447] Age of moon at Crucifixion: this calculation adds nothing to the cross-checking, but restates the conclusions of the calculation at *CP* pp. 414-15. The age of the moon at the first Easter was a problem in *CP*'s chronology since, whereas the Crucifixion had to occur on a Friday, on the eve of the Jewish Passover (which began when the moon was 14 days old), in *CP*'s *annus mundi* 5540 (year of Crucifixion) the moon was only 13 days old on Friday 23 March. The discrepancy was resolved by a complex reckoning of fractions of days (for which, see Grumel, *Chronologie* 79-80). The significance of the figure 5 (ε) after the age of the moon is unclear to us; it might relate to the hour of the night, which is connected with calculations concerning the Crucifixion at *CP* p. 410. 14.

**617** Indiction 5, year 7, the 6th post-consulship of Heraclius Augustus.[448]

And from 22nd inclusive of the month January it is recorded as year 5 of the reign of Heraclius II Constantine.

**618** Indiction 6, year 8, the 7th post-consulship of Heraclius Augustus.

And from 22nd inclusive of the month January it is recorded as year 6 of the reign of Heraclius II Constantine.

In this year the recipients of the state bread were requested for 3 coins for each loaf as a levy. And after everyone had provided this, straightway in the month August of the same indiction 6 the provision of this state bread was completely suspended.[449]

**619** Indiction 7, year 9, the 8th post-consulship of Heraclius Augustus.

And from 22nd inclusive of the month January it is recorded as year 7 of the reign of Heraclius II Constantine.

## Olympiad 350

**620** Indiction 8, year 10, the 9th post-consulship of Heraclius Augustus.

**[p.712]** And from 22nd inclusive of the month January it is recorded as year 8 of the reign of Heraclius II Constantine.

---

[448] **617** Consul: Theophanes 301. 16-18 records a consulship for Heraclius II Constantine on 1 Jan., but this is not attested by *CP* or *Heracl*. Stein ('Post-consulat' 893-4 n. 1) suggested that Theophanes has inserted the notice one indiction cycle (15 years) early, and this is supported by Nic. 22. 26-23. 1.

[449] **618** Bread ration: as a capital city, Cpl. had received the privilege of a free bread distribution from Constantine (*CP s.a.* 332 with n. 59). Payment was now imposed at a rate of 3 *folles* per loaf (translating *nomismata* as 'coins': cf. p. 706. 9), not 3 *'solidi'* (e.g. Ericsson, 'Date' 19, a confused discussion; Haldon, *Praetorians* 442 n. 354), which would give an impossibly high price for a loaf of bread. (*CP* refers to loaves, not 'bread tickets' as Ericsson loc. cit.) In the famine of 463 bread had sold for 3 *folles* per loaf, according to *CP s.a.* (with n. 281); making allowance for inflation in the intervening 150 years, 3 *folles* was perhaps now not an exceptional charge, and in 626 (cf. *CP s.a.* with n. 456) there was an attempt to increase this to 8 *folles*.

This change, soon to be followed by the suspension of distributions, illustrates both the empire's financial problems and the disruption to the grain supply caused by the Persian capture of Egypt, the normal granary of Cpl.; Persian armies had entered the province in 616, and Alexandria finally surrendered in 619. Nicephorus 12. 4-8 records, not surprisingly, that the loss of Egyptian corn caused a famine and that plague struck soon after.

**621** Indiction 9, year 11, post-consulship of Heraclius Augustus year 10. [450]

And from 22nd inclusive of the month January it is recorded as year 9 of the reign of Heraclius II Constantine.

**622** Indiction 10, year 12, post-consulship of Heraclius Augustus year 11.

And from 22nd inclusive of the month January it is recorded as year 10 of the reign of Heraclius II Constantine.

**623** Indiction 11, year 13, the 12th post-consulship of Heraclius Augustus.

And from 22nd inclusive of the month January it is recorded as year 11 of the reign of Heraclius II Constantine.

In this year in month Daisius, on June 5th according to the Romans, a Sunday, the emperor Heraclius was in the Thracian regions with certain officials, and not only certain property-owners and clergy, but also shopkeepers and partisans from each of the two factions and a considerable throng of others, when the Chagan of the Avars approached the Long Wall with an innumerable throng, since, as it was supposedly rumoured, peace was about to be made between Romans and Avars, and chariot races were about to be held at Heracleia. An innumerable throng, misled by this rumour, came out from the all-blessed city. And about hour 4 of this Lord's Day the Chagan **[p.713]** of the Avars signalled with his whip, and all who were with him charged and entered the Long Wall, although he remained outside the wall with some of his men; and supposedly he said that he would have both entered the wall and taken the city except that God prevented him. However, his men who entered on this Lord's Day plundered all whom they found outside the city from the west as far as the Golden Gate, together also with the men and animals of various kinds present for whatever reason in the suburbs. They entered both SS Cosmas and Damian at Blachernae, and the Archangel on the far side in the quarter of Promotus; not only did they remove the ciboria and other treasures, but they also broke up the holy altar itself of the church of the Archangel, and without any opposition transported everyone, along with the things removed, to the far side of the Danube. [451]

---

[450] **621** The MS has a slight variation in the post-consular formula for this year (incorrectly recorded in the Bonn text) the same as in 622; cf. also *s.a.* 626.

[451] **623** Avar attack: on the date of this incident, which we believe that *CP* records correctly, see discussion in Appendix 4.

Heraclius had to establish peace in the Balkans to allow him to concentrate on the Persian campaign to which he was already committed, and his hope in

Olympiad 351

**624** Indiction 12, year 14, the 13th post-consulship of Heraclius Augustus.

And from 22nd inclusive of the month January it is recorded as year 12 of the reign of Heraclius II Constantine.

In this year in the month Dystrus, March according to the Romans, on the 25th of the month, on the day of the Annunciation of our Lady **[p.714]** the Mother of God, the emperor Heraclius departed for the eastern regions, together with his children Heraclius and Epiphania, who was also called Eudocia, and the empress Martina. In their company he kept the Easter festival near the city of Nicomedia; after the festival the emperor Heraclius himself with Martina the empress set out for

organizing the meeting with the Avar Chagan seems to have been that Roman expertise at lavish ceremonial might suggest an opulence and strength which the inadequate Roman military forces could not substantiate (cf. Theophylact i. 3. 8-12 for analogous use of lavish gifts by Maurice). This explains the choice of location: it would have been dangerous to admit the Chagan into Cpl., whereas Heracleia was perhaps the nearest city in the Balkans to possess a hippodrome or similar suitable venue for the grand occasion. Heraclius' entourage, ceremonial rather than military, with the circus factions present to provide organized chanting (Cameron, *Factions* 257), also indicates that fighting was not expected.

This incident is also described by Nicephorus (12. 29-14. 10) and Theophanes (301. 26-302. 4). After securing a preliminary promise of goodwill from the Chagan (Nic. 12. 29-13. 10), Heraclius advanced as far as Selymbria (Nic. 13. 14-15), modern Silivri, at the south end of the Long Walls, 40 miles west of Cpl. (cf. n. 322); the Chagan posted troops to the rear of Heraclius, but the latter discovered this and fled ignominiously carrying his crown, at which point the Avars attacked (Nic. 13. 16-28); they ravaged as far as the Hebdomon and the Golden Gate at the south end of the Theodosian walls and the head of the Golden Horn to the north, and apparently took 270,000 captives (Nic. 13. 28-14. 10). In spite of this misfortune, it seems that Heraclius still made an agreement with the Chagan (Theoph. 302. 15-21; Theod. Sync. 302. 4-5; Nic. 17. 16-24): he had no choice, since he could not fight the Persians and the Avars at the same time. The terms recorded by Nicephorus reveal the desperation of the Romans, an annual payment of 200,000 *solidi*, and the surrender as hostages of illegitimate sons of Heraclius and Bonus the patrician, and of Heraclius' nephew Stephen.

Cosmas and Damian: at or near modern Eyüp on the Golden Horn, so that Blachernae is perhaps used loosely for a wide area; see Janin, *Églises* 286-9. Archangel Michael at Promotus: probably identical with the church at Anaplus on the Bosporus, modern Kuruçeşme. Both had been lavishly rebuilt or extended by Justinian, Janin, *Églises* 344-5, 444-5 with 338-40. This attack will have been the occasion for the removal by the Romans from the church to the Virgin at Blachernae of precious metals and the casket containing the Virgin's Robe, as described in the contemporary text translated and discussed by Averil Cameron, 'Robe'; see also Speck, *Bellum Avaricum* 39-41.

the eastern regions,[452] and Anianus *domesticus* of the *magister* was also with them;[453] but his children returned to Constantinople.

In this year in the month Artemisius, May according to the Romans, in the 12th indiction, under Sergius patriarch of Constantinople, it was decided that there should be a chant after everyone had partaken of the Holy Mysteries, when the clergy were about to replace in the sacristy the precious flabella, patens, chalices, and other holy vessels, after the distribution had also been entirely replaced on the holy altar from the credence tables, and the final verse of the Communion had been chanted: this antiphon too should be recited, 'Let our mouth be filled with praise, Lord, so that we may hymn your glory because you have deemed us worthy to share in your Holy Mysteries. Preserve us

---

[452] 624 Heraclius' second Persian campaign: for the debate about the date, see Appendix 4. Easter 624 fell on 15 April, and Heraclius' departure for the east shortly afterwards can probably be linked with Theophanes' date of 20 April for Heraclius' 'invasion' of Persia (306. 26-7: see Baynes, 'Date' 113, for the interpretation of this expression to mean 'starting on his march for'). In 622, Heraclius had stayed in the capital to celebrate Easter (4 April) before setting out on campaign (Theoph. 302. 32-4); in 624 he chose a propitious day (the Annunciation) on which to leave Cpl., but still celebrated Easter before his campaign properly began. All this emphasized the religious significance of the Persian war (for which, compare the victory dispatch *s.a.* 628). Heraclius was not to return to Cpl. again until after the defeat and overthrow of Khusro in 628.

*CP* does not narrate the intervening campaigns (for which, see Bury, *HLRE* [1] ii. 230-43, Stratos, *Byzantium* 151-222), nor mention the preliminary expedition of 622, but the author took little interest in warfare, unless it directly affected Cpl. (see Introduction pp. xxv-xxvi). There were indeed very few decisive battles in 622–7, and these campaigns consisted mainly of important but confusing manoeuvres in the Armenian highlands and sub-Caucasian regions, interspersed with occasional skirmishes. Theophanes, perhaps following lost works of George of Pisidia, did his best to glamorize these, but it was by no means apparent that Heraclius was winning the war. At the time of the 626 siege of Cpl. defeat might have seemed likely, so that the contemporary chronicler prudently waited for conclusive proof in the form of Heraclius' victory dispatch in 628.

Martina: this is the only reference in *CP* to the empress, who was also Heraclius' niece (their marriage in 613/14 is not recorded); this suggests that the author disapproved of the incestuous union (cf. Nic. 14. 11-15. 2).

[453] Anianus: as *domesticus* he was deputy to the *magister officiorum* Bonus, who remained in Cpl.; see Bury, *IA* 50; Haldon, *Praetorians* 145-7. Bury suggested that Anianus went to command the *scholae*, but they were in Cpl. in May 626 (*CP s.a.*), and were not commanded in action by the *magister* (Jones, *LRE* 368-9). Part of Anianus' role may have been the difficult task of supervising communications between the emperor and the capital. He subsequently became *magister* (Nic. 24. 6).

in your holiness as we rehearse your justice throughout the whole day. Alleluia!'.[454]

**625** Indiction 13, year 15, the 14th post-consulship of Heraclius Augustus.

**[p.715]** And from 22nd inclusive of the month January it is recorded as year 13 of the reign of Heraclius II Constantine.

**626** Indiction 14, year 16, post-consulship of Heraclius Augustus year 15.

And from 22nd inclusive of the month January it is recorded as year 14 of the reign of Heraclius II Constantine.

In this year in the month Dystrus, March according to the Romans, an exceedingly bright star appeared for 4 days in the west after sunset.[455]

In this year in the month Artemisius, on May 14th according to the Romans, a Wednesday, at the holy Mid-Pentecost itself, the *scholae* and many others of the multitude congregated in the most holy Great Church and chanted against John who was called Seismos, because he wished to remove the bread of the *scholae* in the name of the soldiers. And the Patriarch Sergius promised to appease the crowd if only they would allow the sacred liturgy to take place.

On the fifteenth of the same month more people were again present in the most holy Great Church, and chanted against the said John. The patriarch, Alexander the praetorian prefect, and certain other officials, including Leontius the *comes Opsariou* and *spatharius*, went up into the *ambo* of the Great Church, and since many chants were made by the assembly against the stated John who was called Seismos **[p.716]** to the effect that he should no longer participate in affairs of state, that man was demoted and his images were at once destroyed. And Alexander the praetorian prefect made an address, saying, 'From now on you have a grant of bread from me, and I hope that I may speedily make restitution as regards it.' For the said John Seismos, when

---

[454] Liturgical change: cf. *s.a.* 615 (with n. 440) for another change. This chant was introduced at the reverse of the Entrance of the Mysteries at the end of the liturgical celebration: Mathews, *Churches* 159, 173; Brightman, *Liturgies* i. 536-7. Both were intended to emphasize that God was present with the congregation, a reliable source of protection in troubled times.

[455] **626** Star: the sighting of a comet in this year is also reported by Chinese astronomers, J. Williams, *Observations of Comets from B.C. 611 to A.D. 1640 extracted from the Chinese Annals* (London 1871), 40.

a loaf was being sold for 3 *folles*, himself planned to make it cost 8 *folles*. And God destroyed his plan.[456]

It is good to describe how now too the sole most merciful and compassionate God, by the welcome intercession of his undefiled Mother, who is in truth our Lady Mother of God and ever-Virgin Mary, with his mighty hand saved this humble city of his from the utterly godless enemies who encircled it in concert, and redeemed the people who were present within it from the imminent sword, captivity, and most bitter servitude;

---

[456]  Date: for discussion of Ericsson's attempt to redate this passage to 615, see Appendix 3.

John Seismos: the Earthquake (the noun means 'blackmail' or 'extortion' in 2nd-c. BC papyri: LSJ s.v. 3). His official position is unknown, but the reference to his images indicates that he was important; he might have been city prefect, since this official administered a fund for supplementary purchases of grain, but his actions may have exceeded his legitimate powers. Ericsson ('Date' 21) seeks to identify this John with John Tzittas who plotted against Phocas in 605, but both CP (p. 696. 16) and Theophanes (295. 10-11) distinguish John and Tzittas, and record that all named conspirators were executed.

*Scholae*: units of guards (*scholarii*), cf. n. 351. Their military effectiveness had by now declined, as indicated by the attempt to divert their rations to soldiers (presumably the troops who had recently arrived to strengthen Cpl.'s defences, cf. n. 461).

Bread ration: for problems in Cpl.'s food supply, cf. n. 449. Strictly the rations of the *scholae* were part of the distribution of civic bread and, if this were remembered, should have been included in the general suspension of bread distribution in 618; however, the *scholae* had defended their privileged rations on other occasions (*Cod. Theod.* xiv. 17. 8-11 catalogues a dispute in the late 4th c.; cf. Jones, *LRE* 697) and could well have done so again. Justinian is alleged to have persuaded the *scholae* to renounce their stipends by threatening to send them on active military service (Proc. *SH* 24. 21; cf. Theoph. 236. 16-20); this seems to parallel the logic of John's action, namely that the privileges of the *scholae* must be sacrificed to military need.

Great Church: the use of St. Sophia for popular demonstrations and mass meetings (cf. *CP* p. 727. 11) reflects not only the dominance of the Patriarch Sergius, but perhaps also the shrunken population of Cpl. (on which see Mango, *Const.* 53-5) for whom the Hippodrome was now too large an arena.

Alexander: as praetorian prefect he would have controlled the collection and transport of grain, Jones, *LRE* 698.

Leontius: his title was most probably *comes Opsikiou* (C. Diehl, *BZ* ix, 1900, 677); as such he would have commanded the Palace guards (*scholae*) and been an appropriate person to attempt to restore discipline (Haldon, *Praetorians* 174-5). This Leontius must be distinguished (*contra* Ericsson, 'Date' 22) from the city prefect of 615, who died on embassy to Persia (Nic. 20. 17-18): apart from Ericsson's implausible redating, it is most unlikely that the same individual would hold the civilian post of city prefect and the military one of *comes Opsikiou*. For *spatharius*, cf. n. 264.

no-one will find a means to describe this in its entirety.[457] For the accursed Salbaras, commander of the Persian army, while he was awaiting (as it seems and was indeed finally revealed by deeds) the arrival of the utterly godless Chagan of the Avars, had for these very many days past been at Chalcedon; he impiously burnt all the suburbs and palaces and houses of prayer, [p.717] and thereafter remained, awaiting the advent of that man.[458]

And so on the 29th of the month June of the present indiction 14, that is on the day of the Feast of the holy and glorious chief

[457] Siege of Cpl.: there are four other main descriptions of these events, two highly rhetorical accounts by contemporaries, the homily attributed to Theodore Syncellus, and the Bellum Avaricum by George of Pisidia (both of which may have been recited in Cpl. in 627), and two later chronicles, Nicephorus (17. 24-19. 2), who is fairly full and includes a few specific details, and Theophanes, who has a brief and generalized version (316. 16-27); cf. Cedr. i. 728. 14-729. 20. Barišić ('Siège' 371-95) has collated the various accounts to produce a composite version; see also Stratos, Byzantium ch. 14; Tsangadas, Fortifications ch. 9; Speck, Bellum Avaricum.

CP's is the most detailed and the fullest narrative, with an introduction couched in a more elaborate style than is usual (e.g. the opening sentence with tricolon at p. 716. 15-16: cf. p. 704. 15-16), but characteristically supplying precise dates and information on the repeated diplomatic exchanges between Romans and Avars, as well as other details. However, events between Monday 4 and Thursday 7 Aug. are omitted, as a result of a lacuna (cf. n. 472). Speck (Bellum Avaricum 62-3) suggested that the basis for CP's account was an official report intended for the absent Heraclius, which concentrated on political and military aspects of the siege rather than the religious or miraculous.

The Virgin: see n. 476 for her role, and cf. G. Pisid. BA 1-9 for a similar initial reference to the Virgin. In 623 Cpl. was also thought to have received divine help (CP p. 713. 3-5), hence the opening 'now too'.

[458] Arrival of Shahvaraz (Salbaras): cf. Theod. Sync. 300. 27-36; siege of Chalcedon: id. 304. 31-2. Although Barišić (390-1) was inclined to regard the joint presence of Persians and Avars as the chance synchronization of independent military action, it is not implausible that the attack had been co-ordinated (cf. Theoph. 315. 7-11, Cedr. i. 727. 11-15; also Nic. 17. 26-18. 2, reading βάρβαροι with the London MS; Stratos, 'Attack' 370-2). In the 6th c. the Persians had shown themselves to be aware of Roman problems in the Balkans (cf. Whitby, Maurice 278, 280), and it made sense for the Persians to stir up trouble there to force Heraclius to return west. The Avars could be urged to make a pre-emptive strike before the possible return of a victorious emperor, and they might also have been prompted by unrest among their subjects, for which Roman diplomacy could be held responsible (Stratos, Byzantium 315-17). Nevertheless, the siege was primarily an Avar affair, with the Persians as encouraging but ineffectual associates. It marks the high point of Avar power: their intention throughout was to remove the Romans completely from Cpl. (e.g. CP pp. 720. 13-15, 721. 15-21; Nic. 17. 28-18. 2), so that they could take over as the new imperial controller, and their catastrophic humiliation undermined the Chagan's grasp on his subjects and stimulated revolts among subordinate groups.

apostles, Peter and Paul, a vanguard of the God-abhorred Chagan arrived, about 30,000. He had spread the rumour by means of reports that he would capture both the Long Wall and the area within it, and as a result, on the same day, which was a Lord's Day, the excellent cavalry who were present outside the city came inside the new Theodosian wall of this imperial city. The same advance guard remained in the regions of Melantias, while a few of them made sallies at intervals as far as the wall, and prevented anyone from going out or collecting provisions for animals at all.[459]

In the meantime, when as many as ten days in succession had elapsed and none of the enemy appeared near the wall, soldiers went out with camp followers and civilians, with the intention of harvesting a few crops about ten miles distant; it happened that the enemy encountered them, that some fell on either side, and that some of the soldiers' camp followers and of the civilians who had gone out with them were also apprehended. For if it had not happened that the soldiers were diverted to the defence of their camp followers and the civilians, a considerable number of the enemy would have been slaughtered on that day.

Shortly afterwards some of the enemy, as many as 1,000, [p.718] approached the venerated church of the Holy Maccabees on the far side at Sycae; they made themselves visible to the Persians, who had congregated in the regions of Chrysopolis, and they made their presence known to each other by fire signals.[460]

---

[459] Avar vanguard: Stratos (*Byzantium* 180-1 with n. XXVI, p. 372) suggested that the Avars also attacked Thessalonica in 626, a distraction which explained why the Avar vanguard arrived a month before the Chagan and the main army, together with its siege equipment which had already been used at Thessalonica. However, as Stratos recognized, it would have been an unwise diversion of resources to assault the two major cities in the Balkans in the same year, and there is no evidence to prove that Thessalonica was besieged in 626 (most scholars prefer an earlier date). The main Avar army, encumbered by large herds of animals, a heavy siege train and portable boats, would naturally have moved slowly; the vanguard, advancing rapidly, was intended to spread terror and prevent the Romans from making last-minute preparations such as the harvesting of crops outside the Theodosian walls to consolidate their food supply (cf. *Miracula S. Demetrii* secs. 198-9, and Theophylact vi. 4. 6 for similar rapid advances).

Melantias: the first stage on the old (inland) Via Egnatia, 18 or 19 miles outside Cpl. near the Athyras stream (Agathias v. 14. 5: the Kotrigurs had camped there in 559) which flows into the Büyük Çekmece inlet west of Cpl. (Mango, *Const.* 32). It was well inside the Long Walls, so that the vanguard's sallies will have penetrated as far as the Theodosian wall.

[460] Shrine of the Maccabees: at Galata (Janin, *Églises* 313-14), probably on high

In the meantime the accursed Chagan dismissed Athanasius the most glorious patrician from the regions of Adrianopolis, after saying to him, 'Go and see how the people of the city are willing to conciliate me, and what they are willing to give me to make me retire.' And so when the same most glorious Athanasius entered and announced this to Bonus, the most glorious patrician and *magister*, and to the other officials, they reproached him for having thus cringed before the accursed Chagan and for having promised that the people of the city would perform acts of conciliation for him. Then the most glorious Athanasius said that these had been his instructions from the most glorious officials at the time when he was dispatched on embassy; thereafter he had not learnt that the defences had been strengthened thus and that an army was present here; however, he was ready to tell the Chagan without alteration the message given to him. Then, after the same most glorious Athanasius requested that he first wished to inspect the army that was in the city, a muster was held and about 12,000 or more cavalry resident in the city were present. And then the officials gave him a response that was intended by every means to cause the accursed Chagan [p.719] <not> to approach the wall, that is the city. Then, after the most glorious Athanasius had reached the vicinity of that man, he was not received, but the cursed Chagan said that he would not give way at all unless he obtained both the city and those who were in it.[461]

---

ground from which it would have been easy to communicate with the Persians who had moved north from Chalcedon to Chrysopolis (Üsküdar).

[461] Negotiations: it seems that Athanasius had been dispatched to the Chagan to dissuade him from approaching Cpl., perhaps after the appearance of the Avar vanguard. In the meantime, unknown to Athanasius (*CP* p. 718. 15-22), extra defenders had arrived, sent by Heraclius who had divided his army into three and ordered one section to protect the city (Theoph. 315. 11-13; possibly the Armenians mentioned at *CP* p. 724. 11); they were perhaps accompanied by written instructions from the emperor about extra precautions in case of siege (G. Pisid. *BA* 266-92; cf. Theod. Sync. 304. 1-4). Further reinforcements, which arrived at the end of the siege, were brought by Heraclius' brother (*CP* p. 726. 7-8), presumably Theodore with the detachment of the eastern army that had defeated Shahin (Theoph. 315. 13-24). Speck (*Bellum Avaricum* 46-7) conflates these two separate contingents, contrary to the evidence of *CP*. However, in spite of these additions, the Roman defenders relied primarily on the strength of Cpl.'s walls (coupled with the superiority of their navy); they did not try to engage the main Avar army outside the walls, and repeatedly attempted to persuade the Chagan to retire. At p. 719. 1, we have followed Du Cange in supplying a negative, '*not* to approach...'

Bonus: the *magister*, i.e. *magister officiorum*, see Bury, *IA* 29-33; Haldon,

On the 29th of the month July the same God-abhorred Chagan reached the wall with the whole of his horde, and showed himself to those in the city.[462] After one day, that is on the 31st of the same month July, he advanced, arrayed for battle, from the gate called Polyandrion as far as the gate of the Pempton and beyond with particular vigour: for there he stationed the bulk of his horde, after stationing Slavs within view along the remaining part of the wall. And he remained from dawn until hour 11 fighting first with unarmoured Slav infantry, and in the second rank with infantry in corslets.[463] And towards evening he stationed a few siege engines and mantelets from Brachialion as far as Brachialion.[464]

---

*Praetorians* 444-6 n. 361, with the additional point that *CP* does not use *magister* for generals. Together with the Patriarch Sergius, guardian of the young Heraclius II Constantine, he had been entrusted by Heraclius with control of the city (Theoph. 303. 3-6, Nic. 15. 16-17, Theod. Sync. 302. 28-30, 305. 16-18). George of Pisidia composed a panegyric in his honour (*In Bonum patricium*, ed. Pertusi, pp. 161-75). The *Patria* (ii. 72, p. 189; cf. Janin, *Const.* 206-7) credits him with the construction of a cistern, which was perhaps connected with preparations for the siege.

[462] Tuesday 29 July: the Chagan's personal display was intended to intimidate the defenders, and Theodore Syncellus provides an impressionistic account of the terror inspired by the Avars, with their armour glittering in the sun, while the Patriarch Sergius paraded on the walls to counteract this, and Bonus made preparations within the city (305. 13-28); on the next day the Chagan prepared for combat and demanded food, which the defenders graciously supplied without managing to appease him (305. 28-36).

Thereafter the Avars began the siege, which had three main elements: a direct attack against the Theodosian walls where the Avars could deploy their fearsome siege technology and use their subordinates, of whom the most numerous were Slavs, as a human wave; an attempt to bring Persian troops over from Chalcedon by means of Slav canoes; and a naval attack down the Golden Horn, using the Slav canoes to threaten an unprotected (or dilapidated) section of Cpl.'s perimeter.

[463] Attack on walls: Theodore gives a very generalized account of the Avar attack 'on the third day' (i.e. 31 July) which was repulsed through the Virgin's miraculous defence (305. 37-306. 12). The Avars had a formidable reputation as besiegers, see *Miracula S. Demetrii* sec. 200; Whitby, *Maurice* 173. They concentrated their attack on the central hilly section of the land walls, from the gate of the Pempton in the Lycus valley, extending about 1 kilometre south to the Polyandrion gate, the modern Yeni Mevlevihane Kapısı near the summit of Cpl.'s 'seventh' hill (Tsangadas, *Fortifications* 90-1, cf. Mango, *Const.* 32-3 with n. 58, 47). However, to keep the defenders occupied, the dispensable Slav infantry and a few siege machines were stationed along the entire length of the land walls. George of Pisidia (*BA* 217-19) records that about 80,000 barbarians approached the gate of Philoxenus (which is not securely located; see Pertusi, *Giorgio* 215-16).

[464] Brachialia: literally 'bracelets', these were probably short walls that projected

And again on the following day he stationed a multitude of siege engines close to each other against that part which had been attacked by him, so that those in the city were compelled to station very many siege engines inside the wall. When the infantry battle was joined each day, through the efficacy of God, as a result of their superiority our men kept off the enemy at a distance. But he bound together his stone-throwers and covered them outside with hides; [p.720] and in the section from the Polyandrion gate as far as the gate of St. Romanus he prepared to station 12 lofty siege towers, which were advanced almost as far as the outworks, and he covered them with hides.[465] And as for the sailors who were present in the city even they came out to assist the citizens. And one of these sailors constructed a mast and hung a skiff on it, intending by means of it to burn the enemies' siege-towers. Bonus the all-praiseworthy *magister* gave commendation to this sailor for having dismayed the enemy not inconsiderably.[466]

But the same most renowned *magister*, after the enemy's approach to the wall, did not cease from urging him to take not only his agreed tribute but also any other condition for the sake of which he had come as far as the wall. And he did not accept, but said, 'Withdraw from the city, leave me your property, and save yourselves and your families.' He was anxious to launch to sea the canoes which he had brought with him, and was prevented by the cutters. Finally he prepared for these to be launched at the bridge of St. Callinicus after a third day of the fighting. It was for this reason that he prepared for the canoes to be launched there, because the area was shallow and the cutters were unable to approach there. But the cutters remained [p.721]

respectively into the Sea of Marmara and the Golden Horn to prevent access around either end of the land walls (cf. Janin, *Const.* 327, Speck, *Bellum Avaricum* n. 148 at 99-100, *contra* Tsangadas 91-3); Const. Porph. *de caer.* i. 18 (p. 108. 19-20) mentions the Brachialion of the Golden Gate which was accessible by boat; also Theoph. 353. 30. Agathias (*Hist.* v. 22. 2) describes comparable projecting walls at the Chersonese.

465 Friday 1 Aug.: cf. Theod. Sync. 306. 13-19, for the preparation by the Avars of siege engines, and *Miracula S. Demetrii* sec. 272, for Avar engines covered in hides (to reduce risk of fire). The Avar attack was now concentrated on the short stretch of wall north of the Polyandrion gate as far as St. Romanus (the modern Top Kapısı: Janin, *Const.* 280, 420-1).

466 Sailors: presumably the crews not of the Roman warships (who had to be ready to oppose the Slav canoes) but of trading vessels in the capital's harbours; cf. *Miracula S. Demetrii* sec. 209, for sailors from grain ships manning siege engines during an Avar attack on Thessalonica. Heraclius had sent instructions for everyone to be involved in the defence (G. Pisid. BA 293-7).

within sight of the canoes from St. Nicholas as far as St. Conon on the far side at Pegae, preventing the canoes from going past.[467]

On Saturday in the evening, that is on the second of the month August, the Chagan asked for officials to converse with him. And there went out to him George the most glorious patrician, and Theodore the most glorious *commerciarius* for †woad†, and Theodosius the most glorious patrician and logothete, and Theodore *syncellus* most dear to God, and Athanasius the most glorious patrician.[468] And when they had set out, the Chagan brought into their sight three Persians dressed in pure silk who had been sent to him from Salbaras. And he arranged that they should be seated in his presence, while our ambassadors should stand. And he said, 'Look, the Persians have sent an embassy to me, and are ready to give me 3,000 men in alliance. Therefore if each of you in the city is prepared to take no more than a cloak and a shirt, we will make a compact with Salbaras, for he is my friend: cross over to him and he will not harm you; leave me your city and property. For otherwise it is impossible for you to be saved, unless you can become fish and depart by sea, or birds and ascend to the sky. For look – as the Persians themselves say – neither has your emperor invaded Persia nor [p.722] is your army arrived.' But the most glorious George said to him, 'These men are imposters and do not speak a word of truth, since our

---

[467] Naval preparations: the Slavs launched their canoes at the head of the Golden Horn, near the bridge of St. Callinicus over the Barbysses stream (Nic. 18. 18-19, cf. Theod. Sync. 308. 8-10; see also n. 338). They had brought the canoes (*monoxyla*) with them, apparently overland from the Danube (cf. Theoph. 316. 19-21); these may have been simple dugouts, but it is possible that some were rather more sophisticated 'log boats' (for which, see K. Greene, *The Archaeology of the Roman Economy*, London 1986, 20) which could have been dismantled for easier transport, but also been large enough to ferry the Persian cavalry across the Bosporus. The Roman fleet was deployed across the Golden Horn from St. Nicholas at Blachernae to St. Conon in Galata (Janin, *Églises* 369-71, 283-4) to prevent the Slavs sailing down the Golden Horn. Pegae: the Springs, identified with Kasımpaşa north of the Golden Horn (Janin, *Const.* 463-4).

[468] Embassy to Chagan: cf. Theod. Sync. 306. 20-5; G. Pisid. *BA* 311-27. At the same time as resisting Avar assaults, the Romans attempted to restore good relations with the Chagan and so create a favourable climate for the siege to be ended.

Ambassadors: a distinguished group. Theodore the *commerciarius* (a customs officer, Bury, *IA* 88), and the logothete (cf. n. 403) Theodosius were financial officials; Theodore *syncellus* (or cell-mate of the patriarch), is commonly accepted to be the author of the contemporary homily on the siege; the patrician Athanasius had already served on an embassy to the Chagan (*CP* pp. 718. 4-719. 4). On *commerciarii*, see H. Antoniadis-Bibicou, *Recherches sur les douanes à Byzance* (Paris 1963), chs. 6-7; '†woad†', τὴν ἰσατιν, is unexplained.

army is arrived here and our most pious lord is in their country, utterly destroying it.' Then one of the Persians was infuriated and in the presence of the Chagan insulted the said most glorious George, and he himself replied to him, 'It is not you who insult me, but the Chagan.' But the most glorious officials who had come out to him also said this to the Chagan, 'Although you have such great hordes, you need Persian help.' And he said, 'If I wish, they will provide me with men in alliance, for they are my friends.' And again our officials said to him, 'We will never relinquish the city, for we came out to you in the expectation of discussing something material. So if you do not wish to discuss with us peace proposals, dismiss us.' And he dismissed them.[469]

Straightway, during the night preceding the Lord's Day, through the efficacy of the good and mercy-loving God, the same Persians who had been on the embassy to the Chagan, while they were crossing over to Chrysopolis by way of Chalae, encountered our skiffs, in which there were also some of those from the orphanage. And one of these Persians was found after he had thrown himself into a small skiff known as a *sandalos*, face down and beneath the coverings, and was crossing over to Chrysopolis thus; but the sailor who was in this skiff and was steering it, adroitly signalled to those from the [p.723] orphanage who pulled back and removed the coverings, and found this Persian unharmed and lying face down; they slew him and removed his head. They overpowered the other two Persians along with the sailor as well, while they were crossing over in another boat, and these they brought at dawn to the wall.[470] Our

---

[469] Co-operation between Avars and Persians: cf. Theod. Sync. 306. 26-307. 11 (an eye-witness account); G. Pisid. BA 328-54. In view of the large numbers of troops at the Avars' disposal, the presence of the Persians at the embassy was intended partly to demonstrate Cpl.'s utter helplessness, which the Chagan hoped to impress on the Roman envoys. However, the Persians could also contribute their expertise at siege warfare, and the Chagan made a treaty with the Persians to convey them across the Bosporus in Slav canoes (Theod. Sync. 307. 1-7, and cf. n. 458, for Persian–Avar co-operation).

CP's detailed account of the diplomatic exchanges suggests a first-hand informant.

[470] Capture of envoys: cf. Theod. Sync. 308. 1-2, for a vague allusion. After the unsuccessful return of the embassy, the Romans kept a close watch on the sea to prevent further Avar-Persian communications (G. Pisid. BA 355-65).

Chalae: modern Bebek, on the west side of the Bosporus at one of its narrowest points (Janin, *Const.* 470). The Persians were probably being returned via Galata, which the Avars controlled.

Orphanage: the identity is unknown; the best-attested orphanage in Cpl.,

men chopped off the two hands of one of the surviving Persians, tied round his neck the head of the man slain in the skiff, and sent him to the Chagan. The other was thrown into a skiff and taken off alive to Chalcedon; when he had been exhibited to the Persians our men beheaded him just as he was in the skiff, and threw his head onto land with a message that read like this: 'The Chagan, after making terms with us, sent us the ambassadors who were dispatched to him by you; two of them we have beheaded in the city, while look! you have the head of the other.' [471]

On the same Lord's Day the accursed Chagan set out for Chalae and put to sea canoes which were intended to set out for the opposite side and bring the Persians to him, in accordance with their promise. When this was known, in the evening about

---

that of St. Paul located on the acropolis (Janin, *Églises* 567-8; Mango, *Const.* 34), was an official institution presided over by an important cleric; see Dagron, *Naissance* 511-12; Bury, *IA* 103-5. Alternatively Pertusi (*Giorgio* 220) identified the orphanage as that connected with the leper house of Zoticus in Galata. The Patriarch Sergius had been superintendant of poor relief prior to his appointment (*CP s.a.* 610), and may have had a long-standing connection with the orphanage(s). It would appear that in the 626 crisis the beneficiaries of the orphanage had been commandeered to assist in the defence of the city by patrolling the Bosporus to intercept communications between Persians and Avars.

[471] Treatment of Persians: Mango ('Deux Études' 107-9) has suggested that the Persian commander Shahvaraz had already been suborned or deceived into disobedience to Khusro by Heraclius (see Theoph. 323. 22-324. 16 and Michael the Syrian xi. 3; Nic. 16. 26-17. 15 has a different version), and that he made no attempt to participate in the siege. The evidence of *CP* suggests that this is unlikely. Shahvaraz ravaged Chalcedon, attempted to link up with the Avars, and sent envoys who promised alliance, reinforced the Avars' self-confidence, and engaged in mutual insults with the Roman representative George; when the Romans intercepted Persian-Avar contacts they mutilated or killed the Persian representatives, and then pretended to Shahvaraz that the Avar Chagan had double-crossed him (*CP* pp. 716. 20-1; 718. 3-4, cf. 723. 15-19; 721. 10-722. 7; 722. 14-723. 15). Such actions are improbable unless Shahvaraz was still perceived by Avars and Romans as a party to the conflict.

The factor which prevented his participation in the siege was the Bosporus (cf. Theod. Sync. 300. 30-2): the Persians did not have a reputation as sailors, and there is no evidence that Shahvaraz's experience extended to ships; it is also likely that most boats available on the Asiatic shore (e.g. fishing vessels) had been commandeered by refugees fleeing as the Persians approached (or removed by the Roman fleet). At some point towards the end of the war Shahvaraz's loyalty to Khusro was undermined, but the earliest plausible occasion is perhaps the return to Cpl. of the victorious Theodore, Heraclius' brother, at the end of the Avar siege (*CP* p. 726. 7-8) when news and messages might have been passed by him to Shahvaraz.

70 of our skiffs sailed up towards Chalae, even though the wind
was against them, so as to prevent the canoes from crossing over.
And towards evening the accursed Chagan retired [p.724] to the
vicinity of the wall, and some food and wine were sent to him
from the city. Hermitzis, commander of the Avars, came to the
gate, saying, 'You have committed a grave deed in killing those
who ate with the Chagan yesterday, and furthermore in sending
him the head and the other with his hands cut off.' But they
said, 'We are not concerned about him.' In the night then, as
Monday was dawning, their canoes were able to escape our
watch and cross to them...[472]

.   .   .   .   .   .   .   .   .   .   .   .   .   .   .   .   .

...They sank them and slew all the Slavs found in the canoes.
And the Armenians too came out from the wall of Blachernae
and threw fire into the portico which is near St. Nicholas. And
the Slavs who had escaped by diving from the canoes thought,
because of the fire, that those positioned by the sea were Avars,
and when they came out there they were slain by the Armenians.
A few other Slavs who had escaped by diving, and who came
out in the region where the godless Chagan was positioned,
were slain at his injunction. And at God's command through the
intercession of our Lady the Mother of God, in a single instant,
calamity at sea came to him. [473] Our men drove all the canoes

---

[472] Attempt to ferry across Persians: cf. Theod. Sync. 307. 8-308. 2 (attributing
failure to divine intervention). Although the Persians on the Asiatic shore were
visible to the Avars, they were so unskilled in nautical matters that they had to
await the arrival of Slav canoes before attempting to slip across the Bosporus by
night. The canoes reached the Asiatic shore (perhaps while the Roman ships
were delayed by a head wind), but their subsequent manoeuvres, encumbered by
Persian passengers, were thwarted by the Roman fleet; according to Sebeos (ch.
26, p. 79) 4,000 Persians perished in this naval engagement.

Hermitzis: the Hermi were an element in the Avar federation (H. W.
Haussig, 'Theophylakts Exkurs über die skythischen Völker', Byz. xxiii, 1953,
275-462 at 424-5).

Lacuna: the words 'to them' (πρὸς τοὺς, a noun is probably lost) end a folio
in the Vatican MS: at this point one folio is missing (Mercati, 'Study' 409-10), and
the phrase 'they sank...' refers to the Roman defeat of the subsequent Slav naval
attack down the Golden Horn (see n. 473). In the intervening days, the Chagan
made preparations for a concerted land and sea attack; on Wednesday (6 Aug.)
the Romans repulsed an attack on the walls (Theod. Sync. 308. 2-28).

[473] Naval attack: Thursday 7 Aug.; cf. Theod. Sync. 310. 38-40 for day and date,
and for more impressionistic accounts, ibid. 311. 7-312. 5, G. Pisid. BA 441-74
(the latter including details of ploys used by shipwrecked Slavs to escape

onto the land, and after this had happened, the accursed **[p.725]** Chagan retired to his rampart, took away from the wall the siege engines which he had set beside it and the palisade which he had constructed, and began to dismantle the siege towers which he had constructed: by night he burnt his palisade and the siege towers and the mantelets, after removing the hides, and retreated.[474]

Some people said that the Slavs, when they saw what had happened, withdrew and retreated, and for this reason the cursed Chagan was also forced to retreat and follow them.[475]

And this is what the godless Chagan said at the moment of the

destruction; ibid. 409-12, Bulgars on Slav boats). The attack was concentrated in the Golden Horn, on which side the city was probably not protected by a wall (Mango, *Const.* 25 n. 12; cf. above n. 243).

CP's account of the attack is lost in the textual lacuna, but Nicephorus supplies additional evidence (18. 6-23): the Avars hoped that the appearance of the Slav flotilla would cause confusion within the city and allow them to overrun the walls (cf. Theod. Sync. 311. 10-12). The Romans had advance knowledge of the plan of attack and organized their fleet accordingly; the Slavs were misled into launching their assault too soon when the Romans anticipated Avar fire signals from Blachernae (Speck, *Bellum Avaricum* n. 106 at 92-3, unnecessarily doubts this). The Slav boats were destroyed (cf. *Miracula S. Demetrii* secs. 189-91 for a comparable Slav disaster at Thessalonica); survivors who struggled ashore near Blachernae (where they expected to find Avar besiegers) were killed both by the Roman defenders (Armenians, who were probably among the reinforcements sent by Heraclius; cf. n. 461), and by the enraged Chagan. Nicephorus (18. 21-3) mentions that the Slav dead included women.

St. Nicholas: cf. n. 467. The location of the Roman triumph near the church of the Virgin at Blachernae gave rise to stories of divine intervention (see n. 476). According to George of Pisidia (*BA* 403-6) the Avars had initially captured Blachernae, and the Armenians were probably trying to drive them back.

[474] End of siege: Theodore Syncellus records that the Romans collected and burnt the enemies' corpses and canoes, displayed the victims' heads on the walls, and began to sally forth from the city (312. 5-18); 'the guardian of public affairs' (Bonus) had to restrain citizens from rushing out to fire the Avars' engines, and the Theotokos arranged for the Chagan to burn his own machines (312. 19-39).

[475] Postulated transposition: Speck (*Bellum Avaricum* 31-48) has claimed that much of this and the following two paragraphs (CP pp. 725. 6-726. 10), as well as the notice about the Blachernae wall (*s.a.* 627), has been transposed from its proper connection with the Avar surprise (CP *s.a.* 623). The arguments are unconvincing: (i) the Slavs are not in fact prominent in the earlier surprise attack, whereas the humiliation of the Chagan now prompted them to rebel; the reasons given for the retreat of the Slavs and the Chagan are entirely appropriate to 626, but not to 623 (cf. n. 478). (ii) For the destruction of churches and the Blachernae wall, see nn. 478 and 481. (iii) The reference to the recent arrival of the emperor's brother (CP p. 726. 7-8) must relate to 626, as Speck 43-4 concedes, but this undermines his theory of the transposition of a folio from the Avar surprise to the end of the 626 siege.

battle: 'I see a woman in stately dress rushing about on the wall all alone.'[476] When he was on the point of retreating, he declared, 'Do not imagine that I am retreating because of fear, but because I am constrained for provisions and did not attack you at an opportune moment. I am departing to pay attention to supplies, and will return intending to do to you whatever you have accomplished against me.'[477]

On the Friday a rearguard of cavalry remained in the vicinity of the wall, setting fire to many suburbs on the same day up till hour 7; and they withdrew. They burnt both the church of SS Cosmas and Damian at Blachernae and the church of St. Nicholas and all the surrounding areas. However, after approaching the church of our Lady [p.726] the Mother of God and the Holy Reliquary, the enemy were completely unable to damage any of the things there, since God showed favour, at the intercession of his undefiled Mother.[478] And he requested the

---

476  Divine assistance: a key element in Theodore Syncellus' account of the siege (e.g. 304. 4-16, icons of the Virgin set at the gates by Sergius; 311. 17-35, the Virgin sinks the Slav fleet at Blachernae). Nicephorus (18. 4-6) alludes to divine destruction of Avar siege towers, and a subsequent thanksgiving at Blachernae (18. 24-7, cf. Theod. Syn. 320. 10-15, *Anth. Graec.* i. 120-1); Cedrenus (i. 728. 23-729. 12) reports a phantom embassy by a distinguished woman who was mistaken for the empress. The Chagan's mention of his vision is inserted here to confirm the Virgin's intervention; cf. *Miracula S. Demetrii* secs. 222, 260-3 for Demetrius terrifying Slavs at Thessalonica; also *CP s.a.* 350 (Shapur at Nisibis), Zos. v. 6, Evag. iv. 28, Theophylact vi. 5. 7 for comparable apparitions during sieges; and H. Chadwick, *JThS* xxv, 1974, 65 n. 5 for visions of the Virgin as a woman in purple.
During the siege Sergius had maintained the morale of defenders (e.g. Theod. Sync. 303. 14-32), with the Virgin Mary and her precious relics at Blachernae taking pride of place. See N. H. Baynes, 'The Supernatural Defenders of Constantinople', *Byzantine Studies* (London 1955), 248-60; Averil Cameron, 'Robe', and ead. 'Theotokos', although note the cautionary remarks of Speck (*Bellum Avaricum* n. 189 at 105-7), who stresses the pre-eminence of Christ.

477  Avar withdrawal: cf. Theod. Sync. 313. 5-13. After the humiliating failure of his attempts (cf. Theoph. 316. 24), the Chagan needed to restore his authority over the Avar federation, which was in danger of disintegration as Slavs (and other subjects) rebelled, cf. Whitby, *Maurice* 184-6. The Chagan used shortage of supplies as an excuse for withdrawal; this has been doubted by Stratos (*Byzantium* 192-5) who regards it as no more than a face-saving formula: however, organization of food supplies was frequently as much of a problem for besiegers as for the besieged (e.g. Malchus fr. 2, lines 20-1), and the Avars were known to be troubled by supply shortages (Maurice, *Strategicon* xi. 2. 66-7, p. 364), so the Chagan's excuse may have been true.

478  Destruction of churches: SS Cosmas and Damian near Eyüp had already been ravaged, although not burnt, by the Avars in 623, see n. 451. St. Nicholas: cf. n. 467.

most glorious *commerciarius* to converse with him,[479] and Bonus the all-praiseworthy *magister* declared this to him: 'Until the present I had the power to talk and make terms with you. But now the brother of our most pious lord has arrived together with the God-protected army. And look! he is crossing over and pursuing you as far as your territory. And there you can talk with one another.'[480]

**627** Indiction 15, year 17, the 16th post-consulship of Heraclius Augustus.

And from 22nd inclusive of the month January it is recorded as year 15 of the reign of Heraclius II Constantine.

In this year was built the wall around the church of our Lady the Mother of God, outside the so-called Pteron.[481]

---

Church of our Lady: the Blachernae church (Janin, *Églises* 161-71), although unprotected by a wall (Proc. *Bld.* i. 3. 3; cf. n. 481), survived the siege, and the Slav naval assault was defeated in its vicinity; the adjacent chapel of the Holy Reliquary contained the relics of the Virgin deposited by Leo I, see C. Mango, *The Art of the Byzantine Empire 312–1453* (Englewood Cliffs 1972), 34-5; Theophylact viii 5. 1-2 with n. 22 (Whitby).

Speck claimed (cf. n. 475) that this account of church burning has been switched from the earlier Avar attack (*CP s.a.* 623), but there is no sign of a break in the narrative of events in 623, where the reference to ravaging is directly linked to the transport of booty back to the Danube (*CP* p. 713. 9-14). The account here of specific burnings is quite compatible with general references in other sources to burnings at the start of the siege, which probably relate to buildings on the Avars' line of advance from Melantias (Theod. Sync. 304. 32-5: churches, all imperial and private property; Nic. 17. 25-6: all suburbs).

[479] *Commerciarius*: probably the Theodore who participated in George's earlier embassy to the Chagan (p. 721. 7); cf. n. 468. It would be natural for the Chagan to ask for a negotiator whom he already knew (Speck, *Bellum Avaricum* 44).

[480] Reinforcements: their arrival, probably under the command of Theodore brother of Heraclius (cf. n. 461), would have boosted Roman morale. Stratos ('Attack' 375-6) claimed that a Roman army chased the Avars back to the Danube, but there is no evidence that Bonus' threat to the Chagan of pursuit by the emperor's brother was carried out: the presence of a Byzantine commander at Belgrade at some time in Heraclius' reign, probably c.630 (Const. Porph. *DAI* 32. 19-20) does not prove that there was an immediate pursuit.

The movements of the Persian army at Chalcedon are uncertain: according to Theophanes (316. 25-7) they remained there throughout the winter; Theodore Syncellus says (313. 14-27) that they continued to besiege Chalcedon for a further period before withdrawing in shame.

[481] **627** Blachernae defences: the suburb of Blachernae was defended by a bulge at the north-west end of the main Theodosian walls. This outwork, known as the Pteron (Nic. 18. 9) did not incorporate the famous church to the Virgin (cf. n. 478). Nicephorus 18. 27-19. 1 confirms that the wall was extended to include the Virgin's church after the siege of 626. For discussion of the fortifications in the vicinity of Blachernae, see Mango, 'Fourteenth Region' 1-3; Müller-Wiener,

In this year in the month Artemisius, on May 11th according to the Romans, there died Bonus of celebrated memory, who had been *magister*, and his body was laid to rest in the revered monastery of [p.727] St. John the Forerunner and Baptist, the one named that of Studius, near the Golden Gate.[482]

## Olympiad 352

**628** Indiction 1, year 18, the 17th post-consulship of Heraclius Augustus.

And from 22nd inclusive of the month January it is recorded as year 16 of the reign of Heraclius II Constantine.

In the 18th year of the reign of Heraclius, and post-consulship 17, and in year 16 of the reign of Heraclius II Constantine his son, on the 15th of the month May, indiction 1, a Sunday, at the holy Pentecost itself, from the *ambo* in the most holy Great Church were read out dispatches which had been sent from the eastern regions by Heraclius our most pious emperor, which announced the fall of Chosroes and the proclamation of Seiroe as the Persian king. They were as follows:[483]

'Let all the earth raise a cry to God; serve the Lord in gladness, enter into his presence in exultation, and recognize that God is Lord indeed. It is he who has made us and not we ourselves. We are his people and sheep of his pasture. Enter into his courts

*Bildlexikon* 301-7, also pl. 275; the treatment in Tsangadas, *Fortifications* ch. 4, is not entirely clear or accurate.

The Vatican MS has the following version of this notice inserted in the margin by a later hand: 'In the 15th year [*sic*] of the reign of Heraclius was built the wall outside Blachernae, and the temple of the all-holy Mother of God was enclosed inside, together with the Holy Reliquary; for previously it was outside the wall.' The incorrect regnal year (15th year = 624/5) is an error derived from the correct indiction date of the main notice. However, Speck (*Bellum Avaricum* 34-41) has asserted that this extra defence was in fact built before the siege, in direct response to the earlier Avar surprise (*CP s.a.* 623), when precious relics had hurriedly to be removed from the church (cf. n. 451). The claim, contradicted independently by *CP* and Nicephorus, is weakly based, and is entirely dependent on the implausible theory that material connected with the 626 siege has been transposed from the earlier Avar attack (cf. n. 475).

482  Bonus: co-regent with Sergius during Heraclius' absence, see n. 461. Church of St. John: see Janin, *Églises* 430-40, and cf. n. 284.

483  **628** Heraclius' victory dispatch: characteristically *CP*'s only detailed reference to Heraclius' Persian campaigns is occasioned by the public reading of his victory dispatch in the capital. The magnitude of the occasion is signified by the elaborate dating formula; the scribe of the Vatican MS carefully arranged the passage following the date as an ornamental heading. For the use of St. Sophia for the delivery of this dispatch, cf. n. 456.

with hymns and give thanks to him. Praise his name because Christ is Lord, his mercy is unto eternity, his truth for generation upon generation. Let the heavens be joyful **[p.728]** and the earth exult and the sea be glad, and all that is in them.[484]

And let all we Christians, praising and glorifying, give thanks to the one God, rejoicing with great joy in his holy name. For fallen is the arrogant Chosroes, opponent of God. He is fallen and cast down to the depths of the earth, and his memory is utterly exterminated from earth; he who was exalted and spoke injustice in arrogance and contempt against our Lord Jesus Christ the true God and his undefiled Mother, our blessed Lady, Mother of God and ever-Virgin Mary, perished is the profaner with a resounding noise. His labour has turned back upon his head, and upon his brow has his injustice descended. For on the 24th of the past month February, of the current first tax period, disturbance came to him at the hands of Seiroe his first-born son, just as we signified to you in our other missive. And all the Persian officials and troops who were there, along with all the army that had been amassed from diverse places by the cursed Chosroes, gathered to the side of Seiroe, together also with Gurdanaspa, the former commander of the Persian army. That God-abhorred Chosroes proposed to resort to flight and, being arrested, was cast in bonds into the new fort which had been built by him for protecting the wealth amassed by him.

**[p.729]** 'And on the 25th of the same month February, Seiroe was crowned and proclaimed Persian king, and on the 28th of the same month, after keeping the God-abhorred Chosroes bound in irons for 4 days in utter agony, he killed the same ingrate, arrogant, blaspheming opponent of God by a most cruel death, so that he might know that Jesus who was born of Mary, who was crucified by the Jews (as he himself had written) against whom he blasphemed, is God almighty; and he requited

---

[484] Biblical exultation: cf. Psalm 99 (100). The triumphant Biblical tone reflects Heraclius' presentation of his Persian campaign as a crusade, in response to Khusro's attitude to the conflict: although there were influential Christians at the Persian court (e.g. the financier Yazdin, the doctor Gabriel of Sinjar, as well as the family of Shahvaraz, for which see Mango, 'Deux Études' 105-17), Khusro had set out to triumph over Christianity (e.g. Theoph. 301. 22-4), or at least orthodox Chalcedonian Christianity (Agapius of Membij 460). Heraclius, taking up the religious challenge, had used the celebration of Easter in 622 as the ceremonial start for his Persian campaigns; his second departure to the east was similarly highlighted by a religious festival, cf. *CP s.a.* 624 with n. 452.

The sermon of Dometianus of Melitene at Theophylact iv. 16 has a similar tone, and its composition was probably influenced by Heraclius' dispatch, see Whitby, *Maurice* 334-5.

him in accordance with what we had written to him. And thus perished in this life that opponent of God, but he departed on the path of Judas Iscariot, the man who heard from our almighty God, "It were good for that man not to have been born"; he departed to the unquenchable fire which had been prepared for Satan and his peers.[485]

'In our other missive which came to you from us from our camp near Canzacon, which contained moves from the 17th of the month October until the 15th of the month March, we signified how God and our Lady the Mother of God collaborated with us and our Christ-loving contingents beyond mortal understanding, and how the God-abhorred and execrated Chosroes fled our presence, from Dastagard to Ctesiphon, how his palaces, along with many provinces of the [p.730] Persian state were destroyed, and that by this means Seiroe was enabled to make the move against him.[486] After we had produced that missive

---

[485] Overthrow of Khusro: the Biblical tone of the dispatch continues, quoting Ev. Matt. 26. 24 on Judas. For other more detailed accounts, cf. Theoph. 317. 11-327. 10, Sebeos chs. 26-7, and *Anon. Guidi* 26-8. In autumn 627 Heraclius, advancing from the north, had defeated the main Persian army under Rhazates in Mesopotamia near Nineveh, and had then pressed south to reach Dastagard, Khusro's preferred palace, at the beginning of Jan. Khusro meantime had fled to Ctesiphon, and then across the Tigris where he was incapacitated by dysentry, but the Roman victories, coupled with the extensive ravaging of central districts of Persia both in Azerbaijan and Beth Aramaye, had aroused discontent among his entourage. This crystallized the ambitions of his eldest son Shiroe (Seiroe), who was jealous of the favours lavished on the younger Merdanshah, the son of Khusro's favourite wife, the Christian Shirin; consequently Shiroe began to organize a coup and opened negotiations with Heraclius (Theoph. 325. 10-326. 24), using as intermediary the nobleman Aspad-gusnasp (Gurdanaspa or Gusdanaspa in *CP*), whose father was probably the general Rahzadh (Rhazates) killed in the battle at Nineveh in 627 (cf. *CP* p. 731. 8). Heraclius encouraged the plotters; they captured Khusro in a palace garden and imprisoned him in a royal treasury (Theoph. 326. 25-327. 3; *Anon. Guidi* 27, with Tabari pp. 362ff for the location named as the house of Mihraspend); there two Persian nobles, Shamta and Nehormizd, slew him to avenge their fathers (*Anon. Guidi* 28).

[486] Heraclius' strategy: during this plotting, Heraclius had withdrawn his army from Mesopotamia, where further advance had been prevented by Khusro's destruction of key bridges, to Siarsurae (modern Suleimaniyeh) where he spent much of Feb. ravaging the vicinity (Theoph. 325. 5-8). He crossed the Zagros (Zara) probably by the Shirwan pass (rather than via Rowanduz and the Keli Shin pass, further north and higher) to Azerbaijan; in early March he established winter quarters at Canzacon, traditionally located at Takht-i Suleiman, where there are remains of a substantial fire temple with a strong fortress and more ruins outside the walls (H. C. Rawlinson, 'Notes on a Journey from Tabriz...', *Jour. Royal Geog. Soc.* x, 1840, 1-64 at 46-57, and 'Memoir on the Site of Atropatenian Ecbatana', ibid. pp. 65-158; Stratos, *Byzantium* 366, has questioned

and dispatched it on the 15th of the present month March, while we were concerned with the discovery of the sequence of events as regards Chosroes and Seiroe and we were sending to diverse places, both as far as Siarsurae and the Lesser Zab, Chalcas and Iesdem, along the two routes both from our most fortunate contingents and from the Saracens who are subject to our Christ-loving state, for this reason that, as has been said, we might know accurately what moves had been made there,[487] on the 24th of the same month March the men of the watch brought to us in our camp near Canzacon one Persian and one Armenian, who delivered to us a memorandum which came to us from a certain Persian *a secretis*, whose name was Chosdae and rank Rasnan; its contents were that, following Seiroe's proclamation as Persian king, he dismissed him to us, along with other officials and a memorandum which came to us from Seiroe himself; that when Chosdae came to Arman, he resolved to dismiss to us the aforementioned two men, so that some men might be sent in order to escort himself and those with him unharmed; it was made known to us that because he had seen many Persian corpses on the journey who had been killed by our most fortunate [p.731] army, about 3,000 corpses after the Narban, he was terrified as a result of this and was afraid to come to us without the escorts.[488]

---

this, but on inadequate grounds). Canzacon was an administrative as well as a religious centre, serving as the seat of the local governor; Heraclius had rested his army there in 624 (Theoph. 307. 31-308. 1), and it was presumably a good place for collecting supplies.

From Canzacon Heraclius had sent to Cpl. a report covering his victorious autumn campaign and events down to the start of the coup against Khusro (but not including Khusro's death). The present letter provided the next instalment.

[487] Intelligence missions: news filtered slowly across the snow-bound passes over the Zagros, and to collect information Heraclius sent out missions, which returned to Persia in a south-westerly direction towards the valley of the Lesser Zab.

Chalcas: perhaps identical with Karkha d-beth Slokh (modern Kirkuk), the main town of the Lesser Zab. Iesdem: an area named after Yazdin, Khusro's senior finance minister, and located near Karkha d-beth Slokh.

'Two routes': the reference is unclear. In the 6th c. the main Saracen allies of the Romans had been the Ghassanids, whose territory extended south from the Euphrates along the eastern fringes of Syria and Palestine; although most of Heraclius' campaigns had been conducted in the mountains of Armenia and Azerbaijan, it is possible that he had re-established contact with pro-Roman tribes in Mesopotamia and used them to threaten the Persians from two directions at once.

[488] Persian embassy: confirmation of developments in Mesopotamia was only obtained when an offical Persian messenger, Chosdae, arrived. Razban (Rasnan):

'And on the 25th of the same month March we dismissed to them Elias the most glorious *magister militum*, who is called Barsoka, and Theodotus the most magnificent *drungarius*, together with recruits and 20 saddled pack-horses, in order to meet and escort them to us. With them we resolved to send as well Gusdanaspa the son of Rhazes, the chiliarch of the Persian army, who had come to us when the disturbance took place between Seiroe and Chosroes.[489]

And on the 30th of the month March in our same camp near Canzacon we received a dispatch from Elias and Theodotus and Gusdanaspa to the effect that they had found severe winter at the mountain of Zara, that they had taken from the forts Persians and animals and thus cut through the snows; that it had been made known to them that the ambassadors who had been sent by Seiroe the king were nearby in those regions, but that they had been unable to cross the mountain of Zara because of the coming of severe winter. As a result of this we and all the men of our Christ-loving contingents knew even more that the favour and goodness of God had guided us and guides and escorts us. For if it had happened that we had lingered [p.732] for a few days in the regions of Zara and then winter had come like this, our most fortunate contingents could have come to great harm, since such great provisions were not available in those parts: for from the time when we moved from Siarsurae, that is from the 24th of the month February until the 30th of the month March, it did not cease snowing. But by God's aid we came to the regions of Canzacon and found plentiful supplies, both for men and animals, and we have stayed in this city of Canzacon (which lacks nothing and has about 3,000 houses) and in the neighbouring districts, and hence we were able to reside for so many days in one place. And we commanded the men of our Christ-loving contingents that they should put their animals into the houses of the city on account of the winter that had come, and that each one of them should have no more than one horse at our camp: for our rampart is close to this city. For the

---

messenger; *a secretis*: secretary.

Arman: presumably located on the south-west flank of the Zagros. Narban: the Nahr Wahn canal, only 12 miles from Ctesiphon, which marked the furthest point of Heraclius' advance in Jan. 628.

[489] *Drungarius*: a middle-ranking military officer, possibly in charge of the watch, see Bury, *IA* 41-3, 61-2; this is a very early reference to the position. Gusdanaspa: cf. n. 485.

At p. 731. 10 the Bonn text mistakenly reads μετὰ τοῦ ('with the') for the MS μεταξὺ ('between').

commandant of the city of Canzacon and all its men of property had withdrawn and retired to more secure fortresses in the mountainous parts when they learnt that we had crossed the mountain of Zara.

'When we received the two men who had been sent from Seiroe the Persian king, we dismissed one of them, namely the Persian, with some other men as well to the commandant of Canzacon, who was in a strong fort 40 miles away, and [p.733] we made him a memorandum that he should make ready about 60 animals on behalf of the ambassadors, so that they might speedily and without impediment depart to Seiroe the Persian king. And when the commandant had received the men sent by us and our said memorandum, for many hours both he and all those who were present there praised both us and Seiroe the Persian king. For they were assured by the Persian who had been sent by the ambassador that the opponent of God Chosroes had perished and that Seiroe had become Persian king. And the same commandant wrote back to us that with regard to our instructions to him, he was making ready the ambassadors' animals and that, whenever he received a second missive from us in which the arrival of the ambassadors was contained, the commandant himself would come personally to us, bringing the said animals, in order to perform all duty and servitude.

'When we had resided in this camp near Canzacon until the third of the month April, about the second hour there arrived Phaiak the *a secretis*, who is also called Rasnan, it being the Lord's Day. And at the same hour we received him, and he gave us a memorandum from Kabates, who is also called Seiroe, the most clement Persian king, which contained his proclamation and his desire to have peace with us and with every man. We therefore resolved to append a copy of the memorandum of Kabates, who is also called Seiroe the most clement, [p.734] to our present missive, and then likewise to append also the reply from us to him. Until the seventh of the month April, that is for 27 days, we resided in our same camp near Canzacon, and on the eighth of the same month we dismissed the same Phaiak the *a secretis*, who is also called Rasnan; so far as was in our power we had attended on him and all those with him, since he also had with him personages of good repute. And with him we dismissed Eustathius the most magnificent *tabularius*. And thus we have confidence in our Lord Jesus Christ, the good and almighty God, and in our Lady the Mother of God, that they will direct all our affairs in accordance with their goodness.

'And on the 8th of the same month, with God's aid we moved

from our camp in order to make our way to Armenia. But may
you prosper, praying incessantly and fervently on our behalf that
God may deem us worthy of seeing you, as we desire.'[490]

**[p.735]** *Copy of memorandum which came from Kabates, who is also
called Seiroe, the most clement Persian king, to Heraclius our most
pious and God-guarded emperor.*

'From Kabates Sadasadasach to Heraclius the most clement
Roman emperor, our brother.

'We impart greatest joy to the most clement Roman emperor,
our brother.

'Through the protection of God we have by good fortune been
adorned with the great diadem, and have gained possession of
the throne of our fathers and ancestors. Therefore, because we
have thus beneficently been deemed worthy by God of gaining
the said throne and lordship, if there is anything for the benefit
and service of mankind, we have resolved to accomplish this in
so far as it is in our power and, as was proper, we have
beneficently ordered it to be done. Since God sanctified us for
such a great throne and lordship, we have the intention of
releasing each and every man who is confined in prison. And
thereafter, if there is anything for the benefit and service of
mankind and of this state, and it was possible that it be ordered
by us, this we have ordered, **[p.736]** and it has been done. And
we have this intention that we should live in peace and love with
you, the emperor of the Romans and our brother, and the Roman
state and the remaining nations and other princes who surround
our state. Because of the fact that your fraternity the emperor of
the Romans was gladdened by our gaining possession of the
same throne,...'[491]

---

490  Embassy of Phaiak: the local Persian commandant (the Greek βαρισμανᾶς,
translated 'commandant', is a rendition of the Persian title Marzpan) had
prudently awaited confirmation of the change in Persian monarch, which was
now brought by Phaiak. For *a secretis* and Rasnan, cf. n. 488. *Tabularius*: a
military accountant, Jones, *LRE* 564-5.
       At p. 734. 3 ἐπεποιήσαμεν ('resided') should be read instead of ἐποιήσαμεν
('made').

491  Persian letter: The last pages of the MS of *CP* are badly damaged and the
text deteriorates into increasingly disjointed fragments. The most ambitious
attempt at restoration is by N. Oikonomidès, 'Correspondence between Heraclius
and Kavādh-Siroé in the Paschal Chronicle (628)' *Byz.* xli, 1971, 269-81, who has
identified and reconstructed part of Heraclius' reply to Shiroe's letter.
       It is notable that Shiroe addresses Heraclius as a brother, implying equality;
this recalls Khusro II's approach to Maurice in 590, when a Persian king in a

similarly weak position had been prepared to talk in terms of equality with the Romans and not to stress the Persians' traditional belief in their own superiority (cf. Whitby, *Maurice* 204-6 for the diplomatic vocabulary). Shiroe's references to a God in the singular were probably intended to suggest that he was favourably disposed to Christianity, possibly even a candidate for conversion, but Khusro II in 590 had used comparable ambivalent language to elicit Roman help (Theophylact iv. 11). In reply, Heraclius addressed Shiroe as 'son' and, apart from welcoming the Persian approach, he probably demanded the restoration of the Holy Cross and asked about the fate of the Roman ambassadors sent to Khusro in 615 (Nic. 20. 5-20). For Shiroe's promise to release prisoners, cf. Theoph. 326. 20-4, and 327. 10-16 for Shiroe's letter and settlement.

Heraclius' ambition was to achieve a secure settlement with the new Persian monarch, and possibly to install a Christian on the Persian throne. These aims were briefly achieved when the Christian Shahvaraz (the general who had operated against the Romans at Chalcedon in 626) seized the throne, but the rapid turnover of Persian monarchs undermined stability; see Mango, 'Deux Études' 105-18. Shiroe reigned for 6 or 7 months, his young son Ardashir for a few months, Shahvaraz for 40 days, and Boran the wife of Shiroe and daughter of Khusro for less than 2 years. In 631 Yazdgard the last Sassanian king succeeded, but had to overcome two rivals before confronting the Arab invasions.

## THE TERMINAL DATE OF *CP*

In our Introduction AD 630, the date attested in *CP*'s title, is accepted as the terminus of the work, but this has been challenged and the alternatives of 628 and 639 proposed.

Beaucamp ('Chronique' 463-5) has advocated 628, but the arguments are unconvincing. First, it is assumed that the text of *CP* originally terminated with Heraclius' letter in 628, whereas this is merely the point at which the Vatican MS disintegrates: the only indication that we have for the terminal date is provided by the title (quoted on p. xi above), and there is no reason to doubt its statement that the chronicle extended to some point in 630. Second, a distinction is drawn between an 'imperial' and a 'patriarchal' attitude to the Persian wars: the 'imperial', represented by George of Pisidia and Theophanes, portrayed Heraclius' campaigns as a crusade, stressing the religious element and with the restoration of the Cross in 630 as public affirmation that the emperor had subsumed Christian symbolism for imperial purposes; the 'patriarchal', supposedly represented by *CP* and Nicephorus, was not particularly interested in the Persian wars and ignored the restoration of the Cross, thereby refusing to sanction the imperial exploitation of Christianity. This distinction is not convincing, because under Heraclius emperor and patriarch were closely united in the struggle for the survival of the Christian empire; the emperor exploited the material wealth of the Church, but the patriarch was arguably the greater beneficiary in terms of prestige and power since Sergius was appointed guardian of Heraclius' children, St. Sophia became a focus for public life in Cpl. (e.g. the popular demonstrations of 626), and credit for the repulse of the Avar siege of Cpl. in 626 was accorded to religious and divine factors as much as to secular and imperial. The union of interests in *CP* is clear both in the narrative of the 626 siege and through the inclusion of Heraclius' victory dispatch (*s.a.* 628), a message which repeatedly proclaims the Christian role of Heraclius: an author who, for whatever reason, found this role unacceptable could easily have paraphrased the letter in less explicit terms. As for *CP*'s failure to report all Heraclius' Persian campaigns in detail, the author was not particularly interested in foreign military events (see Introduction, sec. iii); furthermore, the obscurity of manoeuvres in the Armenian highlands in 624-7, and the lack of proof of Roman success, might have acted as a deterrent. As a result, all attention in *CP* is focused on the moment of triumph, which is treated at great length with full emphasis on the crusading aspects of the war.

The later terminal date, 639, has been advocated by Pernice (*L'Imperatore Eraclio*, Florence 1905, pp. xiv-xv), followed by Ericsson ('Date' 18). Pernice claimed that accounts of two imperial ceremonies datable to 638/9, which are preserved in Constantine Porphyrogenitus (*de caer.* ii. 27-8), originated in *CP*; but, apart from being beyond proof, this is implausible, as was pointed out by Mercati ('Study' 410), who noted that both language and dating method were inconsistent with *CP*. The first ceremony is described in much greater detail than is normal in *CP*'s accounts even of contemporary ceremonies such as the coronations of Epiphania Eudocia in 612 or Heraclius II Constantine in 613. Constantine's researchers had access to archives that contained highly detailed accounts of specific ceremonies from the 5th c. onwards: these archives are the obvious source at this point (in fact *de caer.* ii. 27-8 form part of a longer sequence drawn from a single source), whereas there is no ceremony in *de caer.* which can be shown to be copied from an extant part of *CP*. A complication was introduced by Pertusi (*Giorgio* 234), who identified the ceremony of *de caer.* ii. 28, a procession to St. Sophia on 1 Jan., as a victory celebration organized by Heraclius in 629, on the grounds that the MSS of *de caer.* give the date as indiction 2, i.e. 629. But the simple emendation of Reiske to indiction 12 (639), printed in the Bonn text (p. 629. 1), is essential: this procession was followed on 4th Jan. by acclamations addressed to the imperial family (*de caer.* ii. 29), in which the younger Heraclius and David are described as Augustus and Caesar respectively, titles which they only received on 4 July 638 (*de caer.* ii. 27).

Ericsson elaborated on Pernice's thesis to suggest that the end of *CP* was deliberately mutilated by an orthodox copyist who wanted to remove from the historical record all references to Heraclius' Monotheletism; the scribe then adapted the introductory heading to take account of this change, an example of thoroughness that would be uncommon (Pernice had attributed the title to a copyist). It is also alleged that Anastasius' reign was treated in the same way, in order to disguise that emperor's Monophysite sympathies. This theory, like Pernice's, is beyond the scope of proof or disproof, but is equally implausible. There are several gaps in the text of *CP*: the start of the Nika Riot in 532 (*s.a.* 531) is lost, but there is no reason to suspect mutilation by an orthodox copyist; rather, it seems that not only the Vatican MS of *CP* but its archetype as well were defective at some points (see above n. 320 and note A at p.112).

Indeed in the two places where the hypothetical orthodox copyist was faced by a heretical emperor, it would have been sensible for him to have left the text complete: if the chronicle had ever covered the 630s it would presumably have contained references to Arab successes, including their capture of Jerusalem, which could have been exploited to demonstrate divine anger at the emperor's religious innovations, while in the decade 507–17 lost in the Anastasian lacuna there was a report of a major religious riot that could have been used to similar effect. A further indication that the Anastasian lacuna was in fact accidental is provided by the incorrect indiction and regnal years for 518 and 519: it looks as though the copyist did not understand that there had been a jump of 10 years and so continued the sequences directly from 507 until the realization that Anastasius was no longer on the throne (he died in 518) prompted him to stop altering the correct numerals in his exemplar; as a result there is a 10-year jump between 519 and 520. A copyist responsible for creating this muddle in his text is most unlikely to have had the capacity to emend the heading which introduces the chronicle.

There is no good reason to doubt the evidence of the title that *CP* originally terminated in 630.

## THE GREAT CHRONOGRAPHER

At two points in the 10th-c. Vatican MS of *CP*, extracts from a historical source referred to as the Great Chronographer (GC) have been inserted by a later scribe (probably 11th c.: see Whitby, 'Chronographer' 10). Fourteen extracts are inserted at folios 241v–242v, where the copyist had left blank pages in the hope of finding material to fill the lacuna in his archetype's account of the Nika Riot (cf. n. A at p. 112 above), and a fifteenth extract is included in the margin of the MS in the context of *CP*'s narrative of the overthrow of Maurice in 602. The majority of the extracts are concerned with earthquakes, though other forms of disaster (plagues, riots) are also treated.

For the Greek text, discussion and citation of parallel passages in Byzantine chroniclers, see A. Freund, *Beiträge zur antiochenischen und zur konstantinopolitanischen Stadtchronik* (Jena 1882), 38-53 (omitting the extract on Maurice), and Whitby, 'Chronographer'. The identity and date of this unknown source, and its links with extant chronicles, are major problems. It is difficult to do more than establish limits for speculation, since from a period of 300 years there survive only 15 scattered extracts. Furthermore it would be imprudent to assume that these have always been excerpted accurately, and that they can be taken as they stand to be literal quotations from the original. One obvious area of contamination is in the initial formulae, 'In the reign/time of...', most of which were probably composed by the excerptor, as suggested by the lack of grammatical cohesion at the beginning of GC 2. Hence conclusions about the chronicle's date cannot safely be drawn from the fact that Constantine V is twice called Copronymus in introductory phrases: for analogous additions in the Constantinian *Excerpta*, see *Exc. de insid.* G. Mon. 35, 'Justinian who built St. Sophia', or *Exc. de virt.* G. Mon. 36, 'Constantine the son of Leo the icon-fighter, the Isaurian'.

Another possible source of distortion is that the scribe copying the extracts into the MS of *CP* may have thought that he was running out of space towards the end of the series: both extracts 12 and 13 (located at the foot of folio 242r; cf. note A at p.112 above) contain somewhat garbled and abbreviated accounts in comparison with parallel texts in Theophanes and Nicephorus (see further below), and extract 14 (on folio 242v) is out of chronological sequence. These indications encourage the suggestion that extracts 12 and 13 might be somewhat abridged, as if the scribe began to compress his material into what he believed was a limited space (cf. Whitby, 'Chronographer' 13 n. 32), while extract 14 might have been inserted as an afterthought, when the scribe turned over and realized that he still had some more space available.

The first eleven extracts probably originated ultimately in a 6th-c. chronicle, since seven of them relate to the reign of Justinian. They provide evidence for assessing the relationship of GC with the Malalas tradition of information, though discussion is complicated by the loss of the complete version of Malalas. There is substantial overlap with Malalas, but the lack of parallels for extracts 2,

3, and especially 10 (the Great Plague of 542–3), suggests that GC also had at least one independent source of evidence. Extracts 7, 8 and 11, though they have some links with the Malalas tradition, are connected more closely with the series of 6th-c. chronicle extracts appended to the abbreviated version of the lost ecclesiastical history of Theodore Lector (*Anecdota Cramer*), which suggests that the chronicle represented by *Anec. Cramer* was probably one additional source for GC; Theophanes also supplemented Malalas with information from the *Anec. Cramer* tradition. But there could also have been a further source which, for example, provided the account of the plague.

Extracts 12–14 record 8th-c. events, and present different problems from the first part of the sequence, while the isolated extract from Maurice's reign should be considered in the same context since it casts light on GC's links with later chronicles, by indicating that at this point GC was following one of Theophanes' sources, but not Theophanes himself. A definite *terminus post* for the composition of the chronicle represented by the extracts is provided by the birth of Leo son of Constantine V in 750 (the latest recorded event; extract 13), but the only secure *terminus ante* is provided by the insertion of the extracts into the Vatican MS of *CP* in the 11th c. Within this space of about three centuries, the main decision to be made is whether GC preceded and influenced, or postdated and used, Nicephorus (late 8th c.) and Theophanes (early 9th c.). Both positions have been promoted, and a definite solution is perhaps impossible. The earlier date was favoured by E. Gerland (*Byz.* viii, 1933, 100-1), H. Hunger (*Literatur* 337, 345), and Whitby, 'Chronographer'. Maas ('Akklamationen' 47-8), discussing the *Akta dia Kalopodion* (on which, cf. note C at p.113-14 above), claimed that the *Akta* was an extract from the Great Chronographer, and that it derived from Theophanes. Maas was not primarily concerned with the GC extracts themselves (brief allusion at 47 n. 2), and his attribution of the *Akta* to GC was based on the mistaken belief that the *Akta* and GC were inserted in the Vatican MS by contemporaneous hands, whereas in fact they are separated by about a century. Cameron (*Factions* 322-9 esp. 325) followed Maas and confidently connected the GC extracts as well as the *Akta* with Theophanes. Mango ('Nicephorus' 545-8, discussing only extracts 12 & 13) argues afresh for the late date.

The dating decision is determined by the assumptions which are made: whether the extracts are assumed to be exact transcriptions from the original GC, or whether considerable garbling and/or abbreviation has occurred (particularly in extracts 12 & 13); whether GC was hostile to iconoclasts because of the references to Constantine as Copronymus ('shit by name') but yet inexplicably excluded the anti-iconoclast interpretation of the plague of 747 (GC 12) which is evident in Theophanes, or whether the inclusion of the epithet Copronymus in the introduction to extracts 12 & 13 is irrelevant since the start of the extracts was probably composed by the scribe responsible for their extraction from the original text; whether GC was an eclectic compiler who sometimes followed Theophanes (extracts 12 & 14), sometimes Nicephorus (13), sometimes the source of Theophanes without reference to Theophanes himself (extract on Maurice), and sometimes an unidentified text (2, 3, 10), or whether GC represents, however inaccurately, one of the sources used by Nicephorus and Theophanes.

*Alternatively from the Great Chronographer:*

1. In the reign of Zeno, an earthquake occurred in Rhodes and destroyed its *gymnasia* and all the beauty of the city. And not long afterwards, in autumn, a great earthquake occurred at Byzantium so that many houses, churches, and porticoes fell down; countless multitudes of men too were buried. The orb of the statue in the Forum also fell and the monument of the great Theodosius, the one on the column at the Taurus, and the sea became furious, rushed up very far, and engulfing a part of what had formerly been land it brought down several houses. And stars fell down into the sea like orbs of fire and made its water hot. The said earthquake persisted for 30 days continuously, with the result that a considerable part of the walls also fell down, all the towers and many buildings were overturned, and the city stank from the corpses; and the areas outside the city and the Golden Gates were all demolished.[1]

2. In the reign of the same Zeno; for when a strong movement occurred, it wrought substantial damage. For at the Hellespont strait it afflicted the greater part of the cities of Abydus and Lampsacus, and in the Thracian district Callipolis and Sestus fell down and most of the city of Tenedos fell down; and 50 towers of the Long Walls were also demolished, and all who had fled there were buried in them. In the area round Sestus a sort of mud welled up from the earth which immediately became stiff and solid.[2]

---

[1]    These tremors, which probably struck Cpl. on 25/26 Sept. 478 (cf. n. 310), are recorded more briefly in several chronicles, although with no mention of the preceding Rhodian quake, the tidal wave or shooting stars: Mal. 385. 3-8; *Anec. Cramer* 112. 11-18; *CP* p. 605. 16-18; Theoph. 125. 29-126. 5; Leo Gramm. 116. 21-117. 1; Cedr. i. 618. 16-22. The unnamed Forum should refer to the Forum of Constantine, which was dominated by the porphyry column with its statue of Constantine holding in the left hand a globe surmounted by a winged victory (Dagron, *Naissance* 38; cf. n. 54, and GC 8). For the equestrian statue of Theodosius in his Forum ( = Forum Tauri), cf. n. 174. The Golden Gate was located near the south end of the Theodosian walls.

[2]    There are no parallel passages, but this is probably part of the same series of tremors (Croke, 'Long Wall' 62), since the 478 earthquake also affected Bithynia (Mal. 385. 5-8) and could easily have extended to the Hellespont. For the suggestion that the Long Walls are those of Cpl. rather than the defence at Gallipoli (which probably did not have 50 towers), see Whitby, 'Long Walls' 570-5.

3. In the reign of Anastasius Dicorus, balsam rained on the imperial city itself and several other places.[3]

4. In the time of Justin the emperor, a great earthquake occurred in Antioch, at about hour 2 of the day; for, as agitations as well as tremors of the earth joined in movement, it became a grave for almost all the inhabitants.[4]

5. In the time of Justinian, the great Antioch again suffered an earthquake from divine wrath, two years after the occurrence of the first earthquake. And the earthquake prevailed for one hour with the result that the walls of the city and great houses fell to their foundations, and 4,000 men died as well. And a fearful roaring from the heaven occurred as well as a terrible and most severe winter.[5]

6. In the reign of Justinian, Pompeiopolis suffered from divine wrath, for it was split by the earthquake and half of the city was destroyed along with the inhabitants. And they were under the ground, and their voices were heard shouting, and the emperor made great donations for them to be brought up. And he lavished generosity on the victims.[5]

7. In the 5th year of the reign of Justinian occurred the insurrection of Nika as it is called. And the people crowned as emperor Hypatius, the kinsman of the emperor Anastasius. And when a popular riot occurred in the Hippodrome, a crowd of up to 35,000 perished. And a great part of the city was also burnt, including the Great Church and St. Irene and the hospice of Samson and the Augustaeum and the porch of the Basilica and the Chalce of the Palace, and there was great fear.[7]

---

[3] No parallel passages, and the shower (probably ash, στάκτη, rather than balsam, στακτή): Mango, 'Nicephorus' 548 n. 19) is not precisely datable; cf. CP s.a. 469 for a shower of ash from Vesuvius at Cpl.

[4] The great Antioch earthquake of May 526, of which Mal. 419. 5-421. 21 provides a long account, mentioning the entombment of many victims; also Theoph. 172. 11-19, G. Mon. 626. 8-15, Leo Gramm. 123. 19-24, Cedr. i. 640. 23-641. 19.

[5] The Antioch earthquake of Nov. 528; described by Mal. 442. 18-443. 7 (5,000 casualties); also Theoph. 177. 22-178. 5, Cedr. i. 646. 5-19 (both with 4,870 casualties and reference to the winter); G. Mon. 643. 4-10, Leo Gramm. 126. 1-5.

[6] Destruction of Pompeiopolis in 528/9; cf. Mal. 436. 17-437. 2, Theoph. 216. 17-22; also G. Mon. 626. 15-19, Leo Gramm. 123. 24-124. 2, Cedr. i. 641. 21-3 (all of whom place the earthquake in Justin I's reign). Pompeiopolis was located in Pontus in the valley of the river Amnias, modern Gök Irmak in northern Turkey.

[7] The Nika Riot of Jan. 532; for this synopsis, cf. Anec. Cramer 112. 19-27, Theoph. 181. 24-31, Leo Gramm. 126. 6-17, Cedr. i. 647. 11-17. For detailed narrative, cf. CP s.a. 531 with notes, esp. nn. 351, 354 for the buildings destroyed,

8. In the reign of the same Justinian, a great earthquake occurred in Constantinople. And there fell churches and houses and the wall, particularly that at the Golden Gate. And there also fell the spear which the statue that stood in the Forum grasped, and the right hand of the statue of the Xerolophus, and many died, and great fear seized all.[8]

9. In the reign of Justinian, a great earthquake occurred throughout the whole world with the result that half of Cyzicus was ruined.[9]

10. In the reign of Justinian, a varied and grievous disease fell upon mankind; and some who encountered phantoms by supernatural power at once shared the disease, so that even the emperor himself was apportioned the disease but was saved by the good favour of God; others who wandered in their dreams got the pestilence. Others, when a feverish onset came on unseen, were lacerated by deranging disease and overpowering sleep; of these, some perished from hunger since they were intent on sleep, but others went to destruction through sleeplessness. A vomiting of blood came upon others and quickly deprived them of life. As many as did not meet with the affliction of derangement, these people, after a swelling came on, either in a part of the body or particularly inside the armpit, in the pangs threw away even life. For some too, blistering carbuncles broke out on the body: immediately they escorted them to death. But because of the multitude of the dying, the corpses were neither carried out with an escort nor were they buried with psalmody according to custom, but they were cast into the pits.[10]

and n. 366 on casualties.

8    Earthquake at Cpl. in Aug. 554; cf. Mal. 486. 23-487. 5; *Anec. Cramer* 113. 24-30; Theoph. 222. 25-30, 229. 5-9; G. Mon. 642. 7-9; Cedr. i. 656. 2-5. For Constantine's statue in his Forum, see n. 54 and GC 1; it held a lance or sceptre in the right hand (Dagron, *Naissance* 38). The statue at the Xerolophus was that of Arcadius, which stood in his Forum (cf. *CP s.a.* 421 with n. 231). Golden Gate: cf. GC 1.

Theophanes records the destruction under both 541/2 and 553/4 as a result of his reliance on two separate sources, the *Anec. Cramer* for the earlier entry, Malalas for the later one. The placing of the extract in GC, before the Cyzicus earthquake in 543 (extract 9), and the affinities with *Anec. Cramer*, indicate that GC was using a source other than Malalas, one which had already misdated the earthquake.

9    Earthquake at Cyzicus in Sept. 543; cf. Mal. 482. 12-13; Theoph. 224. 11-13; Cedr. i. 656. 16-18.

10   The Great Plague of 542-3; there are no parallel passages for this, and the plague is described very briefly by chronicles (e.g. Mal. 482. 4-11; Theoph. 222.

11. In the reign of the same man, while the dome of the Great Church was being repaired – for it had been cracked by the earthquakes which occurred – the eastern part of the holy sanctuary fell. And it crushed with it the *ciborium*, and the holy altars, and the *ambo*.[11]

12. In the reign of Copronymus, an earthquake occurred in Palestine and the Jordan and all the Syrian land. And many tens of thousands, innumerable people indeed, are dead, and churches and monasteries are fallen. And at the same time a pestilential disease, starting from Sicily and Calabria and spreading like a fire, crossed to Greece and the islands. It also took hold of Constantinople, bringing frequent apparitions as well. And such a great multitude came to death from the said disease that planks were laid upon dumb animals and the corpses loaded up; and when the mules were exhausted, carts too were loaded up and led away like this; and when the graves had run out, even the waterless cisterns were filled with dead bodies. And things unseen were made manifest: very many oily crosses both on the clothes of men and on the holy vestments, and visions came to many men. As a result of these things, it came about that entire houses were shut up and there was no-one to perform burials.[12]

---

22-3), with most attention being paid to burial arrangements (e.g. G. Mon. 641. 1-17; Leo Gramm. 127. 17-128. 1), rather than the symptoms of the disease.

[11] Collapse of the dome of St. Sophia in May 558; cf. Mal. 489. 19-490. 5; *Anec. Cramer* 114. 14-22; Theoph. 232. 27-233. 3; Cedr. i. 676. 20-677. 19.

[12] Earthquake in Levant and plague at Cpl. in 747; cf. Nic. 62. 24-64. 9; Theoph. 422. 25-424. 3; Cedr. ii. 7. 17-9. 1.

GC is closer to Theophanes than to Nicephorus in that it records an earthquake in the Levant before turning to the plague, but both the other two have more information than is preserved in GC (including an exact date for the earthquake in Theophanes). The earthquake is not mentioned by Nicephorus, but he regularly omitted information that was available in the chronicle source which he shared with Theophanes. This common source did record some major events in the near east, including the earthquake of 750 (Nic. 64. 22-65. 7, Theoph. 426. 16-26; see below on GC 13), so that it could have contained a reference to the earthquake of 747. Theophanes also had an independent eastern chronicle source, which has parallels with Syriac chronicles down to 746, and contained further information probably added by a writer in Palestine c.780 (see E. W. Brooks, 'The Sources of Theophanes and the Syriac Chroniclers', *BZ* xv, 1906, 578-87), but the example of the 750 earthquake shows that not all eastern information in Byzantine chronicles should be traced to it.

GC 12, *as it stands*, cannot have been the common source of Theophanes and Nicephorus because of their fuller treatment (cf. Whitby, 'Chronographer' 11-12). However, GC's account of the plague is disordered when compared with the other versions, in that it mentions the burial arrangements for the victims before

13.  At the time of the birth of Leo the son of Constantine
Copronymus, all the stars of the heavenly place seemed to be
shifting and moving downwards throughout the whole night.
But those which came near the earth were immediately
destroyed. And many say that the said extraordinary sight was
displayed throughout all the world.[13]

the apparition of oily crosses on the garments of the afflicted, and it does not
contain any of the anti-iconoclast interpretations of the plague included by the
orthodox authors. One must assume, therefore, either (i) that it is an inaccurate
derivation from Theophanes by an excerptor who deliberately eliminated
Theophanes' anti-iconoclast interpretation of the plague, although this would
run counter to the excerptor's use of the epithet Copronymus for Constantine; or
(ii) that it is an inaccurate and abbreviated version of the common source used by
Theophanes and Nicephorus, the distortions being caused by the excerptor's
belief that he was running out of space on folio 242r (cf. p.192 above). We find
the latter assumption easier, but for the alternative, see Mango, 'Nicephorus' 546-
7.

[13]  Shooting stars in 750/1; cf. Nic. 65. 13-23; Theoph. 426. 14-29.

The GC extract is close to Nicephorus, and he has been identified as GC's
source by Mango ('Nicephorus' 547-8). But Nicephorus linked the shooting stars
with Leo's coronation (AD 751), the siege of Melitene and the death of the
empress Maria (65. 8-13), whereas he connected Leo's birth (64. 21-2) with the
Syrian earthquake of 750 and the prodigy of the talking mule (64. 22-65. 7): GC's
association of the stars with Leo's birth rather than coronation is a difficulty for
the belief that this extract is derived from Nicephorus, unless it is assumed that
the excerptor was working carelessly. Theophanes, who uses the same source as
Nicephorus for the earthquake of 750 and the prodigy of the talking mule (426.
16-26; cf. Nic. 64. 21-65. 7), mentions Leo's coronation but not the stars (though at
435. 5-7 he has a report of shooting stars 14 years later, using different language).
We would suggest that the common source of Theophanes and Nicephorus
recorded all the various strange events of 750/1, and that Theophanes,
Nicephorus and GC 13 represent independent but overlapping selections from it.
In support of his argument for the priority of Nicephorus over GC, Mango
(loc. cit.) advances two linguistic considerations, traces of incongruous high style
in GC and the superior quality of Nicephorus' phraseology. With regard to style,
there are also traces of elevation in Theophanes' description of the earthquake:
Theophanes describes the effect of the earthquake in an elaborate sentence with
tricolon structure and some grand language (e.g. ὑποκείμενα πεδία), which he
shares with Nicephorus. Chronicles do sometimes highlight certain events with
a grander literary style (cf. GC 10, the plague of 542; CP pp. 704. 13-705. 2 with n.
437, the loss of Jerusalem in 614), and it seems that the common chronicle source
attempted to grace the various disasters and prodigies of 750/1 with some
expansive or grand language. With regard to quality of phraseology, Nicephorus
was attempting to compose a rhetorical work in elevated Greek, so that his
language is likely to have been more elegant than GC's, but this does not prove
his priority. Thus Nicephorus' expression, 'It seemed to them that all the stars
were moving from the heavenly place appointed for them and being brought
down to earth', could be regarded as an elaboration of the clause in GC 'all the

14. In the reign of Leo a great and terrible earthquake occurred in Constantinople on 26th of the month October, indiction 9, a Wednesday at hour 8. And churches and monasteries were ruined, and a great host died. And the statue of the great Constantine which stood at the gate of Attalus together with the same Attalus also fell, as did the monument of Arcadius which stood on the Xerolophus column, and the statue of the great Theodosius at the Golden Gate, and the land walls, and cities and estates in Thrace, and in Bithynia Nicomedia and Praenetus and Nicaea: in the last, one church survived. And the sea withdrew from its proper boundaries at certain spots. And the earthquake persisted for 12 months. Therefore the emperor, seeing the walls of the city ruined, commanded the administrators to demand by way of supplement to the tax assessment 1 *miliaresion* for each *nomisma* for rebuilding the walls of the city. And thereafter custom prevailed that the two *keratia* should also be demanded annually by the adminstrators.[14]

stars...': an excerptor copying Nicephorus is unlikely to have altered the verb παρακινούμενοι to μετακινεῖσθαι, or to have advanced the phrase 'of the heavenly place' to the start of the clause (where its reference is ambiguous), whereas corresponding changes by Nicephorus wculd be in character.

In this extract, as in 12, there appears to be a substantial degree of inaccurate compression, which makes it impossible to prove whether GC was loosely derived from Nicephorus or from the common source. Overall, the latter seems more likely, and avoids the hypothesis that GC was an eclectic compiler who followed Theophanes for events of 747 but then switched to Nicephorus for similar information in 750.

[14] Earthquake at Cpl. and environs in Oct. 740; cf. Nic. 59. 2-14; Theoph. 412. 6-21; G. Mon. 744. 11-16; Leo Gramm. 180. 6-16; Cedr. i. 801. 9-22. The gate of Attalus, probably to be identified with the Exokionion gate, was located at the intersection of the Mese with the Constantinian wall (Janin, *Const.* 28-9, 317); the nearby column of the Exokionion was surmounted by a statue of Constantine (*Patria* ii. 54, pp. 180-1). There is no confirmation for a statue of Theodosius I (the Great) at the Golden Gate, although *Patria* ii. 57 (p. 182) records a statue of Theodosius II at the Sigma, which was relatively close (cf. Mango, *Const.* 50 n. 81); for Arcadius' statue, cf. GC 8 above. On Leo's new *dikeraton* tax, see Hendy, *Economy*, 238, 503-4, who takes this passage to indicate that the value of a *miliaresion* was two *keratia*.

GC is here identical to Theophanes, except that the latter has used direct speech to describe Leo's arrangements for raising the money for reconstructions: such introduction of short snatches of direct speech is characteristic of Theophanes' rephrasing of his sources (cf. 134. 27-8, and see Whitby, 'Chronicle Source' 315), so that GC is here more likely to be parallel to Theophanes' source than to have been derived from Theophanes. Nicephorus' version is based ultimately on the same source, but with considerable stylistic reworking and the introduction of some additional material (damage to St. Irene, inhabitants camp

*On wonders; from the Great Chronographer*

Maurice the emperor commanded the general Comentiolus to
hand over the Roman army to its enemies on account of its
mutinies. The latter did this in the middle of the night, and
ordered the army to equip itself, without having disclosed to the
masses that they were about to join battle. Since they imagined
that he had ordered them to don their weapons for the purpose
of an exercise, they did not arm for battle as they should have: as
a result, when day came, confusion overtook the army. And the
barbarians disrupted the ranks of the army; after finding the men
leaderless, some they slaughtered without mercy, others they
enslaved, and they took many captives in Thrace. Then, after
taking the captives, the barbarian Chagan granted the emperor a
ransom for them of one *nomisma* per head. But he bore a grudge
against his own army and did not consent to grant it. And again
the Chagan asked to receive half a *nomisma* for each life, but,
when Maurice refused to take the prisoners even for four *keratia*,
the Chagan became enraged and killed them all. He imposed on
the Romans tribute of 50,000 *solidi*. And on account of the said
impiety Maurice underwent the punishment of slaughter, since
he was rent asunder with his women and children and
relatives. [15]

---

outside walls).

    The opening phrase of the extract exactly parallels the previous 13 and does
not begin with ὅτι ('that') as printed in Whitby, 'Chronographer' 20.

[15]  Extract from Maurice's reign (inserted at *CP s.a.* 602); cf. <u>Theoph. 278. 32-
280. 10</u>. For discussion, see Whitby, 'Chronographer' 2-9 and *Maurice* 121-4.
This story of imperial treachery, whose veracity is very doubtful, is linked with
the Balkan campaign of 598 when Comentiolus was worsted by the Avars while
attempting to relieve Priscus who was under siege at Tomi. Comparison of this
extract with Theophanes and Theophylact (vii. 13. 8-15. 2) reveals that
Theophanes' text is an amalgam of two different sources, Theophylact and a text
that was extremely close to GC. Such is the overlap that it is reasonable to
conclude that GC either was one of Theophanes' two sources at this point or
exactly reproduces that source (with no material derived from Theophanes).

    This extract provides by far the best opportunity for determining the
relationship of GC with Theophanes; it suggests that GC did not have access to
Theophanes at this point, and this indication should perhaps help to tilt the
balance when examining the other extracts, particularly 12 and 13 where internal
evidence alone is not conclusive.

# APPENDIX 3

## ERICSSON'S POSTULATED TEXTUAL TRANSPOSITION

### A: AD 615

Ericsson ('Date') claimed that all CP's information for the year 615 down to and including the reference to Shahin at the Bosporus (CP pp. 705. 18-706. 13) correctly belongs in 626 but has been switched with the account of unrest among the *scholae* in Cpl. recorded *s.a.* 626 (pp. 715. 9-716. 8). The complex argument, though supported by Haldon (*Praetorians* n. 354 at 442-3), is unconvincing, and is not substantiated by any evidence for transposition in the Vatican MS. With regard to the information *s.a.* 615, Ericsson was concerned (pp. 22-5) that CP does not provide any details about events between Shahin's arrival at Chalcedon and the interview with Heraclius, and thought that the liturgical change ('a hymn of jubilation') was more appropriate in 626. But:

(i) a Persian army under Shahin did reach the Bosporus near the start of Heraclius' reign (see n. 442), and it is typical of CP that the Persian actions are recorded only as they impinged on the perceptions of a Constantinopolitan observer: CP's account of Heraclius' coup similarly begins with the appearance of ships near the Hebdomon.

(ii) The liturgical change did not involve the composition of 'a hymn of jubilation', but a morale-boosting chant that is consonant with the acquisition of relics of the Crucifixion in 614 (cf. *s.a.* 624 for a comparable addition to the liturgy); thus there is no reason to transpose it to 626 on the grounds that triumph was impossible in 615. (Haldon appears to believe that the introduction of the hymn in Lent 626 would follow the successful repulse of the Avar siege, but the latter took place in July/Aug.) The indiction date is one year out (Easter of indiction 4 = AD 616, p. 705. 19), and either it is incorrect or the notice has been inserted one year early; CP does sometimes provide in the text indiction dates which are at variance with the indiction date of the year heading, although such cases usually involve events dated to the period Oct.–Dec. when a new indiction year had begun (e.g. CP p. 699. 20; cf. Ericsson, p. 23 n. 15). Ericsson postulated that the notice was originally dated to indiction 14 (AD 626), and that when the sequence of notices was transposed the indiction date was altered to 4 (even though this was one year out of step with its new location): this is over-subtle.

(iii) The date of the coinage reform (reported between the liturgical notice and that on Shahin) cannot be corroborated, but it is likely to have preceded the large-scale striking of silver coins in 622 (Hendy, *Economy* 494-5); 615 is an appropriate occasion for such an economy measure, since the bronze currency was devalued *c.*616 (see n. 441).

### B: AD 626

There is equally little reason to advance to 615 the account of the unrest at Mid-Pentecost, 14 May 626. (In both 615 and 626 Easter fell on 20 April, hence Mid-

Pentecost on 14 May.) The arguments urged in favour of the transposition are: (i) bread tickets had already been abolished, after the cost had been raised to 3 '*solidi*' in 618 (*CP s.a.*); (ii) John Seismos wished to remove the rations from the *scholae* for the benefit of the soldiers, which presupposes the presence in Cpl. of troops; (iii) the specific officials named (Alexander and Leontius) are not mentioned in any accounts of the 626 siege; (iv) this riot would not have received popular support in the crisis of the Persian War or 'during or shortly after' a major siege like that of 626. The following points can be made. (i) In 618 bread (not bread tickets) had been priced at 3 *nomismata* 'coins' (i.e. *folles* not *solidi*, cf. n. 449), a price which should antedate the plan attributed to John of increasing the price from 3 to 8 *folles*. Although public bread distribution had been suspended in 618, the rations of the *scholae* may have been exempt, cf. n. 456. (ii) In 626 Heraclius detached part of his army to return to Cpl. to meet the threat posed by Shahvaraz (Theoph. 315. 7-13), and John may have been trying to arrange provisions for these newly arrived troops (cf. *CP* p. 718. 20-2 for 12,000 cavalry present in the city). (iii) Accounts of the 626 siege deliberately highlight the roles of the Patriarch Sergius and the patrician Bonus, but other leading men were involved in crucial decisions even though they are not always named (e.g. *CP* p. 718. 10-11). (iv) This unrest occurred nearly seven weeks before the Avar siege began at the end of June, and although the city's inhabitants may have regarded Shahvaraz's approach to the Bosporus as a danger, the Persians did not yet pose a direct threat to the capital: the prospect of a massive increase in the general price of bread might have seemed much more worrying, and would explain why the removal of the privileged rations of the *scholae* attracted popular support and provoked a more general riot on the second day.

## APPENDIX 4

## THE DATE OF HERACLIUS' ENCOUNTER WITH THE AVARS
### (CP s.a. 623)

The year in which Heraclius encountered the Avars on Sunday 5 June is a problem. CP, writing within a decade of the incident, places it in 623, a year in which 5 June did fall on a Sunday. However, this Balkan encounter appears to disrupt the sequence of Heraclius' Persian campaigns, which began in 622 and terminated in 628: it has been assumed that Heraclius must have been in the east fighting the Persians in 623, and so alternative dates have been considered for the Avar incident. Nicephorus, who also reports the encounter at length (12. 29-14. 10), does not give a date but places it quite early in Heraclius' reign, after the Persian capture of Egypt and the consequent famine but before the start of the major campaigns against Persia. No conclusions can, however, be drawn from this, since Nicephorus seems to have arranged this section of his narrative thematically rather than chronologically, with the result that Heraclius' incestuous marriage to Martina in 614 is placed after the loss of Egypt (616-19) and this Avar incident. Nicephorus' intention was to group together all Heraclius' misfortunes, so that Heraclius, the incestuous sinner, was shown to be properly afflicted with failure. Nicephorus (or at least the Vatican MS which varies slightly from the alternative tradition of the London MS) portrays Heraclius and his reaction to the Avar surprise unfavourably (e.g. 13. 22-28). Theophanes preserves a briefer notice of the encounter (301. 26-302. 4) which he puts in *a.m.* 6110, the ninth year of Heraclius' reign, i.e. AD 618-19, one year before Heraclius agreed terms with the Avars in order to facilitate the campaign against the Persians (302. 15-21).

Theophanes' date has had some champions, recently Averil Cameron ('Robe' 43-6, esp. n. 7, following A. Vasilievski, *Viz. Vrem.* iii, 1896, 83-95, and A. Wenger, *L'Assomption de la T.S. Vièrge dans la tradition byzantine du VIe au Xe siècle*, Archives de l'Orient chrétien 5, Paris 1955). Neither of these scholars, however, discussed the discrepancy between 619 and 623, and the chronological problem does not affect the substance of Cameron's article. The purpose of Vasilievski's article was to prove that the account of the rediscovery of the Virgin's Robe should not be connected with the Russian attack on Cpl. in 842 (as argued by K. M. Loparev, *Viz. Vrem.* ii, 1895, 592ff), but that it must be early 7th c., before the construction in 627 of the wall to protect the church at Blachernae; this argument is quite correct, but Vasilievski (93ff) did not concern himself with the debate between 619 and 623 and seems unaware that there was a problem. Wenger (119) offered no arguments at all and merely cited CP, incorrectly, for the date 5 June 619.

The accuracy of Theophanes' chronology for the early part of Heraclius' reign is not good: the majority of notices (including the Avar ones) are simply introduced 'in this year' without a more precise date, and some of them are certainly in the wrong year (e.g. 300. 30-301. 5, the capture of Jerusalem, dated *a.m.* 6106 = 614/5, i.e. one year late); his only precise information relates to the births of imperial children, and in other respects his evidence is limited and somewhat vague (e.g. the reports, adjacent to the Avar incident, for *a.m.* 6109, 6111, 6112). It seems that at this point his source did not present him with a clear chronological framework, and as a result it is unsafe to rely on his dates without corroboration. A significant problem for Theophanes' date is the precise day reference in *CP*: in 623, 5 June did fall on a Sunday, whereas in 619 it fell on a Tuesday, so that if 619 were the correct year *CP* must be wrong about either the day (Sunday) or the date (5 June). Although 5 June might be emended to 3 June (a Sunday in 619), this creates the somewhat extraordinary coincidence that the author of *CP* reported the day of the month incorrectly but also located this incorrect date in a year when it fitted the day of the week. It is possible that he took trouble to cross-check his days of the week while remaining unaware that he had misplaced this recent event by four years, but such tinkering with *CP* does not provide corroboration for Theophanes: the date of 619 must stand or fall solely on the reliability of Theophanes.

An alternative date of 617 was proposed by Baynes ('Date'). He argued strongly that *CP*'s date of Sunday 5 June was correct (122-5, citing the evidence of a 9th/10th-c. *typikon* for an anniversary celebration), but advanced the year to 617, the nearest previous occasion for this conjunction, postulating the accidental switch of one leaf of the MS archetype. This suggestion is ingenious, and was widely accepted before Cameron reverted to Theophanes' date, but it still raises the problem that *CP*'s notice, although *accidentally* switched away from its correct year was still *accurately* located so that the day of the month fitted the day of the week. Before resorting to either solution it is worth reviewing the much-discussed question of the chronology of Heraclius' Persian campaigns (e.g. Stratos, *Byzantium* chs. 10, 12-13, with notes), to consider if this really is incompatible with *CP*'s date of 623 for the Avar encounter.

Heraclius' first Persian campaign is securely dated to 622: he left Cpl. on the Monday after celebrating Easter on 4 April of indiction 10 (622; Theoph. 302. 32-4). N. Oikonomidès ('A Chronological Note on the First Persian Campaign of Heraclius (622)', *BMGS* ii, 1976, 1-9) has suggested that there was little military activity in the campaign: Heraclius was mainly concerned to improve his army's training and organization; there was some skirmishing in July–Aug. culminating in a Roman success in a minor engagement; after the campaign, Heraclius was summoned back to Cpl. by a threat in the west (G. Pisid., *Exp. Pers.* iii. 311-40).

The second campaign poses the major problem. *CP* (pp. 713. 19-714. 8) records that Heraclius set out on 25 March, the day of the Annunciation, in indiction 12, regnal year 14 (i.e. 624), celebrated Easter at Nicomedia (15 April in 624), and then proceeded east: during the three weeks at Nicomedia, Heraclius may have been awaiting a response from Khusro to a diplomatic initiative (Baynes, 'Date' 114-15), or simply organizing his expeditionary force. Theophanes (306. 19-27) states that Heraclius left Cpl. on 15 March in indiction 11 (623), quickly reached Armenia, and after attempting to negotiate with Khusro took the offensive against Persia on 20 April (cf. n. 452). Both sources are recording the same departure, so that it is a question of deciding which date is correct, that of the contemporary *CP* or that of Theophanes who, though writing two centuries later, had the poems of George of Pisidia (also contemporary) among his sources, and who (unlike *CP*) provides a long, detailed account of Heraclius' campaigns.

A compromise chronology might be adopted, whereby Heraclius left Cpl. on

25 March 623 (Good Friday), celebrated Easter at Nicomedia on 27 March, and then proceeded at once to the east; however, it seems improbable that Heraclius would have set out on Good Friday, an ill-omened day of lamentation (even if somewhat alleviated in 623 by coincidence with the Feast of the Annunciation), instead of waiting an extra two days to celebrate Easter in the capital as he had in 622. A choice should be made between the years in Theophanes and *CP*.

The most secure date in the sequence of Persian campaigns is their conclusion in 628 following the death of Khusro (see *CP s.a.* with notes). Theophanes, however, inserts Khusro's death one year early (*a.m.* 6118 = AD 626/7); furthermore he provides an incorrect indiction date for the start of the manoeuvres between Heraclius and the Persian general Rhazates (317. 26: 9 Oct. indiction 15 = 626), whereas the correct date for their decisive battle at Nineveh was Saturday 12 Dec. 627: Theophanes subsequently (318.16-17) gives the day and date, which are accurate for 627, not 626. Once Theophanes' error over the end of the campaign is corrected, then counting back campaign years in Theophanes' text gives 624 as the year of Heraclius' second campaign, recorded under *a.m.* 6114, where Theophanes' indiction date is again one year early (306.19: March indiction 11, instead of indiction 12), and was perhaps calculated by reference to the incorrect date at 317. 26. Thus there is good reason to distrust Theophanes' chronology and indiction dates.

There may, however, be more serious problems in the order of Theophanes' narrative. The Avar siege of Cpl. is correctly located in *a.m.* 6117, and eastern military events associated with this (e.g. Heraclius' tripartite division of the army, 315. 11-16) are also placed in the correct year. The sources for Theophanes' military narrative in the 620s are unknown, but included George of Pisidia whose poems would not have provided precise chronological indications. Theophanes perhaps had to create his own chronological divisions, as he did in his account of the 590s Balkan campaigns, where he attempted to clarify the obscure chronology of Theophylact's narrative and created spurious year divisions in the process (Theoph. *a.m.* 6085-7; cf. Whitby, 'Chronicle Source' 333). As a result Theophanes' distribution of material between different years cannot be trusted without external corroboration. It would not be surprising if Theophanes failed to realize that there was a gap of a whole year after the first campaign in 622: consequently he produced a garbled date for the second campaign, inventing incorrect indiction dates both for this and for the final campaign year.

If this argument is correct, Heraclius did not campaign against the Persians in 623. A suitable explanation for this break would be the need to negotiate a binding agreement with the Avars in the Balkans (the western threat to which George of Pisidia alludes at the end of the first campaign, *Exp. Pers.* iii. 311-40); the ill-fated meeting at Heracleia formed part of this process. Hence there is no need to alter *CP*'s date for the meeting: *CP* gives precise detail (e.g. 'about hour 4', p. 712. 21), and his contemporary knowledge of the event should be allowed some authority. The same solution was adopted by E. Gerland ('Die persischen Feldzüge des Kaisers Herakleios', *BZ* iii, 1894, 330-73), and Stratos (*Byzantium* 361-5, though his discussion is not entirely clear). The extremely complicated question of the Persian campaigns is currently being re-examined in detail by Dr James Howard-Johnston.

## SELECT BIBLIOGRAPHY
(Works cited in full in the notes are not included here)

*Primary Sources*

Agapius of Membij, *Histoire Universelle*, pt. ii, French tr. A. A. Vasiliev, *PO* viii (1912).

Agathias, *History*, ed. R. Keydell (Berlin 1967); English tr. J. D. C. Frendo (Berlin and New York 1975).

Ammianus Marcellinus, *Res Gestae*, ed. and tr. J. C. Rolfe, 3 vols. (Loeb, London 1936-9).

*Anecdota Cramer* = J. A. Cramer, *Anecdota Graeca e codd. manuscriptis Bibliothecae Regiae Parisiensis* ii (Oxford 1839).

*Anon. Guidi* = *Chronicon Anonymum de Ultimis Regibus Persarum*, ed. with Latin tr. I. Guidi, *Chronica Minora, CSCO* Scr. Syri iii/4 (Paris 1903).

*Anonymus Valesianus*, ed. and tr. J. C. Rolfe in Ammianus Marcellinus iii (Loeb 1939), 506-69.

*Anthologia Graeca*, ed. with German trans. H. Beckby, 4 vols. (Munich 1957-8); English tr. W. R. Paton, 5 vols. (Loeb, London and New York 1916-18).

Antiochus Strategius, *La Prise de Jérusalem par les Perses en 614*, ed. with French tr. G. Garitte, *CSCO* cciii, Scr. Iberici xii (Louvain 1960).

Aurelius Victor, *De Caesaribus*, ed. Fr. Pichlmayr, rev. R. Gruendel (Leipzig 1961).

Candidus, ed. and tr. Blockley, *Historians* (see *Secondary Sources*).

Cedrenus, *Historiarum Compendium*, ed. E. Bekker (*CSHB* 1838-9).

*Chronicon Miscellaneum ad Annum Domini 724 pertinens*, ed. with Latin tr. E. W. Brooks and J.-B. Chabot, *CSCO* Scr. Syri iii/4 (Paris 1903), 61-119.

*Chronicon Paschale*, ed. L. Dindorf (*CSHB* 1832).

*Codex Theodosianus*, ed. T. Mommsen and P. M. Meyer (Berlin 1905); English tr. C. Pharr (New York 1952).

Constantine Porphyrogenitus, *de Administrando Imperio*, ed. G. Moravcsik, tr. R. J. H. Jenkins (Budapest 1949).

_____, *de Caerimoniis*, ed. J. J. Reiske (*CSHB* 1829); French tr. (incomplete) A. Vogt, 2 vols. (Budé, Paris 1935-40).

_____, *Excerpta de Insidiis*, ed. C. de Boor (Berlin 1905).

_____, *Excerpta de Virtutibus*, ed. C. de Boor (Berlin 1906-10).

*Corpus Iuris Civilis*, i *Codex Iustinianus*, ed. P. Krüger and T. Mommsen (16th ed., Berlin 1954); iii *Novels*, ed. R. Schoell and W. Kroll (6th ed., Berlin 1954).

Cosmas Indicopleustès, *Topographie chrétienne* i, ed. with French tr. W. Wolska-Conus (Paris 1968).

208     CHRONICON PASCHALE

Daniel the Stylite, *Life*, tr. E. Dawes and N. H. Baynes, *Three Byzantine Saints* (London and Oxford 1948), 1-84.
*Doctrina Iacobi nuperbaptisati*, ed. N. Bonwetsch, *Abhandl. des. k. Ges. der Wissens. zur Göttingen*, xii/3 (1910).

Eusebius, *Kirchengeschichte*, ed. E. Schwartz (*GCS*, Leipzig 1908); *Ecclesiastical History* ed. and tr. K. Lake and J. E. L. Oulton, 2 vols. (Loeb 1926-32).
_____, *Praeparatio Evangelica*, ed., tr., and comm. E. H. Gifford (Oxford 1903).
_____, *Triakontaeterikos*, ed. I. A. Heikel (*GCS*, Leipzig 1902); English tr. H. A. Drake, *In Praise of Constantine* (Berkeley 1976), 83-127.
_____, *Vita Constantini*, ed. F. Winkelmann (*GCS*, Berlin 1975); English tr. E. C. Richardson in *Library of Nicene and Post-Nicene Fathers*, 2nd ser., i (Oxford and New York 1890), 481-540.
Eutropius, *Breviarium*, ed. F. Ruehl (Leipzig 1919).
Evagrius, *Ecclesiastical History*, ed. J. Bidez and L. Parmentier (London 1898); French tr. A. J. Festugière in *Byz.* xlv, 1975, 187-488; English tr. (with Theodoret) in Bohn's Ecclesiastical Library (London 1854).

*Fasti Heracliani*, ed. H. Usener, *MGH Auct. Ant.* xiii, *CM* iii. (Berlin 1898), 386-410.
*Fasti Hydatiani*, ed. T. Mommsen, *MGH Auct. Ant.* ix, *CM* i (Berlin 1892), 197-247.
*Fragmenta Historicorum Graecorum*, vols. iv-v, ed. C. Müller (Paris 1851-70).

George of Pisidia, ed. with Italian tr. and comm. A. Pertusi, *Giorgio di Pisidia Poemi*, i *Panegyrici epici* (Ettal 1960).
Georgius Monachus, *Chronicon*, ed C. de Boor, re-ed. P. Wirth (Stuttgart 1978).
Goleniščev Papyrus, ed. A. Bauer and J. Strzygowski, *Denkschrift der kaiserlichen Akademie der Wissens. zu Wien, Phil.-Hist. Klasse* li (1906).

*Inscriptiones Latinae Selectae*, ed. H. Dessau, 3 vols. (Berlin 1892-1916).

Jerome, *Chronicle*, ed. R. Helm (*GCS*, Berlin 1956).
John Lydus, *de Magistratibus Populi Romani*, ed. R. Wuensch (Leipzig 1903); English tr. A. C. Bandy, *Ioannes Lydus, On Powers* (Philadelphia 1983).
John of Antioch, *FHG* iv. 535-622, v. 27-38.
John of Ephesus, *Iohannis Ephesini Historiae Ecclesiasticae pars tertia*, ed. with Latin tr. E. W. Brooks, *CSCO* cv-vi, Scr. Syri liv-v (Louvain 1935-6).
_____, *The Third Part of the Ecclesiastical History of John of Ephesus*, English tr. R. Payne-Smith (Oxford 1860).
John of Nikiu, *Chronicle*, tr. R. H. Charles (London 1916).
Jordanes, *Romana et Getica*, ed. T. Mommsen, *MGH Auct. Ant.* v/1 (Berlin 1882).

# BIBLIOGRAPHY 209

Julian, *Works*, ed. and tr. W. C. Wright, 3 vols. (Loeb, London 1913-23).

Lactantius, *de Mortibus Persecutorum*, ed. J. Moreau (*Sources chrétiennes* xxxix, Paris 1954); ed. with English tr. J. L. Creed (Oxford 1984).
Leo Grammaticus, *Chronographia*, ed. E. Bekker (*CSHB* 1842).

Malalas, *Chronographia*, ed. L. Dindorf (*CSHB* 1831).
_____, Australian Malalas = English tr. E. Jeffreys, M. Jeffreys, and R. Scott (Byzantina Australiensia iv, Melbourne 1986).
_____, Slavonic Malalas, see Australian Malalas, pp. xxxviii-xl.
_____, Tusculan fragment, ed. A. Mai, *Spicilegium Romanum* ii (Rome 1839), Appendix, 6-28.
Malchus, ed. and tr. Blockley, *Historians* (see *Secondary Sources*).
Marcellinus Comes, ed. T. Mommsen, *MGH Auct. Ant.* xi, *CM* ii (Berlin 1894), 39-101.
Maurice, *Strategicon*, ed. G. T. Dennis, German tr. E. Gamillscheg (Vienna 1981); English tr. G. T. Dennis (Philadelphia 1984).
Michael the Syrian, *Chronique*, French tr. J. B. Chabot, ii (Paris 1901).
*Miracula S. Demetrii*, ed. with French tr. P. Lemerle *Les plus anciens Recueils des Miracles de Saint Démétrius*, i Le Texte (Paris 1979).
Moses of Khoren, *History of the Armenians*, English tr. R. W. Thomson (Harvard 1978).

Nicephorus, *Opuscula historica*, ed. C. de Boor (Leipzig 1880).
*Notitia Urbis Constantinopoleos*, ed. O. Seeck, *Notitia Dignitatum* (Berlin 1876), 227-43.

Olympiodorus, ed. and tr. Blockley, *Historians* (see *Secondary Sources*).

*Parastaseis Syntomoi Chronikai*, ed., tr. and comm. Averil Cameron and Judith Herrin, *Constantinople in the Early Eighth Century: The Parastaseis Syntomoi Chronikai* (Columbia Studies in the Classical Tradition x, Leiden 1984).
*Patria Constantinopoleos*, ed. T. Preger, *Scriptores Originum Constantino-politanarum*, 2 vols. (Leipzig 1901-7).
Philostorgius, *Kirchengeschichte*, ed. J. Bidez, rev. F. Winkelmann (*GCS*, Berlin 1981); English tr. E. Walford (with Sozomen) in Bohn's Ecclesiastical Library (London 1855).
Priscus, ed. and tr. Blockley, *Historians* (see *Secondary Sources*).
Procopius, *Works*, ed. and tr. H. B. Dewing, 7 vols. (Loeb 1914-40).

Sebeos, *Histoire de Héraclius*, French tr. F. Macler (Paris 1904).
Socrates, *Ecclesiastical History*, ed. and Latin tr. R. Hussey (Oxford 1853); English tr. in Bohn's Ecclesiastical Library (London 1853).
Sozomen, *Kirchengeschichte*, ed. J. Bidez and G. C. Hansen (*GCS*, Berlin 1960); English tr. E. Walford in Bohn's Ecclesiastical Library (London 1855).

*Suda = Suidae Lexicon*, ed. A. Adler (Leipzig 1928-38).
*Synaxarium Ecclesiae Constantinopolitanae*, ed. H. Delehaye, *Propylaeum ad Acta Sanctorum Nov.* (Brussels 1902).

Tabari, *Geschichte der Perser und Araber zur Zeit der Sasaniden aus der arabischen Chronik des Tabari*, German tr. T. Nöldeke (Leiden 1879).
Theodore Lector, *Ecclesiastical History* = Theodoros Anagnostes, *Kirchengeschichte*, ed. G. C. Hansen (*GCS*, Berlin 1971).
Theodore Syncellus, ed. L. Sternbach, *Analecta Avarica* (Cracow 1900).
Theodoret, *Historia Religiosa*, ed. and tr. P. Canivet and A. Leroy-Molinghen (Paris 1977-9).
_____, *Kirchengeschichte*, ed. L. Parmentier, re-ed. F. Scheidweiler (Berlin 1954); English tr. in Bohn's Ecclesiastical Library (London 1854).
Theophanes, *Chronographia*, ed. C. de Boor (Leipzig 1883-5); English tr. (AD 602–813) H. Turtledove (Philadelphia 1982).
Theophylact, *History*, ed. C. de Boor, re-ed. P. Wirth (Stuttgart 1972); English tr. and notes, Michael and Mary Whitby (Oxford 1986).

Victor Tonnensis, ed. T. Mommsen, *MGH Auct. Ant.* xi, *CM* ii (Berlin 1894), 178-206.

Ps.-Zachariah of Mitylene, *Ecclesiastical History*, tr. F. J. Hamilton and E. W. Brooks (London 1899).
Zosimus, *Histoire Nouvelle*, ed. with French tr. and comm. F. Paschoud, vols. i-iii/2 (Paris 1971-89); English tr. R. T. Ridley (Byzantina Australiensia ii, Canberra 1982).

*Secondary Sources*

Allen, 'Eustathius' = P. Allen, 'An Early Epitomator of Josephus: Eustathius of Epiphaneia', *BZ* lxxxi, 1988, 1-11.
____, *Evagrius* = P. Allen, *Evagrius Scholasticus the Church Historian* (Spicilegium Sacrum Lovaniense, études et documents xii, 1981).
Avi-Yonah, *Jews* = M. Avi-Yonah, *The Jews of Palestine* (Oxford 1976).

Bagnall, *Consuls* = R. S. Bagnall, Alan Cameron, S. R. Schwartz, K. A. Worp, *Consuls of the Later Roman Empire* (Philological Monographs of the American Philological Association xxxvi, Atlanta, Georgia 1987).
Baldwin, *Studies* = B. Baldwin, *Studies on Late Roman and Byzantine History, Literature and Language* (Amsterdam 1984).
Barišić, 'Siège' = F. Barišić, 'Le Siège de Constantinople par les Avares et les Slaves en 626', *Byz.* xxiv, 1954, 371-95.
Barnes, *CE* = T. D. Barnes, *Constantine and Eusebius* (Camb., Mass. 1981).
____, *NE* = T. D. Barnes, *The New Empire of Diocletian and Constantine* (Camb., Mass. 1982).

Baynes, 'Date' = N. H. Baynes, 'The Date of the Avar Surprise', *BZ* xxi, 1912, 110-28.

Beaucamp, 'Chronique' = J. Beaucamp, R. Cl. Bondoux, J. Lefort, M. Fr. Rouan-Auzépy, I. Sorlin, 'La Chronique Pascale: le temps approprié', in *Le Temps chrétien de la fin de l'Antiquité au Moyen Age* (Colloques du CNRS dciv, 1984), 451-468.

Beck, *Studien* = ed. H-G. Beck, *Studien zur Frühgeschichte Konstantinopels* (Miscellanea Byzantina Monacensia xiv, Munich 1973).

Bidez, *Julien* = J. Bidez, *La Vie de l'Empereur Julien* (Paris 1930).

Blockley, *Historians* = R. C. Blockley, *The Fragmentary Classicising Historians of the Later Roman Empire*, i-ii (Liverpool 1981, 1983).

Brightman, *Liturgies* = F. E. Brightman, *Liturgies Eastern and Western*, i *Eastern Liturgies* (Oxford 1896).

Browning, *Julian* = R. Browning, *The Emperor Julian* (London 1975).

_____, 'Language' = R. Browning, 'The Language of Byzantine Literature', *Byzantina kai Metabyzantina* i, 1978, 103-33.

Brunt, 'Epitomes' = P. A. Brunt, 'On Historical Fragments and Epitomes', *CQ* xxx, 1980, 477-94.

Bury, *HLRE* [1] = J. B. Bury, *A History of the Later Roman Empire from Arcadius to Irene (395 A. D. to 800 A. D.)* (London 1889).

_____, *HLRE* [2] = J. B. Bury, *A History of the Later Roman Empire from the Death of Theodosius I to the Death of Justinian* (London 1923).

_____, *IA* = J. B. Bury, *The Imperial Administrative System in the Ninth Century* (British Academy Supplemental Papers i, London 1911).

_____, 'Riot' = J. B. Bury, 'The Nika Riot', *JHS* xvii, 1897, 92-119.

Cameron, *Claudian* = Alan Cameron, *Claudian: Poetry and Propaganda at the Court of Honorius* (Oxford 1970).

_____, 'Empress' = Alan Cameron, 'The Empress and the Poet: Paganism and Politics at the Court of Theodosius II', *YCS* xxvii, 1982, 217-89.

_____, *Factions* = Alan Cameron, *Circus Factions* (Oxford 1976).

Averil Cameron, *Continuity* = Averil Cameron, *Continuity and Change in Sixth-Century Byzantium* (Variorum, London 1981).

_____, 'Robe' = Averil Cameron, 'The Virgin's Robe: an Episode in the History of Early Seventh-Century Constantinople', *Byz.* xlix, 1979, 42-56 [ = *Continuity* XVIII].

_____, 'Sophiae' = Averil Cameron, 'Notes on the Sophiae, the Sophianae, and the Harbour of Sophia', *Byz.* xxxvii, 1967, 11-20 [ = *Continuity* XIII].

_____, 'Theotokos' = Averil Cameron, 'The *Theotokos* in Sixth-Century Constantinople', *JThS* xxix, 1978, 79-108 [ = *Continuity* XVI].

Carrié, 'Distributions' = J. M. Carrié, 'Les Distributions alimentaires dans les cités de l'empire romain tardif', *Mélanges de l'école française de Rome: Antiquité* lxxxvii, 1975, 995-1101.

Chadwick, *Church* = H. Chadwick, *The Early Church* (Penguin, London 1967).

Conybeare, 'Chronicle' = F. C. Conybeare, 'The Relation of the Paschal Chronicle to Malalas', *BZ* xi, 1902, 395-405.

Conybeare, 'Codex' = F. C. Conybeare, 'The Codex of the *Paschal Chronicle* used by Holstein', *JThS* vii, 1906, 392-7.

Croke, 'Basiliscus' = B. Croke, 'Basiliscus the Boy-Emperor', *GRBS* xxiv, 1983, 81-91.

_____, 'Chronicles' = B. Croke, 'The Origins of the Christian World Chronicle', in (edd.) B. Croke and A. M. Emmett, *History and Historians in Late Antiquity* (Pergamon Press 1983), 116-31.

_____, 'Earthquakes' = B. Croke, 'Two Early Byzantine Earthquakes and their Liturgical Commemoration', *Byz.* li, 1981, 122-47.

_____, 'Long Wall' = B. Croke, 'The Date of the "Anastasian Long Wall" in Thrace', *GRBS* xxiii, 1982, 59-78.

Dagron, *Naissance* = G. Dagron, *Naissance d'une capitale: Constantinople et ses institutions de 330 à 451* (Bibliothèque Byzantine, études vii, Paris 1974).

Downey, *Antioch* = G. Downey, *A History of Antioch in Syria* (Princeton 1961).

Du Cange, *Glossarium* = C. du Fresne du Cange, *Glossarium ad Scriptores Mediae et Infimae Graecitatis* (Lyons 1688, repr. Graz 1958).

Dvornik, *Apostolicity* = F. Dvornik, *The Idea of Apostolicity in Byzantium and the Legend of the Apostle Andrew* (Dumbarton Oaks Studies iv, Camb., Mass. 1958).

Ericsson, 'Date' = K. Ericsson, 'Revising a Date in the Chronicon Paschale', *JÖBG* xvii, 1968, 17-28.

Fiey, *Nisibe* = J-M. Fiey, *Nisibe: métropole syriaque orientale et ses suffragants des origines à nos jours* (*CSCO* ccclxxxviii, Subs. liv, Louvain 1977).

Finegan, *Handbook* = J. Finegan, *Handbook of Biblical Chronology* (Princeton 1964).

Fliche and Martin, *Église* = (edd.) A. Fliche and V. Martin, *Histoire de l'Église* iii (Paris 1945).

Frank, *Scholae* = R. I. Frank, *Scholae Palatinae: the Palace Guards of the Later Roman Empire* (Papers and Monographs of the American Academy in Rome xxiii, 1969).

Frend, *Monophysite* = W. H. C. Frend, *The Rise of the Monophysite Movement* (Cambridge 1972).

Grierson, 'Tombs' = P. Grierson, 'The Tombs and Obits of the Byzantine Emperors (337-1042)', *DOP* xvi, 1962, 1-63.

Grumel, *Chronologie* = V. Grumel, *La Chronologie* (Bibliothèque byzantine, Traité d'études byzantines i, Paris 1958).

Guilland, *Études* = R. Guilland, *Études de topographie de Constantinople byzantine* i-ii (Berliner byzantinische Arbeiten xxxvii, Amsterdam 1969).

_____, *Recherches* = R. Guilland, *Recherches sur les institutions byzantines* i-ii (Berliner byzantinische Arbeiten xxxv, Amsterdam 1967).

Haldon, *Praetorians* = J. F. Haldon, *Byzantine Praetorians: An Administrative, Institutional and Social Survey of the Opsikion and Tagmata, c.580-900* (Poikila Byzantina iii, Bonn 1984).

_____, 'Recruitment' = J. F. Haldon, *Recruitment and Conscription in the Byzantine Army c.550-950: A Study on the Origins of the* Stratiotika ktemata, (Sitzungsb. der österreichischen Akad. der Wissens., phil.-hist. Klasse ccclvii, Vienna 1979).

Hendy, *Economy* = M. F. Hendy, *Studies in the Byzantine Monetary Economy c.300-1450* (Cambridge 1985).

Honoré, *Tribonian* = T. Honoré, *Tribonian* (London 1978).

Hunger, *Literatur* = H. Hunger, *Die hochsprachliche profane Literatur der Byzantiner* i (Handbuch der Altertumswissenschaft xii/5.1, Munich 1978).

Hunt, *Pilgrimage* = E. D. Hunt, *Holy Land Pilgrimage in the Later Roman Empire AD 312-460* (Oxford 1982).

Janin, *Const.* = R. Janin, *Constantinople byzantine* (2nd ed., Paris 1964).

_____, *Églises* = R. Janin, *La Géographie ecclésiastique de l'empire byzantin*, i *Le Siège de Constantinople et le Patriarcat oecumenique*, 3 *Les Églises et les monastères* (2nd ed., Paris 1969).

_____, *Monastères* = R. Janin, *Les Églises et les monastères des grands centres byzantins* (Paris 1975)

Jones, *LRE* = A. H. M. Jones, *The Later Roman Empire, 284-602: A Social, Economic and Administrative Survey* (Oxford 1964).

Justi, *IN* = F. Justi, *Iranisches Namenbuch* (Marburg 1895).

Karlin-Hayter, *Studies* = P. Karlin-Hayter, *Studies in Byzantine Political History: Sources and Controversies* (Variorum, London 1981).

Lampe, *Lexicon* = G. W. H. Lampe, *A Patristic Greek Lexicon* (Oxford 1968).

Liddell and Scott = H. G. Liddell and R. Scott, *Greek-English Lexicon*, rev. H. S. Jones and R. McKenzie (Oxford 1968).

Maas, 'Akklamationen' = P. Maas, 'Metrische Akklamationen der Byzantiner', *BZ* xxi, 1912, 28-51.

Mango, *Brazen House* = C. A. Mango, *The Brazen House: A Study of the Vestibule of the Imperial Palace of Constantinople* (Arkaeol. Kunsthist. Medd. Dan. Vid. Selsk. iv/4, Copenhagen 1959).

_____, *Const.* = Cyril Mango, *Le Développement urbain de Constantinople (IVe-VIIe siècles)* (*TM* Monographies ii, Paris 1985).

_____, 'Deux Études' = Cyril Mango, 'Deux Études sur Byzance et la Perse Sassanide', *TM* ix, 1985, 91-118.

_____, 'Diippion' = C. A. Mango, 'Le Diippion', *REB* viii, 1950, 152-61.

Mango, 'Fourteenth Region' = Cyril Mango, 'The Fourteenth Region of
Constantinople', in (edd.) O. Feld and U. Peschlow, *Studien zur
spätantiken und byzantinischen Kunst: Friedrich Wilhelm Deichmann
gewidmet* ii (Bonn 1986), 1-5.
_____, 'Nicephorus' = Cyril Mango, 'The Breviarium of the Patriarch
Nicephorus', in ed. N. A. Stratos, *Byzantium: Tribute to Andreas N.
Stratos* ii (Athens 1986), 539-52.
Mathews, *Churches* = T. F. Mathews, *The Early Churches of Constantinople:
Architecture and Liturgy* (Pennsylvania State UP 1971).
Mercati, 'Study' = G. Mercati, 'A Study of the *Paschal Chronicle*', *JThS* vii,
1906, 397-412.
Montgomery, *Samaritans* = J. A. Montgomery, *The Samaritans*
(Philadelphia 1907, repr. 1968).
Müller-Wiener, *Bildlexikon* = W. Müller-Wiener, *Bildlexikon zur
Topographie Istanbuls* (Tübingen 1977).

Pertusi, *Giorgio* = George of Pisidia (see *Primary Sources*).
*The Prosopography of the Later Roman Empire*, i, edd. A. H. M. Jones, J. R.
Martindale, J. Morris (Cambridge 1971); ii, ed. J. R. Martindale
(Cambridge 1980); iii, forthcoming.
A. S. Proudfoot, 'The Sources of Theophanes for the Heraclian Dynasty',
*Byz*, xliv, 1974, 367-439.

Rabello, *Samaritani* = A. M. Rabello, *Giustiniano, Ebrei e Samaritani alla luce
delle fonti storico-letterarie, ecclesiastiche e giuridiche* i (Milan 1987).
Richard, 'Comput'= M. Richard, 'Le Comput Pascal par Octaétéris', *Le
Muséon* lxxxvii, 1974, 307-339.
Rubin, 'Church' = Z. Rubin, 'The Church of the Holy Sepulchre and the
Conflict between the Sees of Caesarea and Jerusalem', in (ed.) L. I.
Levine, *The Jerusalem Cathedra* (Jerusalem and Detroit 1982), 79-105.

Scott, 'Easter', = R. Scott, 'Justinian's Coinage and Easter Reforms and the
Date of the Secret History', *BMGS* xi, 1987, 215-21.
_____, 'Justinian' = 'Malalas and Justinian's Codification', in (edd.) E. and
M. Jeffreys and A. Moffat, *Byzantine Papers* (Byzantina Australiensia i,
Canberra 1981) 12-31.
_____, 'Malalas' = R. Scott, 'Malalas, *The Secret History*, and Justinian's
Propaganda', *DOP* xxxix, 1985, 99-109.
Speck, *Bellum Avaricum* = P. Speck, *Zufälliges zum Bellum Avaricum des
Georgios Pisides* (Miscellanea Byzantina Monacensia xxiv, Munich 1980).
Stein, *BE* = E. Stein, *Histoire du Bas-Empire* i-ii (Paris 1949-59).
_____, Stein, 'Post-Consulat' = E. Stein, 'Post-Consulat et αὐτοκρατορία',
*Mélanges Bidez* ii (Brussels 1934), 869-912.
Stratos, 'Attack', = A. N. Stratos, 'The Avars' Attack on Byzantium in the
Year 626', *Byzantinische Forschungen* ii ( = *Polychordia*, Festschrift F.
Dölger), 1967, 370-6.

Stratos, *Byzantium* = A. N. Stratos, *Byzantium in the Seventh Century* i, tr. M. Ogilvie-Grant (Amsterdam 1968).

Taft, *Great Entrance* = R. F. Taft, *The Great Entrance* (Orientalia Christiana Analecta cc, Rome 1978).

Tiftixoglu, 'Helenianai' = V. Tiftixoglu, 'Die Helenianai nebst einigen anderen Besitzungen im Vorfeld des frühen Konstantinopel', in Beck, *Studien* 49-120.

Thomson, *Artsrunik* = R. W. Thomson, *Thomas Artsruni, History of the House of Artsrunik*, English trans. and comm. (Detroit 1985).

Tsangadas, *Fortifications* = B. C. P. Tsangadas, *The Fortifications and Defense of Constantinople* (East European Monographs lxxi, New York 1980).

Mary Whitby, 'Ceremony' = Mary Whitby, 'On the Omission of a Ceremony in mid-sixth century Constantinople: *candidati, curopalatus, silentiarii, excubitores* and others', *Historia* xxxvi, 1987, 462-88.

Whitby, 'Chronicle Source' = L. M. Whitby, 'Theophanes' Chronicle Source for the Reigns of Justin II, Tiberius and Maurice (AD 565-602)', *Byz.* liii, 1983, 312-45.

_____, 'Chronographer' = L. M. Whitby, 'The Great Chronographer and Theophanes', *BMGS* viii, 1982-3, 1-20.

_____, 'Long Walls' = L. M. Whitby, 'The Long Walls of Constantinople', *Byz.* lv, 1985, 560-83.

_____, *Maurice* = Michael Whitby, *The Emperor Maurice and his Historian: Theophylact Simocatta on Persian and Balkan Warfare* (Oxford 1988).

_____, *Theophylact* = Michael and Mary Whitby, *The History of Theophylact Simocatta: An English Translation with Introduction and Notes* (Oxford 1986).

Young, *Nicaea* = F. M. Young, *From Nicaea to Chalcedon* (London 1983).

# INDICES

Page references are to pages in our translation, not to the Bonn text (the latter can be obtained by referring to the **bold** numbers inserted in the translation). References to page numbers include notes on that page; additional references to notes are arranged in a separate sequence at the end of each entry.

Cilicia 9, 36, 87, 88
Cosila n. 171
Cotyaeum 3; n. 261
Crimea n. 331
Ctesiphon 41, 184; n. 488
Cucusus n. 304
Cyrrhestike/Cyrrhus 40
Cyzicus 54, 95, 196; nn. 115, 374

Dacia Mediterranea n. 325
Dadastana 44
Dalmatia n. 33
Damascus 50
Danube 15, 77, 165; nn. 124, 190, 246, 382, 401, 467, 478, 480
Dara/Doras 100; nn. 317, 391
Dardania n. 33
Dastagard 184
Diadromoi 143; n. 403
Dorostolon (Silistra) 39; n. 124
Drepanum = Helenopolis

Edessa 149; nn. 88, 115
Egypt/-ians 9, 37, 39, 128, 203; nn. 2, 8, 48, 218, 258, 292, 368, 373, 416, 422, 434, 438, 449
Emesa 37, 82; n. 171
Ephesus 33, 71, 76, 128; nn. 258, 268, 442
Epidamnus (Dyrrachium) n. 315
Epiphania 37
Epirus (New) 98; n. 315
Euphrates n. 487
Europe 18; n. 188
Eutropius, harbour of 146; n. 402

Flanona n. 99
Frigidus n. 175

Galatia n. 130
Gargarides (Garizim) 96
Gaul 21, 26, 31, 32; nn. 9, 75, 159, 216, 259
Gaza 37
Greece xii, 197

Helenopolis 15; n. 310
Heliopolis (Baalbek) 3-4, 37, 50
Hellespont 95, 194; n. 188
Heraclea (Asiana) n. 249
Heracleia 18, 65, 165, 205; nn. 157, 348, 451
Hierapolis (Syria) n. 115
Holy Land/Places 74-5, 157

Iberia/-ns nn. 331, 337
Iesdem 185
Illyricum/Illyria 73, 128; nn. 90-1, 374
Isauria/-ns 91, 92, 93, 94, 119; nn. 289, 316
Istria/Istrus 32
Italy xxv, 6, 21, 27, 29; nn. 75, 91, 98, 208, 259, 281, 309, 349-50, 364, 382

Jerusalem xii, xxvii, 31, 74-5, 128, 149, 156, 191, 203; nn. 249, 438, 440, 442
  Golgotha 31
  Holy Sepulchre 19-20
  Mount of Olives 31
Jordan 197
Justinianopolis n. 374

Keli Shin Pass n. 486

Lampsacus 194
Lazica/Laz 105-6, 109; n. 331
Libanensis 3
Limnae (Sasina/Gölcük) 94
Lugdunum (Lyons) 32; n. 159

Marcianopolis 76
Mariamme 4
Marmara, Sea of nn. 192, 203, 243, 261, 284-5, 296, 322, 352, 367, 421, 464
Melantias 171; nn. 264, 478
Melitene 198 n. 13
Mesopotamia 21, 22, 27, 43, 100; nn. 485-8
Milan 55; nn. 6, 99, 159
Mompsus 36
Montus Seleucus 32

## INDEX 3: TITLES AND OFFICES

Theophanes (contd.)
and Arians xvi, xviii; nn. 69,
89, 91, 94
Theophanes Continuatus n.
338
Theophylact xiii, xxv, 200 n.
15; nn. 393, 399, 401-3, 406,
408, 415, 444, 451, 459, 476,
484
Theotokos = Virgin Mary

Vandals 70, 72, 73; nn. 272-3,
281, 292, 382
Victor Tonnensis n. 367
Virgin Mary (Our Lady)/
Theotokos 71, 78, 96, 129-30,
166, 169, 178, 180, 181, 183,

Virgin Mary (contd.)
184, 187; nn. 261, 375, 435, 457,
463, 474, 476; see also relics
Visigoths nn. 208, 216, 221, 259
visions 9, 28, 31, 41, 42, 44, 81,
102-3, 135, 180
Vitalians 38

weather, natural phenomena xxi,
46, 58, 60-1, 66, 69, 89-90, 90-1,
104-5, 168, 198
Xylocircites 59

Zachariah nn. 363, 367
Zosimus nn. 59, 91, 131, 159, 186-
7, 190, 195-6, 476

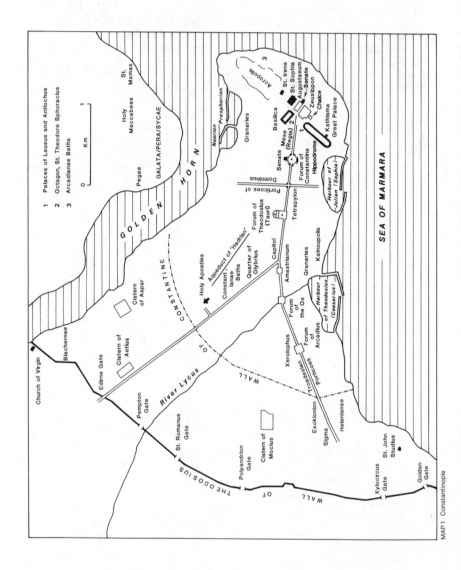

MAP 1 Constantinople

Legend:
1 Palaces of Lausus and Antiochus
2 Octagon, St. Theodore Sphoracius
3 Arcadianae Baths

Labels on map:
GOLDEN HORN
SEA OF MARMARA
River Lycus
St. Mamas
Holy Maccabees
Pegae
GALATA/PERA/SYCAE
Neorion
Prosphorian
Granaries
Acropolis
St. Irene
St. Sophia
Augustaeum
Zeuxippon
Chalke
Senate
Basilica
Mese
(Regia) 2
Kathisma
Great Palace
Senate
Forum of Constantine
Hippodrome
Harbour of Julian (Sophia)
Porticoes of Domninus
Forum of Theodosius (Tauri)
Tetrapylon
Kainoupolis
Granaries
Harbour of Theodosius (Caesarius)
Amastrianum
Forum of the Ox
Capitol
Quarter of Olybrius
Aqueduct of 'Hadrian'
Constantianae Baths
Holy Apostles
Cistern of Aspar
Church of Virgin
Blachernae
Cistern of Aetius
Edirne Gate
Pempton Gate
WALL OF CONSTANTINE
St. Romanus Gate
Polyandrion Gate
Cistern of Mocius
Forum of Arcadius
Xerolophus
Troadesian Porticoes
Exokionion
Helenianae
Sigma
Xylocircus Gate
St. John Studius
Golden Gate
WALL OF THEODOSIUS

0 Km 1

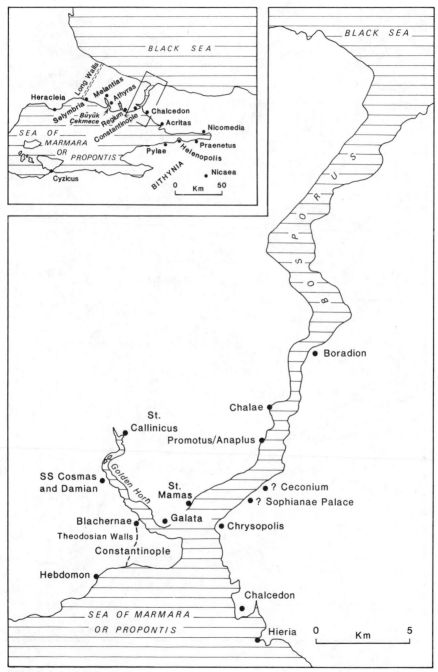

MAP 2 Environs of Constantinople

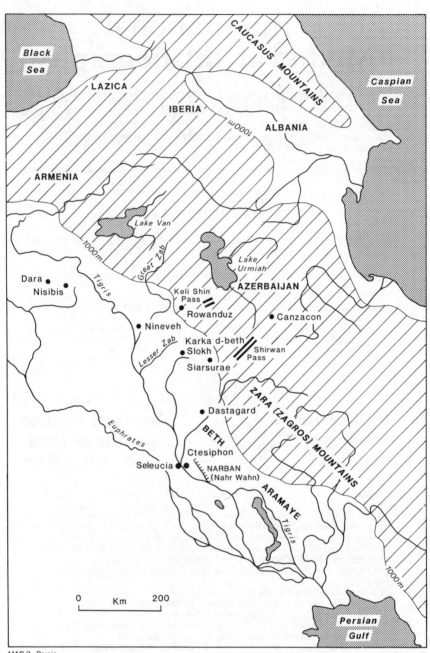

Black
Sea

LAZICA

CAUCASUS MOUNTAINS

Caspian
Sea

IBERIA

ALBANIA

1000m

ARMENIA

Lake Van

Great Zab

1000 m

Lake
Urmiah

AZERBAIJAN

Dara
Nisibis

Tigris

Keli Shin
Pass

Rowanduz

Canzacon

Nineveh

Lesser Zab

Karka d-beth
Slokh

Siarsurae

Shirwan
Pass

ZARA (ZAGROS) MOUNTAINS

Dastagard

Euphrates

BETH

Ctesiphon

Seleucia

NARBAN
(Nahr Wahn)

ARAMAYE

Tigris

0    Km    200

1000 m

Persian
Gulf

MAP 3  Persia